A BLACK COMMUNIST
IN THE FREEDOM STRUGGLE

A BLACK COMMUNIST IN THE FREEDOM STRUGGLE

THE LIFE OF HARRY HAYWOOD

Harry Haywood

EDITED BY GWENDOLYN MIDLO HALL

University of Minnesota Press

Minneapolis

London

Published by the University of Minnesota Press
111 Third Avenue South, Suite 290
Minneapolis, MN 55401-2520
http://www.upress.umn.edu

Library of Congress Cataloging-in-Publication Data

Haywood, Harry, 1898–1985.
    A Black communist in the freedom struggle : the life of Harry Haywood / Harry Haywood ; edited by Gwendolyn Midlo Hall.
    Includes bibliographical references and index.
    ISBN 978-0-8166-7905-8 (hc : alk. paper)
    ISBN 978-0-8166-7906-5 (pb : alk. paper)
1. Haywood, Harry, 1898– 2. Communists—United States—Biography. 3. African Americans—Biography. 4. Communism—United States—History. I. Hall, Gwendolyn Midlo. II. Haywood, Harry, 1898–1985. Black Boshevik. III. Title.
HX84.H38A32   2012
335.43092—dc23
[B]

2012001305

Printed in the United States of America on acid-free paper

The University of Minnesota is an equal-opportunity educator and employer.

18 17 16 15 14 13 12   10 9 8 7 6 5 4 3 2 1

To my family, Gwen, Haywood Jr., and Becky

CONTENTS

INTRODUCTION

Gwendolyn Midlo Hall

The struggle against power "is the struggle of memory against forgetting."
—Milan Kundera

These stories from the autobiography of Harry Haywood can give you confidence that you can help make a better world. His life and his battles for African American freedom and for justice for the poor and disempowered throughout the world need to be better known. This beautifully written book is a remarkable document of his times. That said, I chose to edit to this condensed version of his original seven-hundred-page book to make it easier to read and easier for a new generation to understand his life, what he achieved for humanity, and the example he set. I cut much of the long theoretical debates, polemics, and personal and political conflicts that have little meaning for most readers today. Those who want to read the unabridged book can find the original edition in almost any university library. With this introduction, I hope to share some of what we have learned about the times he lived in since this book was published thirty-five years ago and to add a few of my own thoughts about his work and his legacy.

I presume to make the difficult choices involved in substantially shortening his original autobiography for several reasons. First, I am a professional historian. Second, we were married during the last thirty years of his life, and he is the father of my two youngest children. Such a close personal relationship could undermine my objectivity, I know. But I am a native of New Orleans with childhood memories of the civil rights and trade union battles of the 1930s and 1940s. I was a veteran of the World War II democratic awakening with experience in the Communist Party, which was, to a great extent, a movement of Black maritime and port workers in my culturally rich hometown. I was elected as a white token member of the Executive Board of the Southern Negro Youth Congress (SNYC) at its Southern Youth Legislature in 1946 and was an active member of the Civil Rights Congress in New Orleans until 1949. I was a foot soldier in the historic Henry A. Wallace 1948 presidential campaign in the South. Another advantage is that I have been a post-Marxist since 1963. My conversion was fueled by the process of becoming a historian, which made me see the world as richly concrete, complex, and changing over space and time. My belief in ideology plunged as my understanding of consciousness and the role of the individual in history grew. But I never told Harry because I did not want to hurt him. I hope this combination of experience, involvement, and detachment will compensate somewhat for questionable objectivity due to my close relationship with Harry. You, the reader, will have to be the judge.

If we discuss the validity of ideas in the abstract, as many philosophers, historians, and sociologists do, we cannot begin to appreciate Harry's contribution to the Black freedom movement. His life and ideas send important messages from the past. He was part of a long Black radical tradition of armed resistance to racist terror. Blacks had long experience defending themselves with arms, especially in the Deep South. Black Civil War veterans and postwar militiamen often kept their arms and defended themselves and others from Ku Klux Klan terror. The courage, determination, and indignation of the ancestors were passed down to their descendants. Long before Rosa Parks refused to give up her seat on a bus in Montgomery, Alabama, many devoted, courageous people fought for African American freedom; they remain forgotten and unsung. Rosa Parks herself was a veteran of this older tradition. During slavery, the Civil War, and Radical Reconstruction, there were massacres and violent battles in the Deep South. There were also usually unpublicized underground Black power movements for cultural resistance as well as armed self-defense against racist terror.[1] Ida B. Wells began national and international campaigns against lynching, spanning the twentieth century.[2] During and after World War I, the African Blood Brotherhood agitated for self-determination for the Black nation and for armed self-defense against the racist massacres that escalated after World War I.[3] The New Negro movement and the Harlem Renaissance of the 1920s stood up for Black identity and pride. Scholars, teachers, and the media rarely mention this silenced history.[4] Now conscientious, open-minded historians are only beginning to research, write about, and publish on these movements.

Harry's stories tell us how to fight for power for the powerless, a lesson the vast majority of people of the world still urgently need to learn. He played a major role in starting massive street protests for African American freedom getting powerful international support. These protest tactics laid a foundation for the Black power, armed self-defense, gender equality, and peace movements of the 1950s through 1970s. Street protests, marches, civil disobedience, and boycotts led by Dr. Martin Luther King Jr., the Student Nonviolent Coordinating Committee (SNCC), the Congress of Racial Equality (CORE), Robert F. Williams, the Deacons for Defense and Justice, the Black Panthers, and Malcolm X, combined with the federal government's concern about internal stability and the image of the United States abroad during the Cold War, brought real change. Legalized racial segregation and discrimination finally ended. The right to vote was secured for all. A brake was put on police brutality and on job, housing, and gender discrimination, and the war in Vietnam was ended. Some scholars believe the most crucial factor in the victories of the civil rights movement was that our racist system was spoiling our image abroad during the Cold War.[5] King is rightly celebrated as the leader of the civil rights movement. But the movement he led did not emerge out of the blue. The world-famous movement beginning with the Montgomery Bus Boycott in 1955 was rooted in many lesser-known, older, and varied forms of protest.[6]

Unlike many other leaders of the movements of the 1920s—the New Negro movement, the Harlem Renaissance, the African Blood Brotherhood, and the Marcus Garvey movement—Harry Haywood was not a Caribbean immigrant to New York City. He was a son of the Black working class of the industrial Midwest with deep roots in the Black Belt South. With little formal education, he became a self-taught working-class intellectual-activist. He lived through the worst years of racist oppression in the United States. Born in 1898 in Omaha, Nebraska, his parents were both born enslaved in 1860. His father was a beef-lugger at the Cudahy meat-packing plant, and his mother was a domestic and a caterer. The most violent and exploitative conditions prevailed in the Deep South, especially in the Black Belt, where 80 percent of black folks lived and worked as sharecroppers or small farmers. But the Black Belt South was also the source of the richest culture, traditions, and history of resistance to racist terror.

Harry served in the U.S. Army during World War I, training in the South and then going on to fight on the battlefields of France. He and his fellow Black troops became increasingly defiant of the racist status quo. During and after the war they defended Black communities against racist terror with arms. Along with other members of the African Blood Brotherhood, he joined the Communist Party of the United States (CPUSA) in 1923. He was sent to Moscow in 1926 to train as a revolutionary and found himself in a strategic position to get badly needed help for the Black freedom movement. The timing was perfect. Joseph Stalin was consolidating his power against his chief rival, Leon Trotsky, who minimized the peasant and anticolonial movements and instead prioritized working-class revolutions in the advanced, industrial world. The Russian czarist empire was composed of many oppressed and exploited ethnicities and nations. The Soviet Union was established to win their loyalty by being sensitive to their cultures and giving them the right to use their own languages in education, culture, and government. The Communist International (Comintern) was highly motivated to support the struggle for the freedom of Black people in the United States, the Caribbean, and Africa and was willing and able to organize massive international support.

While Harry was studying in Moscow (1926–30), the Comintern was indoctrinating and giving financial aid and military training to revolutionaries throughout the world. Asian revolutionaries were especially important in stressing Black liberation in the United States. Sen Katayama (1859–1933), the famous Japanese writer, activist, and revolutionary, was a founder of both the Communist Party of the United States and the Communist Party of Japan. He actively promoted support for the Black freedom movement in the Comintern. Both Sen Katayama and Ho Chi Minh (1890–1969) of Vietnam had spent years living and working in the United States. Ho Chi Minh worked in Harlem, Brooklyn, and Boston in the United States and in London, England, and he was exposed to the Marcus Garvey movement at its apex. Both Ho Chi Minh and Katayama knew the sting of American racism firsthand and understood the powerful potential of revolutionary Black nationalism in the United States. The Communist Party of China was founded in Moscow, and many of its leaders were studying at Comintern schools at the same time as Harry. Pioneer leaders of the independence movement of India and the Black freedom movements in South Africa and Ghana were also there.

Harry helped write a Comintern resolution that helped the Communist Party of South Africa (CPSA) play an important role in the successful struggle against apartheid.[7] Nelson Mandela forthrightly acknowledged the unwavering support the CPSA gave the African National Congress (ANC) in the fight to end apartheid. He wrote, "For many decades Communists were the only political group in South Africa who were prepared to treat Africans as human beings and their equals; who were prepared to eat with us; talk with us, live with and work with us." The CPSA emerged as a major political party in Mandela's government. The Communist Parties of China and Vietnam eventually took power. We now know the amazing military success of Vietnam against all odds and the rise of Communist China to become one of the greatest economic powers in the world.[8]

Although Harry never finished elementary school, he learned to speak, read, and write Russian better than any other U.S.-born Communist. He could even read literature in Russian. His mastery of the major language of the Comintern increased his influence. His marriage to his first love—Ina, a Russian ballet dancer and interpreter of English—enhanced his understanding of and love for Russia.

His greatest achievement was adapting Marxist–Leninist theory to benefit the Black freedom struggle in the United States. The Black movement was defined as a revolutionary movement in its own right, which could triumph at its own pace independently of the working-class revolution for socialism. By defining Blacks as an oppressed nation within the heartland of one of the most powerful capitalist countries in the world and with strong backing by the Comintern, he convinced reluctant white Communists in the United States that the only road to a successful socialist revolution was by uncompromising support for the Black freedom struggle. In 1928 and 1930 he helped draft two Comintern resolutions prioritizing the fight for freedom in the most repressive regions of the South, with the Black working class in the lead. The Black elite was viewed as too eager to compromise by accepting white patronage. They kept the movement under safe control in return for gains most attractive to themselves rather than addressing the needs of Black workers, sharecroppers, and farmers. Following the tradition established by Cyril B. Briggs and his African Blood Brotherhood, these resolutions also opposed Black separatism, with its social base in the "ghetto bourgeoisie."[9] Garveyism was characterized as an escapist movement distracting from the struggle for rights for Blacks where they actually lived and would remain. The slogan of self-determination for the oppressed Black nation continues to resonate.[10] As the recent experience of Africa shows, independent nations can be thoroughly subverted and torn apart, and their peoples and resources can be exploited without overt foreign occupation. Although much has changed during the twentieth and twenty-first centuries, the role of class forces in the struggle for Black liberation speaks to current and future issues, including the need for structural change in society to benefit the poor and the powerless.

Before the "Negro question" was officially defined by the Comintern in Moscow as a vital aspect of colonial oppression in 1928, most American socialists and Communists considered southern workers and farmers, both Black and white, hopelessly backward and saw them predominantly as strikebreakers. Black and white Communists were extremely reluctant to work in the South on the grounds that it was impossible to organize in such a dangerous and oppressive environment. Claude McKay's report to the Comintern in Moscow in 1922 stated:

If we send white comrades into the South they are generally ordered out by the Southern oligarchy and if they do not leave they are generally whipped, tarred and feathered; and if we send black comrades into the South they generally won't be able to get out again—they will be lynched and burned at the stake.[11]

Lovett Fort-Whiteman, one of the first Black members of the CPUSA, remained in the Soviet Union mainly to avoid organizing in the South. He died in a Siberian forced-labor camp instead.[12]

The Comintern forced a reluctant Communist Party to organize in the South after Blacks were declared an oppressed nation in the Black Belt entitled to the right of self-determination. Harry Haywood was the first African American to understand and accept this concept. He played a major role in drafting these resolutions and then in enforcing their implications after he returned in 1930 to the United States, where he led the Communist Party's Negro work. The Communist Party began to organize in the South beginning with the Gastonia, North Carolina, textile strike of mainly white women in 1929. Glenda E. Gilmore has written a definitive book about the impact of these resolutions on the CPUSA's organizing work in the South.[13]

As the leading Black member of the CPUSA and with great influence with the Comintern in Moscow, Harry Haywood helped launch militant Black protest movements during the 1930s, most notably the campaign to save and free the Scottsboro Boys. These nine Black youths falsely accused of raping two white girls were quickly found guilty by an all-white jury in Alabama and were sentenced to death. The Scottsboro case exposed legal lynching, challenged the exclusion of Blacks from juries, and undermined the deeply embedded image of Black men as rapists lusting after white women. Street demonstrations for the lives and freedom of the Scottsboro Boys became a huge, international campaign spearheaded by the CPUSA and firmly supported by the Comintern. All the Scottsboro Boys were finally freed. Impressed by the Scottsboro campaign, in 1931 some sharecroppers in Alabama contacted the *Southern Worker,* a new newspaper published by the Communist Party in Memphis, Tennessee, and asked for organizers.[14] The local people knew all about how to organize, including how to defend themselves with arms. They were seeking effective outside help and received it, at least for a few years. This powerful, largely underground movement survived and grew despite widespread terroristic tortures and murders of their members in Alabama. It won a few economic victories and spread throughout the Black Belt South, most notably to Louisiana.

These events occurred during the Great Depression, beginning with the Wall Street crash of 1929. The southern district of the CPUSA organized interracial Unemployed Councils and hunger marches, teaching whites the need for unity among all workers. Racial integration was strictly enforced in all organizations, meetings, and socials. By 1936, the Congress of Industrial Organizations (CIO) was organizing interracial industrial unions in the South, relying heavily on experienced Communist organizers who insisted on racially integrated unions. Conflicts among Black, Latino, and white workers were defused.[15] The Communist Party didn't use the word "multiculturalism." It said "worker solidarity" and "fighting white chauvinism." But it was way ahead of its time, everywhere both North and South.[16]

Some writers have dismissed Harry as a soulless bureaucrat within the CPUSA. This portrayal is wrong. Harry was a totally devoted, loyal, disciplined Communist. He insisted upon leaving the center of power in New York City to organize coal miners in Pennsylvania and West Virginia, worked with the Sharecroppers Union in Alabama, began Communist Party activity in Memphis, and then returned to Chicago organizing Black workers on the Southside. He was one of the few Black Communist leaders who did not depend on having a job in the party bureaucracy. He could make a living working as a waiter, and he often did until he was well into his sixties.

In 1933 the Comintern policy shifted to the right. The escalating fascist threat dampened Soviet support for revolutions abroad. In 1919, Benito Mussolini began the fascist movement in Italy and took power by terrorizing the Left and all supporters of democracy. Adolf Hitler and his Fascist thugs took power in Germany in 1933 with a vicious racist ideology. German persecution and extermination policies first targeted Jews within Germany. But Hitler also targeted Slavs, viewing them as inferior to Germans, and marked them for extermination. By killing them off and occupying their territories throughout eastern Europe, Germans would have more living space. This immediate threat to the existence of the Soviet Union and its people led it to seek alliances with the Western democracies, softening its support for class struggle and revolutions abroad. At its Seventh World Congress in 1935, the Comintern adopted a new policy: the United Front against Fascism. It failed. Spain fell to fascism in 1939 despite Soviet military invention to save the Spanish Republic. Hitler's "unstoppable" blitzkrieg occupied all of western Europe with breathtaking speed. In June 1941 Germany invaded the Soviet Union. At the cost of nearly 30 million lives, the Soviet Union crushed the German invasion. Stalin's micromanagement of the Red Army's military campaign defeating the "unstoppable" Nazi war machine is now indisputable, thanks to documents released from the Russian archives.[17] But by 1935 Comintern support for world revolution, including Black liberation in the United States and its leading proponents, had dried up, which had an immediate impact in the Black Belt South.

Harry wrote:

> In the years that had followed my visit to Alabama, the Sharecroppers Union had continued to grow. In 1936, it had a membership of roughly 10,000, spread over five counties in the Alabama Black Belt. It was growing throughout the lower South with 2,500 members in Mississippi, Georgia, Louisiana and North Carolina. But in October 1936, the SCU was dissolved and its membership merged into the Agricultural Workers Union and the Farmers Union of Alabama. This latter was an organization of predominantly white small farm owners and tenants based in the northern part of the state, outside the plantation area. This union was strongly influenced by the racist and right-wing Coughlinite forces.[18]

The United Front against Fascism presaged the end of the Comintern. William Chase's impressive book demonstrates its utter destruction by deadly, xenophobic, hysterical witch hunts between 1934 and 1939; confessions were obtained through torture and execution, and surviving victims were exiled to Siberian forced-labor camps.[19] Without support from the Comintern, Black Communists were faced with a dilemma that Harry never came to grips with. Black working-class members had no self-determination within the Communist Party, so their ability to exert autonomous leadership of the Black freedom struggle became crippled.

The Soviet Union's necessities for survival and the destruction of the Comintern precipitated Harry Haywood's fall from leadership in the CPUSA. He became an indirect victim of the purges of the Soviet military in Moscow while he served as a commissar in the International Brigades in Spain. While recruiting volunteers to defend the Loyalist government during the Spanish Civil War, he decided he could not ask others to do what he did not do himself, so he volunteered to go to Spain. Earl Browder, then general secretary of the CPUSA, strongly objected and prevented his departure for several months. Browder evidently understood at least some of the thick, murky politics in Spain that were fueled by Soviet military incompetence and even more by Red Army commanders' fear for their lives in the purges, which wiped out many of the Red Army officers as well as the entire Comintern. Failure, criticism, even suspicion meant recall to Moscow for torture, execution, or exile to Siberian slave-labor camps. Harry should have taken Browder's advice. His experiences in Spain nearly destroyed him. His chapter about the Spanish Civil War is informative, but he could never see beyond the false images hiding Soviet incompetence. He died without ever understanding what had happened to him in Spain. An FBI agent of "known reliability" wrote that Harry was made a "scapegoat for Soviet mistakes in Spain and then his rivals [mentioning James W. Ford] took advantage to advance themselves into higher leadership positions."

Harry told me only once, when he was very drunk, that he walked across a battlefield in Brunete and saw the mangled corpses of many of the U.S. volunteers, some of whom he no doubt had recruited. He never got over it. His discussion of the Spanish Civil War weeps for the invaluable lives needlessly lost in Spain. New research lends support to some of what he wrote. Red Army officers not only commanded the International Brigades but controlled the planes, tanks, artillery, rifles, and ammunition sent by the Soviet Union; the supplies were often pledged but never arrived at the right place and time or in the promised numbers. All the contentious publications about the Spanish Civil War agree that time and again the Internationals, often unarmed, were uselessly slaughtered. Harry rightfully did his best to protect his troops and became the scapegoat for the Soviet officers' incompetence and their fear not of the enemy but of the purges in Moscow. "General Walter"—actually a Polish-born Red Army general named Karol Wacław Świerczewski, one of the very few Polish Communists to survive the terror in Moscow—was the highest-ranking Soviet general in Spain. He explained these defeats partially by the nationalist and linguistic insensitivity of Soviet military personnel and partially by fifth-column infiltration behind their lines. Harry's version coincides with "General Walter's" intelligence reports about the disasters at Brunete:

> In the Brunete operation we did not show enough tenacity in using the very favorable conditions of the first few days, but then had more than was necessary later on when we were too late. We stubbornly tried to compensate for being caught yawning with local and futile attacks at Villafranca and Mosquite by 18th corps units that had little fighting value.[20]

Harry never blamed the Soviet Union for his fall from leadership after he returned to the United States. His loyalty to communism and to the Soviet Union was unshakable. He had great integrity, but he was a true believer and a bit naive. He fared much better than most of his mentors at the Comintern: at least he survived physically and lived to fight another day.

Harry did indeed formally protest the useless slaughter of American troops at the Jarama front. A diary entry by the Comintern commander Vladimir Copic dated June 18, 1937, reports that the American commissar Harry Haywood led a delegation of American officers including Steve Nelson. Haywood informed Copic

> that as a delegate of the Party it is his duty to tell me that the men have no confidence in the co of the Brigade and want to replace me. That if that lack of confidence is justified or not is another question and he does not want to explore it but says it has to be considered and taken into account as the opinion of the mass. [Harry] has already in previous discourses in the battalion incited against the co. I told him he could communicate his views to the Division co but if he tried again to organize factional meetings in the battalion against the command, he would be arrested and sent to Albacete.[21]

When Harry wrote that Copic was concerned about loss of prestige, he did not know that for Soviet officers in Spain, being recalled to the Soviet Union was a fatal event. Rumors, slanders, and deliberate disinformation were thick. Ernest Hemingway wrote, "Then there was Gall, the Hungarian who ought to be shot if you can believe half you heard . . . make it if you can believe ten percent of what you heard."[22]

Both Copic and Janos Gal were high-ranking commanders of the International Brigades. They suffered the same fate. Gal was relieved of his command shortly after the Battle of Brunete and disappeared into the pit of the purges in Moscow. Copic followed him shortly after.

Harry Haywood was formally removed from the Politbureau, the top leadership body of the CPUSA, in 1938 after he returned from Spain. His dismissal was based upon false, enduring racist reports about his supposed cowardice there. The slander still persists that he left the Brunete battlefront without permission and continues to resonate in almost every publication about the International Brigades. Some of these reports are based on interviews with survivors who demonstrate racist attitudes toward Blacks. Harry and others were resented because they were the first Black officers to lead white troops. He was criticized for wearing an officer's uniform and insisting on dressing neatly and properly, in contrast to Steve Nelson, a white officer who was praised for wearing jeans.

Oliver Law, a Black officer who died leading his troops into battle, was resented when he was promoted to officer status.

> "Why Law?" Jarama veterans asked. "Law was not a Negro as I thought of Negroes," recalled a New York furrier. "Law was an illiterate southern darkie, The kind you picture with a watermelon."[23]

Harry drank a lot in Spain and was frightened by enemy machine-gun and artillery fire and by bombings and strafing from German and Italian planes. But so was everybody else. The best, most unvarnished account by a soldier in the field is by Alvah Bessie.[24] Harry was no coward. He fought in three foreign wars and in class warfare in the United States. During World War II, he joined the National Maritime Union (NMU) and served on ships bringing troops and supplies to fighting fronts around the world. He treats us to his sea tales about life both aboard the ships and in port, including the especially dangerous Murmansk run bringing desperately needed supplies to the Soviet Union.

When Harry's autobiography turns to the post–World War II period, it becomes burdened with inner-party struggles and polemics, which are of little interest today except to specialists in Communist history. I will try to summarize the most important background here. The CPUSA was dissolved in 1944, a dissolution inspired by delusions that the wartime alliance between the United States and the Soviet Union would continue after the war. After the CPUSA was restored in 1945 under the leadership of William Z. Foster, Harry was formally cleared of all charges of deserting the front in Spain. The slogan of self-determination in the Black Belt was revived, and Harry was encouraged to write a book. His first book, *Negro Liberation,* contributed greatly to reviving the Communist Party in the South, which reached its highest membership (two thousand) after World War II. Despite vicious legal, and sometimes violent, attacks on militant leftists beginning almost immediately after the war ended, the revived CPUSA accomplished a lot. The Southern Negro Youth Congress held its Southern Youth Legislature in Columbia, South Carolina, in 1946, with wide representation from a wide range of Black youth groups. Many of those attending became active throughout the later and more famous civil rights movement. The Civil Rights Congress was organized in 1946 under the leadership of William L. Patterson. It was especially active in the South, reviving the work of the International Labor Defense (ILD) that had led the Scottsboro defense years before. Harry helped Patterson with research for *We Charge Genocide,* the Civil Rights Congress petition to the United Nations that documented and called world attention to the oppression of Blacks in the United States.[25] Henry A. Wallace and Paul Robeson toured the South during the 1948 presidential election campaign and broke new ground enforcing racially integrated public meetings.[26]

The CPUSA was largely destroyed by the wave of witch hunts after World War II. Many of its leaders were jailed for supposedly plotting to overthrow the government of the United States by force and violence. The Taft–Hartley Act demanded that union leaders swear oaths that they were not Communists, removing some of the best, most militant, and most experienced unionists from leadership. A vacuum of militant leadership was left within the labor movement, undermining interracialism and militant worker-led Black liberation movements in the North as well as the South.[27]

This vacuum was partially filled by the National Negro Labor Council (NNLC) established in 1951. It arose from the Black caucus movement within labor unions mainly in the industrial Midwest and then the Northeast. It fought job discrimination against Black workers in a range of business enterprises as well as within labor unions. During its five short years, it grew rapidly in membership and influence. The NNLC focused especially on the right of Black women to hold any job, pushed by Vicki Garvin. Unfortunately this badly needed organization was battered to death by the red scare and dissolved in 1956.[28]

The red scare was most enthusiastically embraced to defend racial segregation in the South. When the U.S. Supreme Court outlawed racial segregation in schools in 1954, southern politicians unleashed their Massive Resistance campaign to defend racial segregation. The House Un-American Activities Committee and the Senate Internal Security Committee, both authorized by the U.S. Congress, held public hearings throughout the South, accusing all those who advocated racial equality of being Communist subversives and demanding that they identify others they knew to be Communists. Southerners who supported racial equality were publicly exposed, denounced, and persecuted. They lost their jobs and were often jailed as Communists by these investigating committees of the U.S. Congress as well as by state and local governments enforcing antisubversive laws. These persecutions largely succeeded in driving the last few remaining Communists out of the South, including the southern whites most devoted to African American freedom. Even the NAACP, which vigorously endorsed red baiting in an effort to maintain its respectability during the Cold War, was outlawed in many southern states.[29]

Harry and I were married in 1956 in the midst of the worst phase of the red scare. I took his legal name Hall to enhance my anonymity. That didn't help much when Gus Hall became the leader of the Communist Party. Just about everyone who has heard of me over the years believes I was married to Gus Hall. Although Harry was thirty-three years older than I, he lived long enough to see our son Dr. Haywood Hall attend Baylor College of Medicine and our daughter Dr. Rebecca Hall graduate from Swarthmore College.

During the years we lived together in Brooklyn both before and after our legal marriage we did our best to encourage an impressive network of experienced Black and white working-class organizers. Many of them were Harry's old friends, who stuck together and continued the militant struggle for Black liberation. They defied the CPUSA, which beat a hasty retreat, most drastically in the sensitive issues of Black liberation. Harry vigorously opposed this retreat, and in 1957 he completed and we informally circulated *For a Revolutionary Position on the Negro Question*. Michael C. Dawson discussed Black Communists' battles for self-determination within the CPUSA during the 1950s and its implication in his outstanding book *Black Visions*.[30]

As the CPUSA collapsed, we formed the Provisional Organizing Committee to Reconstitute the Communist Party (POC) at a founding convention held in New York City in August 1958. Its membership was impressive. Almost all Black and Puerto Rican party members and waterfront workers joined, including Al Lannon, founder and director of the Waterfront Section of the CPUSA, as did coal miners from Williamsport, Pennsylvania, and workers from Philadelphia and Cleveland and elsewhere. Coleman Young, a leader of the Auto Workers Union in Detroit and of the recently dissolved NNLC and later the first Black mayor of Detroit, also joined. Theodore W. Allen, a young organizer from West Virginia, went on to create the white-skin privilege theory during the 1960s, and during the 1990s he published the very influential and respected two-volume book *The Invention of the White Race*.[31]

One of the best things the Communist Party did was to teach its members how to organize. Black Communist merchant seamen who were veterans of the NMU became active and influential civil rights leaders after the Communist Party was destroyed. Jack O'Dell, a former Communist merchant seaman, became an important organizer for Martin Luther King Jr.'s Southern Christian Leadership Conference. He was red-baited out and then rehired later to lead its voter-registration drive, which he steered to the Black Belt South.[32] Vernon Bowen, a former MNU member and a veteran of the Spanish Civil War, was jailed in Louisville, Kentucky, with six other armed whites who stationed themselves on the front porch of a Black family who were threatened with violence for moving into a white neighborhood.

When they sailed together on NMU ships, Harry mentored young Jesse Gray from Baton Rouge, Louisiana, and taught him how to organize. They led wildcat strikes "to bring their ships down," which in maritime worker talk meant stopping them from sailing by unauthorized work stoppages. After World War II, the U.S. Coast Guard screened merchant seamen and took those suspected of being Communists off the ships on the grounds they were security risks. Although this blacklisting was finally declared illegal, it was too late because the U.S. merchant marine became an early victim of globalization. After being barred from the ships, they brought their organizing skills to Harlem, where Jesse led rent strikes and organized for welfare rights. Josh Lawrence, former NMU rivers and lakes port agent, and James Haughton organized Harlem Fight Back, which fought for skilled jobs for Black construction workers in New York City. In 1964 they all began working with Malcolm X's Organization of African Unity, continuing until he was murdered in February 1965. Jesse Gray was elected to the New York State Assembly, where he served between 1972 and 1974.

The Black radical tradition of armed self-defense remained an essential counterpoint to the passive resistance strategy and ideals of Martin Luther King. During the mid-1950s Robert F. Williams loudly advocated and practiced armed self-defense against Ku Klux Klan violence in Monroe, North Carolina. Recent research has revealed that in the Mississippi Black Belt, underground armed self-defense movements were organized after the murder of Emmett Till in 1954.[33] In Jonesboro, Louisiana, the Deacons for Defense and Justice was organized in 1964. It spread to Bogalusa, Louisiana, in 1965 and then all over the South. One of the founding deacons was a veteran of the Sharecroppers Union. Deacons in Louisiana loudly advocated armed self-defense against the Ku Klux Klan, while other organized groups elsewhere, some calling themselves Deacons and others without names or publicity, armed themselves and ran the KKK out.[34]

There was a powerful civil rights movement in the North that advocated self-determination as well. The Revolutionary Action Movement (RAM) was organized by Max Stanford in Cleveland. Robert F. Williams was invited to return from China to lead it.[35] In early 1964 Harry and I completed the manuscript "Towards a Revolutionary Program for Negro Freedom." It was dedicated to Williams and was widely circulated in mimeographed form, mainly in California and in the South. Excerpts were serialized during 1965 and 1966 in *Soulbook* magazine, a precursor to the Black Panther Party published in Berkeley, California. Bobby Seale was distribution manager.[36] It did not advocate a reconstituted Communist Party and contained a phrase repeated by word of mouth throughout the movement: "The *only* effective weapon Negroes have at this point is to pose their own threat to internal stability."[37] Harry went to Oakland for several months and eventually returned to Detroit with Ernie Allen, one of the magazine's young editors. By 1966 Harry's main base was in Detroit, where he was living at John Watson's house and serving as elder statesman of the Dodge Revolutionary Union Movement (DRUM) and the Black Workers Congress (BWC).[38] During 1970 he was in residence at the Institute for the Black World in Atlanta, invited by Vincent Harding.

Harry's ideas enjoyed a major revival after China broke with the Soviet Union during the 1960s and the battle between these two leading Communist powers intensified during the 1960s and 1970s.[39] This was during the period of the Great Cultural Revolution, which kept China isolated, backward, self-satisfied, and anti-intellectual. Almost all its teachers and educated people were destroyed. Starting from scratch, the Chinese educational system became open to new ideas from around the world, laying the basis for the spectacular growth of her economy and influence during the past thirty years.[40]

Outside China during the Great Cultural Revolution a plethora of New Communist movement organizations arose internationally, many of them rivals for the "Chinese franchise," as they sometimes called it. Some organizations enjoyed shifting Chinese support based on their unquestioning support for China's foreign policy. Harry joined the Communist Party Marxist Leninist (CPML) during the 1970s. Liberator Press, the CPML's publishing house, reissued or published some of his most important writings. It published *For a Revolutionary Position on the Negro Question* twenty years after he had completed it. It is now available free on the Internet.[41] Liberator Press reissued his first book, *Negro Liberation*. CPML members helped him complete his autobiography, *Black Bolshevik*, which Liberator Press published in 1978. The book received wide attention from a broad range of people both in and out of academia both at home and abroad.

Many, if not most of the Maoists or New Communist organizations in the United States embraced the theory of the oppressed Black nation in the Black Belt and its right to self-determination. The CPML absorbed remnants of the Students for a Democratic Society (SDS), the BWC in Detroit, and finally the Congress of African Peoples (CAP) in Newark, New Jersey.[42] Chicanos began to embrace the slogan of self-determination for themselves, and so did Puerto Ricans.

The death of Mao Tse-Tung ended the Great Cultural Revolution in China and among its supporters abroad. The CPML fell into intense factional fighting with other New Communist (Maoist) groups and eventually cannibalized itself with internal splits. The real Communist Party he believed he had finally found disintegrated shortly before Harry died, a terrible blow to him. The last article he published questioned the Maoist orthodoxy in international relations, denying that the Soviet Union was an empire-building social imperialist country and calling on Communists to focus on winning legitimacy within their own countries rather than seeking validation from abroad.[43]

Harry's ideas certainly did not explain all the realities of the world he lived in and even less the world we live in now. But his thought contains a core of truth with deep roots in African American history and traditions that helped make the Black freedom movement work. International protest against racist violence, segregation, and discrimination against Blacks in the United States, along with the crucial work of the unsung militants at home who brought thousands of protesters into the streets, allowed for some important victories and advances toward true democracy in our country. We can now more rightfully boast about our tradition of civil liberties and our growing multiculturalism. But we still have a long, long way to go.

Harry Haywood was one of the most influential among the thinkers, writers, organizers, and activists who helped make the world conscious of the virulent racism staining our democracy. Now capitalism, with its indiscriminate robbery through financial manipulation and its blind, conscienceless destruction of the environment, is turning out to be much worse than any Communist predicted. Our entire middle class is threatened with destruction, and our young people have little faith in their futures. Methods of struggle have changed as the rise of the Internet and social networking vastly accelerates and democratizes communications. Hopefully, change can come more peacefully and with less top-down control than in the past. With new technology our voices can now be less dependent on the money of lobbyists or institutions or bureaucracies and be infinitely faster and louder. But we can benefit from looking backward to learn how it was done in the past, so that we can move forward to end the dispossession of all of us and take back our world. The poor and the dispossessed of our country, and indeed everywhere, need to find their advocates and their own voices again.

ABBREVIATIONS

ABB	African Blood Brotherhood
ACTC	American Consolidated Trades Council
AFL	American Federation of Labor
AME	African Methodist Episcopal Church
ANC	African National Congress
ANLC	American Negro Labor Congress
AWOL	absent without leave
BWC	Black Workers Congress
CAP	Congress of African Peoples
CI	Communist International
CIO	Congress of Industrial Organizations
COINTELPRO	Counter Intelligence Program
CORE	Congress of Racial Equality
CP	Communist Party
CPML	Communist Party Marxist Leninist
CPSA	Communist Party of South Africa
CPUSA	Communist Party of the United States
DRUM	Dodge Revolutionary Union Movement
ECCI	Executive Committee of the Communist International
FEPC	Fair Employment Practices Committee
ILD	International Labor Defense
IWO	International Workers Order
IWW	Industrial Workers of the World
KKK	Ku Klux Klan
KUTVA	Universitet Trydyashchiysya Vostoka Imeni Stalina (University of the Toilers of the East Named for Stalin)
LSNR	League of Struggle for Negro Rights
MP	military police, military policeman
NAACP	National Association for the Advancement of Colored People
NMU	National Maritime Union
NMU	National Miners Union

NNC	National Negro Congress
NNLC	National Negro Labor Council
OAU	Organization of African Unity
POC	Provisional Organizing Committee to Reconstitute the Communist Party
POUM	Workers Party of Marxist Unification
RAM	Revolutionary Action Movement
RILU	Red International of Labor Unions
SCLC	Southern Christian Leadership Conference
SDS	Students for a Democratic Society
SIU	Seamen's International Union
SNCC	Student Nonviolent Coordinating Committee
SNYC	Southern Negro Youth Congress
TUEL	Trade Union Education League
TUUL	Trade Union Unity League
UMWA	United Mine Workers of America
UNIA	Universal Negro Improvement Association
USO	United Service Organizations
WPA	Works Progress Administration
YCI	Young Communist International
YCL	Young Workers (Communist) League

A BLACK COMMUNIST
IN THE FREEDOM STRUGGLE

PROLOGUE

On July 28, 1919, I literally stepped into a battle that was to last the rest of my life. Exactly three months after mustering out of the army, I found myself in the midst of one of the bloodiest race riots in U.S. history. It was certainly a most dramatic return to the realities of American democracy.

It came to me then that I had been fighting the wrong war. The Germans weren't the enemy—the enemy was right here at home. These ideas had been developing ever since I landed home in April, and a lot of other Black veterans were having the same thoughts.

I had a job as a waiter on the Michigan Central Railroad at the time. In July, I was working the Wolverine, the crack Michigan Central train between Chicago and New York. We would serve lunch and dinner on the run out of Chicago to St. Thomas, Canada, where the dining car was cut off the train. The next morning our cars would be attached to the Chicago-bound train and we would serve breakfast and lunch into Chicago.

On July 27, the Wolverine left on a regular run to St. Thomas. Passing through Detroit, we heard news that a race riot had broken out in Chicago. The situation had been tense for some time. Several members of the crew, all of them Black, had bought revolvers and ammunition the previous week when on a special to Battle Creek, Michigan. Thus, when we returned to Chicago at about 2:00 p.m. the next day (July 28), we were apprehensive about what awaited us.

The whole dining-car crew, six waiters and four cooks, got off at the Twelfth Street Station in Chicago. Usually we would stay on the car while it backed out to the yards, but the station seemed a better route now. We were all tense as we passed through the station on the way to the elevated that would take us to the Southside and home. Suddenly a white trainman accosted us.

"Hey, you guys going out to the Southside?"

"Yeah, so what?" I said, immediately on the alert, thinking he might start something.

"If I were you I wouldn't go by the avenue." He meant Michigan Avenue, which was right in front of the station.

"Why?"

"There's a big race riot going on out there, and already this morning a couple of colored soldiers were killed coming in unsuspectingly. If I were you I'd keep off the street, and go right out those tracks by the lake."

We took the trainman's advice, thanked him, and turned toward the tracks. It would be much slower walking home, but if he were right, it would be safer. As we turned down the tracks toward the Southside of the city, toward the Black ghetto, I thought of what I had just been through in Europe and what now lay before me in America.

On one side of us lay the summer warmness of Lake Michigan. On the other was Chicago, a huge and still-growing industrial center of the nation, bursting at its seams; brawling, sprawling Chicago, "hog butcher for the nation," as Carl Sandburg had called it.

As we walked, I remembered the war. On returning from Europe, I had felt good to be alive. I was glad to be back with my family—Mom, Pop, and my sister. At twenty-one, my life lay before me. What should I do? The only trade I had learned was waiting tables. I hadn't even finished the eighth grade. Perhaps I should go back to France, live there and become a French citizen? After all, I hadn't seen any Jim Crow there.

Had race prejudice in the United States lessened? I knew better. Conditions in the States had not changed, but we Blacks had. We were determined not to take it anymore. But what was I walking into?

Southside Chicago, the Black ghetto, was like a besieged city. Whole sections of it were in ruins. Buildings burned and the air was heavy with smoke, reminiscent of the holocaust from which I had recently returned.

Our small band, huddled like a bunch of raw recruits under machine-gun fire, turned up Twenty-Sixth Street and then into the heart of the ghetto. At Thirty-Fifth and Indiana, we split up to go our various ways; I headed for home at Forty-Second Place and Bowen. None of us returned to work until the riot was over, more than a week later.

The battle at home was just as real as the battle in France had been. As I recall, there was full-scale street fighting between Black and white. Blacks were snatched from streetcars and beaten or killed; pitched battles were fought in ghetto streets; hoodlums roamed the neighborhood, shooting at random. Blacks fought back.

As I saw it at the time, Chicago was two cities. The one was the Chamber of Commerce's city of the "American Miracle," the Chicago of the 1893 World Columbian Exposition. It was the new industrial city that had grown in fifty years from a frontier town to become the second-largest city in the country.

The other, the Black community, had been part of Chicago almost from the time the city was founded. Jean Baptiste Point du Sable, a Black trapper from French Canada, was the first settler. Later came fugitive slaves, and after the Civil War—more Blacks, fleeing from post-Reconstruction terror, taking jobs as domestics and personal servants.

The large increase was in the late 1880s through World War I, as industry in the city expanded and as Blacks streamed north following the promise of jobs, housing, and an end to Jim Crow lynching. The Illinois Central tracks ran straight through the Deep South from Chicago to New Orleans, and the Panama Limited made the run every day.

Those that took the train north didn't find a promised land. They found jobs and housing, all right, but they had to compete with the thousands of recent immigrants from Europe who were also drawn to the jobs in the packing houses, stockyards, and steel mills.

The promise of an end to Jim Crow was nowhere fulfilled. In those days, the beaches on Lake Michigan were segregated. Most were reserved for whites only. The Twenty-Sixth Street Beach, close to the Black community, was open to Blacks—but only as long as they stayed on their own side.

The riot had started at this beach, which was then jammed with a late-July crowd. Eugene Williams, a seventeen-year-old Black youth, was killed while swimming off the white side of the beach. The Black community was immediately alive with accounts of what had happened—that he had been murdered while swimming, that a group of whites had thrown rocks at him and killed him, and that the policeman on duty at the beach had refused to make any arrests.

This incident was the spark that ignited the flames of racial animosity that had been smoldering for months. Fighting between Blacks and whites broke out on the Twenty-Sixth Street Beach after Williams's death. It soon spread beyond the beach and lasted over six days. Before it was over, 38 people—Black and white—were dead, 537 injured, and over 1,000 homeless.

The memory of this mass rebellion is still very sharp in my mind. It was the great turning point in my life, and I have dedicated myself to the struggle against capitalism ever since. In the following pages of my autobiography, I have attempted to trace the development of that struggle in the hopes that today's youth can learn from both our successes and failures. It is for the youth and the bright future of a socialist USA that this book has been written.

A CHILD OF SLAVES

I was born in South Omaha, Nebraska, on February 4, 1898—the youngest of the three children of Harriet and Haywood Hall. Otto, my older brother, was born in May 1891, and Eppa, my sister, in December 1896.

The 1890s had been a decade of far-reaching structural change in the economic and political life of the United States. These were fateful years in which the pattern of twentieth-century subjugation of Blacks was set. A young U.S. imperialism was ready in 1898 to shoulder its share of the "white man's burden" and take its "manifest destiny" beyond the Pacific Coast and the Gulf of Mexico. In the war against Spain, it embarked on its first "civilizing" mission against the colored peoples of the Philippines and the "mixed breeds" of Cuba and Puerto Rico. In the course of the decade and a half following the Spanish–American War, the two-faced banner of racism and imperialist "benevolence" was carried to the majority of the Caribbean countries and the whole of Latin America.

"The echo of this industrial imperialism in America," said W. E. B. Du Bois, "was the expulsion of Black men from American democracy, their subjection to caste control and wage slavery."[1] In 1877, the Hayes–Tilden agreement had successfully aborted the ongoing democratic revolution of Reconstruction in the South. Blacks were sold down the river, as northern capitalists, with the assistance of some former slaveholders, and gained full economic and political control in the South. Henceforward, it was assured that the future development of the region would be carried out in complete harmony with the interests of Wall Street. The following years saw the defeat of the southern-based agrarian populist movement, with its promise of Black and white unity against the power of monopoly capital. The counterrevolution against Reconstruction was in full swing.

Beginning in 1890, the southern state legislatures enacted a series of disenfranchisement laws. Within the next sixteen years, these laws were destined to completely abrogate the right of Blacks to vote. This same period saw the revival of the notorious Black Codes, the resurgence of the hooded terror of the Ku Klux Klan (KKK), and the defeat for reelection in 1905 of the last Black congressman surviving the Reconstruction period. Jim Crow laws enforcing segregation in public facilities were enacted by southern states and municipal governments. The U.S. Supreme Court upheld Jim Crow in the *Plessy v. Ferguson* decision in 1896, declaring that legislation is powerless to eradicate "racial instincts" and establishing the principle of "separate but equal." This decision was only reversed in 1954, when the U.S. Supreme Court held that separate facilities were inherently unequal.

At the time when I was born, the Black experience was mainly a southern one. The overwhelming majority of Black people still resided in the South. Most of the Black inhabitants of South Omaha were refugees from the twenty-year terror of the post-Reconstruction period. Omaha itself, despite its midwestern location, did not escape the terror completely, as indicated by the lynching of a Black man, Joe Coe, by a mob in 1891. Many people had relatives and families in the South. Some had trekked up to Kansas in 1879 under the leadership of Henry Adams of Louisiana and Moses "Pap" Singleton of Tennessee, and many had then continued further north to Omaha and Chicago.

My parents were born slaves in 1860. They were three years old at the time of the Emancipation Proclamation. My father was born on a plantation in Haywood County, Tennessee, north of Memphis. The plantation was owned by Colonel Haywood Hall, whom my father remembered as a kind and benevolent man. When the slaves were emancipated in 1863, my grandfather, with the consent of Mr. Hall, took both the given name and surname of his former master.

I never knew Grandfather Hall, as he died before I was born. According to my father and uncles, he was—as they said in those days—"much of a man." He was active in local Reconstruction politics and probably belonged to the Black militia. Although Tennessee did not have a Reconstruction government, there were many whites who supported the democratic aims that were pursued during the Reconstruction period.

But Tennessee was also the home of the Ku Klux Klan, where it was first organized after the Civil War. In the terror that followed the Hayes–Tilden agreement, these "night riders" had marked my grandfather out as a "bad nigger" for lynching. At first they were deterred because of the paternalism of Colonel Hall. Many of Hall's former slaves still lived on his plantation after the war ended, and the colonel had let it be known that he would kill the first "son of a bitch" that trespassed on his property and tried to terrorize his "nigrahs."

But the anger of the night riders, strengthened by corn liquor, finally overcame their fear of Colonel Hall. My father, who was about fifteen at the time, described what happened. One night the Klansmen rode onto the plantation and headed straight for Grandfather's cabin. They broke open the door and one poked his head into the darkened cabin. "Hey, Hall's nigger—where are you?"

My grandfather was standing inside and fired his shotgun point-blank at the hooded head. The Klansman, half his head blown off, toppled onto the floor of the cabin, and his companions mounted their horses and fled. Grandmother, then pregnant, fell against the iron bed.

Grandfather got the family out of the cabin and they ran to the "big house" for protection. It was obvious they couldn't stay in Tennessee, so the colonel hitched up a wagon and personally drove them to safety, outside of Haywood County. Some of Grandfather's family were already living in Des Moines, Iowa, so the Hall family left by train for Des Moines the following morning. The shock of this experience was so great that Grandmother gave birth prematurely to their third child—my Uncle George, who lived to be ninety-five. Grandmother, however, became a chronic invalid and died a few years after the flight from Tennessee.

Father was only in his teens when the family left for Des Moines, so he spent most of his youth there. In the late 1880s, he left and moved to South Omaha, where there was more of a chance to get work. He got a job at Cudahy's Packing Company, where he worked for more than twenty years—first as a beef-lugger (loading sides of beef on refrigerated freight cars), and then as a janitor in the main office building. Not long after his arrival, he met and married Mother— Harriet Thorpe—who had come up from Kansas City, Missouri, at about the same time.

Father was powerfully built—of medium height, but with tremendous breadth (he had a forty-six-inch chest and weighed over two hundred pounds). He was an extremely intelligent man. With little or no formal schooling, he had taught himself to read and write and was a prodigious reader. Unfortunately, despite his great strength, he was not much of a fighter, or so it seemed to me. In later years, some of the old slave psychology and fear remained. He was an ardent admirer of Booker T. Washington, who, in his Atlanta Compromise speech of 1895, had called on Blacks to submit to the racist status quo.

Uncle George was the opposite. He would brook no insult and had been known to clean out a whole barroom when offended. The middle brother, Watt, was also a fighter and was especially dangerous if he had a knife or had been drinking. I remember both of them complaining of my father's timidity.

My mother's family also had great fighting spirit. Her father, Jerry Thorpe, was born on a plantation near Bowling Green, Kentucky. He was illiterate, but very smart and very strong. Even as an old man, his appearance made us believe the stories that were told of his strength as a young man. When he was feeling fine and happy, his exuberance would get the best of him and he'd grab the largest man around, hoist him on his shoulders, and run around the yard with him.

Grandfather Thorpe was half Creek Indian and had an Indian profile with a humped nose and high cheekbones. His hair was short and curly, and he had a light brown complexion. He had a straggly white beard that he tried to cultivate into a Vandyke. He said his father was a Creek Indian and his mother a Black plantation slave. No one knew his exact age, but we made a guess based on a story he often told us.

He was about six or seven years old when, he said, "The stars fell."

"When was that, Grandpa?"

"Oh, one night the stars fell, I remember it very clearly. The skies were all lit up by falling stars. People were scared almost out of their wits. The old master and mistress and all the slaves were running out on the road, falling down on their knees to pray and ask forgiveness. We thought the Judgment Day had surely come. Glory Hallelujah! It was the last fire! The next day, the ground was all covered with ashes!"

At first we thought all of that was just his imagination, something he had fantasized as a child and then remembered as a real event. But when my older brother Otto was in high school, he got interested in astronomy and came across a reference to a meteor shower of 1833. We figured out that was what Grandfather Thorpe had been talking about, so we concluded that he was born around 1825 or 1826.

Grandfather Thorpe was filled with stories, many about slavery.

"Chillen, I've got scars I'll carry to my grave." He would show us the welts on his back from slave beatings (my Grandmother also had them). Most of his beatings came from his first master in Kentucky. But he was later sold to a man in Missouri, who he said treated him much better. This may have been due in part to his value as a slave—he was skilled as both a carpenter and a cabinetmaker.

Grandfather had many stories to tell about the Civil War. He was in Missouri at the time, living in an area that was first taken by a group known as Quantrell's Raiders (a guerrilla-like band of irregulars who fought for the South) and then by the Union forces.

When the Union soldiers first came into the plantations, they would call in slaves from the fields and make them sit down in the great drawing room of the house. They would then force the master and mistress and their family to cook and serve for the slaves. Grandfather told us that the soldiers would never eat any of the food that was served, because they were afraid of getting poisoned.

The master on the plantation was generally decent when it became clear that the Union forces were going to control the area for a while. At that time, Grandfather and my Grandmother Ann lived on adjacent plantations somewhere near Moberly, Missouri. Grandfather was allowed to visit Ann on weekends. Often on Sundays when he went to make a visit, he was challenged by Union guards. They would roughly demand to know his mission. My Grandfather and Grandmother got married, with the agreement of their two masters, and eventually had a family of five daughters and two sons. Grandfather Thorpe was given a plot of land in return for his services as a carpenter, but the family soon moved into Moberly. As the children reached working age, the family began to break up, but the girls always remained very close. They came back to visit frequently and never broke family ties as the boys had.

My mother, Harriet, was born when Grandmother was a slave on the plantation of Squire Sweeney in Howard County, Missouri. After the family moved into Moberly, Mother worked for a white family in town. She later went to St. Joseph, Missouri, to work for another white family. One day, while she was at work in St. Joseph, she heard a shot and then screams from down the street. She ran out to see what had happened. There was a great commotion and a crowd of people was gathering in front of the house next door.

The family living there went by the name of Howard—a man, wife, and two children. Both the man and his wife were church members; they appeared to be a most respectable couple. Mrs. Howard had been very active in church affairs and socials. Her husband was frequently absent because, she said, he was a traveling salesman and his work took him out of town for long periods of time.

What the neighbors were not aware of was that "Mr. Howard" was none other than the legendary Jesse James. He was shot in the back while hanging a picture in his house. The man who killed him was Robert Ford—a member of Jesse's own gang who had turned traitor for a bribe offered by the Burns Detective Agency.

When my Mother did the laundry, I remember she would often sing the "Ballad of Jesse James"—a song that became popular after his death.

Jesse James was a man—he killed many a man,
The man that robbed that Denver train.
It was a dirty little coward
Who shot Mr. Howard,
And they laid Jesse James in his grave.
Oh the people held their breath

When they heard of Jesse's death,
And they wondered how he came to die.
He was shot on the sly
By little Robert Ford,
And they laid poor Jesse in his grave.

In 1893, my mother went to Chicago to visit her sister and see the exposition. She said she saw Frank James, Jesse's brother. He was out of prison then, a very dignified old man with a long white beard. He had been hired to ride around as an attraction at one of the exhibitions.

Mother kept moving up to the north by stages. After the job in St. Joseph, she found work in St. Louis. She arrived to find the city in a tense situation— the whole town was on the verge of a race riot. The immediate cause was the murder of an Irish cop named Brady. The Black community was elated, for Brady was a "nigger-hating cop" who carved notches on his pistol to show the number of Blacks he had killed. Brady finally met his end at the hands of a "bad" Black man who ran a gambling house in Brady's district.

The gambling, of course, was illegal. But as was often the case, the cops were paid off with a "cut" from the takings of the house. As the story was told to me, Brady and the gambler met on the street one day and got into an argument. Brady accused the gambler of not giving him his proper cut. This was denied vehemently. Brady then threatened to close the place down. The Black man told him, "Don't you come into my place when the game's going on!" He then turned and walked off. The scene was witnessed by several Blacks, and the news of how the gambler had defied Brady spread immediately throughout the Black district.

This was bad stuff for Brady. It might lead to "niggers gettin' notions," as the cops put it. A few days passed, and Brady made his move. He went to the gambling house when the game was on and was shot dead.

Some anonymous Black bard wrote a song about it all:

Brady, why didn't you run,
You know you done wrong.
You came in the room when the game was going on!
Brady went below looking mighty curious.
Devil said, "Where you from?"
"I'm from East St. Louis."
"East St. Louie, come this way.
I've been expecting you every day!"

The song was immediately popular in the Black community and became a symbol of rebellious feelings. Mother said that when she arrived in St. Louis, Blacks were singing this song all over town. The police realized the danger in such "notions" and began to arrest anyone they caught singing it. Forty years later, I was pleasantly surprised to hear Carl Sandburg sing the same song as part of his repertoire of folk ballads of the Midwest. I had not heard it since Mother had sung it to us.

Mother later moved to Kansas City, Missouri, and then to South Omaha. Her marriage there to my father was her second. As a very young girl in Moberly, she had married John Harvey, but he was, to use her words, "a no-good yellah nigger, who expected me to support him." They had one child, Gertrude, before he deserted her.

Gertie came to Omaha some time after my mother and married my father's youngest brother, George. I have a feeling that Mother promoted this match; the two hard-working, sober Hall brothers must have been quite a catch!

As I remember Mother in my childhood years, she was a small, brown-skinned woman, rather on the plumpish side, with large and beautiful soft brown eyes. She had the humped, Indian nose of the Thorpe family.

My first memory of her is hearing her sing as she did housework. She had a melodious contralto voice and what seemed to me to be an endless and varied repertoire. Much of what I know about this period, I learned from her songs. These included lullabies ("Go to Sleep You Little Pickaninny, Mamma's Gonna Swat You if You Don't") and many spirituals and jubilee songs. There were also innumerable folk ballads, and the popular songs of her day, like "Down at the Ball" and "Where Did You Get That Hat?" Then there was the old song the slaves sang about their masters fleeing the Union Army, "The Year of Jubilo."

Oh darkies, have you seen the Massah with the mustache on his face?
He was gwine down de road dis mornin' like he's gwine to leave dis place.
Oh, Massah run, ha ha!
And the darkies sing, ho ho!
It must be now the Kingdom comin' and de year of Jubilo!

Mother never went to school a day in her life, but she had a phenomenal memory and was a virtual repository of Black folklore. My brother Otto taught her to read and write when she was forty years old. She told stories of life on the plantations, of the "hollers" they used. When a slave wanted to talk to a friend on a neighboring plantation, she would throw back her head and half sing, half yell, "Oh, Bes-sie, I wa-ant to see you." Often you could hear one of the "hollers" a mile away.

When Mother was a girl, camp meetings were a big part of her life. She had songs she remembered from the meetings, like "I Don't Feel Weary, No Ways Tired," and she would imitate the preachers with all of their promises of fire and brimstone. Later, when we lived in South Omaha, she was very active in the African Methodist Episcopal Church. As a means of raising funds, she used to organize church theatricals. Otto would help her read the plays; she would then direct them and usually play the leading role herself. She was a natural mimic. I heard her go through entire plays from beginning to end, imitating the voices (even the male ones) and the actions of the performers.

In addition to caring for Otto, Eppa, and myself, Mother got jobs catering parties for rich white families in North Omaha. She would bring us back all sorts of goodies and leftovers from these parties. Sometimes she would get together with her friends among the other domestics, and they would have a great time panning their employers and exchanging news of the white folks' scandalous doings.

Mother had the great fighting spirit of her family. She was a strong-minded woman with great ambition for her children, especially for us boys. Eppa, who was a plain Black girl, was sensitive but physically tough, courageous, and a regular tomboy. Worried about her future, Mother insisted that she learn the piano and arranged for her to take lessons at twenty-five cents each. Though she learned to play minor classics such as "Poet and Peasant" and arias from such operas as *Aida* and *Il Trovatore,* accompanied the choir, and so on, Eppa never liked music very much and was not consoled by it the way Mother was.

As a wife, Mother had a way of making Father feel the part of the man in the house. She flattered his ego and always addressed him as "Mr. Hall" in front of guests and us children.

Life in South Omaha

You ask what town I love the best.
South Omaha, South Omaha!
The fairest town of all the rest,
South Omaha, South Omaha!
Where yonder's Papillion's limp stream
To where Missouri's waters gleam.
Oh, fairest town, oh town of mine,
South Omaha, South Omaha!

In the early part of the century, the days of my youth, South Omaha was an independent city. In 1915, it was annexed to become part of the larger city of Omaha. Like many midwestern towns, the city took its name from the original inhabitants of the area. In this case, it was the Omaha Indians of the Sioux tribal family. The area was a camping ground of the Lewis and Clark Expedition of 1804. It grew in importance when it became a licensed trading post and an important outfitting point during the Colorado Gold Rush. But the main growth of South Omaha came in the 1880s as the meatpacking industry developed.

In 1877, the first refrigerated railroad cars were perfected. This made it possible to slaughter livestock in the Midwest and ship the meat to the large markets in eastern cities. As a result, the meatpacking industry grew tremendously.

The city leaders saw the opportunity and encouraged the expanding packing industry to settle there—offering them special tax concessions and so forth. The town, situated on a plateau back from the Big Muddy (the Missouri River), began to grow. Soon it was almost an industrial suburb of Omaha and was one of the three largest packing centers in the country. All of the big packers of the time—Armour, Swift, Wilson, and Cudahy—had big branches there. Cudahy's main plant was in South Omaha.

The industry brought with it growing railroad traffic. As a boy, I watched the dozens of lines of cars as they carried livestock in from the West and butchered meat to ship out to the East. The Burlington; the Chicago and Northwestern; the Chicago, Milwaukee, St. Paul, and Pacific; the Illinois Central; the Rock Island; the Union Pacific—all of these lines had terminals there. By 1910, Omaha was the fourth-largest railway center in the country.

When I was born in 1898, South Omaha was a bustling town of about twenty thousand. Most of these twenty thousand people were foreign-born and first-generation immigrants. The two largest groups were the Irish and the Bohemians (or Czechs). There was a sprinkling of other Slavic groups—Poles, Russians, Serbs—as well as Germans, Greeks, and Italians.

The Bohemians were the largest ethnic group in town. They lived mainly in the southern part of town, toward the river, in the Brown Park and Albright sections. One thing that impressed me was their concern with education. They were a cultured group of people. I can't remember any of them being illiterate, and they had their own newspaper. They were involved in the political wheelings and dealings of the town and were successful at it. At one time, both the mayor and chief of police were Bohemians.

The Irish were the second-largest group, scattered throughout the town. The newly arrived poor "shanty" Irish would first settle on Indian Hill, near the stockyards. There were two classes of Irish—the "shanty" Irish on the one hand, and the "old settlers" or "lace-curtain" Irish on the other. This second group, who had settled only one generation before, was mostly made up of middle-class, white-collar, civil service, and professional workers who lived near North Omaha. There were also a few Irish who were very rich, managers and executives who lived in Omaha proper. They had become well assimilated into the community. The tendency was for the poorer Irish to live in South Omaha, and those who had "made it" to one degree or another would move up to North Omaha or Omaha proper.

There were only a few dozen Black families in South Omaha, scattered throughout the community. There was no Black ghetto and, as I saw it, no "Negro problem." This was due undoubtedly to our small numbers, although there was a relatively large number of Blacks living in North Omaha. The Black community there had grown after Blacks were brought in as strikebreakers during the 1894 strike in the packing industry, but no real ghetto developed until after World War I.

Our family lived in the heart of the Bohemian neighborhood in South Omaha. Nearly all our neighbors were Bohemians. They came from many backgrounds; there were workers and peasants, professionals, artists, musicians, and other skilled artisans, all fleeing from the oppressive rule of the Austro-Hungarian Empire.

They were friendly people and kept up their language and traditions. On Saturdays, families would gather at one of the beer gardens to sing and dance. I remember watching them dance schottisches and polkas, listening to the beautiful music of their bands and orchestras, or running after their great marching bands when they were in a parade. On special occasions, they would bring out their colorful costumes. Much of their community life centered around the gymnastic clubs—Sokols or Turners' Halls—that they had established.

There were differences in how the ethnic groups related to each other and to the Blacks in town. In those days, Indian Hill was the stomping ground of teenage Irish toughs. One day, a mob of predominantly Irish youths ran the small Greek colony out of town when one of their members allegedly killed an Irish cop. I remember seeing the Greek community leaving town one Sunday afternoon. There were men, women, and children (about a hundred in all) walking down the railroad tracks, carrying everything they could hold. Some of their houses had been burned, and a few of them had been beaten up in town.

We should have seen the danger for us in this, but one Black man even boasted to my father about how he had helped run the Greeks out. My father called him a fool. "What business did you have helping that bunch of whites? Next time it might be you they run out!" The incident was an ominous sign of tensions that were to come many years later.

At the time, however, our family got along well with all the immigrant families in our immediate neighborhood. I loved the sweet haunting melodies of the Irish folk ballads: "Rose of Tralee," "Mother Machree," and many of the popular songs, like "My Irish Molly-O" and "Augraghawan, I Want to Go Back to Oregon."

There was a Bohemian couple living next door. On occasion, Mr. Rehau would get a bit too much under his belt. He'd come home and really raise hell. When this happened, Mrs. Rehau scurried to Officer Bingham, the Black cop, to get some help. I remember one afternoon when Bingham came to lend a hand in taming him. The Bohemian was a little guy compared to him. Officer Bingham threw him down out in the yard and plunked himself down on Rehau's back.

Dust flew as he kicked and thrashed and tried to get out from under the Black man. Bingham just "rode the storm," and when Rehau raised his head, he'd smack him around until the rebellion subsided.

"Had enough?" he'd yell at his victim. "You gonna behave now and mind what Mrs. Rehau says?" All the while, she was running around them, waving her apron.

"Beat him some more, Mr. Bingham, please! Make him be good."

Finally, either Bingham got tired or Mr. Rehau just gave out and peace returned to the neighborhood.

"Police and community relations" were less tense then. The cops knew how to control a situation without using guns. Often this meant they'd get into actual fist fights. In those days, there was a big Black guy in town named Sam, a beef-lugger like my father. Sam was a nice quiet guy, but on occasion he'd go on a drunk and fight anyone within arm's length (which was a big area). The cops generally handled it by fighting it out with him.

But I remember one time Sam really caused a row. He was outside a bar on J Street, up in Omaha proper. During the course of his drunk, he'd beaten up five or six of the regular cops. This called for extreme measures. Briggs, the chief of police, came to the scene to restore law and order. He marched up to Sam and threw out his chest.

"Now Sam, it's time for you to behave, you hear?" He even pulled out his thirty-eight to show he meant business.

But Sam wasn't ready to behave. He came at Briggs, intending to lay him out like he'd done with the other officers. Briggs backed up one step at a time.

"Sam, you stop. You hear me Sam? Time to stop, now."

Sam forced Briggs all the way back to his carriage. Once Briggs was in, he delivered his final threat: "Sam, you come down to City Hall on Monday and see me. This just can't happen this way."

Briggs drove off. Monday morning came and Sam went down to City Hall. He was fined for being drunk and disorderly. He didn't fight the court and willingly paid the fine. It seemed like an unwritten agreement. The cops wouldn't shoot when Sam went on a spree. When it was over, Sam would go and pay his fine, and that would end the whole business.

Our family was the only Black family in our neighborhood, and we were pretty well insulated from the racist pressures of the outside world. As children we were only very dimly aware of what Du Bois called the "veil of color between the races."

I first became aware of the veil, not from anything that happened in the town, but from what my parents and grandparents told me of how southern whites had persecuted Blacks and of how they had suffered under slavery. I remember Grandfather and Grandmother Thorpe showing me the scars they had on their backs from the overseer's lash. I remember Pa reading newspaper accounts of the endless reign of lynch terror in the South, and about the 1908 riots in Springfield, Illinois.

In 1908, Jack Johnson, the first Black heavyweight champion, defeated the "great white hope," Jim Jeffries. Pa said that it was the occasion for a new round of lynchings in the South. There were other great Black fighters—Sam Langford, Joe Jeanette, and Sam McVey, for instance—but Johnson was the first Black heavyweight to be able to fight for the championship and the first to win it.

He was conscious that he was a Black man in a racist world. "I'm Black, they never let me forget it. I'm Black, I'll never forget it." Jeffries had been pushed as the hope of the white race to reclaim the heavyweight crown from Johnson. When Johnson knocked out Jeffries, it was a symbol of Black defiance and self-assertion. To Blacks, the victory meant pride and hope. It was a challenge to the authority of bigoted whites and to them it called for extra measures to "keep the niggers in their place."

To us children, Black repression seemed restricted to the South, outside the orbit of our immediate experience. As I saw it then, there was no deliberate plot of white against Black. I thought there were two kinds of white folk: good and bad, and the latter were mainly in the South. Most of those I knew in South Omaha were good people. Disillusionment came later in my life.

The friendly interracial atmosphere of South Omaha was illustrated by the presence of Officer Bingham and Officer Ballou, two Black cops in the town's small police force. Bingham was a big, Black, and jolly fellow. His beat was our neighborhood. Ballou was a tall, slim, ramrod-straight, and light-brown-skinned Black. He was a veteran of the Black Tenth Cavalry. He had fought in the Indian wars against Geronimo and had participated in the chase for Billy the Kid. Ballou was also a veteran of the Spanish–American War. All the kids, Black and white, regarded him with a special awe and respect. Both Black officers were treated as respectable members of the community, liked by the people because they had their confidence. While they wore guns, they never seemed to use them. These cops fought tough characters with fists and clubs, pulling a gun only rarely, and then only in self-defense. It seemed that a large part of their duty was to keep the kids out of mischief.

"Officer Bingham," the Bohemian woman across the alley would call, "would you please keep an eye on my boy Frontal. See he don't make trouble."

"Don't worry, Mrs. Brazda. He's a good boy."

"Has Haywood been a good boy?"

"Oh yes, Mrs. Hall. He's all right." And he would stop for a chat. My sister Eppa, a lad called Willy Starens, and I were the only Black kids in the Brown Park Elementary School. My brother Otto had already graduated and was in South Omaha High. Our schoolmates were predominantly Bohemians, with a sprinkling of Irish, German, and a few Anglo-Americans. My close childhood chums included two Bohemian lads, Frank Brazda and Jimmy Rehau; an Anglo-Irish kid, Earl Power; and Willy Ziegler, who was of German parentage. We were an inseparable fivesome, in and out of each other's homes all the time.

During my first years in school, I was plagued by asthma and was absent from school many months at a time. The result was that I was a year behind. I finally outgrew this infirmity and became a strong, healthy boy. By the time I reached the eighth grade, I had become one of the best students in my class, sharing this honor with a Bohemian girl, Bertha Himmel. Both of us could solve any problem in arithmetic, both were good at spelling, and at interschool spelling bees our school usually won the first prize. My self-confidence was encouraged by my teachers, all of whom were white and yet uniformly kind and sympathetic.

Of course, like all kids, I had plenty of fights. But race was seldom involved. Occasionally, I would hear the word "nigger." While it evoked anger in me, it seemed no more disparaging than the terms "bohunk," "sheeny," "dago," "shanty Irish," or "poor white trash." All were terms of common usage, interchangeable as slurring epithets on one's ethnic background, and usually employed outside the hearing of the person in question.

In contrast to the daily life of the neighborhood, however, the virus of racism was subtly injected into the classroom at the Brown Park School I attended. The five races of mankind illustrated in our geography books portrayed the Negro with the receding forehead and prognathous jaws of a gorilla. There was a complete absence of Black heroes in the history books, supporting the inference that the Black man had contributed nothing to civilization. We were taught that Blacks were brought out of the savagery of the jungles of Africa and introduced to civilization through slavery under the benevolent auspices of the white man.

In spite of my father's submissive attitude, it is to him that I must give credit for scotching this big lie about the Negro's past. His attitude grew out of his concern for our survival in a hostile environment. He felt most strongly that the Negro was not innately inferior. He perceived that his children must have some sense of self-respect and confidence to sustain them until that distant day when, through "obvious merit and just desert," Blacks would receive their award of equality and recognition.

Father possessed an amazing store of knowledge that he had culled from his readings. He would tell us about the Black civilizations of ancient Egypt, Ethiopia, and Cush. He would quote from the Song of Solomon: "I am Black and comely, oh ye daughters of Jerusalem." He would tell us about Black soldiers in the Civil War; about the massacre of Blacks at Fort Pillow and the battle cry they used thereafter, "Remember Fort Pillow! Remember Fort Pillow!"[2] He knew about the Haitian Revolution, the defeat of Napoleon's army by Toussaint-Louverture, Dessalines, and Jean Christophe. He told us about the famous Zulu chief Shaka in South Africa; about Alexandre Dumas, the great French romanticist, and Pushkin, the great Russian poet, who were both Black.

Father said that he had taught himself to read and write. He had an extensive library, which took up half of one of the walls in our living room. His books were mainly historical works—his favorite subject. They included such titles as *The Decisive Battles of the World, The Rise and Fall of the Roman Empire,* and many histories of England, France, Germany, and Russia. He had *Stanley in Africa,* and a number of biographies of famous men, including Napoleon, Caesar, and Hannibal (who Father said was a Negro). He had Scott's *Ivanhoe* and his Waverly novels; Bulwer-Lytton; Alexandre Dumas's novels and the *Life and Times of Frederick Douglass,* and *Up from Slavery,* by Booker T. Washington.

On another wall there was a huge picture of the charge of the Twenty-Fifth Black Infantry and the Tenth Cavalry at San Juan Hill, rescuing Teddy

Roosevelt and the Rough Riders. There were pictures of Frederick Douglass and, of course, his hero, Booker T. Washington. He would lecture to us on history, displaying his extensive knowledge. He was a great admirer of Napoleon. He would get into one of his lecturing moods and pace up and down with his hands behind his back before the rapt audience of my sister Eppa and myself.

Talking about the Battle of Waterloo, he would say, "Wellington was in a tough spot that day. Napoleon was about to whip him; the trouble was Blucher hadn't shown up."

"Who was he, Pa?"

"He was the German general who was supposed to reinforce Wellington with thirteen thousand Prussian troops. Wellington was getting awful nervous, walking up and down behind the lines and saying, 'Oh! If Blucher fails to come! Where is Blucher?' "

"Did he finally get there, Pa?"

"Yes, son, he finally got there and turned the tide of battle. And if he hadn't shown up and Napoleon had won, the whole course of history would have been changed."

It was through Father that I entered the world of books. I developed an unquenchable thirst to learn about people and their history. I remember going to the town library when I was nine or ten and asking, "Do you have a history of the world for children?"

My first love became the historical novel. I loved George Henty's books; they always dealt with the exploits of a sixteen-year-old during an important historical period. Through Henty's heroes, I too was with Bonnie Prince Charlie, with Wellington in the Spanish Peninsula, with Gustavus Adolphus at Lützen in the Thirty Years' War, with Clive in India, and under Drake's flag around the world. I was also fascinated by romances of the feudal period, such as *When Knighthood Was in Flower* and *Ivanhoe*. I read Twain's *Huckleberry Finn* and *Tom Sawyer* and the works of H. Rider Haggard.

I went through a definite Anglophile stage, in part due to the influence of a Jamaican named Mr. Williams who worked as assistant janitor with my father. Mr. Williams was a huge Black man with scars all over his face. He was a former stoker in the British navy. I was attracted by his strange accent and haughty demeanor. Evidently he saw in me an appreciative audience. I would listen with open mouth and wonder at the stories of the strange places he had seen, of his adventures in faraway lands. He was a real British patriot, a Black imperialist, if such was possible.

He would declare, "The sun never sets on the British Empire," and then sing

"Rule Britannia! Britannia rule the waves." He quoted Napoleon as allegedly saying, "Britain is a small garden, but she grows some bitter weeds" and "Give me French soldiers and British officers, and I will conquer the world." I pictured myself as a British sailor, and I read *Two Years before the Mast* and *Battle of Trafalgar*.

"Do you think they would let me join the British navy?" I asked Mr. Williams.

"No, my lad," he answered. "You have to be a British citizen or subject to do that." I was quite disappointed.

But it was not only British romance that fascinated me. At about the age of twelve I became a Francophile. I read all of Dumas's novels and quite a number of other novels about France. I had begun to read French history, which to me turned out to be as interesting as the novels and equally romantic. I read about Joan of Arc, the Hundred Years' War, Francis I; about Catherine de Medici, the Huguenots and Admiral Coligny, the Duc de Guise, the massacre of St. Bartholomew Eve or the night of the long knives; then the French Revolution, *A Tale of Two Cities*, the guillotining of Charlotte Corday, and the assassination of Marat.

Occasionally, the ugly reality of race would intrude upon the dream world of my childhood. I distinctly remember two such occasions. One was when a white family from Arkansas moved across the alley from us. Mr. Faught, the patriarch of the clan, was a typical rednecked peckerwood. He would sit around the storefront, chewing tobacco, telling how they treated "niggers" down his way.

"They were made to stay in their place—down in the cotton patch—not in factories taking white men's jobs."

As I remember, his racist harangues did not make much of an impression on the local white audience. Apparently at that time there was no feeling of competition in South Omaha because there were so few Blacks. I would also imagine that his slovenly appearance did not jibe with his white supremacist pretensions.

One day a substitute teacher took over our class. I was about ten years old. The substitute was a southerner from Arkansas. During history class she started talking about the Civil War. The slaves, she said, did not really want freedom because they were happy as they were. They would have been freed by their masters in a few years anyway. Her villain was General Grant, whom she contrasted unfavorably with General Robert E. Lee.

"Lee was a gentleman," she put forth. "But Grant was a cigar-smoking liquor-drinking roughneck."

She didn't like Sherman either, and talked about his "murdering rampage" through Georgia. I wasn't about to take all of this and challenged her.

"I don't know about General Grant's habits, but he did beat Lee. Besides, Lee couldn't have been much of a gentleman; he owned slaves!"

Livid with rage, she shouted, "That's enough—what I could say about you!"

"Well, what could you say?" I challenged.

She apparently saw that wild racist statements wouldn't work in this situation and that I was trying to provoke her to do something like that. She cut short the argument, shouting, "That's enough."

"Yes, that's enough," I sassed.

During the heated exchange, I felt that I had the sympathy of most of my classmates. After school, some gathered around me and said, "You certainly told her off!"

When I told Mother she supported me. "You done right, son," she said.

But Father was not so sure. "You might have gotten into trouble."

I feel now that one of the reasons for my self-confidence during my childhood years, and why the racist notions of innate Black inferiority left me cold, was my older brother Otto. His example belied such claims. He was the most brilliant one in our family, and probably in all of South Omaha. He had skipped a grade both in grade school and in high school and was a real prodigy. He was a natural poet and won many prizes in composition. His poem on the charge of the Twenty-Fifth Black Infantry and Tenth Cavalry at San Juan Hill was published in one of the Omaha dailies. Otto was praised by all of his teachers. "An unusual boy," they said, "clearly destined to become a leader of his race."

One day, one of his teachers and a Catholic priest called on Mother and Father to talk about Otto's future. Otto was about fourteen at the time. They suggested that he might be good material for the priesthood and that there was a possibility of his getting a scholarship for Creighton University, Omaha's famous Jesuit school. The teacher suggested that if this were agreed to, he should take up Latin. My parents were extremely flattered, despite the fact that they were good Methodists (AME). Even Father, who did not seem ambitious for his children, was impressed.

But when the proposition was placed before Otto, he vehemently disagreed. He did not want to become a priest, nor did he want to study Latin. He wanted, he said, to be an architect! Doctors, dentists, teachers, and preachers—these were the professions for an ambitious Black in those days.

"An architect!" they exclaimed in amazement. "Who ever heard of a Black architect?"

"Who ever heard of a Black priest?" Otto retorted. (At that time there were only two or three Black priests in the entire United States.)

"But Otto," Mother argued, "you'll have the support of a lot of prominent white folks. They'll help you through college."

But Otto would have none of it. Undoubtedly, my parents thought that they could finally wear down his opposition and that he would become more amenable in time. They did force him to take Latin, a subject he hated.

Otto stayed in school but no longer seemed interested in his studies. He dropped out of school suddenly in his senior year. He was sixteen. He left home and got a job as a bellhop in a hotel in North Omaha's Black community. This move cut completely the few remaining ties he had with his white age group in South Omaha.

Otto's drop-out from high school evidently signified that he had given up the struggle to be somebody in the white world. He had become disillusioned with the white world and therefore sought identity with his own people. During my childhood years, our relationship had never been close. There was, of course, the age gap—he was seven years older. But even in later years, when we were closer and had more in common, we never talked about our childhood. I don't know why. As a child I had been proud of his academic feats and boasted about them to my friends.

At the time he left high school, Otto was the only Black in South Omaha High and was about to become its first Black graduate. Highly praised by his teachers and popular among his fellow students, he was a real showpiece in the school.

What caused him to drop out of school in his senior year? Thinking back on it, I don't believe that it had anything to do with the attempt to make him a priest. I think he had won that battle a couple of years before. At least, I never heard the matter mentioned again.

Otto undoubtedly had high aspirations at one time, as evidenced by his desire to become an architect. Somewhere along the line they disappeared. Perhaps a contributing factor was the accumulating effect of Otto's malady. On occasion, Mother would remind us that Otto had water on the brain and that he was different from Eppa and myself. At the time, he seemed smarter than us, more independent and in rebellion against Pa's lack of encouragement and moral support and his parental authority. Certainly in adult life Otto used to sleep about ten hours a day and very often fell asleep in meetings. He seemed to lack the ability of prolonged concentration, although whatever brain damage he may have suffered never affected the quickness of his mind and ability to grasp the nub of any question or the capacity for leadership that he showed on a number of occasions.

But more debilitating, probably, than any physical disease was the generation gap of that era—between parents of slave backgrounds and children born free, particularly in the north. Otto's dropping out of school and his later radical political development were undoubtedly related to a conflict more intense than the ones of today.

Father was an ardent follower of Booker T. Washington. His ambitions for his sons were very modest, to put it mildly. He undoubtedly would have been satisfied if we could become good law-abiding citizens with stable jobs. He thought of jobs a notch or two above his own station, like a postal employee, a skilled tradesman, or a clerk in the civil service. The offer of a scholarship for the priesthood was, therefore, simply beyond his expectations, and I guess the old man was deeply disappointed at Otto's rejection of it.

Otto was quite independent and would not conform to Father's idea of discipline. For example, he was completely turned off on the question of religion, and Father could not force him to go to church. I don't remember Otto ever going to church with the family. Father claimed that Otto was irresponsible and wild. As a result, there was mutual hostility between them. There were numerous thrashings when Otto was young and violent quarrels between them as he grew older. Mother would usually defend Otto. Grandpa Thorpe, himself a strict disciplinarian, would warn Mother, "Hattie, you mark my words, that boy is going to lan' in the pen."

At some point, Otto came to the conclusion that there was no use in continuing his education. He must have felt that it was irrelevant. Opportunities for educated Blacks were few, even in North Omaha's Black community, where there were only a few professionals. In that community there were a few preachers, one doctor, one dentist, and one or two teachers. Black businesses consisted of owners of several undertaking establishments, a couple of barbershops, and a few pool rooms. The only other Blacks in any sort of middle-class positions were a few postal employees, civil service workers, and Pullman porters and waiters.

Then too, Otto had passed through the age of puberty and was becoming more and more conscious of his race. Along with the natural detachment and withdrawal from childhood socializing with girls—in his case white girls who were former childhood sweethearts—Otto experienced a withdrawal and nonsocialization because of his race. He ended up quite alone because there were not many Black kids his age in South Omaha. There wasn't much contact with the Black kids from North Omaha either. As a very sensitive person on the verge of manhood, I imagine he began to feel these changes keenly.

After he dropped out of school in 1908, Otto was soon attracted to the "sportin' life"—the pool halls and sporting houses of North Omaha. He wanted to be among Black people; he was anxious to get away from Father. Thus, he left home and got jobs as a bellhop, shoeshine boy, and busboy. He began to absorb a new way of life, stepping fully into the social life of the Black community in North Omaha. He'd evidently heeded the "call of the blood" and gone back to the race. It was not until a few years later, when I had similar experiences, that I understood that Otto had arrived at the first stage in his identity crisis and had gone to where he felt he belonged.

He would come home quite often, though, flaunting his new clothes, a "box-backed" suit—"fitting nowhere but the shoulders," high-heeled Stacey Adams button shoes, and a Stetson hat. He'd give a few dollars to Mother and some dimes to me and my sister. Sometimes he would bring a pretty girlfriend with him. But most of the time, he would bring a young man, Henry Starens, who was a piano player. He played a style popular in those days, later to be known as boogie-woogie, in which the piano was the whole orchestra. He played Ma Rainey's famous blues "Make Me a Pallet on Your Floor, Make It Where Your Man Will Never Know," and the old favorite "Alabama Bound":

> Alabama Bound,
> I'm Alabama Bound.
> Oh, babe, don't leave me here,
> Just leave a dime for beer.

A boy of ten at the time, I was tremendously impressed. There is no doubt that Otto's experience served to weaken some of my childish notions about making it in the white world.

Halley's Comet and My Religion

On May 4, 1910, Halley's comet appeared flaring down out of the heavens, its luminous tail switching to earth. It was an ominous sight.

A rash of religious revival swept Omaha. Prophets and messiahs appeared on street corners and in churches preaching the end of the world. Hardened sinners "got religion." Backsliders renewed their faith. The comet, with its tail moving ever closer to the earth, seemed to lend credence to forecasts of imminent cosmic disaster.

Both my mother and father were deeply religious. Theirs was that "old time religion," the fire-and-brimstone kind that leaned heavily on the Old Testament. It was the kind that accepted the Bible and all its legends as the literal, gospel truth. We children had the "fear of the Lord" drilled into us from early age. My image of God was that of a vengeful old man who demanded unquestioned faith, strict obedience, and repentant love as the price of salvation:

I the Lord thy God am a jealous God, visiting the iniquity of the fathers upon the children unto the third and fourth generation of them that hate me, and showing mercy unto thousands of them that love me and keep my commandments.

Thou shalt love the Lord thy God with all thy heart, and with all thy soul, and with all thy might.

Every Sunday, rain or shine, the family would attend services at the little frame church near the railroad tracks. For me, this was a torturous ordeal. I looked forward to Sundays with dread. We would spend all of eight hours in church. We would sit through the morning service, then the Sunday school, after which followed a break for dinner. We returned at five for the Young People's Christian Endeavor and finally the evening service. It was not just boredom. Fear was the dominant emotion, especially when our preacher, Reverend Jamieson, a big Black man with a beautiful voice, would launch into one of his fire-and-brimstone sermons. He would start out slowly and in a low voice; gradually raising it higher, he would swing to a kind of singsong rhythm, holding his congregation rapt with vivid word pictures. They would respond with "Hallelujah!" "Ain't it the truth!" "Preach it, brother!" He would go on in this manner for what seemed an interminable time and would reach his peroration on a high note, winding up with a rafter-shaking burst of oratory. He would then pause dramatically amid moans, shouts, and even screams of some of the women, one or two of whom would fall in a dead faint. Waiting for them to subside he would then, in a lowered, scarcely audible voice, reassure his flock that it was not yet too late to repent and achieve salvation. All that was necessary was to "repent, sinners, and love and obey the Lord. Amen." Someone would then rise and lead off with an appropriate spiritual, such as

Oh, my sins are forgiven and my soul set free-ah,
Oh, glory Halelua-a-a-a!
Just let me in the kingdom when the world is all a'fi-ah,
Oh glory Halelu!
I don't feel worried, no ways tiahd,
Oh, glory Halelu!

I remember the family Bible, a huge book that lay on the center table in the front room. The first several pages were blank, set aside for recording the vital family statistics: births, deaths, marriages. The book was filled with graphic illustrations of biblical happenings. Leafing through Genesis (which we used to call "the Begats"), one came to Exodus, and from there on, a pageant of bloodshed and violence unfolded. Portrayed in striking colors were the interminable tribal wars in which the Israelites slew thousands and Pharaoh's soldiers killed little children in search of Moses. There was the great God, Jehovah himself, white-bearded and eyes flashing, looking very much like our old cracker neighbor, Mr. Faught.

Just a couple of weeks before Halley's comet appeared, Mother had taken us to see the silent film *Dante's Inferno*, through which I sat with open-mouth horror. Needless to say, this experience did not lessen my apprehension.

The comet continued its descent, its tail like the flaming sword of vengeance. Collision seemed not just possible, but almost certain. What had we poor mortals done to incur such wrath of the Lord?

My deportment underwent a change. I did all my chores without complaint and helped Mama around the house. This was so unlike me that she didn't know what to make of it. I overheard her telling Pa about my good behavior and how helpful I had become lately. But I hadn't really changed. I was just scared. I was simply trying to carry out another one of God's commandments, "Honor thy father and thy mother that thy days may be prolonged, and that it may go well with thee in the land which the Lord thy God giveth thee."

Then one night, when the whole neighborhood had gathered as usual on the hill to watch the comet, it appeared to have ceased its movement toward the earth. We were not sure, but the next night we were certain. It had not only ceased its descent but was definitely withdrawing. In a couple more nights, it had disappeared. A wave of relief swept over the town.

"It's not true!" I thought to myself. "The fire and brimstone, the leering devils, the angry vengeful God: None of it is true."

It was as if a great weight had been lifted from my mind. It was the end of my religion, although I still thought that there was most likely a supreme being. But if God existed, he was nothing like the God portrayed in our family Bible. I was no longer terrified of him. Later, at the age of fourteen or fifteen, I read some of the lectures of Robert G. Ingersoll and became an agnostic, doubting the existence of a god. From there, I later moved to positive atheism.

Two years later, the great event was the sinking of the *Titanic*. This was significant in Omaha because one of the Brandeis brothers, owners of the biggest department store in North Omaha, went down with her. In keeping with the custom of Blacks to gloat over the misfortunes of whites, especially rich ones, some Black bard composed the "Titanic Blues":

When old John Jacob Astor left his home,
He never thought he was going to die.
Titanic fare thee well,
I say fare thee well.

But disaster was more frequently reserved for the Black community. On Easter Sunday, 1913, a tornado struck North Omaha. It ripped a two-block swath through the Black neighborhood, leaving death and destruction in its wake. Among the victims were a dozen or so Black youths trapped in a basement below a pool hall where they had evidently been shooting craps. Mother did not fail to point out the incident as another example of God's wrath. While I was sorry for the youths and their families (some of them were friends of Otto), the implied warning left me cold. My God-fearing days had ended with Halley's comet.

Misfortune, however, was soon to strike our immediate family. It happened that summer, in 1913. My father fled town after being attacked and beaten by a gang of whites on Q Street, right outside the gate of the packing plant. They told him to get out of town or they would kill him.

I remember vividly the scene that night when Father staggered through the door. Consternation gripped us at the sight. His face was swollen and bleeding, his clothes torn and in disarray. He had a frightened, hunted look in his eyes. My sister Eppa and I were alone. Mother had gone for the summer to work for her employers, rich white folks, at Lake Okoboji, Iowa.

"What happened?" we asked. He gasped out the story of how he had been attacked and beaten.

"They said they were going to kill me if I didn't get out of town."

We asked him who "they" were. He said that he recognized some of them as belonging to the Irish gang on Indian Hill, but there were also some grown men.

"But why, Pa? Why should they pick on you?"

"Why don't we call the police?"

"That ain't goin' to do no good. We just have to leave town."

"But Pa," I said, "how can we? We own this house. We've got friends here. If you tell them, they wouldn't let anybody harm us."

Again the frightened look crossed his face.

"No, we got to go."

"Where, where will we go?"

"We'll move up to Minneapolis. Your uncles Watt and George are there. I'll get work there. I'm going to telegraph your Mother to come home now."

He washed his face and then went into the bedroom and began packing his bags. The next morning he gave Eppa some money and said, "This will tide you over till your Mother comes. She'll be here in a day or two. I'm going to telegraph her as soon as I get to the depot. I'll send for you all soon."

He kissed us goodbye and left.

Only when he closed the door behind him did we feel the full impact of the shock. It had happened so suddenly. Our whole world had collapsed. Home and security were gone. The feeling of safety in our little haven of interracial goodwill had proved elusive. Now we were just homeless "niggers" on the run.

The cruelest blow, perhaps, was the shattering of my image of Father. True enough, I had not regarded him as a hero. Still, however, I had retained a great deal of respect for him. He was undoubtedly a very complex man, very sensitive and imaginative. Probably he had never gotten over the horror of that scene in the cabin in Haywood County, Tennessee, where as a boy of fifteen he had seen his father kill the Klansman. He distrusted and feared poor whites, especially the native born and, in Omaha, the shanty Irish.

Mother arrived the next day. For her it was a real tragedy. Our home was gone and our family broken up. She had lived in Omaha for nearly a quarter of a century. She had raised her family there and had built up a circle of close friends. With her regular summer job at Lake Okoboji and catering parties the rest of the year, she had helped pay for our home. Now it was gone. We would be lucky if we even got a fraction of the money we had put into it, not to speak of the labor. Now she was to leave all this. Friends and neighbors would ask why Father had run away.

Why had he let some poor white trash run him out of town? He had friends there. Ours was an old respected family. He also had influential white patrons. There was Ed Cudahy of the family that owned the packing plant where he worked. The Cudahys had become one of the nation's big three in the slaughtering and meatpacking industry. Father had known him from boyhood. There was Mr. Wilkins, general manager at Cudahy's, whom Father had known as an office boy and who now gave Father all his old clothes.

A few days later, Mr. Cannon, a railroad man in charge of a buffet car on the Omaha and Minneapolis run and an old friend of the family, called with a message from Father. He said that Father was all right, that he had gotten a job for himself and Mother at the Minneapolis Women's Club. Father was to become caretaker and janitor, Mother was to cater the smaller parties at the club and to assist at the larger affairs. They were to live on the place in a basement apartment.

The salary was ridiculously small (I think about sixty dollars per month for both of them), and the employers insisted that only one of us children would be allowed to live at the place. That, of course, would be Eppa. He said that Father had arranged for me to live with another family. This, he said, would be a temporary arrangement. He was sure he could find another job and rent a house where we could all be together again. As for me, Father suggested that since I was fifteen, I could find a part-time job to help out while continuing school. Mr. Cannon said that he was to take me back to Minneapolis with him, and that Mother and Eppa were to follow in a few days.

With regards to our house, Mr. Cannon said that he knew a lawyer, an honest fellow, who for a small commission would handle its sale. Mother later claimed that after deducting the lawyer's commission and paying off a small mortgage, they only got the paltry sum of three hundred dollars! This was for a five-room house with electricity and running water.

The next day, Mr. Cannon took me out to his buffet car in the railroad yards. He put me in the pantry and told me to stay there, and if the conductor looked in, "Don't be afraid, he's a friend of mine." Our car was then attached to a train that backed down to the station to load passengers. I looked out the window as we left Omaha. I was not to see Omaha again until after World War I, when I was a waiter on the Burlington Railroad.

My childhood and part of my adolescence was now behind me. I felt that I was practically on my own. What did the world hold for me—a Black youth?

Arriving in Minneapolis, I went to my new school. As I entered the room, the all-white class was singing old darkie plantation songs. Upon seeing me, their voices seemed to take on a mocking, derisive tone. Loudly emphasizing the Negro dialect and staring directly at me, they sang,

Down in de caun fiel—HEAH DEM darkies moan,
All de darkies AM a weeping
MASSAHS in DE cold cold ground.

They were really having a ball.

In my state of increased racial awareness, this was just too much for me. I was already in a mood of deep depression. With the breakup of our family, the separation from my childhood friends, and the interminable quarrels between Mother and Father (in which I sided with Mother), I was in no mood to be kidded or scoffed at.

That was my last day in school. I never returned. I made up my mind to drop out and get a full-time job.

I was fifteen and in the second semester of the eighth grade.

2

A BLACK REGIMENT IN WORLD WAR I

On the Negroes this double experience of deliberate and devilish persecu-
tion from their own countrymen, coupled with a taste of real democracy
and world-old culture, was revolutionizing. They began to hate prejudice
and discrimination as they had never hated it before. They began to real-
ize its eternal meaning and complications. . . . They were filled with a bit-
ter, dogged determination never to give up the fight for Negro equality in
America. . . . A new, radical Negro spirit has been born in France, which
leaves us older radicals far behind. Thousands of young Black men have
offered their lives for the Lilies of France and they return ready to offer
them again for the Sun-flowers of Afro-America.

—W. E. B. Du Bois, June 1919

Despite my bitter encounter with racism in school, I liked Minneapolis. I was
impressed by the beauty of this city, with its many lakes and surrounding pine
forests. The racial climate in 1913 was not as bad as my early experience in school
would indicate, either. Blacks seemed to get along well, especially with the
Scandinavian nationalities, who constituted the most numerous ethnic grouping in the city.

Upon quitting school, I became a part of the small Black community and completely identified with it. I found friends among Black boys and girls of my age
group; attended parties, dances, and picnics at Lake Minnetonka; and ice-skated
in the wintertime. Here, as in Omaha, a ghetto had not yet fully formed, though
there were the beginnings of one in the Black community on the north side.

Included in the Black community and among my new friends were a relatively large number of mulattoes, the progeny of mixed marriages between
Scandinavian women and Black men. This phenomenon dated back to the turn
of the century. At that time it was the fashion among wealthy white families to
import Scandinavian maids. Many of these families had Black male servants—
butlers, chauffeurs, and the like—and the small Black population was prepon-
derantly male. The result was a rash of intermarriages between the Scandinavian maids and the Black male house servants. The interracial couples formed

a society called Manasseh, which held well-known yearly balls.[1] As a whole, the children of this group were a hotheaded lot and seemed even more racially conscious than the rest of us.

It was in Minneapolis that I too reached a heightened stage of racial awareness. This was hastened, no doubt, by the tragic events in South Omaha and the fact that I was now an adolescent and there was the problem of girls. I had noticed that it was in the period of pubescence that a Black boy, raised even in communities of relative racial tolerance, was first confronted with the problem of race. It had been so with my brother Otto in Omaha, and now it was so with me.

During the first year after dropping out of school, I worked as a bootblack, barbershop porter, bellhop, and busboy, continuing in the last long enough to acquire the rudiments of the waiter's trade. At the age of sixteen, I got a job as dining-car waiter on the Chicago and Northwestern Railway. The first run was also my first trip to the big city, where I had four aunts (my mother's sisters). All through my childhood my mother had told stories about her first visit there at the time of the Chicago Exposition. Upon arrival, one of the older waiters on the car, Lon Holliday, took me to see the town. I'm sure he looked forward to showing a young "innocent" the ropes. After a visit to my aunts, he took me to a notorious dive on the Southside. It was the back room of a saloon at Thirty-Second and State Streets.

The piano man was playing boogie-woogie style, popular in those days. The few couples on the floor were "walking the dog," "balling the jack," and so on. Then one of the dancers, a woman, called to the pianist, "Oh, Mr. Johnson, please play 'Those Dirty Motherfuckers.'" He enthusiastically complied and sang a number of verses of the bawdy tune. I almost sank through the floor in embarrassment and even amazement. Lon, who was watching, burst out laughing, and he said, "Boy, you ain't seen nothing yet!"

He then took me to the famous Mecca Flats on Federal Street, where a rent party was in process. There he introduced me to a young woman, whom he evidently knew, and slipped her some money, saying, "Take care of my young friend here; be sure you get him back on the car in the morning. We leave for Minneapolis at 10:00 a.m."

The railroads were a way to see the country, and in the months that followed I took advantage of that, working for different lines, on different runs as far west as Seattle. On one run in Montana called the Loop, the dining car shuttled between Great Falls and Butte by way of Helena, stopping at each town overnight. It was known as the "outlaw run," and I soon found out why. It attracted a number of characters wanted by police in other cities, searching for an escape or a temporary hideout.

While laying over in Butte one night, our chef murdered the parlor car porter—cut his throat while he was sleeping in the parlor car. They had been feuding for days. I went through the parlor car that morning and was the first to see the ghastly sight. The police came, but the chef had disappeared. My enthusiasm for the job was gone. It might have been me, I thought, for I had had a number of arguments with the chef about my orders.

I quit and headed back to Minneapolis, arriving there shortly after war broke out in Europe in 1914. I was sixteen and had been avidly following the news, reading of the invasions of Belgium and France, of the Battle of the Marne, and the like.

One day, walking along Hennepin Avenue, I saw a Canadian recruiting sergeant. He was wearing the uniform of the Princess Pat Regiment, bright red jacket and black kilt. A handsome fellow, I thought, looking like Bonnie Prince Charlie himself. He noticed me looking at him and asked, "You want to join up with the Princess Pat, my lad? We've got a number of Black boys like you in the regiment. You'll find you're treated like anyone else up there. We make no difference between Black and white in Canada."

Imagining myself in the red jacket and black kilt, I said, "Sure, I'll join."

Then looking at me closely, he asked, "How old are you?"

"Eighteen," I lied.

"Your parents living?"

"Yes."

"Well, you've got to get their consent."

"Oh, they'll agree," I said.

"They live in the city?"

"Yes."

"Well, you come back here tomorrow and bring one of them with you and I'll sign you up."

"Okay," I said, but I knew that my parents would never agree. And well it was, too, for I later learned that this regiment was among the first victims of the German mustard-gas attack at Ypres, and what was left of them was practically wiped out at bloody Passchendaele on the Somme front.

Life in Minneapolis was beginning to bore me. I was anxious to get back to Chicago, "the big city," so I moved there and stayed with my Aunt Lucy at Forty-Third and State. In 1915 my parents, at the urging of my mother, also moved to Chicago, and I then stayed with them.

In Chicago I got a job as a busboy at the Tip Top Inn, then considered the finest restaurant in town. It was owned by old man Hieronymus, a famous chef, and was noted for its French cuisine and service. In the trade it was taken for granted that if you had been a waiter at the Tip Top Inn you could work anywhere in the country. After a few months I was promoted to waiter and felt that I had perfected my skills. During the next three years I worked at a number of places: the Twentieth Century Limited, the New York Central's crack train; the Wolverine (Michigan Central); the Sherman House; the old Palmer House; and the Auditorium.

During this time in Chicago I saw Casey Jones, a Black man and a legendary character known to at least four generations of Black Chicagoans. As I remember, he was partially paralyzed, probably from cerebral palsy. He would go through the streets with trained chickens, which he put through various capers, shouting, "Crabs, crabs, I got them!" He had a defect in his speech which he exploited. The audience would literally fall out at his rendering of the popular sentimental ballad, "The Curse of an Aching Heart":

> You made me what I am today,
> I hope you're satisfied.
> You dragged and dragged me down until
> The heart within me died.
> Although you're not true,
> May God bless you,
> That's the curse of an aching heart!

Then there was the beloved comedian String Beans, who often appeared at the old Peking Theater at Thirty-First and State Streets. The Dolly Sisters also appeared there; they were very famous at the time. Teenan Jones's lush night spot was at Thirty-Fifth and State Streets. Then at the Panama, another night club, I would listen to Mamie Smith sing "Shim-Me-Sha-Wobble, That's All," a very popular song and dance at the time.

Once, when I wanted to go back to Minneapolis to visit, I caught the Pioneer Limited—riding the rods—out of the station on the west side. This was my first experience in hoboing. I rode the rods as far as Beloit, Wisconsin.

At Beloit I got off, but I was afraid to get back on because a yard dick was going around the cars. I stayed there overnight—a fairly cold night as I remember. I met a white man, a "professional" hobo, who took me in tow and told me about the trains leaving in the morning. He said we could catch a train that would pull us right into Minneapolis. It was a passenger train, and we could "ride the blinds in," that is, the space between the two Pullman cars.

We rode the blinds, reaching La Crosse, Wisconsin. On the way he warned, "You know, there's a bad dick up there in La Crosse. We gotta watch out for him." When the train pulled to a stop in La Crosse, both of us hopped off. Other guys were flying out of the train from all sides—from the rods and the blinds, and there were some on top, too. But this notorious yard dick caught us. He was a rough character and let us know it as he lined us up.

"Hey, up there!"

I was at the end of the line of about a dozen guys and was the only Black there. I had my hands in my pocket.

"Take yer hands outta yer pockets!"

I took my hands out of my pockets.

The engine's fireman was looking out, watching all of this. He called to the yard dick, "Say, Jim, let me have that young colored boy over there to slide down coal for me into Minneapolis."

The dick looked at me and scowled, "All right, you, get up there!"

He shouted to the fireman, "But see that he works!"

"I'll see to that; he'll work."

I scrambled on the engine tender and slid coal all the way to Minneapolis, where I got off at the station.

Among my new friends in Chicago were several members of the Eighth Illinois, Black National Guard Regiment. They would regale me with tall stories of their exploits on the Mexican border in the summer of 1916 when the regiment took part in a "show of force" against the Mexican Revolution. None of us, of course, knew the real issues involved.

I remember reading of the exploits of the famous Black Tenth Cavalry Regiment, which was a part of the force sent by General Funston across the border in pursuit of Pancho Villa. They had been ambushed by Villa, and a number of them were killed. The papers, on that occasion, had been full of accounts of the heroic Black cavalrymen and their valiant white officers. The Eighth, however, had been in the rear near San Antonio, Texas, and saw no action during the abortive campaign.

Intrigued by their experiences, I joined the Eighth Regiment in the winter of 1917. I was nineteen. The regiment, officered by Blacks from the colonel on down (many of them veterans of the four Black regular army regiments), gave me a feeling of pride. They had a high esprit de corps that emphasized racial solidarity. I didn't regard it just as a part of a U.S. Army unit but as some sort of a big social club of fellow race-men. Still, I knew that we would eventually get into the war. That did not bother me; on the contrary, romance, adventure, travel beckoned. I saw possible escape from the inequities and oppression that was the lot of Blacks in the United States. I was already a Francophile. I had read and heard about the fairness of the French with respect to the race issue. It seems now, as I look back upon it, that patriotism was the least of my motives. I was avidly following all the news of the war, and it seemed certain that the United States was going to get involved, despite protestations of President Wilson to the contrary.

Already the press was whipping up war sentiment. Tin Pan Alley joined in with a rash of jingoistic songs: "Don't Bite the Hand That's Feeding You," "Let's All Be American Now," ad nauseam. All this left us cold. However, the song that brought tears to my eyes was "Joan of Arc":

> Joan of Arc, Joan of Arc,
> Do your eyes from the skies see the foe?
> Can't you see the drooping Fleur-de-Lys,
> Can't you hear the tears of Normandy?
> Joan of Arc, Joan of Arc,
> Let your spirit guide us through.
> Awake old France to victory!
> Joan of Arc, we're calling you.

Truly, nothing was sacred to Tin Pan Alley!

The *Lusitania* was sunk; the United States declared war in April 1917. Our regiment was federalized on July 25, 1917, and in the late summer we were on our way to basic training at Camp Logan, near Houston, Texas.

A demagogic promise was widely circulated that things would be better if Blacks fought loyally. For example, there was the statement of President Wilson: "Out of this conflict you must expect nothing less than the enjoyment of full citizenship rights."[2] This propaganda was immediately belied by the mounting wave of new lynchings in the South, which claimed thirty-eight victims in 1917 and fifty-eight in 1918. Worst of all was the East St. Louis riot in September 1917; at least forty Blacks were massacred in a bloody pogrom that lasted several days.[3]

Then there was the mutiny-riot of the Twenty-Fourth Infantry in Houston, Texas, where our regiment was to receive its basic training. Company G of our outfit was already in Houston at the time, having been sent on as an advance detachment to prepare the camp for our occupation. It was through them that I learned exactly what had happened.

Black soldiers of the Twenty-Fourth Infantry, an old regular army regiment, had for months been subjected to insults and abuse by Houston police and civilians. The outfit had stationed its military police in Houston; they were, in theory, supposed to cooperate with local police in maintaining law and order among soldiers on leave. Instead, the Black military police found themselves the object of abuse, insults, and beatings by local police. This treatment of Black MPs by racist cops was evidently encouraged by the fact that they (the Blacks) were unarmed.

A report of the special on-the-spot investigator for the NAACP published in the *Crisis*, its organ, reads:

> In deference to the southern feeling against the arming of Negroes and because of the expected cooperation of the City Police Department, members of the provost guard were not armed, thus creating a situation without precedent in the history of this guard. A few carried clubs, but none of them had guns, and most of them were without weapons of any kind. They were supposed to call on white police officers to make arrests. The feeling is strong among the colored people of Houston that this was the real cause of the riot.
>
> On the afternoon of August 23, two policemen, Lee Sparks and Rufe Daniels—the former known to the colored people as a brutal bully— entered the house of a respectable colored woman in an alleged search for a colored fugitive accused of crap-shooting. Failing to find him, they arrested the woman, striking and cursing her and forcing her out into the street only partly clad. While they were waiting for the patrol wagon a crowd gathered about the weeping woman who had become hysterical and was begging to know why she was being arrested.
>
> In this crowd was a colored soldier, Private Edwards. Edwards seems to have questioned the police officers or remonstrated with them. Accounts differ on this point, but they all agree that the officers immediately set upon him and beat him to the ground with the butts of their six-shooters, continuing to beat and kick him while he was on the ground, and arrested him. In the words of Sparks himself: "I beat that nigger until his heart got right. He was a good nigger when I got through with him."
>
> Later Corporal Baltimore, a member of the military police,

approached the officers and inquired for Edwards, as it was his duty to do. Sparks immediately opened fire and Baltimore, being unarmed, fled. . . . They followed . . . beat him up, and arrested him. It was this outrage which infuriated the men of the Twenty-fourth Infantry to the point of revolt.[4]

When word of this outrage reached the camp, feeling ran high. It was by no means the first incident of the kind that had occurred.

The white officers, feeling that the men would seek revenge, ordered them disarmed. The arms were stacked in a tent guarded by a sergeant. A group of men killed the sergeant, seized their rifles, and under the leadership of Sergeant Vida Henry, an eighteen-year veteran, marched on Houston in company strength.

When the soldiers left camp their slogan was "On to the Police Station!" They entered town by way of San Felipe Street, which ran through the heart of the Black community. The fact that they took this route and avoided the more direct one that led through a white neighborhood disproved the charge by local newspapers and the police that they were out to shoot up the town and kill all whites. Their target was clearly the Houston cops. On the way to the station, they shot every person who looked like a cop.

Finally meeting resistance, a battle ensued that ended with seventeen whites, thirteen of them policemen, killed. The alarm went out, and a whole division of white troops, stationed in the camp, was sent in to round up the mutineers. Finally cornered, the men threw down their arms and surrendered, with the exception of Sergeant Vida Henry, who committed suicide rather than be taken.

The whole battalion of the Twenty-Fourth Infantry, including the mutineers, was hurriedly placed aboard a guarded troop train and sent to Fort Huachuca, Arizona. Immediately upon arrival there, those involved were given a drumhead court-martial. Thirteen were executed, and forty-one others were sentenced to life imprisonment.[5]

The bodies of all the executed men were sent home to their families for burial. I remember reading of the funeral of Corporal Baltimore in some little town in Illinois.

Our regiment entrained for Camp Logan with our ardor considerably dampened by these events. Indeed, we left Chicago in an angry and apprehensive mood that lasted all the way to Texas. We passed through East St. Louis in the middle of the night. Those of us who were awake were brooding about the massacre of our kinsmen that had recently taken place there. The regiment traveled in three sections, a battalion each, in old-style tourist cars (sort of second-class Pullmans).

The next morning we arrived in Jonesboro, Arkansas, our first stop on the other side of the Mason–Dixon Line. We were in enemy territory. For many of us it was our first time in the South. Jonesboro was a division point—all three sections of the train pulled up on sidings while the engines were being changed and the cars serviced.

It was a bright, warm, and sunny Sunday morning. It seemed like the whole town had turned out at the station platform to see the strange sight of armed Black soldiers. Whites were on one side of the station platform, and Blacks on the other. We pulled into the station with the windows open and our 1903 Springfield rifles on the tables in plain view of the crowd.

We were at our provocative best. We threw kisses at the white girls on the station platform, calling out to them, "Come over here, Baby, give me a kiss!" "Look at that pretty redhead over there, ain't she a beaut!" and so forth.

A passenger train pulled up beside us on the next track. There, peering out the open window, was a real stereotype of an Arkansas redneck. The sight of him was provocation enough for Willie Morgan, a huge Black in our company who was originally from Mississippi. Morgan was sitting directly across from the white man. He undoubtedly retained bitter memories of insults and persecutions from the past and quickly took advantage of what was perhaps his first opportunity to bait a cracker in his own habitat.

He reached a big hamlike hand through the window, grabbed the fellow's face and shouted, "What the hell you staring at, you peckerwood motherfucker?" The man pulled back, and his hat flew off. Bending down, he recovered it and then moved quickly to the other side of his car, a frightened and puzzled look on his face. Our whole car let out a big roar.

Then a yard man walking along the side of the car asked, "Where are you boys going?"

"Goin' to see your momma, you cracker son of a bitch!" came the reply.

The startled man looked up in amazement.

All of us were hungry. We had been given only a couple of apples for breakfast and now noticed that there were a number of shops and stores in the streets behind the station. I believe our first thought was to buy some food. The vestibule guards would not allow us to take our rifles off the cars, so we left them on our seats and proceeded to the stores in groups. As the stores became crowded and as the storekeepers were busy serving some of our group, others started to snatch up any article in sight.

Cases of Coca-Cola, ginger ale, and near beer went back to the cars. The path to the train was strewn with loot dropped by some of the fellows. In the stores, some bought as others stole—this spontaneously evolved pattern was employed in raids on all stores in Jonesboro and at other train stops along the road to Houston.

The only serious confrontation that took place that day involved the group I was with. We crowded into a little store and a fellow named Jeffries, one of my squad buddies, approached the storekeeper, who was standing behind the counter. Putting his money down, he demanded a Coke. Whereupon the guy said, "I'll serve you one, but y'all can't drink it in heah."

"Why?" Jeffries asked, innocently.

"'Cause we don't serve niggahs heah."

Just as we were about to jump him and wreck the place, Jeffries, a comedian, decided to play it straight. He turned to us and said, "Now wait, fellahs, let me handle this. What the man is saying is that you don't know your place."

Turning to the storekeeper he put his money down and with feigned meekness said, "All right, mister, give me a Coke. I know my place, I'll drink it outside."

"Thank goodness this nigger's got some sense," the storekeeper must have thought as he placed a Coke on the counter. Jeffries snatched up the bottle and immediately hit him on the head, knocking him out cold.

We then proceeded to wreck the place. We took everything in sight. Rushing back to the train, I heard a loud crash—a plate-glass window someone had smashed as a parting gift to the nigger-hating storekeeper.

Up to this time we had not seen any of our officers. They had been up front in the first-class Pullmans. Many of them, we suspected, were sleeping off the aftereffects of the parties held on the eve of our departure. Major Hunt and Captain Hill now appeared and gave orders to the noncoms and the vestibule guards to allow no one else to leave the train.

We waved goodbye to the Blacks on the station platform. They looked frightened, sad, and cowed. We were leaving, but they had to stay and face the wrath of the local crackers.

The train headed to Texarkana, where the scene was repeated, though on a smaller scale. In Texarkana the train stopped only a few minutes, and we raided one store near the railroad station. I was the last one out, running to the train with a box of pilfered Havana cigars in my hand. Nearing the train, I passed a couple of local whites talking about the raid. One said to the other, "You see all those niggers taking that man's stuff?"

"Yeah, I see it."

"Well, what are we going to do about it?"

I reached the train just as it was pulling out, relieved not to have been left behind to find out the answer.

The next stop was Tyler, deep in the heart of Texas, scene of our most serious confrontation. Here we confronted the law in the person of the county sheriff. Tyler seemed to be a larger town than the others. It was a division point, and all three sections pulled up on the sidings. As in Jonesboro, a large crowd had gathered at the station, Blacks on one side, whites on the other. Again, with our guns in view, we started flirting with the white women, throwing kisses at them and so on.

We were very hungry. There had been some foul-up in logistics, so there wasn't any food on the train. All we had that day was a couple of sandwiches and some coffee. We piled off the train and headed for the stores, elbowing whites out of the way. We didn't carry our guns, but many of us wore sheathed bayonets.

Major Hunt finally appeared, but he was only able to stop a few of us. By that time most of us were already ransacking the stores in the immediate vicinity of the station. The path back to the station was strewn with bottles of soft drinks, hams, fruits, wrappers from the candy and cigarettes, and the like. The major was frantically blowing his whistle and calling the fellows to come back to the cars. Finally we all got back and were eating our pilfered food, drinking our near beer and soda.

Suddenly a large white man stepped forward out of the crowd. He wore a khaki uniform, a Sam Browne belt, and a Colt forty-five in his holster. He approached Major Hunt and identified himself as the sheriff. (Or he might have been chief of police.) He said he intended to search the train and recover the stolen goods.

The major, a short, heavyset Black man, said, "No, you don't. This is a military train. Any searching to be done will be done by our officers."

"I know," he said, "I want to accompany you."

"No you don't. You won't set foot on this train."

The sheriff hesitated and looked around at the crowd of white and Black. It was clearly a bitter pill for him to swallow, having for the first time in his life to take low to a Black man in front of his white constituents, as well as setting a bad example for the Blacks. He pushed the unarmed major aside and walked forward.

"Come on you peckerwood son of a bitch!" we hollered from the car.

He approached the vestibule of our car where Jimmy Bland, a mean, gray-eyed, and light-skinned Black was on guard.

"Back! Get back or I'll blow you apart!" Jimmy pushed the sheriff in the belly with the barrel of his rifle. To further impress upon him that the gun was loaded, he threw the bolt and ejected a bullet. The sheriff, who had doubled over from the blow, straightened up, his face ghastly white. He gasped out something to the effect that he was going to report this affair to the government and walked away. We all let out a tremendous roar.

We arrived in Houston the next day, five days after the mutiny of the Twenty-Fourth. We were informed that five dollars would be docked from each man's pay to cover the damage incurred on the trip down. I believe we all felt that it was a small price to pay for the lift in morale that resulted from our forays on the trip.

We were greeted by our comrades from Company G of our battalion on arriving at Camp Logan. They had been there at the time of the mutiny-riot and gave us a detailed account of what had happened. We expected to be confronted by the hostile white population, but to our surprise, the confrontation with the Twenty-Fourth seemed to have bettered the racial climate of this typical southern town. Houston in those days was a small city of perhaps a hundred thousand people, not the metropolis it has now become. The whites, especially the police, had learned that they couldn't treat all Black people as they had been used to treating the local Blacks.

I can't remember a single clash between soldiers and police during our six-month stay in the area. On the contrary, if there were any incidents involving our men, the local cops would immediately call in the military police. There was also a notable improvement in the morale of the local Black population, who were quick to notice the change in attitude of the Houston cops. The cops had obviously learned to fear retaliation by Black soldiers if they committed any acts of brutality and intimidation in the Black community.

Houston Blacks were no longer the cowed, intimidated people they had been before the mutiny. They were proud of us, and it was clear that our presence made them feel better. A warm and friendly relationship developed between our men and the Black community. The girls were especially proud of us. Local Blacks would point out places where some notorious, nigger-hating cop had been killed.

"See those bullet holes in the telephone pole over there," they'd say. "That's where that bad cop, old Pat Grayson, got his." "Those Twenty-Fourths certainly were sharpshooters!"

I occasionally took my laundry to an elderly woman who had known Corporal Baltimore. She told me what a nice young man he was.

"I hear he was hanged," she said.

"That's right," I replied.

Tears came to her eyes and she cluck-clucked. "He left some of his laundry here; you're about his size, you want it?"

"Yes, I'll take it."

She handed me several pairs of khaki trousers and some underwear and shirts all washed and starched and insisted that I pay only the cost of the laundry.

In Camp Logan, our Black Regiment, a part of the Thirty-Third Illinois National Guard Division, went into intensive training. We had high esprit de corps. Our officers lost no opportunity to lecture us on the importance of race loyalty and race pride. They went out to disprove the ideas spread by the white brass to the effect that Black soldiers could be good, but only when officered by whites.

Our solidarity was strengthened when the army attempted to remove Colonel Charles R. Young from the regiment. Young was the first Black West Point graduate and the highest-ranking Black officer in the regular army. He wanted to go overseas very badly, but it was quite clear that they did not want a Black officer of his rank over there. He was examined by an army medical board and found unfit for overseas service. We all knew it was a fraud. It was in all the Black papers and was known by Blacks throughout the country.

We men didn't let our officers down. We were out to show the whites that we were not only as good in everything as they, but better. In Camp Logan, our regiment held division championships in most of the sports: track, boxing, baseball, and so on. We had the highest number of marksmen, sharpshooters, and expert riflemen. Of course, there was no socializing between Blacks and whites, but it was clear that we had the respect, if not the friendship, of many of the white soldiers in the division.

In fact, despite all the efforts of the command, there was a certain degree of solidarity between Black and white soldiers in our division. In Spartanburg, South Carolina, white soldiers from New York came to the defense of their Black fellows of the Fifteenth New York when the latter were attacked by southern whites. Many of us felt that in the case of a showdown in town with the local crackerdom, we could get support from some of the white members of our division who happened to be around. At least, we felt they would not side with the crackers against us.

The high morale of the regiment, the new tolerance (at least on the part of the local white establishment), and the new spirit of Houston Blacks were all displayed during the parade of our division in downtown Houston. About two months before our departure, we received notice from headquarters that the regiment was to participate in a parade. We were to pass in review before Governor Howden of Illinois, our host governor of Texas, high brass from the War Department, and other notables.

We spent a couple of days getting our clothes and equipment into shape. We washed and starched our khaki uniforms, bleached our canvas leggings snow white, cleaned and polished our rifles and sidearms, shined our shoes to a mirror gloss. On the day of the parade, we marched the five miles into town, halting just before we reached the center of the city. We wiped the dust from our rifles and shoes and continued the march.

Executing perfectly the change from squad formation to platoon front, we entered the main square. With our excellent band playing the "Illinois March," we passed the reviewing stand with our special rhythmic swagger, which only Black troops could affect. We were greeted by a thunderous ovation from the crowds, especially the Blacks.

I believe all of Black Houston turned out that day. The next morning, the *Houston Post,* a white daily, headlined a story about the parade and declared that "the best looking outfit in the parade was the Negro Eighth Illinois."

Given final leave, we bid good-bye to our girls and friends in Houston. After that, security was clamped down, and no one was allowed to leave the camp. A few days later, we boarded the train and were on our way to a port of embarkation. We didn't know where we were headed but suspected it was New York. Instead, five days later, we wound up in Camp Stuart near Newport News, Virginia.

In Newport News, we barely escaped a serious confrontation with some local crackers and the police. The first batches of our fellows given passes to the town were subjected to the taunts and slurs of the local cops.

"Why don't you darkies stay in camp? We don't want you downtown making trouble."

Several fights ensued. Some of the men from our regiment were arrested, and others were literally driven out of town. They returned to the barracks, some of them badly beaten, and told us what had happened. A repetition of the riot of the Twenty-Fourth Infantry at Houston was narrowly averted, as a number of us grabbed our guns and were about to head downtown. We were turned back, however, by our officers, who intervened and pleaded with us to return to our barracks. Among them was Lieutenant Benote Lee, whom we all loved and respected.

"Don't play into the hands of these crackers," he said. "We'll be leaving any day now. All they want is to get us in trouble on the eve of our departure."

"How about our guys who were arrested?" we asked.

"Don't worry. We'll get them out."

We returned to the barracks, and sure enough, our comrades were returned the next day, escorted by white MPs. We spent the next days on standby orders, apparently waiting for our ship to arrive. After that, all leaves were canceled.

It was on the same day, I believe, that we first learned that we had been separated from our Thirty-Third Illinois Division. Henceforth, we were to be known as the 370th Infantry.

One morning shortly after this, we looked down into the harbor and saw three big ships. We knew then that we would soon be on our way. The following morning the regiment marched down to the dockside to board ship. Yet another incident occurred at the dock. We lined up in company front, facing the harbor, and halted a few yards from the fence that ran the entire length of the dock.

Facing us in front of the fence were several groups of loitering white native males, probably dockworkers. They stared at us as if we were some strange species. Our captain apparently wanted to move the company closer to the fence and gave the command "Forward march." But he "forgot" to call "Halt." That was all we needed.

We were still angry about the beating of our comrades in downtown Newport News a few days before. We marched directly into the whites, closing in on them, cursing and cuffing them with fists and rifle butts, kicking and kneeing them; in short, applying the skills of close-order combat we had learned during our basic training. Of course, we didn't want to kill anybody; we just wanted to rough them up a bit.

We were finally stopped by the excited cries of our officers, "Halt! Halt!" We withdrew, opening up a path through which our victims ran or limped away. Then at the command of "Attention! Right face!" we marched along the dock in columns of twos and finally boarded the ship.

3

ON TO FRANCE

We sailed for France in early April 1918, on the old USS *Washington,* a passenger liner converted into a troop ship. I have crossed the Atlantic many times since, but I can truthfully say that I have never experienced rougher seas. Our three ships sailed out of Newport News without escort. Of course, we were worried; there were rumors of German submarines. Our anxiety was relieved when in mid-ocean we picked up two escort vessels, one of which was the battle cruiser *Covington.* When we reached the war zone, about three days out of Brest, France, a dozen destroyers took over, circling our ships all the way into port.

It took us sixteen days in all to reach Brest, where we arrived on April 22. We were so weak on landing that one half of the regiment fell out while climbing the hill to the old Napoleon Barracks where we were quartered. Immediately upon our arrival, we were put to work cleaning up ourselves and our equipment, notwithstanding our weakened condition.

The next morning we passed in review before some U.S. and French big brass. The following day we boarded a train. We crossed the whole of France from east to west and detrained at Granvillars, a village in French Alsace, close to the Swiss frontier. There we found out that we had been brigaded with and were to be an integral part of the French Army.

The reason we were separated from the white Americans was, as the white brass put it, "to avoid friction." But the American command of General Pershing was not satisfied just to separate us; they tried to extend the long arm of Jim Crow to the French. The American Staff Headquarters, through its French mission, tried to make sure that the French understood the status of Blacks in the United States. Their *Secret Information Bulletin concerning Black American Troops* is now notorious, though I did not learn of it until after I had returned from France. The Army of Democracy spoke to its French allies:

> It is important for French officers who have been called upon to exercise command over black American troops, or to live in close contact with them, to have an exact idea of the position occupied by Negroes in the United States. The increasing number of Negroes in the United States (about 15,000,000) would create for the white race in the

Republic a menace of degeneracy were it not that an impassable gulf has been made between them. . . .

Although a citizen of the United States, the black man is regarded by the white American as an inferior being with whom relations of business or service only are possible. The black is constantly being censured for his want of intelligence and discretion, his lack of civic and professional conscience, and for his tendency toward undue familiarity.

The vices of the Negro are a constant menace to the American who has to repress them sternly. For instance, the black American troops in France have, by themselves, given rise to as many complaints for attempted rape as the rest of the army. . . .

Conclusion:

1. We must prevent the rise of any pronounced degree of intimacy between French officers and black officers. We may be courteous and amiable with these last, but we cannot deal with them on the same plane as with the white American officers without deeply wounding the latter. We must not eat with them, must not shake hands or seek to talk or meet with them outside the requirements of military service.

2. We must not commend too highly the black American troops, particularly in the presence of [white] Americans. . . .

3. Make a point of keeping the native cantonment population from "spoiling" the Negroes. [White] Americans become greatly incensed at any public expression of intimacy between white women with black men. . . . Familiarity on the part of white women with black men is furthermore a source of profound regret to our experienced colonials, who see in it an overweening menace to the prestige of the white race.[1]

Apparently this classic statement of U.S. racism was ineffectual with the French troops and people, even though it was supplemented by wild stories circulated by the white U.S. troops. These included the claim that Blacks had tails like monkeys, which was especially told to women, including those in the brothels.

Our regiment was not sorry to be incorporated into the French military. In fact, most of us thought it was the best thing that could have happened. The French treated Blacks well—that is, as human beings. There was no Jim Crow. At the time, I thought the French seemed to be free of the virulent U.S. brand of racism.

The American Command not only wanted its front line to be all white, it also wanted all regiment commanders (even those under the French) to be white. Consequently, our Black colonel, Franklin A. Dennison; our lieutenant colonel, James H. Johnson; and two of our majors (battalion commanders) were replaced by white officers. Colonel Dennison was sent back to the States, kicked upstairs, given the rank of brigadier general, and placed in command of the Officer Training Camp for Colored Men at Fort Des Moines, Iowa. Although our first reaction was anger, we became reconciled to the shift.

Our new white colonel, T. A. Roberts, seemed to be warm, paternalistic, and deeply concerned about the welfare of his men. He would often make the rounds of the field kitchens, tasting the food and admonishing the cooks about ill-prepared food. He even gave instructions on how the various dishes should be cooked. Naturally, this made a great hit with the men. Our confidence in him was high because we felt that he was a professional soldier who knew his business.[2]

I remember the day the new colonel took over. The regiment formed in the village square. Colonel Roberts introduced himself. He seemed quite modest. He said that he was honored to be our new commander and that he knew the record of our regiment dating back to 1892 and its exploits during the Spanish–American War.

"Since West Point," he said, "I have always served with colored troops—the Ninth and Tenth Cavalry." He then turned to Captain Patton, our Black regiment adjutant. "Captain Patton knows me, he was one of my staff sergeants in the old Tenth Cavalry." Patton nodded.

The colonel smiled and pointed to our top sergeant. "Over there is Mark Thompson. I remember him when he was company clerk in Troop C of the Tenth Cavalry." He went on to point out a dozen or so officers and noncoms with whom he had served in the Ninth or Tenth Cavalry. "These men will tell you where I stand with respect to the race issue and everything else. We are going into the lines soon and I am sure that the men of this regiment will pile up a record of which your people and the whole of America will be proud."

The process of integration into the French Army was thorough. The American equipment with which we had trained at home was taken away and we were issued French weapons—rifles, carbines, machine guns, automatic rifles, pistols, helmets, gas masks, and knapsacks. We were even issued French rations—with the exception of the wine, which our officers apparently felt we could not handle. We got all the wine we wanted anyway from the French troops. They were issued a liter (about a quart) a day, and for a few centimes could buy more at the canteen.

The regiment was completely reorganized along French lines, with a machine-gun company to every battalion. My company, Company E of the Second Battalion, was converted into Machine Gun Company no. 2. We entered a six-week period of intensive training under French instructors to master our new weapons. Our main weapon was the old air-cooled Hotchkiss. And we had to master the enemy's gun, the water-cooled Maxim.

The period of French training was not an easy one. It was a miserable spring—dark and dreary—and it rained incessantly the whole time we were there. There was a lot of illness—grippe, pneumonia, and bronchitis. We lost a number of men, several from our company. The men were in a sullen mood as the time approached for the regiment to move up to the front. Disgruntlement was often voiced in the now-familiar form of "What are we doing over here? Germans ain't done nothing to us. It's those crackers we should be fighting." While we were lined up in the square one day, our captain took the occasion to comment on these sentiments.

"Well," he said, "I've been hearing all this stuff about guys saying that they weren't going to fight the Germans. Well, we certainly can't make you fight if you don't want to. But I'll tell you one thing we can and will do is take you up to the front where the Germans are, and you can use your own judgment as to whether you fight them or not."

In early June 1918, we entered the trenches at the Saint-Mihiel salient near the Swiss frontier as a part of the Tenth Division of the French Army under General Mittelhauser. We were intermingled with the French troops in the Tenth Division so that our officers and men might observe and profit by close association with veteran soldiers. At that time Saint-Mihiel was a quiet sector. Except for occasional shelling and desultory machine-gun and rifle fire, nothing much occurred. We lost no men.

It was here, however, that we made our first acquaintance with two pests— the rat and the louse—which thereafter were our inseparable companions for our entire stay at the front. Undoubtedly there were more rats than men; there were hordes of them. Regiments and battalions of rats. They were the largest rats I had ever seen. We soon became tired of killing them; it seemed a wasted effort. Some of the rats became quite bold, even impudent. They seemed to say, "I've got as much right here as you have." They would walk along, pick up food scraps and eat them right there in front of you! The dark dugouts were their real havens. When we slept, we would keep our heads covered with blankets as protection against rat bites. This may seem flimsy protection, but we were so conditioned that we would awake at any attempt on the part of a rat to bite through the blanket. I have often wondered why there were so few rat bites. Probably the rats felt that it was not worthwhile fooling with live humans when there were so many dead ones around. We soon got used to the rats and learned to live with them.

It was the same with the lice. I woke up lousy after my first sleep in a dugout. My reaction to the pests took the following progression: First, I was besieged by interminable itching, followed by depression. Then I began to lose appetite and weight, finally becoming quite ill. All this was within a period of a few days. Most of the fellows exhibited the same symptoms.

One might say that our illness was mainly psychological, but it was nonetheless real. Since this was a quiet front, I had no difficulty in getting permission to go back to the rear for a few hours. Foolishly, I thought if I could get cleaned up just once, I would feel a lot better. I got some delousing soap, took a bath, and washed my clothes. I then returned to the front, stood machine-gun watch, and then went into the dugout for a nap. Needless to say, I woke up lousy again.

I told my troubles to an old French veteran who had been assigned to my machine-gun squad. "Oh, it's nothing! You must forget all about it," he said. "You'll get used to it. I've been at the front for nearly four years and I've been lousy all the time, except when I was in the hospital or at home on leave."

I took his advice, which was all to the good, because I was not to be rid of these pests until six months later during my sojourn in hospitals at Mantes-sur-Seine and Paris after the Armistice. Even then, it was only a temporary respite, for I was reinfected upon rejoining my regiment at the embarkation port of Brest. After a brief stay with the regiment, I was returned to the hospital, again deloused, only to be reinfected again on the hospital ship returning to the States. I parted company with my last louse at the debarkation hospital at Grand Central Palace in New York City.

We remained in the Saint-Mihiel sector about two weeks. We were then withdrawn and moved into a sector in the Argonne Forest near Verdun, site of the great battles of 1916; we arrived there in late July 1918. We were still brigaded with the French Tenth Division. The area around Verdun was a vast cemetery, with a half million crosses of those who had perished in that great holocaust, each bearing the legend *Mort pour la France* (Died for France).

The Argonne at that time was also a quiet sector. But it was here that we suffered our first casualty, Private Robert M. Lee of Chicago. The incident occurred during machine-gun target practice. The first- and second-line trenches ran along parallel hills about a hundred yards apart. The French had set up a makeshift range in the valley in between the trenches. Behind the gun there was a two- or three-foot rise in the earth, on which a number of us French and Blacks were sitting, chewing the rag, awaiting our turn at the machine gun.

Suddenly, there was a short burst of machine-gun fire. It was not from our guns. Bullets whizzed over our heads—they seemed to be coming from behind the target. All of us scrambled to get into the communication trench that opened on the valley. Second Lieutenant Binga DesMond, our platoon commander (and the University of Chicago's great sprinting star), fell from the embankment on top of me. Fortunately, he was not hit. But even with his 180 pounds on my back, I am sure I made that ten or fifteen yards to the communication trench, crawling on my hands and knees, as fast as he could have sprinted the distance!

The fire was coming from behind the target. What obviously had happened was that the Germans had cased the position of our guns and had somehow got around behind the target and waited for a pause in our target practice to open fire on us. We never found out how they did it, for none of us knew the exact topography of the place. The French of course knew it, but they had assured us that the place was safe and that they had been using the range for months.

We were crouched down, panting, in the communication trench for about five minutes after the German guns ceased fire. The French lieutenant (bless his soul) then sent a French gun crew out to get the gun. To our great surprise they also brought back Robert M. Lee. He was quite dead, with bullets right through the heart. He had evidently been hit by the first burst and had fallen forward in front of the embankment. All of us were deeply saddened by the incident.

No one spoke as we bore his body back to the rear. He was only nineteen, a very sweet fellow, and he was our first casualty. We buried him down in the valley, beside the graves of those fallen at Verdun. The funeral was quite impressive. He was given a hero's burial, with representatives both from our regiment and from our French counterparts. We were especially impressed by the appearance of General Mittelhauser, who came down from division headquarters to express condolences and appreciation to the Black troops now under his command.

The Soissons Sector

Despite the fact that we had been in a quiet sector, it was still on the front line, with its daily tensions of anticipated attack. In the middle of August, we were pulled out of the Argonne sector and sent to rest behind the lines near Bar-le-Duc. We were deeply pleased by the hospitality and kindness extended to us by the townspeople there. They invited us into their homes and plied us with food and wine. Half-jokingly they told us to come back after the war, and we could have our pick of the girls. As we did throughout our stay in France, we deported ourselves well. For pleasures of the flesh, there were a number of legal houses of prostitution, or "houses of pleasure" as they were called by the French. It was with regret that we left that area.

By this time, we had become an integral part of the French Army. Along with our French equipment, training, and so forth, we had affected the style of the French *poilu* (doughboy). The flaps of our overcoats were buttoned back in order to give us more legroom while on the march, as was their style. Like the French infantry, we used walking sticks, which helped to ease the burden of our seventy pounds of equipment. French peasants along the road, hearing our strange language and noticing our color, would often mistake us for French colonials. Not Senegalese, who were practically all black, but Algerians, Moroccans, or Sudanese. We would swing along the road to the tune of our favorite marching song:

My old mistress promised me,
Raise a ruckus tonight.
When she died she'd set me free,
Raise a ruckus tonight.

She lived so long her head got bald,
Raise a ruckus tonight.
She didn't get to set me free at all,
Raise a ruckus tonight!

Oh, come along, little children come along,
While the moon is shining bright,
Get on board on down the river flow,
Gonna raise a ruckus tonight.

But we had not escaped the long arm of American racism. We were rudely confronted with this reality upon our arrival in a small town on the Compiègne front in the department of Meuse. We entrained there for our next front. The regiment was confronted dramatically with the effects of the racist campaign launched by the American high brass.

Upon entering the town, the regiment was drawn up in battalion formation in the square. Before being assigned to billets, we were informed by the battalion commander that a Black soldier from a labor battalion had been court-martialed and hanged in the very square where we were standing. It had happened just a few weeks before our arrival. His crime was the raping of a village girl. His body had been left hanging there for twenty-four hours, as a demonstration of American justice.

"As a result," he told us, "you may find the town population hostile. In case this is so," the major warned, "you are not to be provoked or to take umbrage at any discourtesies, but are to deport yourselves as gentlemen at all times." In any case, we were to be there only for a few days, during which time we were to remain close to our barracks. Then, in a lowered voice, he muttered, "This is what I have been told to tell you."

We kept close to our billets the first day or so but then gradually ventured further into town. At first, the townsfolk seemed to be aloof, but the coolness was gradually broken down, probably as a result of our correct deportment, especially our attitude toward the children (with whom we always immediately struck up friendships). Friendly relations were finally established with the villagers. When we asked about the hanging, they shrugged the matter off.

"So what? That was only one soldier. The others were nice enough." When asked why they had been so aloof when we first arrived, they said it was the result of the warnings of the white officers. "They didn't want us to fraternize with the Blacks."

Continuing the conversation, they seemed puzzled about why the sentence had been so severe and the body barbarously left exposed in the square. "Très brutal, très horrible!" they exclaimed. With regard to the girl, "Ah, she had been raped many times before," one of them jeered.

After two weeks of rest, the regiment began to move by stages toward the front lines again. A few days later, we boarded a train consisting of a long line of boxcars. Each car was marked *Quarante hommes ou huit chevaux* (Forty men or eight horses). The last couple of months had been quiet and relatively pleasant, with the exception of the Lee incident and the events just related. But now, we felt, we were going into the thick of it. The premonition was confirmed the very next morning when we woke (that is, those of us who had been able to sleep in such crowded conditions).

We were passing through Château-Thierry. There could be no doubt about it, even though part of the sign had been blown away and only the word "Thierry" remained. The woods around the station and Belleau Wood, a few miles further on, looked like they had been hit by a cyclone: broken and uprooted trees, gaping shell holes, men from the Graves Registration walking around with crosses, Black Pioneers removing ammunition. All were grim reminders of the great battles that had been fought there by American troops only several weeks before.

We were on the Soissons front, where we became part of the famous Armée Mangin. General Mangin (*le boucher,* or "the butcher," as he was called by the French) was commander of the Tenth Army of France, among whom were a number of shock troops: Chausseurs Alpines, Chausseurs d'Afrique (Algerians and Moroccans), Senegalese riflemen, and the Foreign Legion. His army was pivotal in breaking the Hindenburg Line about Soissons. On this front, we were brigaded with the French Fifty-Ninth Division, under the command of General Vincendon.

We bypassed Thierry and Belleau Wood and detrained at the village of Villers-Cotterêts, the birthplace of Alexandre Dumas. The atmosphere was charged with expectancy. Observation balloons hung like giant sausages on the horizon. Big guns rumbled ominously in the distance. A steady stream of ambulances carrying wounded jammed the roads leading from the front. Obviously a big battle was in progress not too far away. But it turned out that we were not going into that sector. We left the village and marched west to Crépy-en-Valois. Turning north through the Compiègne Forest, we reached the Aisne River at a point near Vic-sur-Aisne and continued on to Ressons-le-Long, where we established our depot company. The march from the railhead to Ressons took about three days. It was a forced march and covered about twenty-five kilometers (fifteen miles) a day.

This was pretty rough after the restless night we had spent on the crowded train. As one of the company wags observed, "One thing 'bout these kilomeeters, they sho' will kill you if you keep on meetin' 'em."

Our regiment spent six months in the lines in all. We took part in the fifty-nine-day drive of Mangin's Tenth Army, which ended on the day of the Armistice. During that period, one or another of our units was always under fire or fighting. Our toughest battles were at the Death Valley Jump Off near the Aisne Canal, the taking of Mont des Singes (Monkey Mountain, which was later renamed Hill 370 in honor of our regiment), fighting at a railroad embankment northwest of Guilleminet Farm, and the advance into the Hindenburg Line at the Oise-Aisne triangle.

It was in the battles on the Hindenburg Line that we met the strongest enemy resistance and sustained most of our losses. The enemy resistance was broken in these battles, and they began a general withdrawal, at first orderly and accompanied by brief rearguard actions. Finally, there was the flight to the Belgian frontier, destroying roads and railroads on orders to impede our advance. After Laon, their flight was so precipitous that we had difficulty maintaining contact. We entered many villages which they had left the day before.

Our outfit was the first Allied troops to enter the fortified city of Laon, wresting it from the Germans after four years of war. We were greeted with tremendous elation by the population, who had lived under German occupation the whole of that period.

The regiment was highly praised by the French. It won twenty-one Distinguished Service Crosses, sixty-eight Croix de Guerre, and one Distinguished Service Medal. In the whole two months' drive, casualties were five hundred killed and wounded—a total of about one fifth of the regiment. These casualties were light when compared with those of Black regiments on other fronts. For example, the 371st Infantry of drafted men lost 1,065 out of 2,384 men in three days' fighting during the great September defensive on the Compiègne front. I believe that the German resistance on these other fronts, east and west of Soissons, was more stubborn than on our front.

All of our Black regiments were fortunate to have been brigaded with the French. In this respect, the American High Command did us a big favor, unintentionally, I am sure. For as far as we were able to observe, the French made no discrimination in the treatment of Black officers and men, with whom they fraternized freely. They regarded us as brothers-in-arms.

Similarly, the French people in the villages in which we stopped or were stationed were uniformly courteous and friendly, and we made many friends. I must say that we were also on our best behavior. I don't remember a single incident of misbehavior on the part of our men toward French villagers. The latter were quick to notice this and to contrast our gentlemanly deportment with the rudeness of the white Americans. Many of the white soldiers made no effort to hide their disdain for the French (whom they regarded as inferiors) and commonly referred to them as "frogs."

But even as we fought, we were being stabbed in the back by the American High Command. We were not to learn, however, until our return to the States of the slanderous, racist document issued by the American General Staff Headquarters through its brainwashed French Mission (the *Secret Information Bulletin concerning Black American Troops* referred to earlier).

We learned also that the hanging of the Black soldier on the Compiègne front was not an isolated incident, but part of a deliberate campaign conducted by higher and lower echelons in the American command to influence French civilians against Blacks. The campaign focused on the effort to build up the Black rapist scare among them.

Such was a memorandum issued by headquarters of the Ninety-Second Division (a Black division officered largely by whites) on August 21, 1918. Its purpose was to "prevent the presence of colored troops from being a menace to women." The memorandum read, in part:

> On account of increasing frequency of the crime of rape, or attempted rape, in this Division, drastic preventive measures have become necessary. . . . Until further notice, there will be a check of all troops of the 92nd Division every hour daily between reveille and 11 p.m., with a written record showing how each check was made, by whom, and the result. . . . The one-mile limit regulation will be strictly enforced at all times, and no passes will be issued except to men of known reliability.

This was followed the next day by another memorandum saying that the commander in chief of the American Expeditionary Forces "would send the 92nd Division back to the States or break it up into labor battalions as unfit to bear arms in France, if efforts to prevent rape were not taken more seriously."[3]

As a result, Dr. Robert R. Moton of Tuskegee was sent by President Wilson and the secretary of war to investigate the charges. He found only one case of rape in the whole division of fifteen thousand men. Two other men who were from labor battalions in the Ninety-Second area were convicted. One of these was hanged, and I'm sure that this was the unfortunate soldier whom we saw on the Compiègne front. General headquarters was forced to admit that the crime of rape, as later stated by Moton, "was no more prevalent among coloured soldiers than among white, or any other soldiers."[4]

This whole racist smear of Black troops, I was to conclude later, represented but an extension to France of the anti-Black racist campaign then current in the States. It was designed to maintain Black subjugation and prevent its erosion by liberal racial attitudes of the French. Back in the States, the campaign was marked by an upturn of lynchings during the war years, with thirty-eight Black victims in 1917 and half again that number in the following year. Even then, things were working up to the bloody riots of 1919.

In contrast to all of this, the appreciation of the French for Black soldiers from the United States was shown by the accolade given by the French division commander, General Vincendon, to our regiment. On December 19, 1918, we were transferred from the French Army back to the U.S. Army. On that day, General Order 4785, directed to the Fifty-Ninth Division of the Army of France, was read to the officers and men of the 370th. It commended us for our contributions to France. I remember being struck by the poetry of the language; it was all beautifully French to me:

> We at first, in September at Mareuil-sur-Ourcq, admired your fine appearance under arms, the precision of your review, the suppleness of your evolutions that presented to the eye the appearance of silk unrolling its waves . . .

Further on in remembering our dead, the communiqué read:

> The blood of your comrades who fell on the soil of France, mixed with the blood of our soldiers, renders indissoluble the bonds of affection that unite us.[5]

The Road Home

The road back from Soissons lay through the old battlefields where we had fought a couple of months before. Near Anizy-le-Château, there were crosses marking the graves of some of our comrades who had died in the fighting there. We paused before the graves, seeking out those of the comrades we knew. We all had the same thoughts: "What rotten luck that they should die almost in sight of victory."

Among the crosses, there was one marked "Sergeant Theodore Gamelin." Gamelin hadn't died in combat. I remember the incident clearly. We were all lined up in some hastily dug trenches that morning, waiting for the "over the top" signal. The cooks had just distributed reserved rations. These consisted of a half loaf of French bread (not the crispy white kind, but a coarse grayish loaf baked especially for the troops, which we called "war bread") and a big bar of chocolate. Somehow, Gamelin had missed out on these rations. Jump-off time was drawing near. He looked around and his eyes fixed upon a private named Brown, who was sitting on the firing step, putting his rations in a knapsack. Now, Private Brown was one of those quiet, meek little fellows. He always took low, was never known to fight. But Brown was the type of man, I have observed, who can become dangerous. This is particularly true in a combat situation, where one doesn't know whether one will live five minutes longer. Gamelin, a big bullying type, an amateur boxer, and very unpopular with his men, called to Brown:

"Give me some of that bread, Brown. I didn't get my rations."

"Now, that's just too bad, sergeant," Brown responded. "I'm not going to give you any of this bread. It's not my fault you missed your rations."

Gamelin, with one hand on his pistol, moved as though he were going to seize the bread. Brown had his rifle lying across his lap. He simply raised it and coolly pulled the trigger. The sergeant fell dead!

The platoon commander heard the commotion and ran to the spot, inquiring about what had happened. The men told him that Gamelin was trying to take Brown's reserve rations and had made a move toward his pistol. Brown, they said, had shot in self-defense.

Obviously nothing could be done about Brown in those circumstances. So the lieutenant said, "Consider yourself under arrest, Brown. We will take this matter up after this action."

Unfortunately, Brown was killed a few days later. The memory of this incident was on our minds as we viewed Gamelin's grave. His helmet hung on a cross, which ironically bore the inscription "Sergeant Theodore Gamelin— Mort pour la France, September 1918."

I had gone through six months at the front without a scratch or a day of illness. But as we neared Soissons, I began to feel faint and light-headed. By the time we reached the city, I had developed quite a high fever. It was the period of the first great flu epidemic, which wreaked havoc among U.S. troops in France. I reported to the infirmary and lined up with a group of about fifty men. The medical sergeant took our temperatures and then tied tags to our coats. I looked at mine and it read "influenza." We were evacuated to a field hospital near Soissons, where I remained for about five days. After that, we boarded a hospital train and were told that we were going to the big base hospital in Paris. Now, I liked that.

I had never seen Paris and was most anxious to visit the famed city before going home. There were two of us in the compartment, another soldier from the regiment and myself. I felt a little drowsy, so I told my compartment mate that I was going to take a little nap and to wake me up when the chow came around. I "awoke" five days later in a French hospital at Mantes-sur-Seine, near Paris.

They had put me off the train as an emergency case just before Paris. I came out of a coma to find a number of strange people around my bed—nurses who were Catholic nuns, doctors, and a number of patients. They were all smiling. "Thank God, young man," said the doctor. "We thought we were going to lose you. You've been in a coma for five days, but you're going to be all right now."

"Where am I? Is this Paris?" I asked.

"No, this is Mantes-sur-Seine, close to Paris. They had to put you off here as an emergency case."

"What's wrong with me?" I asked.

"Oh, you've had a little kidney infection and it has affected your heart."

"That sounds bad," I said.

"Well, you're young and have a remarkable constitution. You'll pull through all right—you're out of danger now," he assured me.

I remained in the hospital for about a month, receiving the kindest and most solicitous attention from nurses, doctors, and patients. All seemed to regard me as their special charge. No one spoke English, but I got along all right. It was like a crash course in French. They told me I had a beautiful accent. They brought in an old lady to talk English with me, but she bored me to death. Really, my French was better than her English. She came once and didn't return.

I was feeling much better when the head sister came to me one evening to tell me I was to leave the next morning for Paris and the American hospital at Neuilly.

"You've never been to Paris, have you?" she asked.

"No," I said.

"Well, you've got a treat coming!"

I was filled with great expectations. The next morning, after embracing all my fellow patients and exchanging warm good-byes with the doctor and sisters, the head nurse (or sister) took me out in front of the hospital, where an American ambulance was waiting.

"Hop in, buddy," said the driver.

"Haywood, be sure to write us when you get back to Chicago," said the sister. "Remember we are your friends and want to know how you are getting along."

I promised that I would. As we pulled out, she stood on the road waving a white handkerchief and continued to wave it as long as we were in sight. I never wrote them, but often thought of them.

Paris, you wondrous city! I was feeling good that morning as we pulled into the hospital at Neuilly. The hospital was situated on the Avenue Neuilly near the Boulevard de la Grande Armée, only a few blocks from the Arc de Triomphe. It was a veritable palace. I was assigned to a ward in which there were only four guys, three Australians and one white American from Wisconsin. They greeted me and gave me a rundown on the situation. They were having a ball seeing Paris, taking in all the events, theaters, racetracks, boxing, and girls. I don't believe that I saw a real sick man in that hospital. There were some of course, but they must have been secluded in some out-of-sight wards. We were all convalescents in our ward. A couple were recuperating from wounds received at the front.

"What do you do for money?" I asked.

"Oh, we don't worry about that—just stick around awhile and we'll show you the ropes."

Under their tutelage, it didn't take me long to catch on. At that time there were dozens of rich American women, including a number from the social register, in Paris. They were under the auspices of the Red Cross and had taken over the hospital and its patients as their special "war duty." They would organize excursions, get tickets for shows, sports events, and the like. Coming to the hospital in relays, they would leave huge boxes of chocolates and other goodies.

We were showered with gifts—Gillette razors, Waterman fountain pens, and even some serviceable wrist watches if you asked for them. They would come in waves. Scarcely had one group left when another would come, leaving the same gifts. The guys had it down perfect. They always left one man on watch in the ward. He was there in case the gals came in while the others were out, and he would receive all the presents and gifts for them. He would point to the three unoccupied beds (there were only five of us in an eight-bed ward) and pretend that their occupants were out in the streets. He would suggest that the presents be left for them, also. Old Wisconsin Slim was the real genius in all this. He even hung a couple of crosses over the unoccupied beds to give more substance to the fiction that they were occupied.

Every morning we would gather all our presents, take them to the gate, and sell them for a good price to the French who gathered there to buy them. We would then return to the ward and divide the "swag." Razors and fountain pens seemed to be rare in France at that time. The going rate for razors was about ten francs (two dollars), and for Waterman fountain pens, even more. All this was carried out under the benign gaze of the hospital authorities.

Discipline was lax, almost nonexistent. We could stay out for two days at a time. The attitude seemed to be, Let the boys have a good time; they deserve it; besides, it's essential for their convalescence. When we would get a little money together (about once a week), we would run out to Montmartre and the famous Rue Pigalle, "Pig Alley," to see the girls.

As an old Francophile, I was also interested in French history and culture. I got a guidebook and spent days walking all over Paris, visiting all the historical places about which I had read, mentally reconstructing the events.

Time was passing rapidly. I had been in the hospital about two months when an administrator called me into his office.

"Well, Corporal Hall," he said. "I hope you've been having a good time in Paris."

"Oh yes," I replied.

"That's good," he said. "We're sending you back to your regiment tomorrow."

"Where are they?" I asked.

"They're in Brest, waiting to embark for the voyage home."

The next morning I got on the train at the Gare Ouest and arrived in Brest that evening. In Brest I strolled around a bit on the waterfront and finally sat down at a sidewalk café. I was in no hurry to get back into the old regimental harness. I was about to order a drink when suddenly a big white MP appeared. Glowering at me, he said, "Where's your pass, soldier?"

"Here it is. I've just got back from the hospital in Paris, and I'm going to my outfit up on the hill," I explained.

He grabbed it, glanced at it, and shouted, "Well, get going up that hill right now. You're not supposed to hang around here."

I left without my drink and started climbing the hill to the old Napoleon Barracks where we had been eleven months before. It seemed like that had been years ago, so much had been crowded into the brief intervening period.

I rejoined my outfit. They were living in tents in what seemed to me like a swamp. The weather was miserable, a steady cold rain. The mud was ankle deep. I was greeted warmly by my comrades. I don't think that more than half the old boys of my company were left. The rest were dead, wounded, or ill in hospitals all over France.

A couple of bottles of cognac were produced. The guys started reminiscing about what they were going to do when they got home. The news from home was bad. Discrimination and Jim Crow were rampant, worse than before. Blacks were being lynched everywhere. "Now, they want us to go to war with Japan," observed one of the fellows. (The Hearst newspapers at the time were again raising the specter of the "yellow peril.")

"Well," someone said, "they won't get me to fight their yellow peril. If it comes to that, I'll join the Japs. They are colored." There was unanimous agreement on that point.

I bunked down that night and awoke the next morning with a high fever. I went to the infirmary and again was evacuated to a hospital. I immediately began to worry whether I would be able to return with my outfit. As I was waiting on the side of the road to hitch a ride to the hospital, I heard footsteps behind me. I turned and there was Colonel Roberts, our white commander, whom I had not seen for months.

I started to spring to my feet and salute, but he motioned me to remain seated. "Corporal, you're from our regiment, aren't you?"

"Yes, sir," I said, "I'm sick and going to the hospital."

"What's the matter?"

"I guess I got the flu."

"Well," he said, "you're in no condition to walk that distance." He hailed a passing truck and instructed the driver to take me to the hospital. "Take care, son; we're going home soon. Try to come back with us." That's the last time I saw Colonel Roberts.

A month later, while in the hospital, I picked up the Paris edition of the *Herald Tribune.* The headline read, "The 370th Infantry (the old Eighth Illinois) returns and is given hero's welcome in victory parade down State Street." I felt pretty bad, because I could imagine my old mother standing there waiting for me to pass by. Since I hadn't written in months, she would probably assume the worst.

I had been away from the States for quite a while, in free France so to speak, and I had become less used to the American nigger-hating way of life. But I was thrown abruptly back into reality as soon as I crossed the threshold of the American army hospital in Brest.

It seemed to be manned by an all-southern staff: doctors, nurses, and so on. All of them spoke with broad southern accents. I was assigned a bed at one end of the ward. When I looked around, I could see only Blacks were in that end. Whites were at the other end. There were no screens, no Jim Crow signs. The Jim Crow was de facto, but nonetheless real. I also noticed that there was a large space between the Black and white sections.

After a cursory entrance examination, the doctor seemed to think that I didn't have the flu, and upon hearing my recent medical history, he decided that it was a relapse of the old illness.

I had no sooner gotten settled when I heard a nurse bawling out a Black soldier for being so dirty. The poor fellow had just come in from some mud hole like the one in which my regiment was situated, where there was no opportunity to bathe.

"You don't see any of our white boys that dirty!" she shouted, her eyes flashing indignantly at what she, a white lady, was forced to put up with. For the first time, it occurred to me that our Black regiment had been put in a worse location than the whites. Now, that's pretty hard stuff for a frontline veteran to take. If I had been ill when I came in, I was really sick now. I could feel my blood pressure and fever mount.

There was a Black sergeant from my outfit in the same ward. He was a tall, dignified, and proud-looking man, convalescing from a previous illness. He wasn't a bed patient and was therefore supposed to make his own bed. This he did, but he never seemed to do it to the satisfaction of the nurse, who kept berating him.

"Make it over; that's not good enough."

"I've already made it, and I'm not going to do it again."

"Don't talk back to me," she shouted. "Make that bed!"

"I'm not going to," he said.

"You dare disobey my order?" she yelled.

"I'm a frontline soldier, and you don't have to yell at me."

She turned and walked to the office and returned with the ward doctor, a little pip-squeak of a man. In a stentorian voice he said, "Make that bed, soldier."

The sergeant didn't move. The doctor looked at his watch and said, "I'm giving you two minutes to start making that bed. If you don't, I'm going to prefer charges against you for disobeying your superior officers."

You could see that the proud sergeant was thinking it over and coming to a decision. I could almost read his mind; it seemed that he was thinking that this wasn't the time to die. He only had a couple more months to go.

He finally burst into tears, but he got up and made the bed. I'd seen this sort of situation before, and I feel almost certain that had there been a loaded gun around, the sergeant might have started shooting. It would have been reported in the news as "Another nigger runs amok." All of us, including some of the whites, breathed a sigh of relief at this peaceful culmination of what could have been a dangerous incident. At least the nurse never bothered the sergeant after that. Undoubtedly, she sensed the inherent danger of any further provocation.

After my stay in Paris, I was seized periodically by moods of depression. These deepened and became chronic during my stay at the Brest hospital, especially after witnessing such humiliating incidents. I felt that I could never again adjust myself to the conditions of Blacks in the States after the spell of freedom from racism in France. I did not want to go back, and my feeling was shared by many Black soldiers.

I thought of remaining in France, getting my discharge there and possibly becoming a French citizen. But I did not know how to go about this. Besides, I was ill, and there was my mother, whom I wanted to see again. Probably, some day, if I got well, I would come back—or so I thought as I lay in the hospital at Brest.

Finally, the day came. We were discharged from the hospital and given casual pay (one month's pay), which in my case amounted to thirty-three dollars, and we boarded the ship for home. There was no change in the Jim Crow pattern. We were merely transferred from a Jim Crow hospital to a Jim Crow hospital ship. We Blacks found ourselves quartered in a separate section of the ship. The segregation, however, did not extend to the mess hall or the lavatories (heads). I guess that would have been too much trouble. But the ship's military command passed up no opportunity to let us know our place.

For example, on the first day out we were given tickets for mess—breakfast, lunch, and supper. We were supposed to present them to a checker who stood at the foot of the stairway leading up to the mess hall. A Black soldier who had evidently misplaced his ticket tried to slip by the checker unnoticed, but he was not quick enough. A cracker officer who was standing by the checker hollered, "Hey, Nigger, come back here!"

The guy kept going and tried to merge into a group of us Blacks who had already passed through. Again the officer shouted, "Nigger, come back here. You, I mean. I mean the tall one over there. That nigger knows who I'm calling." The soldier finally turned and walked back. Purple with rage, protected by his bars and white skin, the officer said, "Listen, you Black son of a bitch, where is your ticket?" Clearly, the officer had already gauged his man and concluded that there was no fight in him.

"I couldn't find it," said the soldier. "Well, why didn't you say that in the first place instead of tryin' to slip through heah? Well, you go on back and try to find it. If you can't, see the sergeant in charge. Don't evah try that trick again," said the officer. His anger seemed to ebb, and a glow of self-satisfaction spread across his face. He had done his chore for the day. He had put a nigger in his place.

The seas were rough again. It was a small ship, leased from the Japanese. Most of us were seasick. The sailors were having a ball at our expense. When one of us would rush to the rail to vomit, one of them would holler, "A dollar he comes."

One night, the ship tilted sharply and a number of us were thrown out of our bunks. The bunks were in tiers, and I was in a top one. I got a pretty hard bump. The next morning on deck the sailors were talking loudly among themselves (for our benefit of course).

"Gee," said one, "this is the roughest sea I've ever seen. This old pile is about to come apart. The Japs leased us the worst ship they had."

"It just might be sabotage," another one suggested.

"I hope we make it, but I'm not so sure," said another.

Not being seamen, most of us were taking this seriously. A Black soldier turned to me and said, "You know man, after all I've been through, if this ship were to sink now almost in sight of home, I would get off and walk the water like the good Lord."

Another voice, that of a white sergeant from Florida who had been rather friendly to us: "You know," he drawled, "this reminds me of old Sam down home."

Here it comes, we thought, one of those nigger jokes.

"He was up theah on the gallows with a rope around his neck and the sheriff said, 'Well Sam, is there anything you want to say before you die?'

"'All I got to say sheriff,' said Sam, 'this sho' would be a lesson to me.'"

The voyage proceeded uneventfully, with one exception. The gamblers among us were out to get the soldiers' casual pay. The law of concentration of money into fewer and fewer hands was in process. This was taking place in one of the endless crap games that started in the Bay of Biscay and wound up at Sandy Hook, New Jersey.

I never really gambled, even in the army with room and board guaranteed. If you were broke, you could always borrow some money. The lender knew you couldn't run out on him. His only risk was that you might become a casualty. But motivated by nothing more than sheer boredom, I got into the game this time. After all, what good was thirty-three dollars going to do me? To my surprise, I hit a streak of luck, and over a period of a week in and out of the game, I ran my paltry grubstake up to the tremendous sum of twelve hundred dollars. That was the high point, after which my luck began to peter out. Nevertheless, I left the ship with five hundred dollars. It was my last gambling venture.

That morning, we lined up at the rail as our ship passed Sandy Hook and pulled into New York Harbor. It was my first view of the New York skyline. Overcome with emotion, I felt tears well up in my eyes. Embarrassed, I looked around and found that I was not alone. The guy next to me was obviously crying.

Our landing was a memorable one. Ship stacks were blasting, foghorns were blowing, bells were ringing, and fireboats were sending up great sprays of water. Passengers in ferryboats were waving and shouting greetings.

Upon docking, we were met by two reception committees of young women: a white one to receive the white soldiers and a Black one to greet us. This time segregation didn't bother us at all, we were so pleased to see the pretty Black girls. They drew us aside as we came down the gangplank, ushered us into waiting ambulances, and drove us to Grand Central Palace, which had been converted into a debarkation hospital. Leaving us in the lobby, they said good-bye and promised to come back soon and show us around.

A woman from the Red Cross took our home addresses to notify our families of our arrival. We were then escorted into a large room and told to strip off our clothes. Leaving them in the room, we then went through the delousing process. We were sprayed with some sort of chemical and washed off under showers. We were then given pajamas and a bathrobe and shown to our Jim Crow ward.

The next day, after a physical examination, we were paid off, receiving all of our back pay. In my case, it was for twelve months, amounting to about $450. This, plus the $500 I had won on the ship, seemed to me a small fortune, the largest amount of money I had ever had in my life. I was, so to speak, chafing at the bit, raring to get out and up to famed Harlem.

On the ship, I had met a Black sergeant named Patterson, who was from the 369th, the old Fifteenth New York. He had also won a considerable sum in the crap game. He suggested that we team up and go to Harlem together. He said he knew his way around there, since that was where he had lived before he joined the army.

After the payoff, we were still without clothes. But a clothing salesman came around to take orders for new uniforms. Patterson and I ordered suits, for which we were measured. In a couple of hours the man was back with two brand-new whipcord uniforms with chevrons and service stripes sewed on. We had also ordered shoes, which were promptly delivered. We then sneaked out of the hospital.

After we banked most of our money downtown, we took the subway up to 125th Street and visited several "buffet flats" (a current euphemism for a high-class whorehouse), drinking and looking over the girls. Patterson seemed to be an old friend of all the madams. They greeted him like a long-lost brother. We finally wound up in one real classy joint where we stayed for four days, playing sultan-in-a-harem with the girls.

We returned to the hospital, expecting to be sharply reprimanded and restricted to quarters, but the doctor on his rounds merely asked, "Where have you boys been?" Before we could answer, he simply said, "I suggest that you stick around a day or two; we have some tests to make."

From New York, we left for Camp Grant near Rockford, Illinois, where we were demobilized out of the service. I was discharged on April 29, 1919. After a cursory examination, I was pronounced physically fit. "What about my chronic endocarditis and chronic nephritis?" I protested.

"Oh, you're all right; you've overcome it all. You're young and fit as a fiddle," the doctor answered me. From Camp Grant I returned home to Chicago to see my parents.

Reunion with Otto

Not too long after my discharge, I came home one evening to find Otto. He had just arrived after mustering out of the service at Camp Grant. We were all happy to see him, especially Mother. He showed us his honorable discharge.

"You know," he said, "I'm lucky to get this."

He then told stories about his harrowing experiences in a stevedore battalion in the South and then in France. The main mass of Black draftees had been relegated to these labor units, euphemistically called "service battalions," "engineers," "pioneer infantry," and the like.

Regardless of education or ability, young Blacks were herded indiscriminately into these stevedore outfits and faced the drudgery and hard work with no possibility of promotion beyond the rank of corporal. With few exceptions, the officers were KKK whites, as also were the sergeants. Many of them were plantation riding-boss types, especially recruited for these jobs. Southern newspapers openly carried want ads calling for white men who had "experience in handling Negroes." Black draftees were subjected not only to the drudgery of hard labor but also to insults, abuse, and in many cases blows from white officers and sergeants.

Otto told us his worst experience was in Camp Stuart in Newport News, Virginia, where he was stationed during the terribly cold winter of 1917–18. For a considerable period after their arrival, they were forced to live in tents without floors or stoves. In most cases, they had only a blanket, some not even that.

New arrivals to the camp were forced to stand around fires outside all night or sleep under trees for partial protection from the weather. For months there were no bathing facilities, nor was there clothing for the men. These conditions were subsequently changed as a result of protests by the men and reports by investigators.

His outfit landed in the port of Saint-Nazaire, France, and during the great advance participated in the all-out effort to keep the front lines supplied in the "race to Berlin." They worked from dawn to nightfall unloading supplies, including all kinds of railroad equipment, engines, tractors, and bulldozers. They built and repaired roads, warehouses, and barracks. Discipline was strict; guys were thrown in the guardhouse on the most flimsy pretexts. A Black soldier seen on the street with a French woman was likely to be arrested by the MPs. "The spirit of Saint-Nazaire," said one officer, "is the spirit of the South."[6]

Needless to say, Otto often found himself in the guardhouse as a result of fights, AWOLs, and the like. How he escaped general court-martial or imprisonment I don't know.

His outfit was finally moved to the American military base at Le Mans, about a hundred miles from Paris. Things were somewhat better there. There were even a few "reliable" Black corporals, who were allowed weekend passes to visit Paris. Otto was assigned to mess duty as a cook.

When he applied for leave, he was refused, however. "Well, I didn't intend to come this close to Paris without seeing it," he said, "so I went AWOL."

He did not see much of it, however, before he was arrested by MPs. I was surprised to learn that he had been in Paris during the period that I was in the hospital in Neuilly. Most of his time in the great city was spent in the Hotel Sainte-Anne, the notorious American military jail run by the sadistic Marine captain "hard-boiled Smith." Here now, bitter and disillusioned, Otto continued his rebellion. It led him first to the Garvey movement, where he served for a brief period as an officer in Garvey's Black Legion, and then in succession to the Wobblies, or Industrial Workers of the World (IWW), the African Blood Brotherhood, and finally the Communist Party—joining soon after its unity convention in 1921. After returning from the service, Otto stayed at home only a short time and then moved in with some of his new friends.

4

SEARCHING FOR ANSWERS

Back home in Chicago, I was soon working again as a waiter on the Michigan Central Railroad. As I have already mentioned, the first day of the bloody Chicago Race Riot (July 28, 1919) came while I was working on the Wolverine run up through Michigan. When I arrived home from work that afternoon, the whole family greeted me emotionally. We were all there except for Otto. The disagreements I had had with my father in the past were forgotten. Both my mother and my sister were weeping. Everyone was keyed up and had been worrying about my safety in getting from the station to the house.

Following our brief reunion, I tore loose from the family to find out what was happening outside. I went to the Regimental Armory at Thirty-Fifth and Giles Avenue because I wanted to find some of my buddies from the regiment. The street, old Forrest Avenue, had recently been renamed in honor of Lieutenant Giles, a member of our outfit killed in France. I knew they would be planning an armed defense, and I wanted to get in on the action. I found them, and they told me of their plans. It was rumored that Irishmen from west of the Wentworth Avenue dividing line were planning to invade the ghetto that night, coming in across the tracks by way of Fifty-First Street. We planned a defensive action to meet them.

It was not surprising that defensive preparations were under way. There had been clashes before, often when white youths in "athletic clubs" invaded the Black community. These "clubs" were really racist gangs, organized by city ward heelers and precinct captains.

One of the guys from the regiment took us to the apartment of a friend. It had a good position overlooking Fifty-First Street near State Street. Someone had brought a Browning submachine gun; he'd gotten it sometime before, most likely from the Regimental Armory. We didn't ask where it had come from, or about the origin of the 1903 Springfield rifles (army issue) that appeared. We set to work mounting the submachine gun and set up watch for the invaders. Fortunately for them, they never arrived, and we all returned home in the morning. The following day it rained, and the National Guard moved into the Black community, so overt raids by whites did not materialize.

Ours was not the only group that used its recent army training for self-defense of the Black community. We heard rumors about another group of veterans who set up a similar ambush. On several occasions, groups of whites had driven a truck at breakneck speed up South State Street, in the heart of the Black ghetto, with six or seven men in the back firing indiscriminately at the people on the sidewalks.

The Black veterans set up their ambush at Thirty-Fifth and State, waiting in a car with the engine running. When the whites on the truck came through, they pulled in behind and opened up with a machine gun. The truck crashed into a telephone pole at Thirty-Ninth Street; most of the men in the truck had been shot down, and the others fled. Among them were several Chicago police officers—"off duty," of course!

I remember standing before the Angeles Flats on Thirty-Fifth and Wabash, where the day before four Blacks had been shot by police. It appeared that enraged Blacks had set fire to the building and were attacking some white police officers when the latter fired on them. Along with other Blacks, I gloated over the mysterious killing of two Black cops with a history of viciousness in the Black community. They had been found dead in an alley between State and Wabash. Undoubtedly they had been killed by Blacks who had taken advantage of the confusion to settle old scores with these Black enforcers of the white man's law.

Bewilderment and shock struck the Black community as well. I had seen Blacks standing before the burned-out buildings of their former homes, trying to salvage whatever possible. Apparent on their faces was bewilderment and anger.

The Chicago riot of 1919 was a pivotal point in my life. Always I had been hot-tempered and never took any insults lying down. This was even more true after the war. I had walked out of a number of jobs because of my refusal to take any crap from anyone. My experiences abroad in the army and at home with the police left me totally disillusioned about being able to find any solution to the racial problem through the help of the government, for I had seen that official agencies of the country were among the most racist and most dangerous to me and my people.

I began to see that I had to fight; I had to commit myself to struggle against whatever it was that made racism possible. Racism, which erupted in the Chicago riot—and the bombings and terrorist attacks that preceded it—had to be eliminated. My spirit was not unique—it was shared by many young Blacks at that time. The returned veterans and other young militants were all fighting back. And there was a lot to fight against. Racism reached a high tide in the summer of 1919. This was the "Red Summer," which involved twenty-six race riots across the country—"red" for the blood that ran in the streets. Chicago was the bloodiest.

The holocaust in Chicago was the worst race riot in the nation's postwar history. But riots took place in such widely separate places as Long View, Texas; Charleston, South Carolina; Elaine, Arkansas; Knoxville, Tennessee; and Omaha, Nebraska. The flare-up of racial violence in Omaha, my old hometown, followed the Chicago riots by less than two months. It resulted in the lynching of Will Brown, a packinghouse worker, for an alleged assault on a white woman. When Omaha's mayor, Edward P. Smith, sought to intervene, he was seized by the mob. They were close to hanging the mayor from a trolley pole when police cut the rope and rushed him to a hospital, badly injured.[1]

The common underlying cause of riots in most of the northern cities was the racial tension caused by the migration of tens of thousands of Blacks into these centers and the competition for jobs, housing, and the facilities of the city. Rather than being at a temporary peak, this outbreak of racism was more like a plateau—it never got any higher, but it never really went down, either. Writing in the middle of a riot in Washington, D.C., that summer, the Black poet Claude McKay caught the bitter and belligerent mood of many Blacks:

If we must die, let it not be like hogs
Hunted and penned in an inglorious spot,
While round us bark the mad and hungry dogs,
Making their mock at our accursed lot.
If we must die, O let us nobly die
So that our precious blood may not be shed
In vain; then even the monsters we defy
Shall be constrained to honor us though dead!
O kinsmen! We must meet the common foe!
Though far outnumbered let us show us brave,
And for their thousand blows deal one death blow!
What though before us lies the open grave?
Like men we'll face the murderous, cowardly pack,
Pressed to the wall, dying, but fighting back![2]

The war and the riots of the Red Summer of 1919 left me bitter and frustrated. I felt that I could never again adjust to the situation of Black inequality. But how had it come about? Who was responsible?

Chicago in the early twenties was an ideal place and time for the education of a Black radical. As a result of the migration of Blacks during World War I, the Chicago area came to have the largest concentration of Black workers in the country. It was a major point of contact for these masses with the white labor movement and its advanced, radical sector. In the thirties it was to become a main testing ground for Black and white labor unity.

The city itself was the core of a vast urban industrial complex. Sprawling along the southeast shore of Lake Michigan, the area includes five Illinois counties and two in Indiana. The latter contains such industrial towns as East Chicago, Gary, and Hammond. This metropolitan area contained the greatest concentration of heavy industry in the country.

By the second half of the twentieth century, it had forged into the lead of the steel-making industry, surpassing the great Monongahela River valley of Pittsburgh in the production of primary metals, including steel-mill, refining, and nonferrous metals operations. There was the gigantic U.S. Steel Corporation in Gary, the Inland Steel Company plant in East Chicago, and the U.S. Steel South Works. These were the three largest steel works in the United States. The steel mills of the Chicago area supplied more than 14,000 manufacturing plants.

Chicago was at that time, and remains today, the world's largest railway center. It ranked first in the manufacture of railroad equipment, including freight and passenger cars, Pullmans, locomotives, and specialized rolling stock.

The core city itself was most famous for its wholesale slaughter and meatpacking industry. Chicago was known as the meat capital of the world, or in Carl Sandburg's more homely terms, "hog butcher for the nation."

The city's colossal wealth was concentrated in the hands of a few men, who comprised the industrial, commercial, and financial oligarchy. Among these were such giants as Judge Gary of the mighty U.S. Steel; Cyrus McCormick of International Harvester; the meatpackers Philip D. Armour, Gustavus Swift, and the Wilson brothers; George Pullman of the Pullman Works; Rosenwald and General Wood of Sears and Roebuck; the "merchant prince" Marshall Field; and Samuel Insull of utilities. These were the real rulers. Ostensible political power rested in the notoriously corrupt, gangster-ridden, county political machine headed by Mayor William Hale "Big Bill" Thompson, who carried on the tradition exposed as early as 1903 by Lincoln Steffens in his book, *The Shame of the Cities.*

The glitter and wealth of Chicago's Gold Coast was based on the most inhuman exploitation of the city's largely foreign-born working force. A scathing indictment of the horrible conditions in Chicago's meatpacking industry was contained in Upton Sinclair's novel *The Jungle*, published in 1910. It was inevitable that the wage slave would rebel, that Chicago would become the scene of some of the nation's bloodiest battles in the struggle between labor and capital. The first of these clashes was the railroad strike of 1877, which erupted in pitched battles between strikers and federal troops.

Then in 1886 came the famous Haymarket riot, which grew out of a strike for the eight-hour day at the McCormick reaper plant. During a protest rally, a bomb was thrown that killed one policeman and injured six others. This led to the arrest of eight anarchist leaders; four were hanged, one committed suicide or was murdered in his cell, and the others were sentenced to life imprisonment. Obviously being tried and executed simply because they were labor leaders, these innocent men became a cause célèbre of international labor. Thousands of visitors made yearly pilgrimages to the city, where monuments to the executed men were raised. Haymarket became a rallying cry for the eight-hour day. The martyrs were memorialized by the designation of the first of May as International Labor Day.

Several years later the city was the scene of the great Pullman strike led by Eugene V. Debs and his radical but lily-white American Railway Union, which precipitated a nationwide shutdown of railroads in 1894. Again the federal troops were called in, and armed clashes between workers and troops ensued. These battles were merely high points in the city's long history of labor radicalism. It was the national center of the early anarchosocialist movements. In 1905, the IWW (or Wobblies) was founded there. The IWW maintained its headquarters and edited its paper, *Solidarity*, there. In 1921 Chicago was to become the site of the founding convention of the Workers (Communist) Party, USA, which maintained its headquarters and the editorial offices of the *Daily Worker* there from 1923 to 1927.

Blacks, however, played little or no role in the turbulent early history of the Chicago labor movement. This was so simply because they were not a part of the industrial labor force. Prior to World War I, Blacks were employed mainly in the domestic or personal service occupations, untouched by labor organizations. They were not needed in industry, where the seemingly endless tide of cheap European immigrant labor—Irish, Scots, English, Swedes, Germans, Poles, eastern Europeans, and Italians—sufficed to fill the city's manpower needs.

The only opportunity Blacks had of entering basic industry was as strikebreakers. Thus, in the early part of the century, Blacks were brought in as strikebreakers on two important occasions: the stockyards strike of 1904 and the citywide teamsters' strike in 1905. In the first instance, Blacks were discharged as soon as the strike was broken. After the teamsters' strike, a relatively large number of Blacks remained. As a result of the defeat of the 1904 strike, the packinghouses remained virtually unorganized for thirteen more years, and the animosities that developed toward the Black strikebreakers became a part of the racial tension of the city.[3]

At the outbreak of World War I, the situation with respect to Chicago's Black labor underwent a basic change. Now Blacks were needed to fill the labor vacuum caused by the war boom and the quotas on foreign immigration. Chicago's employers turned to the South, to the vast and untapped reservoir of Black labor eager to escape the conditions of plantation serfdom—exacerbated by the cotton crisis, the boll weevil plague, and the wave of lynchings. The great migrations began and continued in successive waves through the sixties.

During the war, the occupational sector in which Blacks worked thus shifted from largely personal service to basic industry. In the tens of thousands, Blacks flocked to the stockyards and steel mills. During the war, the Black population went from fifty thousand to a hundred thousand. Successive waves of Black migration were to bring the Black population to over a million within the next fifty years; Black labor, getting its first foothold in basic industry during the war, had now become an integral part of Chicago's industrial labor force.[4]

With the tapping of this vast reservoir of cheap and unskilled labor, there was no longer any need for the peasantry of eastern and southern Europe. There was, however, a difference between the position of Blacks and that of the European immigrants. The latter, after a generation or two, could rise to higher-skilled and better-paying jobs, to administrative and even managerial positions. They were able to leave the ethnic enclaves and disperse throughout the city—to become assimilated into the national melting pot. The Blacks, to the contrary, found themselves permanently relegated to a second-class status in the labor force, with a large group outside as a permanent surplus labor pool to be replenished when necessary from the inexhaustible reservoir of Black, poverty-ridden, and land-starved peasantry of the South.

The employers now had in hand a new source of cheap labor, the victims of racist proscription, to use as a weapon against the workers' movement. Indeed, this went hand in hand with the Jim Crow policies of the trade union leaders, who had been largely responsible for keeping Blacks out of basic industry in the first place.

These labor bureaucrats premised their racism on the doctrine of a natural Black inferiority. The theory of an instinctive animosity between the races was a powerful instrument for an antiunion, anti-working-class, divide-and-rule policy. The use of racial differences was found to be a much more effective dividing instrument than the use of cultural and language differences between various white ethnic groups and the native born. As we know, ethnic conflicts proved transient as the various European nationalities became assimilated into the general population. Blacks, on the other hand, remain to this day permanently unassimilable under the present system.

Such were conditions in the days when I undertook my search for answers to the question of Black oppression and the road to liberation. Living conditions were pretty rough then, and I had gone back to my old trade of waiting tables in order to make some sort of living.

But I was restless, moody, short-tempered—qualities ill-suited to the trade. Naturally, I had trouble holding a job. My trouble was not with the guests so much as with my immediate superiors: captains, headwaiters, and dining-car stewards, most of whom were white. In less than a month after the Chicago riot, I lost my job on the Michigan Central as a result of a run-in with an inspector.

The dining-car inspectors were a particularly vicious breed. Their job was to see that discipline was maintained and service kept up to par. These inspectors, whom we called company spies, would board the train unexpectedly anywhere along the route, hoping to catch a member of the crew violating some regulation or not giving what they considered proper service. They would then reprimand the guilty party personally, or if the offense was sufficiently serious, would turn him in to the main office to be laid off or fired. Usually the inspector's word was law from which there was no appeal. The dining-car crew had no unions in those days.

This particular inspector (his name was McCormick) had taken a dislike to me. He had made that clear on other occasions. The feeling was mutual. Perhaps he sensed my independent attitude. He probably felt I was not sufficiently impressed by him and did not care about my job. He was right on both counts.

He boarded the Chicago-bound train one morning in Detroit. We were serving breakfast. It was just one of those days when everything went wrong. People were lined up at each end of the diner, waiting to be served. Service was slow. The guests were squawking, and I was in a mean mood myself. I was cutting bread in the pantry when McCormick peered in and shouted, "Say, Hall, that silver is in terrible condition."

The silver! Why the hell is this man talking about dirty silver when I've got all these people out there clamoring for their breakfast?

"I've been noticing you lately," he continued. "It looks as though you don't want to work. If you don't like your job, why in hell don't you quit?"

I took that as downright provocation. "Damn you and your job!" I exploded, advancing on him.

He turned pale and ran out of the pantry. A friend of mine in the crew grabbed me by the wrist.

"What the hell's the matter with you, Hall? Are you crazy?" It was only then that I realized that I had been waving the bread knife at the inspector.

In a few minutes, the brakeman and the conductor came into the pantry. McCormick brought up the rear.

"That's the one," he said pointing at me.

Addressing me, the conductor said, "The inspector here says you threatened him with a knife. Is that true?"

I denied it, stating that I had been cutting bread when the argument started and had a knife in my hand. I wasn't threatening him with it. My friend (who had grabbed my wrist) substantiated my story.

"Well," said the conductor, "you'd better get your things and ride to Chicago in the coach. We don't want any more trouble here, and the inspector has said he doesn't want you in the dining car." I went up forward in the coach. I got off the train in Chicago at Sixty-Third and Stony Island. I didn't go to the downtown station, thinking that the cops might be waiting there.

So much for my job with the Michigan Central.

I went back to working sporadically in restaurants and hotels and on trains. I didn't stay anywhere very long. The first job I regarded as steady was at the Illinois Athletic Club, where I remained for several months. I was beginning to settle down a little and participate in the social life of the community, attending dances and parties and visiting cabarets. The Royal Gardens, a nightclub on Thirty-First Street, was one of my favorite hangouts. King Oliver and Louis Armstrong were often featured there. At the Panama, on Thirty-Fifth Street between State and Wabash, we went to see our favorite comedians—Butterbeans and Susie.

It was on one of these occasions that I met my first wife, Hazel. She belonged to Chicago's Black social elite, such as it was. Her father had died, and her family was on the downgrade. Her mother was left with four children, three girls and a boy, of whom Hazel was the oldest. The other children were still teenagers, and Hazel and her mother had supported them by doing domestic work and catering for wealthy whites. I was twenty-one and she was twenty-five.

Hazel was attractive, a high school graduate. She spoke good English and, as Mother said, "had good manners." She worked for Montgomery Ward, the first big company to hire Blacks as office clerks. She had a nice singing voice and used to sing around at parties. Her friends were among the Black upper stratum, and the family belonged to the Episcopal church on Thirty-Eighth and Wabash, which at that time was the church of the colored elite. We were married in 1920. I was all decked out in a rented swallowtail coat, striped pants, spats, and a derby. The ceremony was impressive. Photos appeared in the *Chicago Defender*.

In a short time, the romance wore off. Hazel's ambition to get ahead in the world, "to be somebody," clashed with my love of freedom. I soon had visions of myself, a quarter century on, making mortgage payments on a fancy house and installments on furniture, trapped in a drab, lower-middle-class existence, surrounded by a large and quarrelsome family.

The worst of it was having to put up with being kicked around on the job and taking all that crap from headwaiters and captains. I had been working at the Athletic Club for several months before I got married. Then nobody had bothered me. When I asked for time off to get married, the white headwaiter and the captain seemed delighted. "Sure Hall, that's fine. Congratulations. Take a couple of weeks off."

Upon my return, I immediately felt a change in their attitude. Now that I was married, they felt they had me where they wanted me. They became more and more demanding. One day at lunch I had some difficulty getting my orders out of the kitchen, and the guests were complaining—not an unusual occurrence in any restaurant. Instead of helping me out and calming down the guests, or seeing what the hang-up was in the kitchen, the captain started shouting at me in front of the guests: "What's the matter with you, Hall? Why don't you bring these people's orders?"

"Can't you see that I'm tied up in the kitchen?" I said. "Why don't you go out and see the chef instead of hollering at me!"

All puffed up, he yelled out, "Don't give me any of your lip or I'll snatch that badge off you!"

I jerked my badge off, threw both badge and side towel in his face, and shouted, "Take your badge and shove it!"

I was moving on him when a friend of mine, Johnson, a waiter at the next station, jumped between us. I turned away, walked down the steps, through the kitchen and into the dressing room. Johnson followed me into the dressing room a few minutes later. "Hurry up and get out of here. They're calling the cops." I changed and left.

My marriage went down the drain along with the job. That was a period of postwar crisis. Jobs were hard to find, and especially so for me since I had been blacklisted from several places because of my temper. I was no longer the same man that Hazel married, and the truth of the matter was that I wanted it that way. Her hang-ups were typical of Black aspirants for social status—strivers, we called them—who never really doubted the validity of the prejudice from which they suffered. Hazel slavishly accepted white middle-class values. I, on the other hand, was looking around trying to figure out how best to maladjust.

My Rebellion

For me, the breakup of our marriage in the spring of 1920 destroyed my last ties with the old conventional way of life. I was completely disenchanted with the middle-class crowd into which Hazel was trying to draw me. But more important, I not only rejected the status quo, I was determined to do something about it—to make my rebellion count.

I sought answers to a number of questions: What was the nature of the forces behind Black subjugation? Who were its main beneficiaries? Why was racism being entrenched in the North in this period? How did it differ from the South? Could the situation be altered, and if so, what were the forces for change and the program?

I renewed my search for a way to go, pressed by a driving need for a world-view that would provide a rational explanation of society and a clue to securing Black freedom and dignity. My search was to continue during what must have been the most virulent and widespread racist campaign in U.S. history. The forces of racist bigotry unleashed during the riots of the Red Summer of 1919 were still on the march through the twenties. Indeed, they had intensified and extended their campaign.

The whole country seemed gripped in a frenzy of racist hate. Anti-Black propaganda was carried in the press, in magazine articles, in literature, and in the theater. D. W. Griffith's obscene movie *The Birth of a Nation,* which glorified the Ku Klux Klan and pictured Blacks as depraved animals, was shown to millions.[5] Thomas Dixon's two novels, *The Clansman* (upon which Griffith's picture was based) and *The Leopard's Spots* (an earlier book on the theme of the white man's burden) were best sellers. Racist demagogues of the stripe of "Pitchfork" Ben Tillman of South Carolina, James Vardaman of Mississippi, and "Cotton" Ed Smith of South Carolina were in demand on northern lecture platforms.

Closely behind the trumpeters of race hate rode their cavalry. A revived Ku Klux Klan now extended to the North and made its appearance in twenty-seven states.[6] This organization, embracing millions, headed the list of a whole rash of super-patriotic groups who were anti-Catholic, anti-Jew, anti–foreign born, and anti-Black. The apostles of white, Anglo-Saxon, and Nordic supremacy included in their galaxy of ethnic outcasts Asians (the "yellow peril"), Latin Americans, and other foreign-born from southern and eastern Europe. Their hate propaganda pitted Protestants against Catholics, Christians against Jews, native-born against foreign-born, and all against the Blacks, upon whom was fixed the stigma of inherent and eternal inferiority.

It seemed as though the prophets of the "lost cause" were out to reverse their military defeat at Appomattox by the cultural subversion of the North. That they were receiving encouragement by powerful northern interests was self-evident. Tin Pan Alley added its contribution to the attack with a spate of Mammy songs and, along the same vein, "That's Why Darkies Were Born":

Someone had to pick the cotton,
Someone had to plant the corn,
Someone had to slave and be able to sing,
That's why darkies were born.
Though the balance is wrong,
Still your faith must be strong,
Accept your destiny brothers, listen to me.

A main objective of the racist assault was the academic establishment. The old crude forms of racist propaganda proved inadequate in an age of advancing science. The hucksters of race hate conducted raids upon the sciences, especially upon the new disciplines—anthropology, ethnology, and psychology—in an attempt to establish a scientific foundation for the race myth.

The new "science of race" evolved and flourished during the period. Spade-work for this grotesque growth had been done in the middle of the previous century by the Frenchman Arthur comte de Gobineau, in his work, *An Essay on the Inequality of the Human Races* (1853–55). It was carried on by his disciple, the Englishman turned German, Houston Chamberlain, who asserted that racial mixture was a natural crime. In the United States, early efforts in this field were the works of Nott and Glidden. Also, there was Ripley's *Races of Mankind*.

Carrying on in this pseudoscientific tradition during the war and the post-war years were the popular theorists Lothrop Stoddard, *The Rising Tide of Color: Against White World-Supremacy* (1923), and Madison Grant, *The Passing of the Great Race; or, The Racial Basis of European History* (1916). The cornerstone of this pseudoscientific structure was social Darwinism, which was an attempt to subvert Darwin's theory of evolution and arbitrarily apply natural selection in plant and animal society to human society. According to the social Darwinists, led by Herbert Spencer, a British sociologist, history was a continuous struggle for existence between races. In this struggle, the Nordic, Anglo-Saxon, or Aryan civilizations naturally survived as the fittest.

The racists had a field day in history, long the area in which the heroes of the "lost cause" had their greatest, most effective concentration. They had held chairs in some of the nation's most prestigious universities—Columbia, Johns Hopkins, Harvard, and so on. Among such historians was William Archibald Dunning, who during his long tenure at Columbia miseducated generations of students by his distortions of the Reconstruction, Civil War, and slave periods.[7]

In the academic world this pseudoscience of racism held sway with only a few open challengers. The latter seemed to be isolated voices in the wilderness, as the counteroffensive was slow in getting underway. In anthropology there was Franz Boas's antiracist thrust, *The Mind of Primitive Man*. This was written in 1911 and was not widely known at the time. The works of his students and colleagues—most notably Melville Herskovitz (*The Myth of the Negro Past*), Gene Weltfish, Ruth Benedict, Margaret Mead, and Otto Klineberg—were not to appear until the next decade.

In history, the movement for revision was then decades away. It only became a trend with the Black revolt of the sixties. Black scholars had pioneered the reexamination: W. E. B. Du Bois, whose tour de force, *Black Reconstruction in America*, with its epilogue, "The Propaganda of History," which contained a bitter indictment of the white historical establishment, was not to appear until the midthirties. J. A. Rogers, popular Black historian, had not yet appeared on the scene. Young Carter Woodson, who had founded his Association for the Study of Negro History in 1915, only began to publish the *Journal of Negro History* in 1916. His own important historical works were yet to come.

Thus, from its taproots in the southern plantation system, the anti-Black virus had spread throughout the country, shaping the pattern of Black–white relationships in the industrial urban North as well. The dogma of the inherent inferiority of Blacks had permeated the national consciousness to become an integral part of the American way of life. Racist dogma, first a rationale for chattel slavery and then for plantation peonage, was now carried over to the North as justification for a new system of de facto segregation.

Black subjugation, city-style Jim Crow, became fixed by the twenties and continues up to the present day. Its components were the residential segregation of the ghetto with its inferior education and slums, and the second-class status of Black workers in the labor force, where they were relegated to the bottom rung of the occupational ladder and prevented by discrimination from moving into better skills and higher paid jobs.

Although its purpose was not clear to me then, I later realized that the virulent racism of the period served to justify and bulwark the structure of Black powerlessness that was developing in every northern city where we had become a sizable portion of the workforce.

At the time the racist deluge simply revealed great gaps in my own education and knowledge. I knew that the propaganda was a tissue of lies, but I felt the need for disproving them on the basis of scientific fact. I rejected racism—the lie of the existence in nature of superior and inferior races—and its concomitant fiction of intuitive hostility between races. For one thing, it ran counter to my own background of experience in Omaha.

Religion as an explanation for the riddles of the universe I had rejected long before. I knew that our predicament was not the result of some divine disposition and therefore that racial oppression was neither a spiritual nor a natural phenomenon. It was created by man, and therefore must be changed by man. How? Well, that was the question to be explored. I had only a smattering of knowledge of natural and social sciences, much of which I had gathered through reading the lectures of Robert G. Ingersoll. It was through him that I discovered Charles Darwin and his theory of evolution through natural selection.

Armed with a dictionary and a priori knowledge gleaned from Ingersoll's popularizations, I was able to make my way through *On the Origin of Species.* Darwin showed the origin of species to be a result of the process of evolution and not the mysterious act of a divine creation. Here at last was a scientific refutation of religious dogma. I had at last found a basis for my atheism, which had before been based mainly upon practical knowledge.

Continuing my search, I found myself attracted to other social iconoclasts or image destroyers and to their attacks upon established beliefs. I remember staying up all night reading Max Nordau's *Conventional Lies of Our Civilization,* being thrilled by his castigation of middle-class hypocrisy, prejudices, and philistinism. Moving on to the contemporary scene, I discovered H. L. Mencken, "the sage of Baltimore," and his "smart set" crowd.

For a short while, I was an avid reader of the *Mercury,* which he helped to establish in 1920 as a forum for his views. I was particularly delighted by his critical potshots at some of the most sacred cultural cows of what he called "the American Babbitry," "boobocracy," "anthropoid majority"—Menckenian sobriquets for middle-class commoners. Mencken enjoyed a brief popularity among young Black radicals of the day, who saw in his searing diatribes against

WASP cultural idols ammunition with which to blast the claims of white su-premacists. The novelty soon wore off as it became clear that Mencken's type of iconoclasm posed no real challenge to the prevailing social structure. In fact, it was reactionary. He sought to replace destroyed idols with even more reaction-ary ones, as I soon found out.

Mencken's philosophical mentor was none other than the German philoso-pher Friedrich Nietzsche, prophet of the superman, of the aristocratic minor-ity destined to rule over the unenlightened hordes of *Untermenschen*—the "perennially and inherently unequal majority of mankind." Most Blacks then, including myself, who flirted with Mencken never accepted him fully. The one exception was George Schuyler of the *Pittsburgh Courier,* who took Mencken's snobbery and reactionary politics and made a career of them that lasted for forty years.

What confused me most were the contentions of the social Darwinists, who claimed to be the authentic continuators of Darwin's theories. Darwin had not dealt with the question of race per se. But it had seemed to me that his theory of evolution precluded the myth of race. How could Darwin's theory—which had helped me finally and irrevocably throw aside the veil of mysticism and put the understanding of the descent of man within my grasp—how could this be used as an endorsement of racism? Perhaps I had been wrong? Was I reading into Darwin more than what he implied?

It was my brother Otto who finally cleared me up on this point. He and I were running in different circles, but we would meet from time to time and exchange notes. Otto pointed out that social Darwinists had distorted Darwin by mechanically transferring the laws of existence among plants and animals to the field of social and human relations. Human society had its own laws, he as-serted. Ah, what were those laws? That was the subject that I wanted to explore.

"You ought to quit reading those bourgeois authors and start reading Marx and Engels," Otto told me, suggesting also that I read Lewis Henry Morgan's *Ancient Society* and the works of James Redpath.

About this time I got a job as a clerk at the Chicago post office. I heard that jobs were available and that veterans were given preference. Following the ad-vice of friends, I approached S. L. Jackson of the Wabash Avenue YMCA, who at that time was a Black Republican stalwart with connections in the Madden political machines.[8] Jackson gave me a note to some post office official in charge of employment. I passed the civil service examination, in which veterans were given a 10 percent advantage, and was employed as a substitute clerk.

The post office job in those days carried considerable prestige. It was almost the only clerical job open to Blacks. Postal workers, along with waiters, Pullman porters, and tradesmen, were traditionally considered a part of the Black middle class. A number of prominent community leaders came from this group, Many officers of the old Eighth Illinois were postal employees, a good percentage of them mail carriers.

The post office became a refuge for poor Black students and unemployed university graduates. For some of the latter it was a sort of way station on the road to their professional careers. Others remained, settling for regular post office careers. But even here opportunities were limited. Blacks held only a few supervisory positions, as advancement depended solely on the discretion of the white postmaster.

On the job I found the work extremely boring. It consisted of standing before a case eight hours a night, sorting mail. All substitutes were relegated to the night shift. It took years to get on the day shift, which was preempted by the veteran employees. On the other hand, I found the company of my new young fellow workers very stimulating.

In those days the organization of Black postal employees was the Phalanx Forum. Before the war, the organization had played an important political and social role in the community. It was dominated by a conservative crowd of social climbers and political aspirants, who were the most active group among postal employees and had close ties with the local Republican machine. Their leadership was completely ineffective with respect to the job issues of Black rank-and-file employees, and it had little or no influence over the younger group of new employees, which included many veterans and students. The gap between the old, conservative crowd and the new, youthful element was sharp. Among the latter a radical sentiment was growing.

I was immediately attracted to this group, among whom I was to find friends who seemed to be impelled by the same motivations as myself—to find new answers to the problems afflicting our people. Most of those with whom I fraternized considered the postal job as temporary, a step to other careers. Our interest at the time, therefore, was not so much with the immediate economic or on-the-job needs of Black postal workers as with the "race problem" generally. The drive for unionization of postal employees was to come later.[9]

The issue to which we addressed ourselves was the current campaign of white racist propaganda: how to counter it on the basis of scientific truth. We saw the network of racist lies as clearly aimed at justifying Black subjugation and destroying our dignity as a people. On this question we had long, endless discussions on the job while sorting mail, at rest, during lunch breaks, and on

Sundays, when some of us would meet. I soon identified with what I considered the more vocal segment. Among our group of aspirant intellectuals there were a medical student, a couple of law students, a dentist (whom we all called "Doc"), students of education, and some intellectually oriented workers like myself. On one Sunday when we had gathered, it was suggested, I think by Joe Mabley, that we organize ourselves as an informal discussion group and that our purpose would be to answer the racist lies on the basis of scientific truth. The idea was instantly agreed upon.

The discussion circle was loosely organized, not more than a dozen participants in all, and was bent on finding answers. The moving spirits of the group were John Heath, Joe Mabley, and Doc.

Heath was a tall, light-complexioned man with high cheekbones. He was a graduate student in the field of education, and a man whose sterling character and keen intellect we all respected. Then there was Joe Mabley, a brilliant, small Black man. He had large velvety eyes and was a college dropout. He was married and had a family—two or three children—and had settled down to a regular post office job. He and Doc were the only regular postal workers in our group, the rest of us being substitutes. Doc had set up an office on the Southside and was trying hard to build up a clientele while working night shifts.

Originally we had planned to meet every Sunday at noon, as the most convenient time for the fellows on our shift. The meeting places were to alternate between the homes or apartments of the members. When we got to procedure, the group would choose a topic of discussion and ask for volunteers or assign a member to make introductory reports. He would then have a week to prepare the report. Our original plans included the eventual organization of a forum in which the issues of the day could be debated, and the holding of social affairs. All of this proved to be too ambitious. We found it impractical to have weekly meetings and finally agreed that twice a month was more feasible. The forum idea never got off the ground.

Among us I think we had most of the answers on the question of race, that is, to all but the big lie, the one that was most convincing to the white masses and is the cornerstone on which the whole structure stood or fell: the assertion that *Blacks have no history.*

A leading formulator of the lie at that time was John Burgess, professor of political science and history at Columbia University:

> The claim that there is nothing in the color of the skin from the point
> of view of political ethics is a great sophism. A black skin means

membership in a race of men which has never of itself succeeded in subjecting passion to reason, has never, therefore, created any civilization of any kind.[10]

We wanted to refute the slanders on the basis of scientific truth. For this, we needed more ammunition and better weapons, particularly in the field of history. It was about this time that I met George Wells Parker, a brilliant young Black graduate student from Omaha's Creighton University. I was introduced to him by my brother Otto, who had known him in Omaha. He was in Chicago to visit relatives and to conduct research for his dissertation. His major was history, I believe. We found him a virtual storehouse of knowledge on the race question, especially Black history. His major objective in life was apparently to refute the prevalent racist lies and to build Black dignity and pride. He possessed wide knowledge and seemed to have read everything.

Parker called our attention to the writings of the great anthropologist Franz Boas; to the Egyptologist Rudolf Virchow; to Max Müller, the philologist who formulated the Aryan myth and then rejected it; to the Frenchman Jean Finot; to Sir Harry Johnston, a British authority on African history; and to the Italian Giuseppe Sergi and his theory of the Mediterranean races, a refutation of the Aryan mythology. Proponents of this myth claimed all civilizations—Indian, near Eastern, Egyptian—as Aryan. One wonders why the Chinese were left out, but then that would have been too palpable a fraud! It was Parker who called our attention to Herodotus (ancient Greek historian), who had described the Egyptians of his time (around 400 BC) as "Black and with woolly hair."

Otto and I introduced Parker to friends and acquaintances, and I, of course, to our discussion circle. He spoke before numerous groups. Everywhere there was hunger for his knowledge. We even brought him before the Bugs Club Forum in Washington Park, where he led a discussion on the race question.

This brilliant young man returned to Omaha to resume his studies. The next winter he was dead. We heard it was the result of a mental breakdown. Thus was a brilliant career cut short and a potentially great scholar lost. Surviving, I believe, was only one brief paper and some notes.

Garvey's Back to Africa Movement

But time and tide did not stand still to wait for our answers to the social problems of the day, or for the results of our intellectual researches. While we sought arguments with which to counter the racist thrust, the masses were forging their own weapons. Their growing resistance was finally to erupt on the political scene in the greatest mass movement of Blacks since Reconstruction.

Great masses of Blacks found the answer in the Back to Africa program of the West Indian Marcus Garvey. Under his aegis this movement was eventually diverted from the enemy at home into utopian Zionistic channels of peaceful return to Africa and the establishment of a Black state in the ancestral land.

The organizational course of the movement was Garvey's Universal Negro Improvement Association (UNIA). He first launched this organization in Jamaica, British West Indies, in 1914. Coming to the United States, he founded its first section in New York City in 1917. The organization grew rapidly during the war and in the immediate postwar period. At its height in the early twenties, it claimed a membership of half a million. While estimates of the organization's membership vary—from half a million to a million—it was the largest organization in the history of U.S. Blacks. There can be no doubt that its influence extended to millions who identified wholly or partially with its programs.

What in Garvey's program attracted these masses?

Garvey was a charismatic leader and in that tradition best articulated the sentiments and yearnings of the masses of Black people. In his UNIA he also created the vehicle for their organization. Equally important, he was a master at understanding how to use pageantry, ritual, and ceremony to provide the Black peasantry with psychological relief from the daily burdens of their oppression. His apparatus included such high-sounding titles as potentate, supreme deputy potentate, knights of the Nile, knights of distinguished service, the order of Ethiopia, the dukes of Nigeria and Uganda. There were Black gods and Black angels and a flag of black, red, and green: "Black for the race, Red for their blood, and Green for their hopes."

The movement's program was fully outlined in the historic Declaration of Rights of the Negro Peoples of the World, adopted at the first convention of the organization in New York City on August 13, 1920. In the manner of the Nation of Islam and its publication *Muhammad Speaks (Bilalian News)*, the program of Garvey combined a realistic assessment of the conditions facing Blacks with a fantasy and mystification about the solution. Along with the Back to Africa slogan, the document contained a devastating indictment of the plight of the Black peoples in the United States. Expressing the militancy of its delegates, it called for opposition to the inequality of wages between Blacks and whites and it protested their exclusion from unions, their deprivation of land, taxation without representation, unjust military service, and Jim Crow laws.

Anticipating the Black power revolt of the sixties, the document called for "complete control of our social institutions without the interference of any other race or races." Reflecting the rising worldwide anticolonial movement of the period, it called for self-determination of peoples and repudiated the loosely formed League of Nations, declaring its decisions "null and void as far as the Blacks were concerned because it seeks to deprive them of their independence." This latter point was in reference to the assignment of mandates to European powers over African territories wrested from the Germans.

Through this atmosphere of militancy, expressing the desire of the masses to defend their rights at home, ran the incongruent theme of Back to Africa. Declared Garvey:

> Being satisfied to drink of the dregs from the cup of human progress will not demonstrate our fitness as a people to exist alongside others, but when of our own initiative we strike out to build industries, governments, and ultimately empires, then and only then, will we as a race prove to our Creator and to man in general that we are fit to survive and capable of shaping our own destiny.
>
> Wake up, Africa! Let us work toward the one glorious end of a free, redeemed, and mighty nation. Let Africa be a bright star among the constellation of nations.[11]

Who were Garvey's followers?

Garvey's Zionistic message was beamed mainly to the submerged Black peasantry, especially its uprooted vanguard, the new migrants in such industrial centers as New York City, Cleveland, Detroit, Chicago, and St. Louis. These masses made up the rank and file of the movement. They were embittered and disillusioned by racist terror and unemployment, and they saw in Garvey's program of Back to Africa the fulfillment of their yearnings for land and freedom to be guaranteed by a government of their own.

On the other hand, Garveyism was the trend of a section of the ghetto lower middle classes, small businessmen, shopkeepers, property holders who were pushed to the wall, ruined, or threatened with ruin by the ravages of the postwar crisis. Also attracted to Garveyism were the frustrated and unemployed Black intelligentsia: professionals, doctors, lawyers with impoverished clientele, storefront preachers who had followed their flocks to the promised land of the North, and poverty-stricken students.

Garveyism reflected the desperation of these strata before the ruthless encroachments of predatory white corporate interests upon their already meager markets. It reflected an attempt by them to escape from the sharpening racist oppression, the terror of race riots, the lynchings, economic and social frustrations. It was from these strata that the movement drew its leadership cadres.

The immediate pecuniary interests of this element were expressed in the form of ghetto enterprises, the organization of a whole network of cooperative enterprises, including grocery stores, laundries, restaurants, hotels, and printing plants. The most ambitious was the Black Star Steamship Line. Several ships were purchased, and trade relations were established with groups in the West Indies and Africa, including the Republic of Liberia.

The New York City division comprised a large segment of the intensely nationalistic West Indian immigrants. West Indians were prominent in the leadership, in Garvey's close coterie, and in the organization's inner councils. There can be no doubt of the considerable influence of this element on the organization. But the attempt on the part of some writers to brand the movement as a foreign import with no indigenous roots is superficial and without foundation in fact. It is clear that Garveyism had both a social and an economic base in Black society of the twenties. Nor was Garvey's nationalism a new trend among Blacks: nationalist currents had repeatedly emerged, going back even before the Civil War.[12]

A key role in the movement was also played by deeply disillusioned Black veterans, who had fought an illusory battle to "make the world safe for democracy" only to return to continued and even harsher slavery. Veterans were involved in the setting up of the skeleton army for the future African state and in such paramilitary organizations as the Universal African Legion, the Universal Black Cross Nurses, the African Motor Corps, and the Black Eagle Flying Corps. Many Black radicals—even some socialistically inclined—were swept into the Garvey movement, attracted by its militancy.

Despite his hostility toward local Communists, Garvey seemed to regard the Soviet experience with some favor—at least in the early years of his movement. This probably reflected the sentiments of many of his followers. As late as 1924, in an editorial in the *Negro World*, he publicly mourned the passing of Lenin, the founder of the Soviet Union, calling him "probably the world's greatest man between 1917 and . . . 1924." On that occasion, he sent a cable to Moscow "expressing the sorrow and condolence of the 400,000,000 Negroes of the world."[13]

The Garvey movement revealed the wide rift between the policies of the traditional upper class of the National Association for the Advancement of Colored People (NAACP) and associates, and the life needs of the sorely oppressed people. It represented a mass rejection of the policies and programs of this leadership, which during the war had built up false hopes and now offered no tangible proposals for meeting the rampant anti-Black violence and joblessness of the postwar period. This mood was expressed by Garvey, who denounced the whole upper-class leadership, claiming that they were motivated solely by the drive for assimilation and banked their hopes for equality on the support of whites—all classes of whom, he contended, were the Black man's enemy. The policy of this leadership, he maintained, was a policy of compromise.

It was in these conditions that Garvey, as the spokesman for the new ghetto petty bourgeoisie, seized leadership of the incipient Black revolt and diverted it into the blind alley of utopian escapism.

My contact with the movement was limited. I had never seen Garvey. I had missed his appearance in 1919 at the Eighth Regiment Armory. I never visited the organization's Liberty Hall headquarters. In Chicago the movement seemed to spring up overnight. I first took serious notice of it in 1920. I listened to its orators on street corners, watched its spectacular parades through the Southside streets. The black, red, and green flag of the movement was carried at the head of the parade. The parades were lively and snappy; marching were the African Legion and the Universal Black Cross Nurses in their spotless white uniforms and white veils. All marched in step with a band. It was quite impressive, but to me it was unreal and had little or no relevance to the actual problems that confronted Blacks.

From the first, the Garvey movement met heavy opposition in Chicago. The powerful *Chicago Defender,* edited by Robert S. Abbott, took the lead. Even if not the world's greatest weekly, as its masthead proclaimed, it had great influence among Chicago and southern Blacks, due to its role in promoting the migration to the North. It was widely read in the South, where a daily newspaper of Athens, Georgia, called it "the greatest disturbing element that has yet entered Georgia."[14] The *Defender* was relentless in its attack, throwing scorn and contempt on the movement and on Garvey himself.

In addition to the *Defender's* attacks, the so-called Abyssinian affair in the summer of 1920 served to discredit the movement. The Star Order of Ethiopia and Ethiopian Missionaries to Abyssinia was an extremist split-off from Chicago's UNIA branch. The leaders of the group held a parade and rally on Thirty-Fifth and Indiana. Speakers clad in loud African costume called upon the crowd to return to their African ancestral lands.

To show their scorn for the United States, they burned an American flag, and when white policemen sought to intervene, the Abyssinians shot and killed two white men and wounded a third. This incident was blown up in the white press as an armed rebellion of Blacks. It was condemned on all sides in the Black community and by its leaders, including the editors of the *Defender,* who helped authorities in capturing the Abyssinian dissidents.

Despite its repudiation by the official Garvey organization, the Abyssinian affair served to muddy the Garvey image in Chicago. I was working on the New York Central at the time and heard a graphic account of the affair from my aunts when I arrived in town the next day. They lived right around the corner on Indiana Avenue.

Despite the hostile Black press and the Abyssinian affair, the UNIA grew. At its height, it claimed a Chicago membership of nine thousand devoted followers. This is probably exaggerated, but there is no doubt that its sympathizers numbered in the tens of thousands.

Our Sunday discussion group underestimated the significance of the Garvey movement and the strength it was later to reveal. We regarded it as a transient phenomenon. We applauded some of the cultural aspects of the movement— Garvey's emphasis on race pride, dignity, and self-reliance and his exaltation of things Black. This was all to the good, we felt. However, we rejected in its entirety the Back to Africa program as fantastic, unreal, and as a dangerous diversion that could only lead to desertion of the struggle for our rights in the United States. This was our country, we strongly felt, and Blacks should not waive their just claims to equality and justice in the land to whose wealth and greatness we and our forefathers had made such great contributions.

Finally, we could not go along with Garvey's idea about inherent racial antagonisms between Black and white. This to us seemed equivalent to ceding the racist enemy one of his main points. While it is true that I personally often wavered in the direction of race against race, I was not prepared to accept the idea as a philosophy. It did not jibe with my experience with whites.

Although we rejected Garvey's program, our ideas for a viable alternative were still vague and unformed. The most important effect the Garvey movement had on us was that it put into clear focus the questions to which we sought answers.

Who were the enemies of the Black freedom struggle? While Garvey claimed the entire white race was the enemy, it did not escape us that he was inconsistent, being soft on white capitalists. His main target was clearly white labor and the trade union movement. According to Garvey:

> It seems strange and a paradox, but the only convenient friend the
> Negro worker or laborer has, in America, at the present time, is the

white capitalist. The capitalist being selfish—seeking only the largest profit out of labor—is willing and glad to use Negro labor wherever possible on a scale "reasonably" below the standard white union wage . . . but, if the Negro unionizes himself to the level of the white worker . . . the choice and preference of employment is given to the white worker. . . .

If the Negro takes my advice he will organize by himself and always keep his scale of wage a little lower than the whites until he is able to become, through proper leadership, his own employer; by doing so he will keep the good will of the white employer and live a little longer under the present scheme of things.[15]

There is no doubt that Garvey was voicing the sentiments of the vast mass of new migrant workers. And it was not that we had any compunction about strikebreaking in industries from which Blacks were barred. In fact, that had been one of the ways Blacks broke into industries such as stockyards and steel. We were also keenly aware of the Jim Crow policies of the existing trade union leadership and of the anti-Black prejudices rampant among white workers. But in casting Blacks permanently into the role of strikebreakers, Garvey was helping to further divide an already polarized situation and playing into the hands of businessmen, bankers, factory owners, and the reactionary leadership of the trade unions.

My own experience with unions in the waiters' trade was bad. Old waiters would tell us that in the first part of the century they had listened to the siren call of white union leaders. They had gone out on strike, ostensibly to better their conditions, only to find their jobs immediately taken by whites. This had been quite a serious blow because at that time, Black waiters had had jobs in most of the best hotels and in a number of fine restaurants. It is therefore understandable that in 1920, we Black waiters felt not the slightest pang of conscience in taking over the jobs of white waiters on strike at the Marygold Gardens (the old Bismark Gardens) on the Northside, one of the swankiest nightspots in Chicago. It was also probably the best waiter's job in town; in fact, it was so good that some of the German captains who remained on the job used to drive to and from work in Cadillacs. The strike was broken after several months, and Blacks were turned out.

Strikebreaking to me was not a philosophy or principle, as Garvey contended, but an expedient forced upon Blacks by the Jim Crow policies of the bosses and the unions.

Even as Garvey was putting forward such views, times were beginning to change. Large numbers of Blacks had been brought into industry during the war and had joined unions, especially in steel and the packing houses. A new industrial unionism was developing and raising the slogan of Black and white labor unity.

My sister Eppa's experiences in 1919 at Swift Packing Company were a case in point. She was one of the first Black women to join the union during the organizing drive of the Stockyards Labor Council, which was headed by two Communists—William Z. Foster and Jack Johnstone. The drive was supported by John Fitzpatrick, chairman of the Chicago Federation of Labor and a bitter foe of the Jim Crow machine of Samuel Gompers's American Federation of Labor (AFL). Despite inevitable racial tensions fostered by the employers, Eppa had seen the basic unity of interest among all workers and felt strongly that the union was the best place to fight for the interests of Black workers.

In looking back, our study of the Garvey movement must be evaluated in light of the fact that it was our first confrontation with nationalism as a mass movement. Our mistake, which I was to find out later through my own experience and study of nationalist movements, resulted from the failure to understand the contradictory nature of the nationalism of oppressed peoples. This contradiction, or dualism, was inherent in the interclass character of these movements once they assume a popular mass form.

They comprise various classes and social groupings with conflicting interests, tendencies, and motives, all gathered under the unifying banner of national liberation, each with its own concept of that goal and how it should be attained. These conflicts, at first submerged, surface as the movement develops.

They are expressed in two main currents (tendencies) within the movement. First of all, there is the nationalism that reflects the interests of the basic masses—workers and peasants—determined to fight for liberation against the oppressors of the nation. Then there is the nationalism of the Black bourgeoisie, who, while at times in conflict with the white oppressors, tend toward compromise and accommodation to protect their own weak position.

From the very beginning this dualism was reflected in the Garvey movement. A highly vocal and aggressively dominant current within the movement was the drive of the small business, professional, and intellectual elements for a Black-controlled economy. They sought fulfillment of this goal through withdrawal to Africa, where they envisioned the establishment of their own state, their right to exploit their own masses free from the overwhelming competition of dominant white capital. (A historical example of this can be seen in Liberia.) They thought they could accomplish this, presumably with the acquiescence of the American white rulers, and even the active support of some.

On the other hand, there was a grassroots nationalism of the masses, the uprooted, dispossessed soil tillers of the South and their poverty-ridden counterparts in the slum ghettoes of the cities. These masses saw in the Black nationalist state fulfillment of their age-old yearnings for land, equality, and freedom through power in their own hands to guarantee and protect these freedoms. It was this indigenous, potentially revolutionary nationalism that Garvey diverted with his Back to Africa slogan.

We failed to recognize the objective conflict of interests between these class components of the movement, equating the social and political aims of the ghetto nationalists, the bourgeoisie, to that of the masses—condemning the whole as reactionary, escapist, and utopian.

These were the internal contradictions upon which the movement was to flounder and finally collapse. They were brought to a head by the subsiding of the postwar economic depression, the ushering in of the "boom" and subsequent easing of the plight of Blacks, the partial adjustment of migrants to their new environment, and their partial absorption into industry.

The main contradiction inherent in the Garvey movement from its very beginning had been the conflict between the needs of the masses to defend and advance their rights in the United States and the fantastic Back to Africa schemes of the Garvey leadership. Garvey's emphasis on these reflected his resolution of the conflict in favor of business interests and against the interests of the masses. The resources and energy of the organization were increasingly diverted to support racial business enterprises such as the Black Star Line and the Negro Factories Corporation. The concentration on selling stock for the Black Star steamship line by the UNIA leadership from 1921 on neglected the immediate needs of the masses and began to erode the base of support.

Furthermore, Garvey's response to the crisis in the movement exposed the dangerously reactionary logic of a program based upon complete separation of the races and its acceptance of the white racist doctrine of natural racial incompatibility. Pursuing the logic of this idea against the backdrop of the organization's decline inevitably drove Garvey into an alliance of expediency with the most rabid segregationists and race bigots of the period.

Thus, in 1922 Garvey sought the support of Edward Young Clarke, the Imperial Wizard of the Ku Klux Klan. This "meeting of the minds" between Garvey and the Klan was not fortuitous. It was an open secret that it took place on the basis of Garvey's agreement to soft-pedal the struggle for equality in the United

States in return for help in the settlement of Blacks in Africa. This ideological kinship arose from the mutual acceptance of the racist dogmas of natural incompatibility of races, race purity, and so forth.

In 1924 Garvey went so far seeking support for his Back to Africa program as to invite John Powell, organizer of the Anglo-Saxon Clubs, and other prominent racists to speak at UNIA headquarters. Garvey also publicly praised the KKK. According to W. E. B. Du Bois, the Klan issued circulars defending Garvey and declared that the opposition to him was from the Catholic Church.[16] In the late thirties, Senator Bilbo of Mississippi introduced a bill to deport 13 million Blacks to Africa and received the support of the remnants of the Garvey organization.

The final curtain was to drop on the Garvey episode with the failure of the Black Star Line. The movement was torn by factionalism and splits, with some of the leadership and remaining rank and file demanding that the domestic fight for equal rights be emphasized over the Back to Africa scheme of Garvey. The internal struggle drove many out of the organization and others into a multitude of splinter groups, each a variation of Garveyism itself. Taking advantage of this disarray, the government moved in.

In 1925 Garvey was framed on charges of using the mail to defraud in connection with the sale of stocks for the Black Star Line and was sent to the Atlanta federal prison for two years. He was deported to the West Indies upon release from prison. This debacle marked the end of Garveyism as an important mass movement, although the offshoots continued to exist in numbers of smaller groups advocating Garvey's theory.

At the time, I had taken Garvey's peculiar brand as representing nationalism in general and had simply rejected the whole ideology as a foreign import with no roots in the conditions of U.S. Blacks. Seeing only the negative features of nationalism in the UNIA, I was blind to the progressive and potentially revolutionary aspects that were to prove so important in my own later development.

Thus, the great movement that Garvey built passed into history. But nationalism, as a mass trend, persisted in the Black freedom struggle. Existing side by side with the assimilationist trend, it was eclipsed by the latter in so-called normal times while flaring up in times of stress and crisis.

The Garvey movement was the U.S. counterpart of the vast upsurge of national and colonial liberation struggles that swept the world during the war and postwar period. In this period, masses of Blacks had come to consider themselves as an oppressed nation. Garvey's ability to capture leadership of this nationalist upsurge by default was the result of the immaturity of the revolutionary forces,

Black and white. The collapse of the Garvey movement proved conclusively that the petty-bourgeois ghetto nationalist current, left to itself, led only to a hopeless blind alley. Unfortunately, the forces that could give Black nationalism revolutionary content and direction were only in the process of formation.

The Black working class and its spokesmen had not yet arrived on the scene as an independent force in the Black community and, therefore, were not capable of challenging either the assimilationist leadership of the NAACP or the ghetto nationalism of Garvey. Its counterparts among radical, class-conscious white labor were waging an uphill fight against the Jim Crow–minded AFL bureaucracy led by the Gompers machine. These radical sections of white labor were not yet clear as to the significance of the Black freedom struggle as a revolutionary force in its own right, and they regarded it simply as a part of the general labor question. Coalescence of these two forces was then a decade away, destined not to take place until the crisis of the thirties.

The preceding analysis is hindsight. I didn't realize the significance of Garvey's movement until a few years later, when, as a student in Moscow, I was assigned to a commission to prepare a resolution on the Negro question in the United States for the Sixth Congress of the Communist International in 1928. It was in the course of these discussions that I came to the recognition of nationalism as an authentic and potentially revolutionary trend in the movement.

The assimilationist programs of the NAACP had been easy to reject. Garvey was somewhat more difficult. But while the Garvey movement was forcing me to a consideration of nationalism (which at the time I also rejected), I could not help but notice the other political developments of the period.

Most conspicuous was the concerted and vicious attack being carried out against white radicals and the trade union movement. The same forces appeared to be behind the Palmer Raids of 1919 and 1920, behind the wave of racism, and behind the violent union and strike busting that took place. The foreigners who were deported, the radicals who were imprisoned, and the workers throughout the country who were attacked by Pinkerton "private armies" were white as well as Black. In Chicago the strikes at the stockyards and the steel mills in the area particularly attracted my attention.

For me, the Garvey movement, the racists' assault, and the attacks on labor and the radical movement sharpened my political perceptions. The racial fog lifted, and the face and location of the enemy were clearly outlined. I began to see that the main beneficiaries of Black subjugation also profited from the social oppression of poor whites, native and foreign born.

The enemy was those who controlled and manipulated the levers of power;

they were the superrich, white moneyed interests who owned the nation's factories and banks and thus controlled its wealth. They were known by many names: the corporate elite; the industrial and financial (and robber) barons; and so on. Chicago was the home base of a significant segment of this ruling class. Here the chain of command was clear: on the political side, it extended from city hall down to the lowliest ward heeler and precinct captain and was tied in at all levels with organized crime. On the economic side, it was represented by such employer organizations as the Chicago Chamber of Commerce, by trade associations, and by top management in the giant industrial plants, railroads, big commercial establishments, banks, utilities, and insurance firms. Their chain of command extended down to the foremen and department heads and on-the-job supervisors. These levers of power also controlled education, the media, the arts, and all law enforcement agencies, both military and police. At the bottom of this pyramid and bearing its weight were the working people who toiled in the steel mills, the packing plants, the railway yards, and the thousands of other sweatshops. Lowliest among these were the Blacks, pushed to the very bottom by the divide-and-rule policy of the corporate giants and their henchmen and by the complementary Jim Crow policies and practices of the AFL trade union bureaucracy.

Passages

Our postal discussion circle, which had held together scarcely three months, was breaking up. Heath, our chairman and recognized leader, was leaving. He had played the greatest role in keeping the group together. Now he had taken a job at some college in Virginia, his native state.

Differences had already developed in the group, and with Heath gone, the possibilities for reconciling them seemed slim. These differences, as I recall, were not of a political or ideological nature. They were seldom expressed in the open, but were reflected in the opposition of some members to proposals for enlarging the group and moving it into the outside political arena. This opposition evidently reflected the desire of some members to retain the group as a narrow discussion circle with membership restricted by tacit understanding to those whom they considered their intellectual peers. It seemed to me that they sought to reduce it to a sort of elitist mutual admiration society. As a result of this sectarian attitude, the group hardly grew beyond its original membership of a dozen or so.

There was no doubt, though, that our association had been mutually beneficial. All of us had grown in political understanding and awareness. But up to the time of Heath's departure, we had advanced no program for putting our newly acquired political understanding into practice. Our original plans for the organization of a forum to debate the issues of the day never got off the ground. We had not developed a program for involvement in the struggles of the community or, for that matter, in the immediate on-the-job problems of Black postal employees. We never even got around to deciding on a name for the group. One suggestion, that we call ourselves the New Negro Forum, was never acted upon.

Heath, Mabley, Doc, and myself were beginning to feel the pull from the outside, the need for a broader political arena of activity, to play a more active role in the community. We were the ones who most often attended radical forums and lectures and kept abreast of what was going on in the Southside community. We often went to the Bugs Club in Washington Park (Chicago's equivalent of London's Hyde Park) and the Dill Pickle Club on the Northside, which was run by the anarchist Jack Jones.

Heath had gone. Mabley refused the chairmanship, pleading that he was tied down by his family and could not take on additional responsibilities. Doc refused to accept the honor; he was similarly tied down by his job and dental practice. But the real reason for their refusal, which they were to confide to me later, was that they had lost confidence in the group. Without Heath, they saw no future role for it. Like myself, they were attracted to the broader movement. I also declined, giving as my excuse that I was quitting the post office in a few days and was going back to my old job on the railroad. A chairman pro tem was chosen; I don't remember who.

I continued my reading along the lines that Otto had suggested. Among the books I read were Lewis Henry Morgan's *Ancient Society* (which Engels had used as the basis for *The Origin of the Family*), Gustavus Myers's *History of the Great American Fortunes*, John Reed's *Ten Days That Shook the World*, and Jack London's *The Iron Heel*.

I also kept abreast of world events, reading about Lenin and Trotsky in revolutionary Russia. I followed the postwar colonial rebellions of Sun Yat-sen in China, Gandhi in India, and Atatürk in Turkey and the rebellion of the Rif tribes in Morocco led by Abd el-Krim. There were rumblings in Black Africa— strikes and demonstrations against colonial oppression. One heard such names as Clements Kadalie and Josiah Gumede of the South African National Congress, and of Sandino in Nicaragua, who fought the U.S. Marines for many years.

My feet were getting itchy. I was fed up with the post office and the excruciatingly monotonous nature of the work. At the same time, the night shift cramped my social life as well as my growing need for broader political activity. I quit the job without regret.

Soon after, I started work as a waiter on the Santa Fe's Chief, the company's crack train running to Los Angeles. It was an eight-day run: three days to the coast, a two-day layover in Los Angeles, and three days back. Our crew would make three trips a month, and a layover one trip (eight days) in Chicago. This schedule gave me approximately twelve free days a month in Chicago—time enough for both political and social life. It was a hard job, but good money for those days and exciting after the drab routine of the post office.

Los Angeles, "Sweet Los," as we used to call it. The Santa Fe boys, all "big spenders," were very popular with the girls. A bevy would show up to meet us at the station every trip.

I was to remain on that run three years, which up to that time was the longest I had ever remained on one job. Upon my return from the first trip, I called Mabley and he informed me that he thought the discussion circle had dissolved. Only one or two guys showed up at the next scheduled meeting, and the chairman pro tem himself was absent. It was dead.

My political development continued nevertheless. The runs on the Santa Fe gave ample time for discussion with my fellow crew members. Most of them, though somewhat older, were as aware as those at the post office with whom I had worked. I also continued to read, now studying *The Communist Manifesto*, Engels's *The Origin of the Family, Private Property, and the State,* and Marx's *Value, Price, and Profit.*

The first stage of my political search was near an end. In the years since I had mustered out of the army, I had come from being a disgruntled Black ex-soldier to being a self-conscious revolutionary looking for an organization with which to make revolution.

For three years I had listened in lecture halls, at rallies, and in Washington Park to a spate of orators, each claiming to meet the challenge of the times. They included the great "people's lawyer" Clarence Darrow; Judge Fisher of the reform movement; the Socialist leader Victor Berger and sundry other members of his party; the anarchist Ben Reitman; Ben Fletcher, the Black IWW orator and organizer; and assorted Garveyites. Although some had their points—for example, the fighting spirit and sincerity of the IWW impressed me—I rejected them all.

In the spring of 1922 I approached my brother Otto, whom I knew had joined the Workers (Communist) Party shortly after its inception in 1921. I told him that I wanted to join the party.

The fact that Otto was in the party and had advised me from time to time on my reading had undoubtedly influenced my decision. I had a generally favorable impression of the Black Communists I knew; men like Otto, the Owens brothers, and Edward Doty. I was also impressed by whites like Jim Early, Sam Hammersmark, Robert Minor, and his wife, Lydia Gibson. What added great weight to my favorable impression of the Communists, however, was their political identity with the successful Bolshevik Revolution.

At the time it happened, I had been totally unaware of its significance. I first heard of it during an incident that occurred in France in August 1918. My regiment, while marching into positions on the Soissons sector, had paused for a rest. On one side of the road there was a high barbed-wire fence, and behind it loitered groups of soldiers in strange uniforms. Upon closer observation, it became clear that they were prisoners. They spoke in a strange tongue, but we understood from their gestures that they were asking for cigarettes. A number of us immediately responded, offering them some from our packs.

When we asked who they were, one of them replied in halting English that they were Russian Cossacks. He explained that their division, which had been fighting on the western front, had been withdrawn from the lines, disarmed, and placed in quarantine. They were considered unreliable, he said, because of the revolution in Russia. At the time, I was not even sure of the meaning of the word "revolution"—some kind of civil disorder, I conjectured. Giving the matter no further thought, we resumed our march. It was not until I had returned from France that I began reading about the Russian Revolution. From then on, I followed its course, and despite the distorted view in the U.S. press, its significance slowly dawned on me.

Here, I felt, was a tangible accomplishment and real power. Along with other Black radicals, I was impressed—just as a later generation came to look at China, Cuba, and Vietnam as models of successful struggle against tyranny, colonialism, and oppression.

Thus, I was particularly attracted to the Communists. True, the party was largely white in its racial composition, with only a handful of Black members. I felt, nevertheless, that it comprised the best and most sincerely revolutionary and internationally minded elements among white radicals and therefore formed the basis for the revolutionary unity of Blacks and whites. This was so, I believed, because it was a part of a world revolutionary movement uniting Chinese, Africans, and Latin Americans with Europeans and North Americans through the Third Communist International.

The Bolsheviks had destroyed the czarist rule, established the first workers' state, and breached the world system of capitalism over a territory comprising more than one-sixth of the earth's surface. Most impressive as far as Blacks were concerned was that the revolution had laid the basis for solving the national and racial questions on the basis of complete freedom for the numerous nations, colonial peoples, and minorities formerly oppressed by the czarist empire. Moscow had now become the focus of the colonial revolution. In the turbulence of those days, there seemed every reason to think that the energy unleashed in Russia would carry the revolution throughout the world.

In the United States, the deluge of lies and distortions by the media, the red baiting, and the Palmer Raids had not been able to hide this monumental achievement of the Russian Bolsheviks. The uninformed Black man in the street could reason that a phenomenon that evoked such fear and hatred on the part of the white supremacist rulers "couldn't be all bad." As for me, the socialist victory confirmed my belief in the Bolshevik variety of socialism as a way out for U.S. Blacks.

I found the theory behind this achievement all there in Lenin's *The State and Revolution*. He developed and applied the theories of Marx and Engels on the role of the state and the dictatorship of the proletariat. This work was the single most important book I had read in the entire three years of my political search and was decisive in leading me to the Communist Party. In this work, Lenin clarified the nature of the state and the means by which to overthrow it. His approach seemed practical and realistic; it was no longer just abstract theory.

Using *The Origin of the Family* as a departure point, Lenin demystified and desanctified the myth of the state in capitalist society as an impartial monitor of human affairs. Rather, he exposed the state in capitalist society—and its apparatus of military, police, courts, and prisons—as an instrument of ruling-class domination, a dictatorship of the bourgeoisie.

It thus followed that the job of forcibly replacing the state power of the dominant class with that of the proletariat was the paramount and indispensable task of socialist revolution. As far as I could see, the Soviet example appeared to offer a completely clear solution to the problems facing American workers, both Black and white. I saw the elimination of racism and the achievement of complete equality for Blacks as an inevitable by-product of a socialist revolution in the United States. It was at this point that I became fully resolved to make my own personal commitment to the fight for a socialist United States.

The first part of my odyssey was over.

5

AN ORGANIZATION OF REVOLUTIONARIES

Otto was pleased when I first told him of my desire to join the party in the summer of 1922. He said that he had known I had been ready to join for some time, but he suggested I should wait a while before joining. When I asked why, he told me about an unpleasant situation that had arisen in the party's Southside branch.

Most of the few Black members were concentrated in this English-speaking branch, but it seemed that a number of recent Black recruits had dropped out. They resented the paternalistic attitude displayed toward them by some of the white comrades who, Otto said, treated Blacks like children and seemed to think that the whites had all the answers. It was only a temporary situation, he assured me. The matter had been taken up before the party District Committee; if it was not resolved there, they would take it to the Central Committee.

"And if you don't get satisfaction there?" I queried.

"Well, then there's the Communist International!" he replied emphatically. "It's as much our party as it is theirs."

I was properly impressed by his sincerity and by the idea that we could appeal our case to the "supreme court" of international communism, which included such luminaries as the great Lenin.

The Blacks who had remained in the party had decided not to bring any new members into the branch until the matter was satisfactorily settled. I was rather surprised to hear all of this. Clearly, membership in the party did not automatically free whites from white supremacist ideas. Nor, for that matter, did it free Blacks from their distrust of whites. Throughout my lifetime, I found that interracial solidarity—even in the Communist Party—required a continuous ideological struggle.

Otto suggested that until the matter was cleared up I should join the African Blood Brotherhood (ABB). The ABB was a secret, all-Black, revolutionary organization to which some of the Black party members belonged—including Otto. I later learned that the matter of white paternalism was eventually resolved to the satisfaction of the Black comrades. I don't recall the details; I think that Arne Swabeck (the district organizer) or Robert Minor from the Central Committee finally came down and lectured the branch on the evils of race prejudice and threatened disciplinary action to the point of expulsion of comrades guilty of bringing bourgeois social attitudes into the party.

In the meantime, I took Otto's advice and joined the African Blood Brotherhood. He took me to see Edward Doty, then commander of the Brotherhood's Chicago post. Vouched for by Otto and Doty, I was taken to a meeting of the membership committee and went through the induction ceremonies. This consisted of an African fraternization ritual requiring the mixing of blood between the applicant and one of the regular members. The organization took its name from this ritual. Doty performed the ceremony; he pricked our index fingers with a needle (I hoped it was sterilized!), and when drops of blood appeared, he rubbed them together.

Now a Blood Brother, I proceeded to take the oath of loyalty, which contained a clause warning that divulging of any of the secrets of the organization was punishable by death. I was deeply impressed by all this; the atmosphere of great secrecy appealed to my romantic sense. There were two degrees of membership; one was automatically conferred upon joining, and the second, which I took a few days later, involved the performance of some service for the organization. In my case, as I recall, it was a trivial task—selling a dozen or so copies of its magazine, the *Crusader*.

At the time that I joined the African Blood Brotherhood, I knew little about the organization other than the fact that it was in some way associated with the Communist Party. I do remember having read a copy or two of the *Crusader* before I joined the group.

Some of the history of the ABB I got from Otto and other post members, but most of it I found out much later when I met and worked with Cyril P. Briggs, the original founder of the group. The African Blood Brotherhood was founded in New York City in 1919 by a group of Black radicals under the leadership of Briggs. A West Indian (as were most of the founders), he was a former editor of the *Amsterdam News*, a Black New York newspaper. He quit in a disagreement over policy with the owner, who attempted to censor his antiwar editorials. Briggs's own magazine, the *Crusader*, was established in 1919. The Brotherhood was organized around the magazine, with Briggs, as its executive head, presiding over a supreme council.

The group was originally conceived as the African Blood Brotherhood "for African liberation and redemption" and was later broadened to "for immediate protection and ultimate liberation of Negroes everywhere." As it was a secret organization, it never sought broad membership. National headquarters were in New York. Its size never exceeded three thousand. But its influence was many times greater than this; the *Crusader* at one time claimed a circulation of thirty-three thousand.[1] There was also the Crusader News Service, which was distributed to two hundred Black newspapers.

Briggs, his associates—Richard B. Moore, Grace Campbell, and others— and the *Crusader* were among the vanguard forces for the New Negro movement, an ideological current that reflected the new mood of militancy and social awareness of young Blacks of the postwar period. In New York, the New Negro movement also included the radical magazine the *Messenger,* edited by Chandler Owen and A. Philip Randolph, and the *Emancipator,* edited by W. A. Domingo. Many in these groups were members of the Socialist Party or close to it politically. They espoused "economic radicalism," an oversimplified interpretation of Marxism that, nevertheless, enabled them to see the economic and social roots of racial subjugation. Historically, theirs was the first serious attempt by Blacks to adopt the Marxist worldview and apply the theory of class struggle to the problems of Black Americans.

Within this broad grouping, however, there were differences that emerged later. Briggs was definitely a revolutionary nationalist; that is, he saw the solution of the "race problem" in the establishment of independent Black nation-states in Africa, the Caribbean, and the United States. In America, he felt this could be achieved only through revolutionizing the whole country. This meant he saw revolutionary white workers as allies. These were elements of a program that he perceived as an alternative to Garvey's plan of mass exodus.

A self-governing Black state on U.S. soil was a novel idea for which Briggs sent up trial balloons in the form of editorials in 1917 in the *Amsterdam News,* of which he was then editor. Shortly after the entrance of the United States into World War I, he wrote an editorial entitled "Security of Life for Poles and Serbs—Why Not for Colored Americans?"[2]

Briggs, however, had no definite idea for the location of the future "colored autonomous state," suggesting at various times Washington, Oregon, Idaho, California, or Nevada. Later, after President Wilson had put forth his Fourteen Points in January 1918, Briggs equated the plight of Blacks in the United States to that of nations occupied by Germany and demanded:

With what moral authority or justice can President Wilson demand that eight million Belgians be freed when for his entire first term and to the present moment of his second term he has not lifted a finger for justice and liberty for over TEN MILLION colored people, a nation within a nation, a nationality oppressed and jim-crowed, yet worthy as any other people of a square deal or failing that, a separate political existence?[3]

He continued this theme in the *Crusader*. One year after the founding of the Brotherhood, Briggs shifted from the idea of a Black state on U.S. soil to the advocacy of a Black state in Africa, South America, or the Caribbean, where those Blacks who wanted to could migrate. In this, he was undoubtedly on the defensive, giving ground to the overwhelming Garvey deluge then sweeping the national Black community. In 1921, Briggs was to link the struggle for equal rights of U.S. Blacks with the establishment of a Black state in Africa and elsewhere:

> Just as the Negro in the United States can never hope to win equal rights with his white neighbors until Africa is liberated and a strong Negro state (or states) erected on that continent, so, too, we can never liberate Africa unless and until the American Section of the Negro Race is made strong enough to play the part for a free Africa that the Irish in America now play for a free Ireland.[4]

The Brotherhood rejected Garvey's racial separatism. They knew that Blacks needed allies and tied the struggle for equal rights to that of the progressive section of white labor. In the 1918–19 elections, the Brotherhood supported the Socialist Party candidates. The *Crusader* and the ABB were ardent supporters of the Russian Revolution; they saw it as an opportunity for Blacks to identify with a powerful international revolutionary movement.[5] It enabled them to overcome the isolation inherent in their position as a minority people in the midst of a powerful and hostile white oppressor nation. Thus, the *Crusader* called for an alliance with the Bolsheviks against race prejudice. In 1921 the magazine made its clearest formulation, linking the struggles of Blacks and other oppressed nations with socialism:

> The surest and quickest way, then, in our opinion, to achieve the salvation of the Negro is to combine the two most likely and feasible propositions, viz.: salvation for all Negroes through the establishment of a strong, stable, independent Negro State (along the lines of our own race genius) in Africa and elsewhere; and salvation for all Negroes (as well as other oppressed people) through the establishment of a Universal Socialist Co-operative commonwealth.[6]

The split in the world socialist movement as a result of World War I led to the formation of the Third (Communist) International in 1919. This split was reflected in the New Negro movement as well. Randolph and Owen, the whole *Messenger* crowd, remained with the social democrats of the Second International who were in opposition to the Bolshevik Revolution. Members of the *Crusader* group— Briggs, Moore, and others—gravitated toward the Third International and eventually joined its American affiliate, the Communist Party. They were followed in the next year or two by Otto Hall, Lovett Fort-Whiteman, and others.

The decline of the African Blood Brotherhood in the early twenties and its eventual demise coincided with the growing participation of its leadership in the activities of the Communist Party. By 1923–24, the Brotherhood had ceased to exist as an autonomous, organized expression of the national revolutionary trend. Its leading members became communists or close sympathizers, and its posts served as one of the party's recruiting grounds for Blacks.

I first met Briggs upon my return from Russia in 1930. We were to strike up a lasting friendship—one that went beyond the comradeship of the party and that extended over more than three decades, until his death in 1967. Throughout those years, we were associated on numerous projects and found ourselves on the same side of many political issues.

When I first met Briggs, he conformed to the impression that I had been given of him: a tall, impressive-looking man—so light in complexion that he was often mistaken for white. He had a large head and bushy black eyebrows. He was a man possessed of great physical and moral courage, which I was to observe on many occasions. Briggs also had a fiery temper, which was usually controlled in the case of comrades or friends.

He had one outstanding physical defect: he was a heavy stutterer. He stuttered so much that it often took him several seconds to get out the first word of a sentence. When he took the floor at meetings, we would all listen attentively; no one would interrupt him because we knew he always had something important and pertinent to say. While he spoke we would cast our eyes down and look away from him to avoid making him feel self-conscious, though he never seemed to be.

We noticed that he stuttered less when he was angry. One such occasion was when Garvey rejected Briggs's offer of cooperation. The wily Garvey saw the maneuver for what it was—an attempt by Briggs to gain a position from which he could better attack him. Garvey lashed out at Briggs, calling him a "white man trying to pass himself off as a Negro."

Friends told me that this attack sent Briggs into such a rage that he mounted a soapbox at Harlem's 135th Street and Lenox Avenue and assailed Garvey for two hours without a stutter, branding him a charlatan and a fraud. Not content with this verbal lashing of his enemy, Briggs hauled Garvey into court on the charge of defamation of character. He won the case, forcing Garvey to make a public apology and pay a fine of one dollar.

Briggs's real forte, however, was as a keen polemicist, a veritable master of invective. His speech handicap was a pity, because aside from the stutter he had all the qualities of a good orator. Closely associated with Briggs was Richard B. Moore, a fine orator who did much public speaking for the ABB.

What were the reasons for the decline of the ABB and its eventual absorption by the Communist Party? Why did Briggs fail to develop the program for Black self-determination in the United States? In the fifties, I had a series of talks with Briggs and asked his opinion on these questions.

His overall appraisal of the role of the Brotherhood was that it was a forerunner of the contemporary national revolutionary trend and a very positive thing. "Of course, we didn't stop Garvey," he said, but "we were beginning to develop a revolutionary alternative. We did put a crimp in his sails," Briggs added.

For a while, the ABB had been a rallying center for left opposition to Garvey. Its membership included class-conscious Black workers and revolutionary intellectuals, and it drew membership from both disillusioned Garveyites and radicals who never took to Garvey's program in the first place. The main reason for de-emphasizing the idea of Black nationhood in the United States, Briggs stated, was the unfavorable relationship of forces then existing.

Garvey, with his Back to Africa program, had preempted the leadership of the mass movement and had corralled most of the militants. His hold over the masses was strengthened by the anti-Black violence of the Red Summer of 1919. This gave further credence to Garvey's contention that the United States was a white man's country where Blacks could never achieve equality. Indeed, for these masses, his program for a Black state in Africa to which American Blacks could migrate seemed far less utopian than the idea of a Black state on U.S. soil.

As for the South, Briggs did not feel that such a region of entrenched racism could be projected realistically as a territorial focus of a Black nationalist state. It would not have been so accepted by the masses who were in flight from the area. For himself, he reasoned, the very idea of self-determination in the United States presupposed the support of white revolutionaries. That meant a revolutionary crisis in the country as a whole, and in that day no such prospect was in sight. In fact, white revolutionary forces were then small and weak, the target of the vicious anti-red drives of the government and employers.

In other words, he felt that Black self-determination in the United States was an idea whose time had not yet come. The Communists didn't have all the answers, and neither did we, Briggs indicated. Whites, as well as a number of Black radicals, undoubtedly underestimated the national element; socialism alone was seen as the solution. Briggs was impressed, however, by the sincerity and revolutionary ardor of the Communists and by the fact that they were a detachment of Lenin's Third Communist International. He felt that the future of the revolution in the United States and of Black liberation lay in multinational Communist leadership.

Though the ABB ceased to exist as an organized, independent expression of the national revolutionary current, the tendency itself remained, awaiting the further maturing of its main driving force, the Black proletariat. By the end of the decade, the national revolutionary sentiment was to find expression in the program of the Communist Party.

By the time I joined the Brotherhood's Chicago post in the summer of 1922, the *Crusader* had dropped much of its original national revolutionary orientation. Although I was then unaware of it, Briggs and the supreme council were presiding over the absorption of the organization into the Communist Party.

In Chicago, the decline of the organization was slower than elsewhere. Perhaps this was because it had a strong base among Black building tradesmen, plumbers, electricians, and bricklayers. Edward Doty, a plumber by trade, was simultaneously the ABB post commander and a leader and founder of the American Consolidated Trades Council (ACTC). The council was a federation of independent Black unions and groups in the building trades who had formed their own unions for the double purpose of protecting Black workers on the job and counteracting the discriminatory policies of the white AFL craft unions dominant in the field.

Doty, a tall, muscular man, was born in Mobile, Alabama, and had come north in 1912 at the age of seventeen. According to him, most of the Black steamfitters and plumbers had learned their trades in the stockyards during the industrial boom and labor shortage that accompanied World War I. Some, however, had gotten their training at Tuskegee Institute in Alabama. Active in the Brotherhood along with Doty were such outstanding leaders of the Black workers' struggle as Herman Dorsey (an electrician) and Alexander Dunlap (a plumber).

Besides the tradesmen, other members of the ABB post included a number of older radicals such as Alonzo Isabel, Norval Allen, Gordon Owens, H. V. Phillips, Otto Hall, and several others. Together with Doty, they made up the Communist core of the Brotherhood.

My experiences in the ABB marked my first association with Black Communists. I had met some of them before, at forums and lectures; I had heard Owens speak at the Bugs Club and the Dill Pickle forums, but I had never worked together with any of them before.[7] They were mostly workers from the stockyards and other industries. One or two, like myself, were from the service trades. Like Otto, several of them had previously been in the Garvey movement. There was no doubt that they represented a politically advanced section of the Black working class. They were the types who today would be called "political activists," the people who kept abreast of the issues in the Southside community and participated in local struggles.

I was interested to learn their backgrounds and how they had come to the revolutionary movement. I found that some of them had been among Chicago's first Marxist-oriented Black radicals and had been associated with the Free Thought Society. This society was formed immediately after the war and held regular forums. I believe its leader and founder was a young man named Tibbs. He was one of the earliest of Chicago's Black radicals. A victim of police harassment and persecution, Tibbs was arrested during the Palmer Raids in 1919 and spent several years in jail on a fake charge of stealing automobile tires. This continual persecution reduced his political effectiveness, which was as the authorities intended.

Members of the Free Thought Society forum, I learned, had cooperated with the New Negro group of economic radicals centered around the radical weekly the *Whip*, edited by Joseph Bibb, A. C. MacNeal (who later became secretary of the Chicago NAACP), and William C. Linton. The members of this group, unlike their New York counterparts, were not avowed socialists. They were, nevertheless, influenced by socialist ideas and regarded the "race problem" as basically economic.

In 1920 members of the Free Thought Society took an active part in the campaign of the Independent Non-Partisan League, sponsored by the *Whip* and its editors. This coalition ran a full slate of candidates in the Republican primary of that year, in which they challenged the old-guard Republicans of the Second Ward Republican organization as well as the so-called New People's Movement of Oscar DePriest.[8]

The election platform called for abolition of all discrimination, public ownership of utilities, civil service reform, women's suffrage, a children's welfare service, and "organization of labor into one union." While they were not successful in turning back the Republican old guard, the campaign resulted in appreciable gains for some of the league's candidates.

At that time, the main efforts of the ABB were directed at mobilizing community support for the Black ACTC tradesmen. While retaining a secret character, its members participated as individuals in campaigns on local issues. They collaborated with the Trade Union Education League (TUEL), of which Doty was a member, in its drive to organize the stockyards. The TUEL supported the demands of the ACTC. At that time, it was led by William Z. Foster and Jack Johnstone. Later to become the Trade Union Unity League, it was a gathering of the revolutionary and progressive forces within trade unions to fight against the reactionary labor bureaucracy and their collaborationist policies and Jim Crowism.

Other members of the Brotherhood participated in the campaign against high rents that was waged in the Southside community. This was a fight in which a white party member, Bob Minor, and his wife, Lydia Gibson, played leading roles.

I found my experience in the Brotherhood both stimulating and rewarding. In addition to learning a lot from the Communists with whom I was associated, it was here I forged my first active association with Black industrial workers. I found them literate, articulate, and class conscious, a proud and defiant group that had been radicalized by the struggles against the discriminatory practices of the unions and employers. They understood the meaning of solidarity and the need for militant organization to obtain their objectives. In this, they were quite different from the people with whom I had been associated at the post office, as well as from waiters whom I so commonly found to be stamped with a hustler mentality. Doty and his followers in the Trades Council were pioneers in the struggle for the rights of Black workers, a struggle that has continued over half a century and remains unfinished to this day.

The older tradesmen finally fought their way into the unions, the electricians in 1938 and the plumbers in 1947. In the early fifties, Doty became the first Black officer in the plumbers' union. But these gains were only token! The bars are still up against Blacks and other minority workers seeking jobs in the ninety-billion-dollar-a-year industry.

The Young Communist League

My sojourn in the African Blood Brotherhood was brief—about six months. I felt the need to move on. My original goal was the Communist Party. While I was in the ABB, the problem of white chauvinism in the Southside branch had been cleared up. Joining the party was no longer a problem; after all, the Brotherhood had been but a stopover.

I was about to apply for admission when H. V. Phillips asked me to join the Young Workers (Communist) League (YCL), the youth division of the Communist Party. Phillips, I learned, was a member of the district and national committees of the league. When I told him I was just about to join the party, he said, "That's all right, but you're a young fellow and should be among the youth. Besides, more of us Blacks are needed in the League."

I thought the matter over. "Why not? It's all the same, they're all Communists."

The next day Phillips took me to meet John Harvey, a white youth who was district organizer of the league. Harvey told me that I had been highly recommended to them by Phillips and others. He expressed delight at my decision to join and said that it fit right in with their plans since they were anxious to move forward with work among Black youth but were handicapped by the fact that they had only a few Black members.

I expressed doubt that I could be considered a youth at the age of twenty-five.

They replied that there were a number of members my age and older in the organization. All that was needed, they assured me, was for one to have the "youth angle."

"What is that?" I asked.

"Oh, that simply means the ability to understand youth and their problems and to be able to communicate with them."

I was not sure I had all of these qualities, but the proposition appealed to me. So I joined the YCL in the winter of 1923. The league at that time was a close-knit fraternity of idealistic and dedicated young people determined to build a new world for future generations. When we sang the "Youth International" at meetings, we actually felt ourselves to be, as the song proclaimed, "the youthful guardsmen of the proletariat."

The organization was small, with only several hundred members. As I recall, Phillips and myself were the only Blacks. I was still working on the Santa Fe, and on layovers I spent most of the time getting acquainted with my new comrades and attending classes, meetings, and social gatherings. I was impressed by what seemed to me to be a high level of political development and by their use of Marxist terminology. It made me keenly aware of my own sketchy knowledge of Marxism and the revolutionary movement and spurred me to close the gap. A partial explanation for their political sophistication, I felt, was the fact that a large number of them, perhaps a majority, were "red diaper" babies—their parents being old revolutionaries, either members of the party or its supporters. On the whole, they were a spirited, intelligent group, and as far as I could discern exhibited not a trace of race prejudice. Many went on to become leaders of the party.

There was no scarcity of places for meetings or for social affairs. We were on friendly terms with Jane Addams and her people at Hull House, where we sometimes met. Other times we used the halls of various language groups. We participated in and supported the activities of the Anti-Imperialist League, headed by Manny Gomez, the party's Latin American specialist. The main campaign at the time was against the invasion of Nicaragua by the U.S. Marines.

I was particularly impressed by Bob Mazut, a young Russian representative of the Young Communist International (YCI) to the league. A small, dark-complected, and soft-spoken young man, Mazut hailed from Soviet Georgia. His mild manner belied his impressive background. Only twenty-five when I met him, he had fought in the Revolution and Civil War, first as a Red Partisan and then in the Red Army, in which he advanced to the rank of colonel. He spoke what we called "political English," and we were always amused by some of his expressions. For example, I remember how we used to kid Mazut about his being sweet on a certain girl comrade. "She likes you very much," someone would say, "but she's a little overawed by you."

He replied very seriously, "How can I liquidate her suspicions of me?"

He took particular interest in me. I believe Phillips and I were the first Blacks he had ever really known, and for us he was the first real Soviet Communist we had met. I asked questions about Russia and told him I wanted to go there and see it for myself. "You undoubtedly will," he said in a matter-of-fact tone, as if the matter were settled.

On one occasion he told me of a discussion he had had on the eve of his departure from Russia. Grigory Zinoviev, then president of the Communist International, had asked him to look closely into the Afro-American question in the United States and to see if he could find any confirmation for his belief and that of other Russian leaders that the right of self-determination was the appropriate slogan for Black rebellion. Zinoviev added that he had long believed that the question would become the "Achilles heel of American imperialism." I told Mazut that I liked the part about the Achilles heel but that I didn't feel that the slogan of self-determination was applicable for U.S. Blacks. It was my understanding that the principle had to do with nations, and Blacks were not a national but a racial minority. To me, it smacked of Garvey's separatism.

Mazut nevertheless raised the question of self-determination for discussion in a meeting of the Chicago District Committee of the YCL. Desirous of getting the committee's reaction to the question, he was literally shouted down by the white comrades. "Blacks are Americans," they said. "They want equality, not separation." Phillips and I, the only Black members of the committee, were noncommittal. And that was the end of that. They did not pursue the matter further.

In order to move forward in work with Black youth, we struck upon the idea of organizing an interracial youth forum on the Southside. The organizing committee consisted of Chi (Dum Ping), a Chinese student at the University of Chicago; a young woman official of the colored YMCA; Phillips; a white league member; and myself. During this period, I was still working on the Santa Fe, but on my layovers I devoted all time to the forum. We had rented a small hall, decorated it and got out our publicity—leaflets, posters, and an ad in the *Chicago Defender.* Our first speaker was to be John Harden, a Black radical orator. It was our first effort at mass work among young Blacks, and with our youthful enthusiasm, we were certain of success. But the venture proved to be abortive.

I can still remember our shock when we came to our meeting place to find it wrecked. Furniture was smashed; posters were ripped from the walls. There was no doubt in our minds that this was the work of the police, who had unleashed their stool pigeons against us. Some of our non-Communist friends dropped out, and the project collapsed. The idea of a forum was abandoned—temporarily, we hoped. A less ambitious plan was then agreed to.

If we could enlarge our cadres by a few more Blacks, we thought, we would have a better base from which to approach mass work. It was therefore suggested that Phillips and I approach some of our acquaintances and try to recruit them directly into the league. I eliminated my waiter friends, all of whom were too old, and approached one of my former colleagues, a postal worker, who had been in our study circle and whom I considered a likely prospect. I remember that he sat very quietly while I delivered a long lecture on the league's program and activities and the need to get support among Black youth.

Finally interrupting me, he blurted out, "I'm sorry, Hall, but I find being Black trouble enough, but to be Black and red at the same time, well that's just double trouble, and when you mix in the whites, why that's triple trouble."

At first I was rather shocked by his offhand rebuff, considering it to be an expression of cynical opportunism. I felt that he had backslid, even from his position at the post office, but he continued in a more serious tone. Apparently he felt a deep distrust for whites and their motives. He regarded the YCL as just another organization of white "do-gooders," and saw me as their captive Negro. When I interrupted to say something about socialism, he cut me short. He said that he too was for socialism as a final solution, but that was a long way off and he would not put it beyond the whites in the United States to distort socialism in a manner in which they could remain top dogs. In any case, he believed

Blacks would have to be on guard. In the meantime, he believed Blacks should retain their own organizations under their own leadership. Alliances, yes—but we ourselves must decide the terms and conditions, he said.

Our exchange had gotten off on the wrong foot. I was deeply chagrined by his charge that I was a captive of the whites and that the league was a white organization. For me, that meant that he felt that I was a "white folks' nigger." As I recall, I retorted by calling him a Black racialist who saw everything in terms of Black and white.

"Why not?" he replied. "Being a Negro, how else should I see things?"

After this flare-up, our tempers cooled off and we continued our discussion in calmer tones. But I was definitely on the defensive, trying to explain why I was in the league and that it was not an organization of white do-gooders as he had charged. It was a revolutionary, interracial vanguard organization, I asserted. Sure, we only had a few Blacks now, but our numbers would grow, I argued.

He was still skeptical and repeated that he was for socialism, but a special road toward this goal he felt was necessary for Black Americans, under their own leadership and organization.

"Do you mean a Black party?" I queried.

"Why not?" he rejoined. "It might be necessary as a safeguard for our interests."

I had no answers to his position. There was a logic to it that I hadn't thought about.

We finally parted on friendly terms, promising to keep in touch. I left, realizing that I'd come out the worst in our exchange. I felt that I had failed in my first effort to recruit a good Black man to the league and that we still had some study to do with regards to Black nationalism.

My friend had been, as I recalled, a bitter critic of Garvey, and I therefore assumed that he was hostile to Black nationalism. But now it seemed that he expressed some of Garvey's racial separatism. Thinking the matter over, I finally came to the conclusion that the main reason for my inability to counter his arguments was that I sensed that they contained a good measure of truth. What was most disturbing was the sense that his position was less isolated from the masses of Blacks than was my own.

Up to that point, I had failed to understand the contradictory nature of Black nationalism. I had rejected it totally as a reactionary bourgeois philosophy that, in the conditions of the United States, had found its logical expression in Garvey's Back to Africa program. It was therefore a diversion from the struggle for economic, social, and political equality—the true goal of Blacks in the United

States. The fight for equality, I felt, was revolutionary in that it was unattainable within the framework of U.S. capitalist society. Nationalism, moreover, was divisive and played into the hands of the reactionary racists. This, of course, did not exclude the acceptance of some of its features, such as race pride and self-reliance, which were not inconsistent with, but an essential element in, the fight for equality.

While rejecting nationalism, I also rejected the bourgeois–assimilationist position of the NAACP and its associates and their blind acceptance of white middle-class values and culture. What confused me were attempts to amalgamate what I felt were two mutually contradictory elements—socialism and the class struggle on the one hand, and nationalism on the other. Or was the contradiction more apparent than real, I wondered. My friend's nationalism did not go to the point of advocacy of a separate Black nation. He demanded only autonomy in leadership and organization of the Black freedom movement. Was this inconsistent with the concept of equality and class unity? Had not Blacks the right to formulate their conditions for unity? For me, this was the first time I had encountered these questions.

I attempted to reflect on my short experience in the YCL. Was there not a basis for Black distrust of even white revolutionaries? The situation in the league was not as idyllic as I had first thought. There was a certain underestimation of the importance of the Black struggle against discrimination and for equal rights among both the youth and the adults of the Communist movement. Behind that, I sensed there was a feeling that the Black struggle was not itself really revolutionary, but was sort of a drag on the "pure" class struggle.

This was no doubt a legacy of the old Socialist Party. Even such a revolutionary as Debs had said, "We have nothing special to offer the Negro, and we cannot make separate appeals to all the races. The Socialist Party is the party of the working-class, regardless of color."[9] And regarding the Afro-American question: "Social equality, forsooth . . . is pure fraud and serves to mask the real issue, which is not *social equality, but economic freedom.*"[10] "The Socialist platform has not a word in reference to social equality."[11] Evidently, there were a number of theoretical matters still to be cleared up on the question of the struggle for Black equality and freedom.

I joined the party itself in the spring of 1925, recruited by Robert Minor, with the consent of the league. I had quit the Santa Fe the summer before, and, totally committed to the Communist cause, I then decided to devote more time to the work and to eventually becoming a professional revolutionary. I took extra jobs on weekends and worked banquets and an occasional extra trip on the road. I was living at home with my mother, father, and sister, who had an infant child, David. All were employed, with my mother accepting occasional catering jobs.

Minor, whom I had known for some time, was a reconstructed white southerner from Texas, a direct descendant of Sam Houston (first governor of the Lone Star State). He was a former anarchist and one of the great political cartoonists of his day. His powerful cartoons were carried in the *St. Louis Post-Dispatch* and later on in the old *Masses* (a cultural magazine of the Left) and in the *Daily Worker*. Among his many talents, he was a journalist of no small ability. Having traveled widely in Europe as a news correspondent during World War I, Minor had visited Russia during the revolutionary period and had met and spoken with Lenin.

With these impressive credentials, he was now a member of the party's Central Committee and responsible for its Negro work. This was understood as an interim assignment, eventually to be taken over by a Black comrade as soon as one could be developed to fill the position. The person then being groomed for the job was Lovett Fort-Whiteman, who was then in Russia taking a crash course in Communist leadership. He had been an associate of Briggs on the *Crusader* and had also worked with Randolph and Owen on the *Messenger*. Later, as I recall, his selection was the cause for some disgruntlement among the Black comrades.

Why was Fort-Whiteman chosen in preference to such well-known and capable Blacks as Richard B. Moore, Otto Huiswoud, or Cyril P. Briggs, all of whom had revolutionary records superior to Fort-Whiteman's? At that time, there were no Blacks on the Central Committee, and even when Fort-Whiteman returned from Russia in 1925 to take charge of Afro-American work, Minor remained responsible to the Central Committee. While not as flamboyant as Fort-Whiteman, these Black leaders had records comparable to, or better than, those of many whites on the Central Committee.

Be that as it may, of all the white comrades, Minor was best fitted for the assignment because of his wide knowledge of and close interest in the question. His intense hatred of his southern racist background came through in some of the most powerful cartoons of the day. He had a wide acquaintance among Black middle-class intellectuals. Bob and his wife Lydia had turned their Southside apartment into a virtual salon where Black and white friends would gather to discuss the issues of the day. There I met various Black notables, including Dean Pickens, national field secretary of the NAACP, and Abraham Harris, then secretary of the Minneapolis Urban League. Harris would later become chairman of the Economics Department of Howard University and then a full professor of the same subject at the University of Chicago.

In the meantime, Lovett Fort-Whiteman, our man in Moscow, returned to head up the Negro work and to prepare the launching of the American Negro Labor Congress (ANLC). H. V. Phillips, Edward Doty, and I were assigned to the organizing committee for the congress, drafting and circulating the call and approaching organizations for delegates. As I remember, most of the Blacks in the party were assigned to work on the congress. Otto was not involved in these activities, as immediately after the Fourth Party Convention, he had left for Moscow with the first batch of Black students.

Fort-Whiteman was truly a fantastic figure, a brown-skinned man of medium height whose high cheekbones gave him somewhat of an Oriental look. He had affected a Russian style of dress, sporting a *robochka* (a man's long belted shirt) that came almost to his knees, an ornamental belt, high boots, and a fur hat. Here was a veritable Black Cossack who could be seen sauntering along the streets of Southside Chicago. Fort-Whiteman was a graduate of Tuskegee and, as I understood, had had some training as an actor. He had been a drama critic for the *Messenger* and for the *Crusader*. There was no doubt that he was a showman; he always seemed to be acting out a part he had chosen for himself.

Upon his return from the Soviet Union, he held a number of press conferences in which he delineated plans for the American Negro Labor Congress, and as a Black Communist fresh from Russia, he made good news copy.

Fort-Whiteman had taken responsibility for lining up entertainment for the opening night of the congress. Characteristically, with his Russian affectations, he arranged for a program of Russian ballet and theater. The rest of us didn't question what he was doing, and the incongruity of the program didn't occur to us until the opening night.

The meeting took place in a hall on Indiana Avenue near Thirty-First Street, in the middle of the Black ghetto. When I arrived it was packed—perhaps five hundred people or so. Inside, I was suddenly attracted by a commotion at the door. As a member of the steering committee, I walked over to see what was the matter. Something was amiss with the "Russian ballet," which was about to enter the hall. A young blonde woman in the ballet had been shocked by the complexion of most of the audience, which she had apparently expected to be of another hue. Loudly, in a broad Texas accent, she exclaimed, "Ah'm not goin' ta dance for these niggahs!"

Somebody shouted, "Throw the cracker bitches out!" and the "Russian" dance group hurriedly left the hall.

The Russian actors remained to perform a one-act Pushkin play. They, at least, were genuine Russians from the Russian Federation. But alas, the play was in Russian. Of itself, it was undoubtedly interesting, but its relevance to a Black workers' congress was, to say the least, unclear. Although Pushkin was a Black man, he wrote as a Russian, and the characters portrayed were Russian. More significant, however, and perhaps an indication of our sectarian approach, was the fact that no Black artist appeared on the program.

Fort-Whiteman made the keynote speech outlining the purposes and tasks of the congress. He was a passable orator and received a good response. Otto Huiswoud, an associate of Briggs and one of the first Blacks to join the party, also spoke. Richard B. Moore brought the house down with an impassioned speech, which reached its peroration in Claude McKay's poem "If We Must Die." I was spellbound by Moore; I had never heard such oratory.

That night, Phillips and I left the hall in high spirits. In fact, I was literally walking on air. At last, I felt, we were about to get somewhere in our work among Blacks. Phillips, a bit more sober than I, remarked, "Let's wait and see the report of the credentials committee."

His caution was justified, for the big letdown came the following morning. The first working session of the congress convened with about forty Black and white delegates, mainly Communists and close sympathizers. The crowd of five hundred at the opening night rally had been mainly community people. I think it was Phillips who remarked that there was hardly a face in the working session that he didn't recognize; most participants, sadly, were from the Chicago area.

The organizing committee had prepared draft resolutions for the congress to consider. As we had anticipated a much larger turnout, we had made plans for a credentials committee, resolutions committee, and so on. But in light of the small attendance, these resolutions and preparations took on an Alice-in-Wonderland quality. For example, according to the constitution, the group's purpose was to "unify the efforts . . . of all organizations of Negro workers and farmers as well as organizations composed of both Negro and white workers and farmers."[12]

Despite our efforts and work, the ANLC never got off the ground. Few local units were formed; resolutions and plans were never carried into action. Only its official paper, the *Negro Champion*, subsidized by the party, continued for several years.

Among the postmortems undertaken on the organization was the one made by James Ford in his book *The Negro and the Democratic Front*. He commented that "for the period of its existence, it [the ANLC] was almost completely isolated from the basic masses of the Negro people."[13] Disappointment and disillusionment followed, and personal differences surfaced among our group. The fact was that the congress had failed, and with it, the first efforts to build a left-led united front among Blacks.

There was a natural tendency to find scapegoats for the failure. Moore and Huiswoud, the able delegates from New York, seemed to have come to Chicago with a chip on their shoulders. They made no attempt to hide their contempt for Fort-Whiteman, whom they had known in New York. They openly alluded to him as "Minor's man Friday." At the time, I was a bit shocked at what I felt was an attempt to malign these comrades. This was especially true of Bob Minor, whom I regarded with respect and affection. He was sort of a father figure to me.

Fort-Whiteman, on the other hand, was still an unknown quantity. My feelings about him were rather mixed. I was both repelled and fascinated by the excessive flamboyance of the man. But much later, I recalled overhearing a conversation between him and Minor during the preparations for the congress. Minor informed Fort-Whiteman that Ben Fletcher, the well-known Black IWW leader, had expressed a desire to participate in the congress. It was evident that Bob was pleased by the response of such an important Black labor leader. Fletcher, as an IWW organizer, had played a leading role in the successful organization of Philadelphia longshoremen. His attendance would undoubtedly have attracted other Blacks in the labor movement.

Fort-Whiteman, however, vehemently opposed the idea and exclaimed, "I don't want to work with him; I know him. He's the kind of fellow who'll try to take over the whole show." That ended the discussion; Fletcher was not invited.

I didn't know Fletcher at the time, but as I reflected back on the incident some time later, it was clear to me that had he been allowed to participate, Fort-Whiteman would have been overshadowed. I was too new to pass judgment on Fort-Whiteman's qualifications, but I did wonder why he was chosen over such stalwarts as Moore and Huiswoud. Huiswoud, as a delegate to the Fourth Congress of the Comintern in 1922, was the first Black American to attend a congress of that body. (Claude McKay was also a special fraternal delegate to that congress.) Together with other delegates, Huiswoud visited Lenin and became the first Black man to meet the great Bolshevik. He later became the first Black to serve as a candidate member of the Executive Committee of the Communist International.

On the whole, I was very optimistic during my early years in the party—confident we were building the kind of party that would eventually triumph over capitalism.

6

A STUDENT IN MOSCOW

Otto's delegation of Black students to the Soviet Union caused quite a stir in the States. The FBI kept an eye on their activities, and in the late summer of 1925, their departure was sensationalized in the *New York Times*.[1] The article attributed a statement to Lovett Fort-Whiteman to the effect that he had sent ten Blacks to the Soviet Union to study bolshevism and prepare for careers in the Communist "diplomatic service." The article concluded with a statement calling for action against such "subversive activity."

At the time, we all felt that any Black applying for a passport would be subjected to close scrutiny. Therefore, when I learned that I too would soon be studying in Moscow, I applied for one in the first names of my mother (Harriet) and father (Haywood). This name was to stick with me the rest of my life.

Several weeks after I received my passport, I heard that the FBI had been making inquiries about me. By that time, I had become known as one of the founders of the ANLC. Therefore, as the time for my departure drew near, I hid out at the home of comrades on Chicago's Westside until arrangements were made. I went to the national office of the Communist Party, then in Chicago, and was informed by Charles Ruthenberg or Jay Lovestone that I should get ready to leave. Political credentials, typed on silk, were sewn into the lining of my coat sleeve. In order to avoid going through the port of New York, I left by way of Canada.

In the manner of the old Underground Railroad, I was passed on from one set of comrades to the next: from Detroit, Rudy Baker, the district organizer, forwarded me on to the Canadian party headquarters in Toronto, where Jim MacDonald and Tim Buck were in charge. They sent me on to Montreal, where comrades housed me and booked passage for me to Hamburg, Germany. Boarding ship in Quebec in the late spring of 1926, I sailed on the Canadian Pacific liner, the old *Empress of Scotland*. From Hamburg, I took a train to Berlin, arriving on a Saturday afternoon.

I had the address of Hazel Harrison, the wife of a Chicago friend of mine who was a concert pianist studying in Berlin, where she had had her professional debut. (Years later, she was to head the Music Department at Howard University.) At that time, she was living at a boarding house near the Kurfürstendamm, and I stopped there for the remainder of the weekend.

This was the first time I had been in Berlin. Germany was then emerging from postwar crisis, during which currency inflation had reached astronomical heights, resulting in the virtual expropriation of a large section of the middle class. It was common to see shabbily dressed men still trying to keep up appearances by wearing starched white collars under their patched clothing.

The owners of the boardinghouse, two middle-aged widows who were friends of Hazel's, showed me a trunk filled with paper notes—old German marks that were now worthless. This had probably represented a life's savings.

Hazel and her two friends took me out to the Tiergarten—the famous Berlin Zoo. I was attracted by the sight of three lion cubs that had been mothered by a German police dog. The cubs were getting big, and it was clear that the "mother" was no longer able to control them. We watched for some time, fascinated. I turned around and realized that there was a crowd around us. At first I thought they were looking at the cubs, but then it became clear that Hazel and I were the center of attention. Blacks were rare in Berlin in those days—there were only half a dozen or so, mostly from the former German colonies of the Cameroons.

Monday morning I took a cab to the headquarters of the German party, at Karl Marx House on Rosenthallerstrasse. It was a dour, fortress-like structure, with high walls surrounding the main building, which was set in the middle. I entered into the anteroom just inside the walls, in which there were a number of sturdy-looking young men lounging around. When I came in, they jumped up and stood eyeing me suspiciously.

They were unarmed, but I knew their weapons were within arms' reach. This was a symbol of the times, for it was not long after the Beer Hall Putsch of Hitler's brownshirts in Munich, and the battle for the streets of Berlin had already begun. I presented my credentials to a man named Walters, who was undoubtedly the head of security.

It was on this occasion that I first met Ernst Thälmann, a former Hamburg longshoreman and then leader of the German Communist Party. He was passing through the gate and Walters stopped him and introduced us. Thälmann spoke fairly good English (probably acquired in his work as a seaman) and we chatted a while. He asked after Foster, Ruthenberg, and others. Wishing me good luck, he passed on his way.

Walters gave me some spending money and arranged for me to stay with some German comrades, a young couple who had an elaborate apartment. The husband ran a haberdashery store on Friedrichstrasse and was a commander in the Rote Front (the Red Front)—the paramilitary organization that the Communists had organized for defense of workers against the fascists.

One day while walking down the Kurfürstendamm, I saw a cabaret billboard advertising the Black jazz band of Leland and Drayton and their Charleston dancers. It was a well-known band back in the States. I had little money, but I couldn't resist the temptation to stop in and hear them. I sat down at a table and ordered a beer. To my dismay, the waiter said they didn't sell beer, just wine. So I took the wine card and chose the cheapest bottle I could find.

A number of band members and dancers came over to my table and asked where I was going. When I told them I was a student going to Moscow, they said they had just returned from a six-month tour in Russia. They were the first Black jazz group to have gone to the Soviet Union. I asked if they had met Otto and the other Black students there. Yes, they had met them all, and they had had good times together. So we all sat down to exchange news.

As we talked, I began to worry about the bill, and said I was low on money. "Oh, don't worry about that," someone said and ordered more wine. But when it came time to pay for the drinks, I got stuck with the whole tab and had to walk several miles across town to get home.

After a month in Berlin, my visa came through. I was on my way to Stettin, a city on the Baltic Sea, which bordered Poland and where I boarded a small Soviet ship. After three days of some of the roughest seas I have ever experienced, we landed in Leningrad. It was April 1926, and we were already in the season of the "white nights," when daylight lasted until late into the evening.

As we entered the Gulf of Finland the following morning, we passed the naval fortress of Kronstadt, about twenty miles out from Leningrad (the site of the anti-Soviet mutiny of 1920). The ship finally docked in Leningrad. Upon landing, I presented my visa and passport to the authorities. Addressing me in English, a man in civilian dress said, "Oh, you're going to the Comintern school in Moscow?"

"Yes," I replied.

He immediately took me in charge and got my baggage through customs. I assumed he was a member of the security police. We left the customs building and got into an old beat-up Packard. As we drove away from the docks, he informed me that the Moscow train would not leave until eight that evening. He put me up at a hotel where I could rest and go out to see the city.

Leningrad (old St. Petersburg) was built by Czar Peter the Great in the sixteenth century and was now renamed for the architect of the new socialist society. As I walked down the now famous Nevsky Prospekt, I thought of John Reed's *Ten Days That Shook the World*, trying to recapture some of the dramatic scenes in that classic.[2] I passed the Peter and Paul Fortress and then the Winter

Palace—once the home of the czars and now a museum of the people. The storming of the Winter Palace in 1917 had been the crucial event in the taking of St. Petersburg by the Bolsheviks.

The people I saw passing me on the street were plainly dressed. Many of the men wore the traditional *robochka* and high boots; others were in European dress. Most people were dressed neatly, though shabbily, and all appeared to be well fed. They were bright and cheerful. It seemed they went about with a purpose—a sharp contrast to the atmosphere of hopelessness that had pervaded Berlin. People in Leningrad looked at me—and I looked at them. By this time, I had become used to being stared at and took it as friendly curiosity. After all, a Black man was seldom seen in those parts.

After several hours, I returned to my hotel. My friend from the security police showed up promptly at seven with my train ticket and took me to the station to put me on the train to Moscow. Filled with excitement and anticipation, I got little sleep on the train and awoke early to see the Russian landscape flowing by my window—pine forests, groves of birch trees, and swamps. I was in the midst of the great Russian steppes.

When we arrived in Moscow at Yaroslavsky Station, some of my traveling companions hailed a *droshky* and told the driver to take me to the Comintern.

Moscow at last! We drove from the station into the vast sprawling city—once the capital of old Russia and now of the new. It was a bright, sunny morning, and the sun glistened off the golden church domes in the "city of a thousand churches." It seemed a maze of narrow cobblestone streets, intersected by broad boulevards. While Leningrad had been a distinctly European city, Moscow seemed a mixture of the Asiatic and the European—a bizarre and strange combination to me, but a cheerful one. Moscow was more Russian than the cosmopolitan Leningrad. Crowds swarmed in the streets in many different styles of dress.

We arrived at the Comintern, which was housed in an old eighteenth-century structure on Ulitsa Komintern near the Kremlin, across the square from Staraya Konyushnya (the old stables of the czar). I paid the driver and entered the building. The guard at the door checked my credentials and directed me upstairs to a small office on the third floor. After producing my bona fides, I was told to take a seat to wait for my comrades, who would soon be coming for me.

About half an hour later, Otto and another Black man entered the room. I was overjoyed at the sight of him and his friend, who turned out to be a fellow student, Harold Williams. We embraced Russian style, and I began to feel more at home in this strange land.

Otto asked about the family. An expression of sadness crossed his face, however, when I asked him about the rest of the Black students. He then informed me of Jane Golden's serious illness. She was at that moment in a uremic coma from a kidney ailment and was not expected to live. Her husband was at her side at the hospital. (Though both were from Chicago, I had not met them before.)

The situation had saddened the whole Black student body, and for that matter, the whole school. In the course of her brief sojourn, Jane had become very popular. Otto described her in glowing terms—a real morale booster, whose spirit had helped all of them through the period of initial adjustment.

I was impressed. Here was a Black woman, not a member of the Communist Party, who had so easily become accustomed to the new Soviet socialist society. It seemed to me that there must be thousands of Black women like her in the United States.

After we had greeted each other, we caught a *droshky* over to the school so that I might register officially. In the course of the ride, the driver lashed his horse and cursed at him. I asked Otto what he was saying, and he gave a running translation: "Get up there, you son of a bitch. I feed you oats while I myself eat black bread! Your sire was no good, you bastard, your momma was no good too!" This verbal and physical abuse, Otto told me, was typical of most Russian *droshky* drivers.

We finally arrived at the school administration, which was housed in another old seventeenth-century structure, built before the revolution. It had been a finishing school for daughters of the aristocracy. Before that, it had been a boys' school where, rumor has it, the great Pushkin had studied.

Otto introduced me to the university rector with what sounded to my untrained ear like fluent Russian. We then went to the office of the chancellor, where I was duly registered. I was now a student at the Universitet Trydyashchiysya Vostoka Imeni Stalina (the University of the Toilers of the East Named for Stalin; Russian acronym KUTVA). Otto and I then walked to the dormitory a few blocks away, where I met the other two Black students, Bankole and Farmer.

We all immediately took a streetcar to the hospital, which was located on the other side of the Moscow River. There we were met by Golden and some other students who informed us that Jane Golden had just passed away that morning. Golden seemed to be in a state of shock, and the doctors had given him some sedatives. We went into the hospital morgue to view her body. Bankole broke down in uncontrollable tears. I learned afterward that Jane had been a close friend—a kind of mother to him during the period of his adjustment to this new land.

We took Golden home to the dormitory. The school collective and its leaders immediately took over the funeral arrangements. The body lay in state in the school auditorium for twenty-four hours, during which time the students thronged past.

The funeral was held the following day, and the whole school turned out. The cortege seemed a mile long as it flowed past Tverskaya toward the cemetery. The students would not allow the casket to be placed upon the cart but, organizing themselves in relays every fifty yards, insisted on carrying it the distance of several miles on their shoulders.

A good portion of the American colony in Moscow was assembled at the cemetery. The chairman of the school collective, a young Georgian, delivered a stirring eulogy at the graveside. One of the students who was standing next to me made a running translation sotto voce which went something like this:

> The first among her race to come to the land of socialism . . . in search of freedom for her oppressed peoples, former slaves . . . to find out how the Soviets had done it. We were happy to receive her and her comrades . . . condolences to her bereaved husband, our Comrade Golden, and to the rest of the Negro students. . . . The whole university has suffered a great loss. Rest in peace, Jane Golden. You were with us only a short time, but all of us have benefited from your presence and comradeship.

Turning to Golden, he said:

> We Soviet people and comrades of oppressed colonial and dependent countries must carry on. We pledge our undying support to the cause of your people's freedom. Long live the freedom fight of our Negro brothers in America! Long live the Soviet Union and its Communist Party, beacon light of the struggle for freedom of all oppressed peoples.

Golden had borne himself well at the graveside, but we didn't want him to return to his room in the students' dormitory, which would only remind him of his grievous loss. So we went to the apartment of MacCloud, an old Wobbly friend of ours from Philadelphia, who had attended the funeral and who lived in the Zarechnaya District, across the river. He was a close friend of Big Bill Haywood and had followed the great working-class leader to the Soviet Union.

There we tried to drown our sorrows in good old Russian vodka, which was in plentiful supply.

Jane Golden's funeral and the school collective's response to her death made a profound impression on me. Through these events, crammed into the first three days of my stay in the Soviet Union, I came to know something about my fellow students and the new socialist society into which I had entered.

The Bolsheviks Fight for Equality of Nations

KUTVA was a unique university. At the time I entered, its student body represented more than seventy nationalities and ethnic groups. It was founded by the Bolsheviks for the special purpose of training cadres from the many national and ethnic groups within the Soviet Union—the former colonial dependencies of the czarist empire—and also to train cadres from colonies and subject nations outside the Soviet Union.

The school was divided into two sections—inner and outer. At the inner section there were Turkmenians, Uzbeks, Tajiks, Bashkirs, Yakuts, Chuvashes, Kazakhs, Kalmucks, Buryat-Mongols, and Inner and Outer Mongolians from Soviet Asia. From the Caucasus there were Azerbaijanis, Armenians, Georgians, Abkhazians, and many others from national and ethnic groups I had never heard of before. There were Tatars from the Crimea and the Volga region.

The national and ethnic diversity found within the Soviet Union is hard to imagine. The revolution had opened up many areas—for example, through the Trans-Caucasus Road—and as late as 1928 the existence of new groups was still being "discovered." These nationalities were all former colonial dependencies of the czars and were referred to as the "Soviet East," "peoples of the East," and "borderland countries." The inner section comprised the main and largest part of the student body in the university.

Otto told me of the discovery he had made on one of his trips to the southern region of the Caucasus. He had originally gone there on the invitation of one of our fellow students, a young woman from the Abkhazian Republic. After meeting some of us, she commented that they too had some Black folk down near her area in a village not very far from Sukhumi, the capital of the republic on the Black Sea.

She invited Otto down to visit the region over his summer vacation, and there he met the people. He described them as being of definite black ancestry—notwithstanding a history of intermarriage with the local people. But the *starsata* (old man) of the tribe was Black beyond a doubt. His story went some generations back, when he and the others joined the Turkish army as Numidian mercenaries from the Sudan. After several forays into this region, they deserted the army and settled there. The *starsata* himself had been in the Czar's cavalry with the Dikhi (that is, "wild") Division of the Caucasus Cossacks.

The people in the village wanted to know what was happening to "our brothers over the mountains." Otto related to them the troubles we had gone through, described the travels "over the mountains and across the big sea." As the evening wore on and the local brandy was consumed, toast after toast was drunk to "our little brother from over the hills." Otto described to them the conditions of Blacks in the United States—the lynchings, racism, and brutality. Incensed, a few jumped up and pulled out their daggers. "You should make a revolution."

"Why don't you revolt?"

"Why do you put up with it?"

We were not the only ones surprised to learn about this group; it was news to the Russians in Moscow too! Several of these tribesmen later visited Moscow as a result of Otto's visit.

We Blacks were of course part of the outer section at the school. It included Indians, Indonesians, Koreans, Filipinos, Persians, Egyptians, Arabs and Palestinian Jews from the Middle East, Arabs from North Africa, Algerians, Moroccans, Chinese, and several Japanese (hardly a colonial people, but as revolutionaries, identified with the East).

The Chinese, several hundred strong, comprised the largest group of the outer section. This was obviously because China, bordering on the USSR, was in the first stage of its own anti-imperialist revolution, a revolution receiving direct material and political support from the Soviet Union. While KUTVA trained the Communist cadres from China, there was also the Sun Yat-sen University, just outside of Moscow, which trained cadres for the Kuomintang.

Among its students was the daughter of the famous Christian general Chang Tso-lin. Several Chinese, including Chiang Kai-shek's son, studied in Soviet military schools during this period. A number of the Chinese students from KUTVA were massacred by Chiang's troops at the Manchurian border when they returned to China shortly after Chiang's bloody betrayal of the revolution in 1927. Otto told me that a former girlfriend of his was among this group.

As I remember, there were no Latin Americans at KUTVA during the time I was there, and the sole Black African was Bankole. The student body was continually expanding, however, and later included many students from these and other areas.

We students studied the classic works of Marx, Engels, Lenin, and Stalin. But unlike schooling we had known in the past, this whole body of theory was related to practice. Theory was regarded not as dogma but as a guide to action.

In May 1925, Stalin had delivered a historic speech at the school outlining KUTVA's purpose and its main task. His lecture was the subject of continuous discussion and study.[3] It was our introduction to the Marxist theory on the national question and its development by Lenin and Stalin.

How did the Bolsheviks transform a territory embracing one-sixth of the earth's surface—known as the "prison-house of nations" under the czar—into a family of nations, a free union of peoples? What was the policy pursued by the Soviets that enabled them to forge together more than a hundred different stages of social development into such extraordinary unity of effort for the building of a multinational socialist state—the kind of unity that enabled them to win the civil war within and to defeat the intervention of seventeen nations, including the United States, from without?

The starting point for us was to understand that the formation of peoples into nations is an objective law of social development around which the Bolsheviks, particularly Lenin and Stalin, had developed a whole body of theory. According to this theory, a nation is a historically constituted stable community of people, based on four main characteristics: a common territory, a common economic life, a common language, and a common psychological makeup (national character) manifested in common features in a national culture. Since the development of imperialism, the liberation of the oppressed nations had become a question whose final resolution would only come through proletarian revolution.[4]

The guiding principle of the Communist Party of the Soviet Union on the national question was to bring about the unity of the laboring masses of the various nationalities for the purpose of waging a joint struggle—first to overthrow czarism and imperialism, and then to build the new society under a working-class dictatorship. The accomplishment of the latter required the establishment of equality before the law for all nationalities—with no special privileges for any one people—and the right of the colonies and subject nations to separate.

This principle was incorporated into the law of the land in the Declaration of Rights of the People of Russia, passed a few days after the seizure of power by the Bolsheviks. Of course, the declaration of itself did not eliminate national inequality, which, as Stalin had observed, "rested on economic inequality, historically formed." To eliminate this historically based economic and cultural inequality imposed by the czarist regimes upon the former oppressed nations, it was required that the more developed nations assist these formerly oppressed nations and peoples to catch up with the Great Russians in economic and cultural development.

In pursuance of this aim, the new government was organized on a bicameral basis. One body was chosen on the basis of population alone; the other, the Council of Nationalities, consisted of representatives from each of the national territorial units—the autonomous Soviet republics, autonomous regions, and national areas. Any policy in regard to the affairs of these formerly oppressed nations could be carried through only with the approval of the Council of Nationalities. The Communist Party, through its members, was involved in both bodies and worked to see that its policy of full equality and the right of self-determination was implemented.

As this theory was put into practice, we learned that national cultures could be expressed with a proletarian (socialist) content and that there was no antagonistic contradiction, under socialism, between national cultures and proletarian internationalism. Under the Soviets, the languages and other national characteristics of the many nationalities were developed and strengthened with the aim of drawing the formerly oppressed nationalities into full participation in the new society. Thus, the Bolsheviks upheld the principle of "proletarian in content, national in form." Through this policy, they hoped to draw all nationalities together, acquainting each with the achievements of the others, leading to a truly universal culture, a joint product of all humanity.

This is in sharp contrast to imperialism's policy of forcibly arresting and distorting the free development of nations in order to maintain their economic and cultural backwardness as an essential condition for the extraction of superprofits. Thus, the oppressed nations can achieve liberation only through the path of revolutionary struggle to overthrow imperialism and in alliance with the working class of the oppressor nations. Stalin, proceeding from the experience and practice of the Soviet Union, emphasized the need for the formation and consolidation of a united revolutionary front between the working class of the West and the rising revolutionary movements of the colonies—a united front based on a struggle against a common enemy. The precondition for forming such unity is that the proletariat of the oppressor nations gives

> direct and determined support to the liberation movement of the oppressed peoples against the imperialism of its "own country," for "no nation can be free if it oppresses other nations." (Engels) . . . This support

implies the advocacy, defense and implementation of the slogan of the right of nations to secession, to independent existence as states.[5]

Without this cooperation of peoples based on mutual confidence and fraternal interrelations, it will be impossible to establish the material basis for the victory of socialism.

All this theory was being proven in practice in the Soviet Union. The experience of the Bolsheviks demonstrably proved to us that socialism offered the most favorable conditions for the full development of oppressed nations and peoples.

At the time of the revolution, there were many nationalities within the borders of the Soviet Union in which the characteristics of nationhood had not yet fully matured, and in fact had been suppressed by the czars. It was the Soviet system itself that became a powerful factor in the consolidation of these nationalities into nations, as socialist industry and collective farming created the economic basis for this consolidation.

I observed this firsthand in the Crimea and the Caucasus during my visits there in the summers of 1927 and 1928. The languages and cultures that had been stifled under the czarist regime were now being developed. The language of the Crimean people was a Turko-Tartar language, but before the revolution, almost all education, such as there was, was in the Russian language. Now there were schools established that used the native language. Otto and other students made similar observations when they traveled to different areas of the Soviet Union.

In the meantime, I was having my own problems with the Russian language. On first hearing it, the language had sounded most strange to me. I could hardly understand a word and wondered if I would ever be able to master it. As the youngest Black American, I applied myself seriously to its study. The first hurdle was the Cyrillic alphabet—its uniquely different characters intimidated me. But the crash course at KUTVA, lasting about an hour and a half per day, soon broke down this initial barrier. In addition, I studied on my own for a couple of hours each day. I would set out to memorize twenty new words a day. Then at night, I would write them out on a sheet of paper and pin them above the mirror in my room. I would then go over them again in the morning while shaving, and during the day I would make sure to use them in conversation with the Russians.

English grammar had always seemed irrelevant to me, but I soon came to appreciate the logic of Russian grammar. In fact, I learned most of my English grammar through the study of Russian. Its rules were consistent and understandable. The language soon ceased to be mysterious and revealed itself as being beautifully and simply constructed. In six months I was able to read *Pravda* with the help of a dictionary.

Blacks in Moscow

We students were a fairly congenial lot, and in particular I got to know the other Black students quite well. Golden was a handsome, jet-black man, a former Tuskegee student and dining-car waiter. He was not a member of the Communist Party, but he was a good friend of Lovett Fort-Whiteman, head of the party's Afro-American work.

Golden told me that his coming to the Soviet Union had been accidental. He had run into Fort-Whiteman, a fellow student at Tuskegee, on the streets of Chicago. Fort-Whiteman had just returned from Russia and was dressed in a Russian blouse and boots.

As Golden related it: "I asked Fort-Whiteman what the hell he was wearing. Had he come off the stage and forgotten to change clothes? He informed me that these were Russian clothes and that he had just returned from that country."

Golden at first thought it was a put-on, but he became interested as Fort-Whiteman talked about his experiences.

> Then out of the blue, he asks me if I want to go to Russia as a student. At first, I thought he was kidding, but man, I would have done anything to get off those dining cars! I was finally convinced that he was serious. "But I'm married," I told him. "What about my wife?" "Why, bring her along too!" he replied. He took me to his office at the American Negro Labor Congress, an impressive setup with a secretary, and I was convinced. Fort-Whiteman gave me money to get passports, and the next thing I knew, a couple of weeks later we were on the boat with Otto and the others on the way to Russia. And here I am now."

He had a keen sense of humor and kidded the rest of us a lot, particularly Otto. His southern accent carried over into Russian, and we teased him about being the only person who spoke Russian with a Mississippi accent.

Then there was Bankole, an African who spent most of his time with the Black Americans. He was an Ashanti, from the Gold Coast (now Ghana), and his family was part of the African elite. The son of a wealthy barrister, his family had sent him to London University to study journalism. From there, he had gone to Carnegie Tech in Pittsburgh.

He had been on the road to becoming a perennial student and had planned to continue at McGill University in Montreal, but he was recruited to the Young Communist League in Pittsburgh. In the States, he was confronted with a racism more blatant than any he had met before. I gathered that this had struck him sharply and had been largely responsible for his move to the left.

My brother Otto had become sort of a character in the school. He was popular among the students, who immediately translated his pseudonym "John Jones" into the Russian "Ivan Ivanovich." Otto had absolutely no tolerance for red tape, and he had become a mortal enemy of the *apparatchiki* (petty bureaucrats) in the school. He had built a reputation for making their lives miserable, and when they saw him coming, they would huddle in a corner: "Here comes Ivan Ivanovich. *Ostorozhno* [Watch out]! *Bolshoi skandal budyet* [This guy will make a big scandal]!"

Harold Williams of Chicago was a West Indian and former seaman in the British merchant marine. He had adopted the name of Dessalines, one of the three leaders of the Haitian revolution of the 1790s. Williams had little formal education and had some difficulty in grasping theory, but he was instinctively a class-conscious guy.

Finally, there was Mahoney, whose name in the USSR was Jim Farmer. Farmer was a steelworker from East Liverpool, Ohio, and a Communist Party member, and he had played a leading role in local struggles in the steel mills.

There were only eight of us Blacks in a city of 4,500,000 people. In addition to the six students, there were also two Black American women who had long residence (since before the revolution) in Moscow.

I only knew one of the women, Emma Harris. We first met on the occasion of the death of Jane Golden. Emma was a warm, outgoing, and earthy middle-aged woman, originally from Georgia. It was evident that she had once been quite handsome, of the type that in the old days we called a "teasin' brown." Emma had first come to Moscow as a member of a Black song-and-dance group, a lowly hoofer in the world of cheap vaudeville. Having been deserted by its manager, the group was left stranded in Moscow.

While the others had evidently made their way back to the States, Emma had decided to stay. She had liked the country. Here, being Black wasn't a liability but, on the contrary, a definite asset. With her drive and ambition to be "somebody," Emma parlayed this asset into a profitable position. She married a Russian who installed her, it seems, as the madam of a house of prostitution. It was no ordinary house, she once explained to me. "Our clients were the wealthy and nobility." To the former hoofer, this was status.

Such was Emma's situation in November 1917, when the Russian Bolsheviks and Red Guards moved in from the proletarian suburbs of Moscow to capture the bourgeois inner city and the Kremlin. During some mopping-up operations, Emma's house was raided by the Cheka (the security police). A bunch of White Guardists had holed up there, and the whole group was arrested, including Emma. They were taken to the Lubyanka Prison, and some of the more notorious White Guardists were summarily executed.

Emma remained in a cell for a few days. Finally she was called up before a Cheka official. He told her that they were looking into her case. Many of the people who had been arrested at her place were counterrevolutionaries and conspirators against the new Soviet state, and some had been shot. Emma disclaimed knowledge of any conspiracy and stated that she was engaged in "legitimate" business and had nothing to do with the politics of her clients.

"You know the only reason we didn't shoot you was because you are a Negro woman," the official said. To her surprise, he added, "You are free to go now. I advise you to try to find some useful work. Keep out of trouble."

When we met Emma, she had become a textile worker. She lived with a young Russian woman—also a textile worker, whom I suspected was a reformed prostitute—in a two-room apartment in an old working-class district near Krasnaya Vorota (Red Gate). Soon after the first Black students arrived, she sought them out and greeted them like long-lost kinfolk.

At least once a month, we students would pool part of the small stipends we received and give Emma money to shop for and prepare some old home cooking for us. On these occasions, she would regale us with stories from her past life. At times one could detect a fleeting expression of sadness, of nostalgia, for her old days of affluence. One could see that she had never become fully adjusted to the new life under the Soviets. While not openly hostile, she was clearly not an ardent partisan of the new regime. Knowing our sentiments, she avoided political discussion and kept her views to herself. Our feelings toward her were warmest when we first arrived, but as we developed more ties with the Russians, we went by to see her less often. But we did continue to visit her periodically; she was a sort of mother figure for us, and we all felt sorry for her. She was getting old and often expressed a desire to return to the States. She was finally able to return home after World War II.

Needless to say, Blacks attracted the curiosity of the Muscovites. Children followed us in the streets. If we paused to greet a friend, we found ourselves instantly surrounded by curious crowds—unabashedly staring at us. Once, while strolling down Tverskaya, Otto and I stopped to greet a white American friend and immediately found ourselves surrounded by curious Russians. It was a friendly curiosity that we took in stride. A young Russian woman stepped forward and began to upbraid and lecture the crowd: "Why are you staring at these people? They're human beings the same as us. Do you want them to think that we're savages? *Eta ne kulturnya!* [That is uncultured!]" The last was an epithet and in those days a high insult. "*Eta ne po-Sovietski!* [It's not the Soviet way!]" she scolded them.

At that point, someone in the crowd calmly responded, "Well, citizeness, it's a free country, isn't it?"

We were not offended, but amused. We understood all this for what it was.

There was one occasion when Otto, Farmer, Bankole, and I were walking down Tverskaya. Bankole, of course, stood out—attracting more attention than the rest of us with his English-cut Savile Row suit, monocle, and cane: a black edition of a British aristocrat. We found ourselves being followed by a group of Russian children, who shouted, "*Jass Band . . . Jass Band!*"

Otto, Farmer, and I were amused at the incident and took it in stride. Bankole, however, shaking with rage at the implication, jerked around to confront them. His monocle fell off as he shouted, "*Net Jass Band! Net Jass Band!*" As he spoke, he hit his cane on the ground for emphasis.

Evidently, to these kids, a jazz band was not just a group of musicians but a race or tribe of people to which we must belong. They obviously thought we were with Leland and Drayton, the musicians I had met in Berlin. They had been a big hit with the Muscovites. We pulled Bankole away, "C'mon man, cut it out. They don't mean anything."

In the Soviet Union, remnants of national and racial prejudices from the old society were attacked by education and law. It was a crime to give or receive direct or indirect privileges, or to exercise discrimination because of race or nationality. Any manifestation of racial or national superiority was punishable by law and was regarded as a serious political offense, a social crime.

During my entire stay in the Soviet Union, I encountered only one incident of racial hostility. It was on a Moscow streetcar. Several of us Black students had boarded the car on our way to spend an evening with our friend MacCloud. It was after rush hour, and the car was only about half filled with Russian passengers. As usual, we were the objects of friendly curiosity. At one stop, a drunken Russian staggered aboard. Seeing us, he muttered (but loud enough for the whole car to hear) something about "Black devils in our country."

A group of outraged Russian passengers thereupon seized him and ordered the motorman to stop the car. It was a citizen's arrest, the first I had ever witnessed. "How dare you, you scum, insult people who are the guests of our country!"

What then occurred was an impromptu, on-the-spot meeting, where they debated what to do with the man. I was to see many of this kind of "meeting" during my stay in Russia.

It was decided to take the culprit to the police station, which, the conductor informed them, was a few blocks ahead. Upon arrival there, they hustled the drunk out of the car and insisted that we Blacks, as the injured parties, come along to make the charges.

At first we demurred, saying that the man was obviously drunk and not responsible for his remarks. "No, citizens," said a young man (who had done most of the talking), "drunk or not, we don't allow this sort of thing in our country. You must come with us to the militia (police) station and prefer charges against this man."

The car stopped in front of the station. The poor drunk was hustled off and all the passengers came along. The defendant had sobered up somewhat by this time and began apologizing before we had even entered the building. We got to the commandant of the station.

The drunk swore that he didn't mean what he'd said. "I was drunk and angry about something else. I swear to you citizens that I have no race prejudice against those Black *gospoda* [gentlemen]."

We actually felt sorry for the poor fellow, and we accepted his apology. We didn't want to press the matter.

"No," said the commandant, "we'll keep him overnight. Perhaps this will be a lesson to him."

Ina

I first met my second wife, Ekaterina—Ina—in December 1926. We were both at a party at the home of Rose Bennett, a British woman who had married M. Petrovsky (Bennett), the chairman of the Anglo-American Commission of the Comintern and formerly Communist International (CI) representative to Great Britain.

Ina was one of a group of ballet students whom Rose had invited to meet some of us KUTVA students. She was a small young woman of nineteen or twenty, shy and retiring, and she sat off removed from the party. After that party, we met several times, and she told me about herself.

She was born in Vladikavkaz (in Northern Caucasus), the daughter of the mayor of the town. It was one of those towns that was taken and retaken during the Civil War, one time by the Whites, then by the Reds. On one occasion when the town fell to the Reds, her father was accused of collaborating with the Whites. The Reds came and arrested him, and she never saw him again. Ina was about eleven at the time; she later learned that her father had been executed.

Her uncle was a famous artist in Moscow, and after her father's execution they went there to live. Ina told me of her trip to Moscow at the height of famine and a typhus epidemic; they rode in freight cars several days through the Ukraine and saw people dying along the road. Her uncle took charge of them and got them an apartment on Malaya Bronnaya. He investigated the case of her father and discovered that a mistake had been made, and her father was posthumously exonerated. As a sort of compensation, she and her mother were regarded as "social activists," and Ina entered school to study ballet. She later transferred from the ballet school to study English in preparation for work as a translator. We lived together in the spring of 1927 and got married the following fall, after my return from the Crimea.

In January 1927, I was stunned by the news of the death of my mother. One morning, when I was at Ina's house, Otto burst in. Overcome by emotion, he could hardly talk, but managed to blurt out, "Mom's dead!" He had a letter from our sister Eppa, with a clipping of Mother's obituary from the *Chicago Defender.*

Under the headline "Funeral of Mrs. Harriet Hall" was her picture and an article that described her, a domestic worker, as a "noted club woman." She had been a member of the Black Eastern Star and several other lodges and burial societies. The article mentioned that she was survived by her husband, daughter, and two sons, the latter in Moscow.

I was overcome with grief and guilt at not being home. I was deeply shocked; I had always assumed that I would return to see mother again. Born a slave, her world had been confined to the Midwest and the upper South. She had once told me, "Son, I sure would like to see the ocean," and I had glibly promised, "Oh, I'll take you there someday, Momma." I felt that I had been her favorite; I was the responsible one, and yet I hadn't been able to do what I had promised. Worse yet, I wasn't even there when she died. It took me some time to get over the shock.

7

SELF-DETERMINATION: THE FIGHT FOR A CORRECT LINE

Toward the end of 1927, N. Nasanov returned to the Soviet Union after a so-journ in the United States as the representative of the Young Communist International. I had known him briefly in the States before my departure for Russia. Nasanov was one of a group of YCI workers who had been sent on missions to several countries. He had considerable experience with respect to the national and colonial question and was considered an expert on these matters.

Nasanov's observations had convinced him that U.S. Blacks were essentially an oppressed nation whose struggle for equality would ultimately take an autonomous direction and that the content of the Black liberation movement was the completion of the agrarian and democratic revolution in the South—a struggle that had been left unresolved by the Civil War and the betrayal of Reconstruction. Therefore, it was the duty of the party to channel the movement in a revolutionary direction by raising and supporting the slogan of the right of self-determination for Afro-Americans in the Black Belt, the area of their greatest concentration.

Upon his return, Nasanov sought me out and it was he, I believe, who first informed me that I had been elected to the National Committee of the YCL back in the States. In the months ahead, we were to become close friends. Through him, I met a number of YCI people, mostly Soviet comrades who held the same position as Nasanov did on the national question. They seemed to be pushing to have the matter reviewed at the forthcoming Sixth Congress of the Comintern. And as it later became clear to me, they were anxious to recruit at least one Black to support their position.

As I have indicated before, the position was not entirely new to me. I was present at the meeting of the YCL District Committee in Chicago in 1924 when Bob Mazut (then YCI rep to the United States), at the behest of Zinoviev, had raised the question of self-determination. At that time, he had been shouted down by the white comrades.

Sen Katayama had told us Black KUTVA students that Lenin had regarded U.S. Blacks as an oppressed nation and referred us to his draft resolution on the national and colonial question that was adopted by the Second Congress of the

Comintern in 1920.[1] Otto and other Black students had also told me that they got a similar impression from their meeting with Stalin at the Kremlin shortly after their arrival in the Soviet Union.

All of this seemed tentative to me. No one had elaborated the position fully, and Nasanov was the first person I met who attempted to argue it definitively. But all of these arguments, and especially Nasanov's prodding, set me to thinking and confronted me with the need to apply concretely my newly acquired Marxist–Leninist knowledge on the national–colonial question to the condition of Blacks in the United States.

To me, the idea of a Black nation within U.S. boundaries seemed far-fetched and not consonant with American reality. I saw the solution through the incorporation of Blacks into U.S. society on the basis of complete equality, and only socialism could bring this to pass. There was no doubt in my mind that the path to freedom for us Blacks led directly to socialism, uncluttered by any interim stage of self-determination or Black political power. The unity of Black and white workers against the common enemy, U.S. capitalism, was the motor leading toward the dual goal of Black freedom and socialism.

I felt that it was difficult enough to build this unity, without adding to it the gratuitous assumption of a nonexistent Black nation, with its implication of a separate state on U.S. soil. To do so, I felt, was to create new and unnecessary roadblocks to the already difficult path to Black and white unity.

Socialism, I reasoned, was not in contradiction to the movement for Black cultural identity, expressed in the cultural renaissance of the twenties and in Garvey's emphasis on race pride and history (which I regarded as one of the positive aspects of that movement). Socialism for U.S. Blacks did not imply loss of cultural identity any more than it did for the Jews of the Soviet Union, among whom I had witnessed the proliferation of the positive features of Jewish culture—theater, literature, and language.

The Jews were not considered a nation because they were not concentrated in any definite territory; they were regarded as a national minority, and Birobidzhan was set aside as a Jewish autonomous province. Such a bolstering of self-respect, dignity, and self-assertion on the part of a formerly oppressed minority people was a necessary stage in the development of a universal culture that would amalgamate the best features of all national groups. This was definitely the policy of the Soviet Union with regard to formerly oppressed nationalities and ethnic groups.

Like the Jews, I reasoned, Blacks were in the position of an oppressed race, though at the time I am sure I would have been hard-pressed to define precisely what was meant by that phrase. The main factor in the oppression of Jews under the czar had been the religious factor; the main factor with U.S. Blacks was race. Blacks lacked some of the essential attributes of a nation as it had been defined by Stalin in his classic work *Marxism and the National Question.*[2]

Most assuredly, one could argue that among Blacks there existed elements of a special culture and also a common language (English). But this did not add up to a nation, I reasoned. Missing was the all-important aspect of a national territory. Even if one agreed that the Black Belt, where Blacks were largely concentrated, rightfully belonged to them, they were in no geographic position to assert their right of self-determination.

I could see many analogies between the national problem in the old czarist empire and the problem of U.S. Blacks, but the analogy floundered on this question of territory. The subject nations of the old czarist empire were situated either on the border of the oppressing Great Russian nation or were completely outside it. But American Blacks were set down in the very midst of the oppressing white nation, the strongest capitalist power on earth. Faced with this, it was no wonder that most nationalist movements up until then had taken the road of a separate state outside the United States. How then could one convince U.S. Blacks that the right of self-determination was a realistic program?

Nasanov and his young friends answered my arguments over the course of a series of discussions and were quick to pick out the flaws in my position. They contended that I was guilty of an ahistoric approach with respect to the elements of nationhood. Certainly, some of the attributes of a nation were weakly developed in the case of U.S. Blacks. But that was the case with most oppressed peoples precisely because the imperialist policy of national oppression is directed toward artificially and forcibly retaining the economic and cultural backwardness of the colonial peoples as a condition for their superexploitation. My mistake had been to ignore Lenin's dictum that in the epoch of imperialism it was essential to differentiate between the oppressor and the oppressed nations.

They further contended that I had presented the matter as though self-determination were solely a question for Blacks. I had therefore separated the Black rebellion from the struggle for socialism in the United States. In fact, it was a constituent part of the latter struggle or, more precisely, a special phase of the struggle of the American working class for socialism.

My argument added up to a defense of the current position of the U.S. party, although I had embellished the position somewhat against Nasanov's criticisms. Up to this point, the Black students had not challenged the party's line on Afro-American work. We reasoned that the party's default in the work among Blacks was not the result of an incorrect line, but came from a failure to carry out in practice its declared line. We believed that this failure was due to an underestimation of the importance of work among Blacks, which came from an underestimation of the revolutionary potential of the struggle of the Black masses for equality. All this resulted from the persistence of remnants of white racist ideology within the ranks of the party, including some of its leadership.

Nasanov and some of his friends agreed with us that the American Communist Party (CP) did underestimate the revolutionary potential of the Black struggle for equality. But, they maintained, this underestimation came from a fundamentally incorrect social-democratic line rather than from white chauvinism. They said that I had stood the whole matter on its head: I had presented the incorrect policies as the result of subjective white chauvinist attitudes, whereas, they pointed out, the white chauvinist attitudes persisted precisely because the party's line was fundamentally incorrect in that it denied the national character of the question.

"Our American comrades seem to think that only the direct struggle for socialism is revolutionary," they told me, "and that the national movement detracts from that struggle and is therefore reactionary." This, they pointed out, was an American version of the "pure proletarian revolution" concept; they referred me to Lenin's polemic against Karl Radek on the question of self-determination.

The Bolsheviks also criticized my formulation of the matter as primarily a race question. To call the matter a race question, they said, was to fall into the bourgeois liberal trap of regarding the fight for equality as primarily a fight against racial prejudices of whites. This slurred over the economic and social roots of the question and obscured the question of the agrarian democratic revolution in the South, which was pivotal to the struggle for Black equality throughout the country. They pointed out that it was wrong to counterpose the struggle for equality to the struggle for self-determination. For in fact, in the South, self-determination for Blacks (political power in their own hands) was the guarantee of equality.

In a speech at the Sixth Congress, James Ford counted nineteen communications from the Comintern to the U.S. party on Negro work, none of which had been put into effect or brought before the party. He further observed that "we have no more than 50 Negroes in our Party, out of the 12 million Negroes in America."[3]

All of these factors strengthened the determination of the Comintern to make the Sixth Congress the arena for a drastic reevaluation of work and policy in this area.

In the winter of 1928, preparations were already afoot for the Sixth Congress, which was to convene the following summer. The Anglo-American Secretariat of the CI set up a special subcommittee on the Negro question, which was to prepare a draft resolution for the official Negro Commission of the congress.

As I recall, the subcommittee consisted of Nasanov and five students: four Blacks (including my brother Otto and myself) and one white student, Clarence Hathaway, from the Lenin School. In addition, there were some ex-officio members: Profintern rep Bill Dunne and Comintern rep Bob Minor. They seldom attended our sessions. James Ford, who was then assigned to the Profintern, also attended some sessions.

Our subcommittee met and broke the subject down into topics; each of us accepted one as his assignment to research and report on to the committee as a whole. The high point in the discussion was the report of my brother Otto on Garvey's Back to Africa movement. In his report, he concluded that the nationalism expressed in that movement had no objective base in the economic, social, and political conditions of U.S. Blacks. It was, he asserted, a foreign importation artificially grafted onto the freedom movement of U.S. Blacks by the West Indian nationalist Garvey.

U.S. Blacks, Otto concluded, were not an oppressed nation but an oppressed racial minority. The long-range goal of the movement was not the right of self-determination but complete economic, social, and political equality, to be won through a revolutionary alliance of Blacks and class-conscious white labor in a joint struggle for socialism against the common enemy, U.S. capitalism.

Up to that point, I was still not certain as regarded the applicability of the right of self-determination to the problems of Blacks in the United States, but my misgivings about the slogan had been shaken somewhat by the series of discussions I had had with my Russian friends. Otto, in his report, had merely restated the CP's current position. But somehow, against the background of our discussion of the Garvey movement, the inadequacy of that position stood out like a sore thumb. Otto, however, had done more than simply restate the position; he brought out into the open what had been implicit in the party's position all along: that is, that any type of nationalism among Blacks was reactionary.

This view, it occurred to me, was the logical outcome of any position that saw only the "pure proletarian" class struggle as the sole revolutionary struggle against capitalism. The party had traditionally considered the Afro-American question as that of a persecuted racial minority. They centered their activity almost exclusively on Blacks as workers and treated the question as basically a simple trade union matter, underrating other aspects of the struggle. The struggle for equal rights was seen as a diversion that would obscure or overshadow the struggle for socialism.

But how could one wage a fight against white chauvinism from that position? I thought at the time that viewing everything in light of the trade union question would lead to a denial of the revolutionary potential of the struggle of the whole people for equality. Otto's rejection of nationalism as an indigenous trend brought these points out sharply in my mind.

In the discussion, I pointed out that Otto's position was not merely a rejection of Garveyism but also a denial of nationalism as a legitimate trend in the Black freedom movement. I felt that it amounted to throwing out the baby with the bathwater. With my insight sharpened by previous discussions, I argued further that the nationalism reflected in the Garvey movement was not a foreign transplant, nor did it spring full-blown from the brow of Jove. On the contrary, it was an indigenous product, arising from the soil of Black superexploitation and oppression in the United States. It expressed the yearnings of millions of Blacks for a nation of their own.

As I pursued this logic, a totally new thought occurred to me, and for me it was the clincher. The Garvey movement is dead, I reasoned, but not Black nationalism. Nationalism, which Garvey diverted under the slogan "Back to Africa," was an authentic trend, likely to flare up again in periods of crisis and stress. Such a movement might again fall under the leadership of utopian visionaries who would seek to divert it from the struggle against the main enemy, U.S. imperialism, and lead it onto a reactionary separatist path. The only way such a diversion of the struggle could be forestalled was by presenting a revolutionary alternative to Blacks.

To the slogan "Back to Africa," I argued, we must counterpose the slogan "right of self-determination here in the Deep South." Our slogan for the U.S. Black rebellion therefore must be the "right of self-determination in the South, with full equality throughout the country," to be won through revolutionary alliance with politically conscious white workers against the common enemy— U.S. imperialism.

Nasanov was seated across the table from me during this discussion, and, elated at my presentation, he demonstratively rose to shake my hand. I was the first American Communist (with perhaps the exception of Briggs) to support the thesis that U.S. Blacks constituted an oppressed nation.

The struggle for this position had now begun; there remained its adoption by the Comintern and its final acceptance by the U.S. party. Our draft resolution, which summed up these points, was turned over to Petrovsky (Bennett), chairman of the Anglo-American Secretariat. He seemed quite pleased with it, expressed his agreement, and suggested some minor changes. He agreed to submit it to the Negro Commission at the forthcoming Sixth Congress. I continued to work with Nasanov on preparations for the congress. By that time, we had become quite a team.

Our next project was the South African question, a question that also fell under the jurisdiction of the Anglo-American Secretariat. We were assigned to work with James La Guma, a South African Colored comrade who had come to Moscow to attend the November 7, 1927, celebrations of the tenth anniversary of the Russian Revolution and had stayed on to discuss with the Executive Committee of the Communist International (ECCI) and the Anglo-American Secretariat the problems of the South African party. Specifically, we were to draft a new resolution on the question, restating and elaborating the Comintern line of an independent Native South African Republic. (The word "Native" was in common usage at the time of the Sixth Congress, though today it is considered derogatory and has been replaced with Black republic or Azania.)

This line, formulated the year before with the cooperation of La Guma during his first visit to the Soviet Union in the spring of 1927, had been rejected by the leadership of the South African party.

La Guma, as I recall, was a young brown-skinned man of Malagasy and French parentage. In South Africa, this placed him in the Colored category, a rung above the Natives on the racial ladder established by the white supremacist rulers. Colored persons were defined as those of mixed blood, including descendants of Javanese slaves, mixed in varying degrees with European whites.

La Guma, however, identified completely with the Natives and their movement. He had been general secretary of the Industrial and Commercial Union (ICU; the federation of Native trade unions) and also secretary of the Capetown branch of the African National Congress (ANC). Later, after his expulsion from the ICU by the red-baiting clique of Clements Kadalie (a Native social democrat), La Guma became secretary of the non-European trade union federation in Capetown.

La Guma was the first South African Communist I had ever met. I was delighted and impressed with him and was to find, in the course of our brief collaboration, striking parallels between the struggles of U.S. Blacks for equality and those of the Native South Africans. In both countries, the white leadership of their respective parties underestimated the revolutionary potential of the Black movement.

La Guma had made his first trip to Moscow the year before. He and Josiah Gumede, president of the ANC, had come as delegates to the inaugural conference of the League against Imperialism, which had convened in Brussels, Belgium, in February 1927. Gumede attended as a delegate from the ANC, while La Guma was a delegate from the South African Communist Party. It was La Guma's first international gathering, and he had the opportunity to meet with leaders from colonial and semicolonial countries and discuss the South African question with them. Madame Sun Yat-sen and Pandit Nehru were among those present. The conference adopted the resolutions of the South African delegates on the right of self-determination through the complete overthrow of imperialism. The general resolutions of the congress proclaimed: "Africa for the Africans, and their full freedom and equality with other races and the right to govern Africa."[4]

After Brussels, La Guma went on a speaking tour to Germany, after which he came to Moscow. Although the Brussels conference had called for the right of self-determination, it left unanswered many specific questions that are raised by that slogan. Were the Natives in South Africa a nation? What was to be done with the whites?

La Guma was to find the answer to these questions in Moscow, where he consulted with ECCI leaders, including Nikolai Bukharin, who was then president of the Comintern. He participated with ECCI leaders in the formulation of a resolution on the South African question, calling for the return of the land to the natives and for "an independent native South African republic as a stage towards a workers' and peasants' republic with full, equal rights for all races."[5]

La Guma returned to South Africa with the resolution in June 1927; Gumede also arrived home in the same month. But the resolution was received hostilely by Sidney P. Bunting and was rejected by the South African party leadership at its annual conference in December 1927. Bunting was a British lawyer who had come to South Africa some years before. An early South African socialist and a founder of the Communist Party, he was the son of a British peer. As Bunting later commented, he nearly used up the small fortune he had inherited in the support of party work and publications.

Bunting and his followers insisted that the South African revolution, unlike those in the colonies, was a direct struggle for socialism without any intermediary stages. To the Comintern slogan "Native South African Republic," Bunting counterposed the slogan "Workers' and Peasants' Republic." This concept of "pure proletarian revolution" was an echo of what we had found in the U.S. party with respect to Blacks. But here, the error stood out grotesquely given the reality of the South African situation, with its overwhelming Native majority. It was against this background that La Guma and Gumede left to go to Moscow to attend the tenth anniversary celebrations of the Bolshevik Revolution and the Congress of the Friends of the Soviet Union. La Guma apparently was not in Moscow on that occasion; he was probably out on a tour of the provinces. Both he and Gumede traveled widely during their visit to the Soviet Union. Our purpose at this time was to develop and clarify the line laid down in the resolution formulated the previous year. Our draft, with few changes, was adopted by the Sixth Congress of the Comintern and the ECCI.

As already noted, Bunting had put forward the slogan "[South African] Workers' and Peasants' Government." Bunting's formulation denied the colonial character of South Africa. He failed, therefore, to see the inherent revolutionary nature of the Natives' struggle for emancipation. As opposed to this, our resolution began with a definition of South Africa as "a British dominion of the colonial type" identifying, among others, the following colonial features:

1. The country was exploited by British imperialism, with the participation of the South African white bourgeoisie (British and Boer),
   with British capital occupying the principal economic position.
2. The overwhelming majority of the population was Natives and
   Colored (five million Natives and Colored, with one and a half
   million whites, according to the 1921 Census).
3. Natives, who held only one-eighth of the land, were almost completely landless, the great bulk of their land having been expropriated by the white minority.
4. The "great difference in wages and material conditions of the white
   and black proletariat," and the widespread corruption of the white
   workers by the racist propaganda and ideology of the imperialists.[6]

These features, we held, determined the character of the South African revolution, which, in its first stage, would be a struggle of Natives and non-European peoples for independence and land. As the previous resolution had done, our draft (in the form adopted by the Sixth Congress and the ECCI) held that as a result of these conditions, in order to lead and influence that movement, Communists—Black and white—must put forth and fight for the general political slogan "an independent Native South African Republic as a stage towards

a workers' and peasants' republic, with full, equal rights for all races, black, coloured and white."

"South Africa is a black country," the resolution went on to say, with a mainly
Black peasant population, whose land had been expropriated by the white colo-
nizers. Therefore, the agrarian question lies at the foundation of the revolution.
The Black peasantry, in alliance with and under the leadership of the working
class, is the main driving force. Thus, alongside the slogan "Native Republic,"
the party must place the slogan "return of the land to the Natives."

This latter formulation does not appear in the resolution as finally adopted.
Instead, it includes the following two formulations:

1. Whites must accept the "correct principle that South Africa belongs
   to the native population."
2. "The basic question in the agrarian situation in South Africa is the
   land hunger of the blacks and . . . their interest is of prior importance
   in the solution of the agrarian question."[7]

With the new resolution completed, La Guma returned to South Africa. In
the year since the first resolution, the opposition to the line had intensified and
had already come to a head at the December party congress—even before La
Guma's return.

Bunting put forward his position in a fourteen-page document in the early
part of 1928. He equated the nationalism of the Boer minority to the nationalism of the Natives and justified his opposition to nationalism on the basis that
all national movements were subject to capitalist corruption and that, in the
case of South Africa, a national movement among Natives "would probably
only accelerate the fusion, in opposition to it, of the Dutch and British imperialists."[8] Since it would thus only consolidate the forces against it, it was not to
be supported.

Bunting not only underrated nationalism, he played on the whites' fear of
it and raised the specter of Blacks being given free reign, with a resulting campaign to drive the whites into the sea. He was echoing the specter that was
haunting whites who remembered the song of the Xhosas:

To chase the white men from the earth
And drive them to the sea.
The sea that cast them up at first
For Ama Xhosa's curse and bane

Howls for the progeny she nursed
To swallow them again.[9]

According to Bunting, the elimination of whites seemed to be implied in the slogan "Native Republic." He regarded the phrase "safeguards for minorities" as having little meaning, since whites would assume that the existing injustices would be reversed; that, in effect, Blacks would do to them what they had been handing out for so long.

While Bunting had held that all nationalism was reactionary, La Guma distinguished between the revolutionary nationalism of the Natives and the "nationalism" of the Boers (which in reality was simply a quarrel between sections of the ruling class). He argued that the Communists must not hold back on the revolutionary demands of the Natives in order to pacify the white workers who are still "saturated with an imperialist ideology" and conscious of the privileges they enjoy at the Natives' expense.[10]

Bunting held that the road to socialism would be traveled under white leadership; to La Guma, the securing of Black rights was the first step to be taken. As the Simonses described it, "First establish African majority rule, he argued, and unity, leading to socialism, would follow." La Guma called on Communists to "build up a mass party based upon the non-European masses," put forward the slogan "Native Republic," and thus destroy the traditional subservience to whites among Africans.[11] This argument continued up through the Sixth Congress.

Discussion in the Sixth Congress

Interest was keen when the Sixth Congress's Negro Commission, which was to take up the problem of the U.S. Blacks and the South African question, moved to the latter point. Here again it was a fight against the denial of the national liberation movement in the name of socialism, the same right deviation on new turf. In the South African setting, where four-fifths of the population were Black colonial slaves, the deviation was particularly glaring.

It was true that in the preceding year or so the South African party had intensified its work among the Natives, a "turn to the masses." As the Simonses noted, by 1928 there were 1,600 African members out of a total of 1,750 in the party. The year before there had been only 200 African members.[12]

The party had pursued a vigorous policy in the building of Black trade unions, in conducting strikes, and in fighting the most vicious forms of national oppression—pass laws and the like. The party's official organ, the *South African*

Worker, had been revived on a new basis. More than half the articles were now written in three Bantu languages: Xhosa, Zulu, and Tsotho.

Sidney Bunting, leader of the South African party, had emerged as a stalwart fighter for Native rights in the defense of Thibedi, a framed-up Native Communist leader. As a result, about a hundred Natives had been recruited into the party, and two were now on the Central Committee. On the whole, the party was making a turn toward the Native masses. But it still lacked the theory that would enable it to tap their tremendous revolutionary potential.

As did most of the white leading cadre, Bunting exhibited a paternalism with respect to the Natives. This paternalism was rooted in an abiding lack of faith in the revolutionary potential of the Native movement. They saw the South African revolution in terms of the direct struggle for socialism. This white leadership, brought up in the old socialist traditions and comprised mainly of European immigrants, had not yet absorbed Lenin's teachings on the national and colonial questions.

These shortcomings had been brought sharply to the attention of the Comintern by La Guma. The result was the resolution on the South African question that La Guma, Nasanov, and I had worked on the previous winter. It recommended that the party put forward and work for an independent Native South African Republic with full and equal rights for all races as a stage toward a workers' and peasants' republic. This was to be accompanied by the slogan "Return the land to the Natives."

Not only did the party leadership reject the resolution, but they had now sent a lily-white delegation to the congress to fight for its repeal. The delegation consisted of Sidney Bunting, party chairman; his wife Rebecca; and Edward Roux, a young South African Communist leader who was then studying at Oxford. Whatever their hopes were when they arrived in Moscow, they now seemed dejected and subdued. Having sat through the discussion on the Afro-American question, they undoubtedly saw the handwriting on the wall.

From the start, the South African delegation was on the defensive, having been confronted by other delegates with the inevitable question, Where are the Natives?

What answer could they give? It was evident to all that theirs was a mission on which Natives could not be trusted, even those "brought up in the old tradition," to use the phrase of Roux.

We Blacks asked about La Guma, and they replied, "Oh, he was here just a short while ago and had his say. We felt that the other viewpoint should be represented."

After copies of the ECCI resolution on South Africa had been distributed, the South African delegates took the floor before the entire congress to challenge the line of the resolution. The South African revolution, they argued, was a socialist revolution with no intermediate stage, an argument that posed a sort of South African exceptionalism.

The argument ran that South Africa was not a colonial country. Bunting then contended, "South Africa is, owing to its climate, what is called a 'white man's country' where whites can and do live not merely as planters and officials, but as a whole nation of all classes, established there for centuries, of Dutch and English composition."[13]

Bunting's statement came under attack on the floor of the congress, notably by Bill Dunne. Bunting defended himself, holding that his description was solely factual and was not an "advocacy of 'White South Africa,' ... the very view we have combatted for the last thirteen years."[14]

In essence, Bunting's views liquidated the struggle of the Black peasantry in South Africa. He declared that they were "being rapidly proletarianized" and further that "the native agrarian masses as such have not yet shown serious signs of revolt." Hence the slogan "Return the land to the Natives" would antagonize white workers with its implication of a *"black race dictatorship."*[15]

Rebecca Bunting spoke in the commission sessions. Addressing herself to the land question, she denied that the land belonged to the Bantu in the first place. Both the Bantu from central Africa and the Afrikaners coming up from Capetown had forced the aboriginal Hottentots and Bushmen off their land. Thus, there was no special Native land question.

The real question on Rebecca Bunting's mind, however, was not of land but of the position of the white minority in a Native South African Republic. She came right to the point. Who would guarantee equality for the whites in an independent Native republic? Their slogan, she said, was, "Drive the whites into the sea." We listened to her in amazement, and a laugh went through the audience.

The cat was finally let out of the bag, and a mangy, chauvinistic creature it was. Manuilsky stepped forward, his eyes twinkling. "Comrade Bunting has raised a serious question, one not to be sneezed at. What is to become of the whites? My answer to that would be that if the white Party members do not raise and energetically fight for an independent Native Republic, then *kto znaet?* [Who knows?] They may well be driven into the sea!" That brought the house down.[16]

The commission finally affirmed the resolution for a Native South African

Republic. It was then passed onto the floor of the congress, where the fight continued and our position was eventually accepted.[17]

Essence of the New Line

The CI's new line on the Afro-American question was released by the ECCI in two documents. The first was the full resolution of the commission, which addressed itself to the concrete issues raised in the discussion. The second was a summary of the full resolution, worked out in the commission under the direction of Ottomar Kuusinen, for incorporation in the congress thesis on the "Revolutionary Movement in the Colonies and Semi-Colonies."[18]

The resolution rejected the assimilationist race theories upon which the line of the party had been based. It defined the Black movement as "national revolutionary" in character on the grounds that "the various forms of oppression of Negroes ... concentrated mainly in the so-called 'Black Belt' provide the necessary conditions for a national revolutionary movement."

Stressing the agrarian roots of the problem, it declared that southern Blacks "[were] ... not reserves of capitalist reaction," as Jay Lovestone had contended, but that they were, on the contrary, "reserves of the revolutionary proletariat" whose "objective position facilitates their transformation into a revolutionary force under the leadership of the proletariat."

The new line committed the party to championing the Black struggle for "complete and real equality ... for the abolition of all kinds of racial, social, and political inequalities." It called for an "energetic struggle against any exhibition of white chauvinism" and for "active resistance to lynching."

At the same time, the resolution stressed the need for Black revolutionary workers to resist "petty bourgeois nationalist tendencies" such as Garveyism. It declared that the industrialization of the South and the growth of the Black proletariat was the "most important phenomenon of recent years." The enlargement of this class, it asserted, offered the possibility of consistent revolutionary leadership of the movement.

It called upon the party to "strengthen its work among Negro proletarians," drawing into its ranks the most conscious elements. It was also to fight for the acceptance of Black workers into unions from which they were barred, but this fight did not exclude the organization of separate trade unions when necessary. It called for the concentration of work in the South to organize the masses of soil tillers. And finally, the new line committed the party to putting forth the slogan of the right of self-determination:

In those regions of the South in which compact Negro masses are living, it is essential to put forward the slogan of the Right of Self-determination. . . . A radical transformation of the Agrarian structure of the Southern States is one of the basic tasks of the revolution. Negro Communists must explain to the Negro workers and peasants that only their close union with the white proletariat and joint struggle with them against the American bourgeoisie can lead to their liberation from barbarous exploitation, and that only the victorious proletarian revolution will completely and permanently solve the agrarian and national question of the Southern United States in the interests of the overwhelming majority of the Negro population of the country.[19]

In June 1929, Nasanov and I continued our work on the Negro Commission of the Comintern. We both loved the work, which involved a continuous check on the press of the U.S. party (then the *Daily Worker* and the *Communist*), the minutes and resolutions of the party's leading committees, and other labor and progressive publications in which party members were active.

This included *Labor Unity,* the organ of the Trade Union Unity League (TUUL), and *Labor Defender,* which was put out by the International Labor Defense (ILD). This material was to be found in the Comintern Information Department, whose American representative at the time, as I remember, was A. G. Bosse.

As I acquainted myself with the material, I became pleased and excited at the advances the party had made in work among Blacks. The United States, it seemed, had experienced a rapid decline of the economy and growth of mass unemployment. Most impressive was the widespread resistance of workers to "rationalization" (wage cutting, stretch-out, and speedup), and the antiunion terror campaign of employers backed by the federal, state, and local governments. The resistance was reflected in the needle trades, mining, automobile, and textile industries.

All this was two months before the October 1929 stock market crash and the onset of the economic crisis that was to embrace the whole capitalist world. The party, now freed from factionalism, had united on the basis of the Comintern political line and was vigorously moving forth to organize and lead the mounting struggles of the workers. Nasanov and I felt the best evaluation of the party's work among Blacks was put forward by Cyril Briggs in a series of articles that appeared in the June, July, and September 1929 issues of the *Communist.*[20]

Briggs characterized the Sixth Congress of the CI as a major turning point for the party in carrying out a revolutionary program in Afro-American work. Using the struggle against white chauvinism as a barometer of the effectiveness of the party's work in this area, he pointed out that "prior to the Sixth Congress, white chauvinism in the American Party (in both factions!), unmasked at that Congress by Comrade Ford, and mercilessly condemned by that supreme revolutionary body, made progress in Negro work well-nigh impossible."[21]

Before the Sixth Congress there were only a handful of Blacks in the party, but since then the Central Committee had set up a National Negro Department to help in the formulation of policies and in the direction of the work nationally. District and section Negro committees were formed in most areas of party concentration. At the Sixth Party Convention, Black comrades were elected to the highest body in the party, the Central Committee, and to the National Executive Committee of the Young Communist League. They were also elected to the party's Politburo and the National Bureau of the League and were added to district committees and section committees. Another step forward was registered at the founding convention of the TUUL in September 1929: of the eight hundred–plus delegates, sixty-eight were Black.

Nevertheless, this was only a beginning. White chauvinism was still pervasive and represented a powerful influence in the party. Briggs then turned a critical spotlight on the most dramatic struggle of the period—the strike of southern textile workers at Gastonia, North Carolina, which took place in the spring of 1929. This strike—led by the party and the National Textile Workers Union, an affiliate of the TUEL—was the party's first mass activity in the South. It was therefore a test for the new line on the unions and on the Afro-American question.

The southern textile industry—and Gastonia's mills were no exception—was traditionally a white industry, with Blacks about five percent of the workforce. The whites were new proletarians from the mountains and farms, employed by northern mill owners who had moved their mills south to exploit the cheap and unorganized labor of the region. In Gastonia, these workers responded to their exploitation by striking against stretch-out and starvation conditions. The bosses used the old battle cry of white supremacy to divide the Black and white workers and try to break the strike. It created an atmosphere of reeking race hatreds and suspicion, and this was the state of things when the National Textile Workers Union launched its organizing campaign in Gastonia. The mill owners and their local myrmidons—the sheriff, police, militia, foremen, and managers and extralegal arms of the KKK—sought to maintain the status quo threatened by the strikers. The strike speedily took on a political character, reaching the point of armed conflict.

The heroic woman strike leader Ella May Wiggins was pursued and shot down in broad daylight. The Gastonia chief of police was killed and several deputies wounded when they attacked a tent colony that strikers had formed after being evicted from their company-owned homes. Sixteen strike leaders, including some Communists, stood trial for the murder of the police chief. The reign of terror that ensued made the situation extremely difficult for our organizers. Clearly there could be no retreat from the principle of organizing Blacks and whites into one union on the basis of complete equality, yet there were some union and party leaders who wanted to back down in the face of the prevailing chauvinism among the white workers. The Central Committee firmly laid down the line against such a retreat. Following the line of the ECCI resolution, it insisted that the new union embrace all nationalities and colors and that separate unions for Blacks were to be organized only in those trades from which they were barred by the reactionary policies of white union leaders. After their initial wavering, the local leadership rallied to the correct line. Blacks and whites were organized into the same union.

Testimony to this is a dramatic incident involving my brother Otto. I hadn't heard much of Otto since he'd returned to the States, only that he'd been placed on the Central Committee at the Sixth Convention and was working in the Negro Department of the TUUL. As a TUUL organizer, he had been sent to Gastonia. He was at nearby Bessemer City at the time of the attack on the strikers' tent colony and the shooting of the police chief. Otto was unaware of what had happened and that the stage had been set for his lynching should he return. As an article in the *Daily Worker* described the incident:

> Otto Hall . . . was on his way . . . to Gastonia on the night of the raid. . . .
> The white workers, realizing the grave danger to which Hall was ex-
> posed if he happened to get into Gastonia that night, formed a body
> guard and went to meet Hall and warned him to keep away. They met
> Hall two miles out of town and took him in a motorcar to Charlotte
> where they collected enough money among themselves to pay his
> railroad fare to New York. No sooner had Hall embarked on the train
> a mob broke into the house where he hid before his departure. It was
> only timely action on the part of these white workers that saved the life
> of their Negro comrade.[22]

The Gastonia struggle signaled a new period in the party's trade union work—a period that characterized the thirties overall. Under the leadership of the Communist Party and our left trade unions, Black and white workers were organized into the same unions on the basis of equality and in the common fight against the capitalists. The party was able to mobilize mass support for the strike and the sixteen leaders framed for murder, in cities throughout the South and the country as a whole. Otto personally spoke in some twenty-seven cities.

But what was to be said about the needle trades union, long a bastion of the Left? Briggs pointed out the "criminal" apathy of the comrades working in this area. The Needle Trades Industrial Workers' Union only organized Blacks in times of strike, and as a result, had very few Black members. While the union had special departments and scores of functionaries for Greek, Italian, Jewish, and other immigrant workers, there was no Afro-American department and not a single Black functionary. This, at a time when in New York alone there were several thousand Black needle trades workers.

Comrades in the Miners Union made a similar underestimation of work among Afro-Americans. This union operated in an industry that had a large number of Black miners—in some fields even outnumbering the white workers—but had not yet appointed a single Black organizer. In Illinois District Eight (my old district), there occurred a particularly blatant case of white chauvinism. William Kruse, the district organizer, refused to share the pool of funds available for wages with Comrade Alonzo Isabel, the Black functionary. He persisted in this practice despite the demands of the National Secretariat that the funds be shared equitably.[23]

Despite the numerous examples of white chauvinism, there was no doubt that the party was making advances in regards to Negro work. In fact, it was precisely because of these advances that chauvinistic practices that hitherto had gone under wraps were brought out into the open and attacked. Briggs's series of three articles was the sharpest attack on white chauvinism ever published by the party.

Their publication reflected that despite the many shortcomings in our work, there was a growing awareness in the party leadership of the seriousness of the question. The rapid deterioration of economic conditions affecting both Black and white workers allowed no complacency. If the party was going to play a leading role in the coming struggles, it would have to carry on a continuous struggle against white chauvinist ideology and practices.

I was heartened by Briggs's articles. At the same time, however, I was somewhat disturbed. While Briggs evoked the Comintern resolution on the Negro question in his blast against white chauvinism, he was curiously silent on the theory and program underlying the resolution. It was certainly true, as Briggs said, that among revolutionary white workers, white chauvinism was often manifested in the "general underestimation of the role of the Negro masses in the revolutionary struggle." But to say no more than that was to avoid the essence of the question.

My three-year term at the Lenin School was drawing toward a close in June 1930. I began thinking about home and what awaited me on my return. I had had little organizational experience in the party before coming to the Soviet Union and now began to wonder what type of work I would be doing.

But I was to find that Nasanov had other immediate plans for me. He felt that I should stay for a few months longer and work with the CI. It was felt (I presumed by Kuusinen and others) that the Comintern should intervene once more on the Black question. Clearly the brief resolution adopted at the Sixth Congress two years previous was not sufficient. Now a more detailed statement of the question was needed. They had in mind another CI commission on the question that would meet after the Seventh Convention of the U.S. party—one set up to discuss and work out such a statement when all the proceedings from that convention were available. The convention would undoubtedly point up remaining areas of confusion.

"Wouldn't it be best for you to stay, Harry?" asked Nasanov. "Eventually everything will work out," he said, "but it would be better for you to return with a new CI resolution. That way you'll be off to a good start. If you left now, you might get battered about in the fights there."

A monthly publication, the *Negro Worker,* was established with George Padmore as the editor. Headquarters of the organization were set up in Hamburg. Many Black sailors came into that international port—the second largest in Europe—and the organization's literature later was circulated there by these sailors throughout Africa.

The International Trade Union Committee of Negro Workers was the first attempt to bring together Black workers on a world scale. Though the founding conference was small, it was historically important, because it was the first time Black workers from Africa and the Americas had gotten together. It was a wedge into Black Africa, which hitherto, with the exception of South Africa, had been isolated from the world revolutionary movement.

The main effort of the organization was to promote trade union organization in Africa and the West Indies, linking them up with the world revolutionary trade union movement led by the Red International of Labor Unions (RILU). Black workers in the United States were to play a vanguard role in this endeavor because of their greater political and organizational experience, the result of their position as an oppressed people in the heartland of the most advanced capitalist country.

Just before my departure, an incident occurred that forcibly brought home to me the contrast between the socialist world that I was leaving and the racist world that I was about to reenter.

The incident occurred in Stalingrad, one of the new huge manufacturing cities of the Soviet Union. The location was Tractorstroi, a basic unit of the Five-Year Plan with a capacity of fifty thousand tractors a year. The plant stretched fifteen miles along the Volga River. They had brought over about 350 highly skilled white mechanics from the United States, who—together with their families—formed a small American colony. They had their own restaurants supplied with the best food, tobacco, and wines that the Soviets could furnish.

Into this situation stepped a lone Black toolmaker, Robert Robinson. A native of Jamaica and a naturalized U.S. citizen, Robinson was a graduate of Cass Technical High School in Detroit. He had come to Moscow under a one-year contract to instruct young Soviet workers in the Stalingrad plant in the art of tool grinding. He had formerly been employed by the Ford Motor Company.

On the morning of his arrival in Stalingrad, he was shown into the American dining room. He sat down at a table for breakfast before starting work; he was immediately insulted, beaten up, and thrown out of the restaurant by two of his white American fellow workers. This attempt to transplant American racism to Soviet soil was met with outrage. It was made a political issue of high order by the Soviet trade unions and party organizations.

Factory meetings were called throughout the Soviet Union that denounced this crime and expressed the outrage of Soviet workers. They adopted resolutions that were sent to Tractorstroi. The slogan of the day became "American technique yes! American race prejudice no!" It was given the widest publicity; the culprits were arrested immediately, not for assault and battery but for white chauvinism, a social crime and therefore far more serious.

A mass public trial, with delegations sent from factories all over the country, was held. The white technicians were sentenced to two years' imprisonment, which was commuted to deportation to the United States.

Pravda Izvestia and all of the provincial papers carried editorials summing up the lessons of the trial. In the building up of our industries, they said, we expected many foreign workers to come to the country on contract to help fulfill the Five-Year Plan. They would inevitably bring with them their prejudices from the capitalist world. Thus it was necessary for the Soviet workers to maintain vigilance against all forms of racism and nationalism, which must be sternly rebuffed.

Robinson himself remained in the Soviet Union, where he became a citizen and eventually an engineer. Later he was a deputy to the Moscow Soviets.

I remember the Robinson incident well. At the time it occurred, some of us from the school were in a restaurant. A group of Russians seated near us pointed to us and exchanged comments.

"You heard about that shameful thing that happened at Tractorstroi?"

Our very presence reminded them of the incident. People were very sympathetic to us.

The incident was a dramatic affirmation by Soviet workers of their country's position on the question of race prejudice.

Ina

The time for my departure was approaching. I thought of Ina and the future of our marriage. She had been much in my mind these last days in Moscow as I reflected back on our three happy years together.

Despite my busy schedule at the school, we managed to spend most weekends together at her mother's apartment on Malaya Bronnaya, a short distance from the school. It was Ina who had introduced me to the cultural life of the Soviet capital. Together we attended theaters, movies, and concerts at the Conservatory of Music and Moscow ballets and operas at the Bolshoi Theater. We often visited the Park of Culture and Rest, a wooded area across from the Kremlin along the Moscow River. It combined restaurants, theaters, and amusements. Exhibitions of all sorts were held there as well. Other times we went boating on the Moscow River.

Ina had given up her ballet school studies a year or so before. She was now attending the Institute of Foreign Languages, where she was studying English. She displayed a great aptitude for languages, and her English was quite good. After only a year of study she had begun to read American literature.

Though not a member of the Communist Party, she was what they called a "nonparty social activist"; that is, sympathetic to the party and actively supporting its aims of building socialism.

As the time for my departure drew near, we earnestly discussed the future of our marriage. We had agreed that it should not be terminated with my departure.

Our idea was that we would eventually get Ina to the States. Of course, I anticipated some difficulties, but to my mind they were not insurmountable. For one
thing, we were—by mutual choice—unencumbered by children.

Ina was a friendly, outgoing person, and I felt she would have little trouble
adjusting to a new environment and would be accepted by the Black community in any of the big urban centers of the North. I would undoubtedly be assigned to national Afro-American work at the center in New York City on my
return.

After all, even professional revolutionaries were not homeless itinerants of
the old Wobbly tradition. Many were married and had families, even in situations where both were full-time professional revolutionaries.

So as we saw it, our separation was to be temporary. We agreed that once
settled in my future work, perhaps in a year or so, I would either send for Ina or
return myself to bring her back to the States.

Just a few days later, Ina, her mother, and fellow students from the school
accompanied me down to the White Russian Station, where I entrained for
Berlin. From there, after a short stopover, I journeyed to Paris and then embarked at Le Havre for home.

The long voyage gave me plenty of time for reflection on my stay in the
Soviet Union. I thought of how I would put into practice some of the lessons
learned during my four-and-a-half-year stay there.

The initial theoretical framework had been set up—now began the difficult task of testing it in practice. How would we build a national revolutionary movement of Blacks in close alliance with the revolutionary working-class
movement? What would be the problems in organizing Blacks? What resistance to the CI position would I find within the party's ranks? These were but a
few of the questions that passed through my mind as I headed home.

8

RETURN TO THE HOME FRONT: WHITE CHAUVINISM UNDER FIRE

I arrived in New York in early November 1930. After four and a half years in the Soviet Union, everything seemed quite strange. While passing through customs, I lit up a cigarette. A cop snarled at me out of the corner of his mouth, "No smoking here, fella." I was so startled by his rude tone that the cigarette dropped from my lips.

Out in the street I caught a taxi to the national office of the party, which was then located on East 125th Street in Harlem. I looked at the people along the way. Despair seemed written on their faces; I don't believe I saw a smile all the way uptown. What a contrast to the gay and laughing crowds in Moscow and Leningrad! I had arrived in the first year of the Great Depression; my own depression deepened as we drove through Harlem. I was overwhelmed by Harlem's shabbiness and the expression of hopelessness on the faces of the people.

Arriving at the office, I was greeted by Earl Browder and my old friend Bob Minor. They introduced me to Jack Stachel, a party leader and national organizer for the TUUL, and Ben Amis, a Black comrade then in charge of Afro-American work. All four men were discussing last-minute plans for the Anti-Lynching Conference called by the American Negro Labor Congress. It was to be held in St. Louis on November 15, a couple of days later.

The party's plan, as I gathered, was to use this occasion to launch a new organization—the League of Struggle for Negro Rights (LSNR). This organization was to replace the now practically defunct ANLC, which had proved inadequate and sectarian. The ANLC had been the subject of sharp criticism as early as the Sixth World Congress in 1928.

The idea of the new organization had been discussed at the party's convention in July. There had also been some discussion at the Negro Commission in the Comintern. The LSNR was conceived as the nucleus of a united front movement around the party's program for Black liberation. The *Liberator* was to be carried over from the ANLC as the official publication of the new organization.

After greeting me, the comrades continued the discussion. I was just in time to participate in the conference and was given the task of writing a draft manifesto and program for the LSNR. I was asked if I had anything to say. I expressed happiness at being back home after such a long absence and said that I would do my best to carry out the new responsibility. I was also happy to hear about the expected southern delegation to the conference, which reflected party work in the South, and made some remarks about the need for an agrarian program for the Blacks in the South.

I noticed that as I spoke some of the comrades were looking at me curiously, as if puzzled or amused. I wondered about it at the time, but I was to find out why only after the meeting. The YCI representative, a young Russian who had been sitting in on the meeting, said, "Harry, you've got a strong Russian accent in your English! If I'd not been looking directly at you I would have sworn some Russian immigrant was speaking." Of course, I reflected; I had been unconsciously rolling my "r's," a habit that was to stick with me for many years.

I traveled to St. Louis via Detroit and Chicago in order to see my family— my three aunts, of whom I was very fond, my sister Eppa, and my nephew David. I chose to travel by bus in order to get a close-up look at the country and the people.

The blight of unemployment and hunger was evident everywhere. It gave the lie to Hoover's slogan "Prosperity is right around the corner." People on the bus were friendly and related their experiences. They seemed hopeless and confused, regarding the Depression as some sort of "natural disaster." They complained about inadequate relief and evictions. From the bus windows I could see Hoovervilles on the outskirts of many towns—vacant-lot communities of shacks, made from discarded boards and boxes and inhabited by homeless families.

I stopped over in Detroit to see Clarence Hathaway, my old Lenin School friend, who was then district organizer. We went into a restaurant downtown on Woodward, a couple of blocks from the party office. We both ordered ham and eggs, and after we waited for what seemed an interminable period, our orders were finally brought to the table. I started to eat but gagged and spit out the first mouthful on my plate.

"What's the matter?" Clarence asked.

"This stuff is as salty as brine!" I said in amazement.

"Yeah?" he said incredulously. "Mine seems to be all right." He tasted some of mine and immediately spat it out, then called the waiter indignantly.

"What's the matter?" the waiter asked.

"My friend's food is so salty it's inedible."

The waiter, with an evil leer, said, "Well, that's the best we can do," and walked away.

It was only then that it struck me that this was their way of discouraging Black patronage. I'd been out of the country so long that I'd forgotten a lot of these things. Clarence and I stalked out of the restaurant, and there was a silence between us. He said, "Let's go to another restaurant in the Black neighborhood."

"I'm not hungry now; I've lost my appetite." I replied. "Clarence, this is your district, you know. You've sure got a lot of work to do!"

I got the bus to Chicago, still angry, and in this mood wrote the first draft of the manifesto and program of the conference. I poured all my anger into the resolution, and the whole thing came together very quickly.

I arrived in Chicago. This great industrial center was hard hit by the crisis, with plants and mills partially closed. There was as yet no public welfare, only soup lines and private relief. Blacks were hardest hit of all.

My elderly aunts, respectable law-abiding people and deeply religious, were forced to sell moonshine whiskey in order to make ends meet. They told me this in an apologetic, shamefaced way—"Everybody's got to do something to get by." This really got to me.

I called on old friends, and they all wanted to know about my experiences in the Soviet Union. I was interviewed by Lucius Harper of the *Chicago Defender*, who was an old friend of the family. I don't remember if the interview was ever published, because I left right afterward for St. Louis.

I arrived in St. Louis on November 15, the opening day of the conference, and met up with Otto, who was a delegate to the meeting. He had been working in the South (probably Atlanta), and he told me of his experiences there and about his near lynching in Gastonia.

I was happy to see so many of my old comrades, like Richard B. Moore and Otto Huiswoud. Then there was Cyril Briggs. I was anxious to make his acquaintance, as I had been in the Chicago post of his African Blood Brotherhood and was a reader of the *Crusader* magazine and his numerous articles in the *Daily Worker*.

There was also Herbert Newton, who had been a student at KUTVA and was now back in the thick of the struggle. He was the only Black member of the Atlanta Six, a group of Communist organizers charged under Georgia's Insurrection Act and facing possible electrocution. They had been arrested at an antilynching and unemployed demonstration in Atlanta. (The other five defendants were Henry Story, Ann Burlack, Mary Dalton, M. H. Powers, and Joe Carr.) Newton and his codefendants had been released on bail as a result of protest all over the country and were now part of the southern delegation to the conference. Ben Careathers of Pittsburgh, Hathaway, Browder, and Baker were some of the party leaders present among the delegates. But there were many new faces at the conference—comrades with whom I was to work in coming years.

The convention was called by the ANLC as a national conference against lynching. In 1930 alone there were thirty-eight lynchings, thirty-six Blacks and two whites. The conference was to be transformed into the founding convention of the League of Struggle for Negro Rights.

The gathering opened with a small but enthusiastic mass meeting. Its declared purpose, as stated in the *Daily Worker* (November 4, 1930), was "to build a powerful fighting mass movement and a militant newspaper to lead the Negro masses in struggle against oppression and for their demands for full political and social equality and the right of self-determination for Negro majorities in the South." In the spirit of working-class solidarity, which characterized the entire conference, a presidium of Black and southern white workers was elected at this session.

The first business session opened on November 15 with forty-four Black and thirty-four white delegates in attendance. A rousing welcome was given the sixteen-member southern delegation, which was led by Mary Dalton—a young white comrade, a National Textile Workers Union organizer, and one of the Atlanta Six. Otto Huiswoud made the report on the economic and political situation, and Herbert Newton reported on organization. The delegates continued to arrive, and by November 17 they numbered 120—seventy-three Blacks and forty-seven whites.

The conference then adopted a name for the new organization: the League of Struggle for Negro Rights. Upon arrival I had submitted my draft of the manifesto for the league to the Resolutions Committee, where it was discussed and approved. The manifesto—a popularization of the party program for full Black liberation—was now dramatically proclaimed by Mary Dalton amid the continuous applause of the delegates. It declared that U.S. Blacks were an oppressed nation struggling against U.S. imperialism and called for unity of Black and white workers in the fight against the common oppressor. It called for complete political equality; an end to oppression and lynching, to be obtained through self-determination of the Black nation in the South; the confiscation of the land in favor of Black and white soil tillers; and state unity of the Black majority area. This could be achieved fully only through socialism.

The immediate program demanded abolition of all forms of discrimination, disenfranchisement, antimarriage laws, and Jim Crow. It urged the establishment of a united trade union movement to include Black workers on the basis of complete equality as an essential step in cementing real fraternal solidarity between Black and white workers on the basis of common interests. It called for "mass violation of all Jim Crow laws" and "death to the lynchers," the banning of the KKK and all extralegal terrorist organizations, and the liquidation of debts and mortgages of the poor farmers. It urged members to organize LSNR chapters in communities throughout the country and to build the *Liberator* as the official organ for the new organization.

Mary's speech was met with rousing cheers and a standing ovation. A national council was elected, of which I was a member; Ben Amis was chosen national secretary. The Communist Party, through Earl Browder, pledged support in mobilizing white masses for the Black liberation struggle.

The meeting adjourned late on the night of November 19. We stood around the hall talking until about two in the morning. Ben Amis, Otto, and myself left the hall with a Jewish couple who had put us up during the conference. They lived in a middle-class white neighborhood and had driven us to and from the conference. Driving home, the conference successfully completed, we were all on top of the world.

The conference had been especially stimulating for me, as it was the first I had attended since my return home.

We pulled up in an alley behind their home to put the car in their garage. Otto, Ben, and I walked the short distance to the street and waited while they locked up. As we stood talking, a squad car cruised by. Its occupants, four white plainclothesmen, were immediately suspicious of three Black guys coming out of an alley in white St. Louis in the middle of the night.

The squad car stopped and the four of them got out. One of them hailed us: "What are you niggers doing here?"

"We're waiting for our friends; we're delegates from a convention. Our friends are putting away their car; we're staying with them," Ben replied.

We were under a big street light and I could see the cops' faces as they stared hostilely at us. Fortunately at that moment our friends came up. They sized up the situation immediately and intervened for us. They explained we were their friends; they even showed the convention badges we all had. "We live just around the corner; they're staying with us," they said.

The cop in charge seemed satisfied with the explanation and turned to his friends, saying, "Okay, let's go."

A little, mean-eyed cop standing next to Otto seemed disappointed at this turn of events, that he would be deprived of the pleasure of shooting or beating up niggers. I figured him as one of the kind that carved notches on his gun for the Blacks he had killed. Looking at Otto he said, "This nigger here seems like a bad nigger to me; you're a bad nigger, ain'tcha?"

I was standing right next to Otto, and knowing his temper, I kept pulling on his sleeve. Otto muttered something like, "Oh, not so bad."

"Yes, you are, you're a bad nigger," the cop responded, trying to bait him. But the head cop urged his partners to leave. Reluctantly they all turned away and got back in their car.

The incident had a sobering effect, cutting through the euphoria of the evening and bringing us back to solid ground. It would have been ironic for us to be the first victims of the police brutality against which we had inveighed at the congress!

I returned to New York via Chicago, revisiting my aunts and sister. My father, now living with a niece in Elgin, Illinois, came into the city to meet me. Age had caught up with him, and his hair had grayed. He was still working as a janitor. I was glad to see him, but I felt sad too—we had so little in common. All he saw for Otto and me was trouble. He was still a Booker T. Washington man, and he didn't think the issue of freedom could be forced. To fight would only cause us grief.

Scottsboro

I followed the Scottsboro issue closely from the beginning. On March 25, 1931, a freight train crowded with young people hoboing from Chattanooga to Memphis in search of work passed through Paint Rock, Alabama. Nine Black youths were pulled off by the local sheriff and his deputies, charged with raping two white girls who happened to be riding the same freight train. The nine were Charles Weems, age twenty; Clarence Norris, nineteen; Haywood Patterson, seventeen; Ozie Powell, fourteen; Eugene Williams, thirteen; Olen Montgomery, seventeen; Andy Wright, eighteen; Willie Roberson, fifteen; and Roy Wright, thirteen.

The situation was made to order for the local henchmen of Alabama's ruling oligarchy. The economic crisis had struck deeply into the entire region of northern Alabama, an area of mainly small, family-size farms and a few textile mills. Many in its largely white population were facing evictions and repossession of tools and livestock by the banks. In the textile mills, layoffs were throwing many out of work. But the sizable Black population in the area suffered even greater hardships.

Moving with lightning speed, the local authorities of Paint Rock lost no time in exploiting the case. The boys were taken to Scottsboro (the county seat), where they were arraigned, indicted, tried, and found guilty of rape in a period of less than three weeks. The trial began on April 6 and ended on the tenth, with the sentencing of eight boys to death in the electric chair. The case of the ninth victim, Roy Wright, was declared a mistrial. The prosecution had requested life imprisonment in view of his youth (he was thirteen), but the jury returned deadlocked with seven jurors insisting on the death penalty.[1]

The trial was carried through in a lynch atmosphere. On the day it opened, mobs of white natives from the surrounding countryside and towns surged around the courthouse. A band was playing "There'll Be a Hot Time in the Old Town Tonight." The National Guard had been called out, ostensibly to preserve order and prevent the mob from attacking the boys. One of the youths, however, was bayoneted by a guardsman.

It was the new-style, legal lynching carried through with the cooperation of the courts and law enforcement agencies. It was intended to guarantee to the mob the same results as would be obtained in an old-fashioned burning and hanging in a public square—the death of the victims.

The courtroom farce at Scottsboro was a part of a wave of racist terror sweeping the South that had resulted in ten known lynchings in the previous three months. Clearly its purpose was to "keep the nigger in his place," to prevent unity of Blacks and poor whites—in other words, to divert the unrest of Black and white workers into channels of interracial strife.

This aim received open and brutal expression by the governor of Texas, Ross Sterling, an arrogant spokesman of the racist rulers of the South. Speaking of a case in his state, he stated, "It may be that this boy is innocent. But it is sometimes necessary to burn down a house in order to save a village."[2]

The Chattanooga Negro Ministers' Alliance retained Stephen R. Roddy, reportedly a member of the Ku Klux Klan, as defense attorney. His defense amounted to little more than pleading for life imprisonment instead of the death penalty. The NAACP kept a low profile on the case, as they were not sure the boys were innocent and they wanted to avoid the possibility of the association being identified with mass rapists. This was their official justification for holding back from the case:

> The N.A.A.C.P. is not an organization to defend Black criminals. We are not in the field to condone rape, murder and theft because it is done by Black men. . . . When we hear that eight colored men have raped two white

girls in Alabama, we are not first in the field to defend them. If they are guilty and have a fair trial the case is none of our business.[3]

It was only when confronted with the dispatch of the ILD and the Communists in taking up the case, and with the widespread outcry against the legal lynching in all sections of the Black population, that the NAACP belatedly tried to enter the case and force the Communists out.

We Communists viewed the case in much broader, class terms. First, we assumed the boys were innocent—victims of a typical racist frame-up. Second, it was a lynchers' court—no one, innocent or guilty, could have a fair trial in such a situation.

From the beginning we called for mass protest against the social crime being acted out by Wall Street's Bourbon henchmen in the South. On April 2, the *Daily Worker* called for protests to free the Scottsboro Boys. Again on April 4, the *Southern Worker* carried an article that characterized the case as a crude frame-up.

I remember distinctly how I became involved in the case. I was sitting in the party's district office on Twelfth Street. I had been reading the newspapers, which were filled with stories of the trial in Scottsboro. It seemed things were going badly there. The first group of boys had already been sentenced to death in the electric chair. I was trying to figure out what our next step should be. It was clear that if we did not take over the defense of at least some of the boys, they were doomed. Suddenly Sol Harper burst in on me.

If there was one person who, before anyone else, understood the significance of the Scottsboro case and what the role of the party should be, it was Sol. Sol Harper was a tall, rangy, stoop-shouldered Black comrade, about thirty-five at the time, with prematurely graying hair. He combined the qualities of a dedicated Communist with the skills of an expert investigative reporter. He seemed to have an inexhaustible store of information about current issues and knew everything that was happening or was about to happen on the Black rights front. He always carried a brief case stuffed with clippings from current newspapers and magazines. When I first arrived in New York it was Sol who guided me through Harlem, explaining what was happening on the streets and introducing me to countless people. One always felt that Sol had his finger on the pulse of the people. He knew what they were thinking and how they would respond to any event.

I had never seen him so agitated as he was that morning. "What's the party going to do?" he demanded. The NAACP was selling these boys out, they were going to the chair, and the Black community was up in arms. "We have to step in now," Sol declared, "We must take over the legal defense. Send our lawyers down and get them to line up the boys and their parents."

Sol got through to me that it was time for a decision. As soon as he left I went up to the national office on the ninth floor of the building to talk with Amis and enlisted his support. Together we went to see Bob Minor in the next office. Bob had just been released from prison after serving one year for his leadership in the March 6 Union Square demonstration against unemployment and for relief.

Bob was keenly sensitive on the Afro-American question and saw "the great mass of Negro people" as one of the greatest and most effective forces for the revolutionary overturn in the United States. He had just finished reading the accounts of the trial and had arrived at the same conclusion we had: the party had to move in on the legal defense.

The three of us went to speak with Browder. He too had been reading about the trial and had just received a firsthand report from Scottsboro, where the legal lynching was taking place. Browder agreed that we must act quickly.

We immediately called a meeting with the ILD and the decision to enter the case was made. The ILD moved with dispatch. Joseph Brodsky, chief lawyer for the organization, and his associate, Irving Schwab, went immediately to Birmingham and Chattanooga, where they got the consent of the parents and the boys to enter the defense. Allen Taub, another ILD attorney, who was already in Chattanooga, engaged the services of a local lawyer, George W. Chamlee.

The ILD had now gained control of the case. On April 10, 1933, the day of the sentencing, the Central Committee issued a statement in the *Daily Worker* exposing the case as a "court house lynching" being carried out by the "Southern white ruling class." It called upon "all working class and Negro organizations to adopt strong resolutions of protest and to wire these to the Governor of Alabama." But wires to such capitalist officials alone, it went on to say, "will do no good; you must organize such at greatest possible speed mass meetings and militant mass demonstrations against this crime."

The statement concluded with the call to build a united front of "all working people and farming masses of this country" and put forward the slogans "Death penalty for lynchers!" and "Stop the legal lynching at Scottsboro!"

On May 23, Bob Minor, Amis, and I left New York to attend the All-Southern Scottsboro Defense Conference, which was to meet on May 24 in Chattanooga. Minor represented the Communist Party, Amis spoke as secretary of the LSNR, and I represented the TUUL.

Upon arrival in Chattanooga, we met with local comrades and Tom Johnson, the party's southern organizer. The four of us formed a steering committee for the conference and set up a command post in the home of a local Black comrade. Tom gave us the rundown on preparations and expectations for the conference.

The atmosphere was tense. Local newspapers had sought to whip up hostility against the meeting, screaming with protests against the new carpetbag invasion from the North. The chief of police assured the white community that his forces were alerted and would take action against any attempt to disrupt the racist status quo.

Tom was not even sure that the conference would be allowed to meet. We learned that police harassment had prevented the arrival of the Alabama delegation; most of them had been picked up by Birmingham police as they were getting into assembled cars to drive to the conference. Since it was early morning, before sunrise, they were charged with a violation of the Birmingham curfew laws. They were later released without fines, but too late to attend the conference. I was disappointed, for I had expected my brother Otto would be part of the Alabama delegation.

Our fear that the police might try to disrupt the conference by arresting its leaders was well grounded. We adopted security measures to prevent this. All of us on the steering committee took turns going to the conference hall one person at a time. When one returned another would go. We adhered to this plan throughout the conference so that the whole steering committee was never present in the hall at any one time.

It was at this conference that I met Angelo Herndon for the first time. Herndon was to become the victim of a frame-up in Atlanta just a year later. I remember the enthusiasm and militancy of the two hundred delegates, especially of the local people. Other delegates told me that when Amis spoke he brought people to their feet as he called on Blacks everywhere to fight for the lives of the nine Scottsboro Boys. In this spirit, he invoked the memory of Nat Turner, Frederick Douglass, and other heroes in the days of slavery. Bob Minor, as I understand, also gave an impressive speech. I too spoke, delivering greetings and support from the TUUL.

The conference ended without incident. We were all enthusiastic—it was the first conference against lynching to be held in the South. Bob, Ben, Tom, and I were exhilarated and dropped our security precautions prematurely. We walked down to the conference hall and stood talking on the sidewalk, less than a block away from the conference. As we stood watching the delegates leave, we congratulated each other on the success of the conference. A patrol wagon swooped down upon us, and the four of us were arrested and charged with "blocking the sidewalk." We spent the night in jail, and next morning Chamlee, our Scottsboro attorney, got us out with a ten-dollar fine each.

Class Warfare in the Mines

In June 1931, the TUUL sent me to Pittsburgh to work as an organizer in a strike led by the National Miners Union (NMU), a TUUL affiliate. It was the largest strike the TUUL had led up to that point, and it involved some forty-two thousand coal miners in the Pittsburgh area (eastern Ohio, northern West Virginia, and western Pennsylvania), six thousand of whom were Blacks. This strike was a part of the whole upsurge of working-class activity led by the Communist Party during this period.[4]

The NMU was founded in 1928 by members of the rank-and-file Save-the-Union Committee of the United Mine Workers of America (UMWA). John Watt was elected president; William Boyce, vice president; and Pat Toohey, secretary-treasurer. When the TUUL was formed in 1929, the NMU affiliated with the new revolutionary labor organization.

Its founding immediately followed the defeat of the UMWA in the bituminous coal strike of 1927, the result of the reactionary policies of John L. Lewis. After a strike that lasted over a year and despite the efforts of the Save-the-Union Committee, Lewis signed a separate agreement for the Illinois district. This move left the men in the Pittsburgh area with nothing to do but go back to work.

Almost overnight, all the gains of the past thirty years of bitter struggle against the mine operators had been wiped out. Splits and dual unions developed throughout the minefields, where the union had once been strong. Conditions for the miners deteriorated very rapidly.[5]

Upon arriving in Pittsburgh, I proceeded immediately to the Yugoslav Hall, where a meeting of the Central Strike Committee was proceeding. Representatives from all fields had assembled to vote on the strike and issue the general strike call. William Z. Foster, Jack Johnstone, Alfred Wagenknecht, and Jack Stachel, from the national TUUL office, were all there, and all spoke. But most impressive to me were the speeches of the organizers from the coalfields.

Ike Hawkins, a veteran Black miner whom I had met as a delegate to the Fifth RILU Congress, and Tom Meyerscough spoke of the miserable conditions in the coalfields and the determination of the miners to fight back. It was a fight for survival dramatically reflected in the strike slogan "Fight against Starvation." To this the miners added another: "As Well to Starve Fighting as to Starve Working in the Mines."

I was assigned as union organizer to the Pricedale region, about thirty miles south of Pittsburgh. The region included some of the largest mines of the Pittsburgh Coal Company, the biggest of all the coal companies. I arrived in town on a late Sunday afternoon in the midst of a big open-air meeting. It seemed that the whole town had turned out. I was delighted to find my friend Bill Dunne there.

He had been sent on a tour of the fields to pep up the morale of the strikers. A veteran of the copper miners' struggles in Butte, Montana, and of the coal miners' strike in Illinois, he was a skilled orator who was able to speak authoritatively on the issues.

I, on the other hand, knew nothing of the mining industry. On the train down from Pittsburgh, I had carefully read the strike call, acquainted myself with the miners' vernacular, and committed the demands to memory. These included an increase in pay, the eight-hour day, and recognition of the NMU.

I was introduced by Cutt Grant, the chairman of the local strike committee. I repeated verbatim what I had learned from the call and summarized the discussion of the strike committee in Pittsburgh. My remarks were on the whole well received. But I had quickly noticed that only a few Black miners were at the meeting. I had been informed that the Pricedale Mine had a large Black force. Where were they?

It seemed that while Blacks were the backbone of the strike in the immediate areas around Pittsburgh (in Library, for example), they had not responded well to the strike in this region. I was later to learn from some Black miners that the probable cause for this was that Blacks around Pittsburgh had come up from the South earlier. They were older in the mines and had become fairly well integrated into the mine force. Many had obtained official posts in the NMU locals. This had its ironical side.

In many locals Blacks worked with recent European immigrants. In some places the latter were even the majority. But Blacks were elected to union positions—president, vice president or secretary—because they were the only ones who could speak English! In Pricedale, however, Blacks had come into the mines later, most of them brought in as strikebreakers, as late as 1927.

Against this background, the difficulties that confronted me as a union leader in the area were obvious. I, a Black man, found myself the leader of a mass of white miners with strong racial prejudices. They didn't understand why the

Blacks had not come out on strike. They seemed to expect that Black miners should forget about racist incidents that occurred during the last strike, job discrimination in the mines, and segregation in the company patches (areas where the mines built company-owned housing and company stores).

Cutt Grant, a slightly built wiry figure, was a strong and courageous fighter of many mine battles and a recognized rank-and-file leader. He was also afflicted with the white chauvinist illness. I remember how his face fell when I stepped on the platform and Bill Dunne introduced me as the NMU organizer. There was a sharp contrast between his enthusiastic introduction of Dunne and his apologetic tone in introducing me.

I must say, however, the attitude of the white miners was cordial and even friendly to me. I was a "union nigger" and therefore different from their Black fellow miners. But I overheard mutterings of "Why don't those damn niggers come out?" And I knew that they expected me to do something about getting them out. It was my first experience in such a situation.

There was a sizable number of South Slavs in the area, including Adam Getto, a young second-generation American who was the party organizer. He immediately took me in tow, introducing me to his father, mother, aunts, and cousins. While the elderly Slavs spoke little or no English, we were able to communicate as I spoke Russian to them and they spoke Croatian to me, a kindred Slav tongue.

I soon became known throughout the area as the Black Slav. It felt good to know I had some sort of a base—however tenuous—in the Yugoslav community, which included a sizable number of the miners in the area. The ethnic picture in my section included a minority of Anglo-Irish (old-timers in the mines, many of whom had come from the South), a sizable number of South Slavs, and the Blacks.

I became immersed in the work of the strike. Our immediate target was to close down the Pricedale Mine. Every day there were picket lines. Finally we called a special day. Every shop in the town closed; all the small merchants turned out for the picket line. The line was led by Cutt Grant, Getto, and myself.

The state police were also out in force. They were a hard-bitten lot—each looked like a one-man army with .30-30 Winchester rifles in their saddle holsters, .45 Colts, long riot clubs, and helmets. I sized them up as ex-marines and former army noncoms. As I passed by, I overheard the corporal say to one of his men, "See that nigger there; he's the union leader. Keep an eye on him!"—trying to scare me off.

In addition to the state police, there were the Coal and Iron Police, private cops employed by the coal companies. They carried on a campaign of terror in the company patches and around the mines. Just a few days before I arrived, they had smashed a picket line at Pricedale using tear gas, clubs, and machine guns. Three miners were shot. It was the "worst rioting in Western Pennsylvania bituminous fields in nine years."[6]

The Black miners were not responding to our organizing efforts, however, and the Pricedale Mine stayed open. It occurred to me that I might use the Scottsboro issue as a handle. I talked it over with Getto and Grant, suggesting that a meeting supporting the Scottsboro Defense be called jointly by the National Miners Union and the League of Struggle for Negro Rights. There was no LSNR in the field, but I felt that as national secretary, I had the authority to use the name.

I suggested we try to get hold of the ILD's famous Black orator Richard B. Moore, who was touring the country on behalf of the Scottsboro Boys. I also suggested we issue a special leaflet to the Black miners, advertising the meeting and asking them to come out and hear the latest on the Scottsboro Boys. They agreed, and we put out a leaflet that also included the special demands of the Black miners against discrimination.

The meeting was held on a hot Sunday afternoon, under a large tree in Fairdale, a neighboring town where our strike headquarters were set up. Several thousand people—miners and their families—turned out, and for the first time Black faces were among them. It seemed the entire Black community had come out.

Richard B. Moore was at his best; he spoke for over two hours about the international situation, the crisis, unemployment, Scottsboro, and the miners' strike. He linked them all up together and was frequently interrupted by applause, as his ideas struck home with the audience. He ended with a rousing plea for unity of Black and white miners in the strike. People were just spellbound.

Cutt Grant came over to me, eyes moist with emotion. He could hardly speak. "My! I've never heard a speaker like that before."

Moore's speech seemed to have purged Grant of his white chauvinism. I believe he joined the party the next day, and the Black miners at Pricedale joined the strike.

Murder in the Coalfields

Every weekend Getto and I would go to Pittsburgh to attend a Central Strike Committee meeting. Often Cutt Grant would accompany us. Organizers from all the fields would be present. We'd get the latest news of the strike, how it was proceeding in other fields, report our own situation, and receive new instructions. We would communicate this to the miners in our region on our return.

Returning one Monday morning, I crossed the bridge at Monessen and was met by some miners from my section. "Have you heard what happened?" they said, rushing up to me.

They informed me that the company goons—the Coal and Iron Police—had killed Filipovich right on his front porch, with his whole family watching.

I was shocked. Filipovich was an ex-miner who had become a small storekeeper. His store was right across the street from the Pricedale company patch. He and his wife and several children lived above the store, and we had our miners' relief station in his basement. Everyone knew him as a strong partisan of the miners, and he was well liked by all except the company thugs who were out to get him.

We proceeded to Fairdale but could only get within several blocks of the store. There were crowds of miners and their families milling around and I found out exactly what had happened. Filipovich and his family had been sitting on their porch the evening before when some company thugs had come out and fired point blank at him from the company patch across the street. He had jumped up and rushed his family through the door, shouting, "Don't kill the children!" It was then that he was shot, though none of his children were hurt.

The reaction was tremendous anger throughout the coalfields at this cold-blooded murder. At the funeral, miners, their families, and sympathizers gathered from all the coalfields around. A Yugoslav priest conducted the service and Adam Getto gave the eulogy.

The anger of the people was so strong that it was clear the operators couldn't get away with it this time. The state prosecutor was forced to try the case; the killers were found guilty and sentenced to long prison terms.

The last holdout mines in our area were two near Bentlyville, Charleroi and Hillman. They were situated on a hill outside the town limits, just off a public highway. Every time we had attempted to picket these mines, the coal and iron thugs would mount machine guns across the road, thus blocking our attempts to close them down. We all knew this crude violation of the rights of the miners could only take place with the collusion of the state police, who were curiously absent on such occasions. Over several weeks we planned and organized for an attack to break through this blockade.

With the help of the Central Strike Committee, we mobilized miners from neighboring coalfields for a march on these mines. The morning of the march, thousands of miners and their wives assembled at the foot of the hill leading up to the mines. The coal and iron thugs had placed across the road three machine guns, which glistened in the morning sun. Cutt Grant, Getto, and myself were to lead the march.

While we were gathering, the state police, who had been conspicuously absent in past confrontations with gunmen, made their appearance in the person of a young lieutenant and a sergeant who drove up in a car.

Standing on the running board, the lieutenant warned us, "Don't march up that hill, you'll all be killed. Don't follow your leaders," he said, pointing at Adam, Cutt, and me. "They are Russian Communists, trying to lead you into a trap."

Voices from the crowd responded, "Isn't this a public road? What right have they to block it? Why don't you clear them off it?" "Let's march," they shouted. The crowd surged forth, with Cutt, Getto, and myself in the lead.

"Here I am," I thought, "over the top again, but in another kind of war this time—against the enemy at home." No weapons, no artillery support; just militant and determined miners. Some had clubs, others picked up rocks, and a few, I'm sure, had handguns concealed under their coats, despite our efforts to discourage them. So we began to march slowly up the hill, expecting at any moment to be blown apart by the company thugs who now had the three machine guns pointing directly at us.

The atmosphere was tense with expectancy. We got about fifty feet from them, when they suddenly picked up their guns and moved them to the side of the road, back onto company property. It had all been a bluff. We surged past with a deafening "hurrah" and established our picket lines on the public road in front of the mines. Bentlyville mines were struck that day. Now all the mines in our section were on strike. The mines were closed tight for several months, during which the miners had excellent morale and fighting spirit.

A back-to-work movement started slowly in the fourth month of the strike. At first, it was scarcely perceptible, but when more and more miners failed to show up at local strike committee meetings, it was clear that demoralization was setting in. Behind this was the stark fact of starvation for the miners and their families. The relief efforts headed by Wagenknecht were inadequate to maintain a long-drawn-out strike.

Getto, an old hand in the minefields, warned me of what to expect. As the feeling that the strike is being lost grows, it is often accompanied by terroristic actions, particularly among the young miners—blowing up tipples, wrecking property and buildings.

We organizers and some of the more militant miners, however, were reluctant to admit defeat. At the beginning of the back-to-work movement, many rank-and-file leaders and even union organizers continued to give rosy reports at the Central Strike Committee meetings.

"Yes, a few scabs are crawling back, but the main mass of miners are solid in support of the strike."

Then the Comintern representative, the German Ewart, appeared at a meeting of the Communist fraction of the strike committee.[7] As I recall, he kept insisting on exact information on the back-to-work movement. Clearly, he was suspicious of the glowing reports from many comrades. He stressed that if the trend was there and growing, we must be prepared for a "strategic retreat."

Retreat! Such a word was strictly taboo. Some organizers looked at him as though he were a scab and argued, "That's just what the operators would like us to do!"

Even Foster seemed unfamiliar with the idea of voluntary retreat. The term was evidently not in his lexicon of strike strategy. If we are facing defeat, we should go down fighting—this seemed to be the common opinion. But Ewart quickly pointed out that if we chose this course, we would find all our militants outside of the mines, blacklisted, and our union destroyed.

On the other hand, if we recognized our defeat and understood that the miners simply could not stay out any longer, we would be able to keep our militants in the mines, prevent ourselves from becoming isolated, and regroup our forces to fight again. The logic of this position was unassailable, and after several meetings we were won over.

We returned to the fields and called meetings of the strikers. The position made sense to them. But our action was not taken soon enough. Thousands of our best miners had already been locked out.

But the rank-and-file movement among miners did not end. Early in 1932, eight thousand miners in the Kentucky fields went out under the leadership of the NMU. This historic strike was carried out under conditions of guerrilla warfare. After a bitter struggle, in which many were killed, this strike was also broken.

9

REUNION IN MOSCOW

I returned to New York from the miners' strike in September 1931. Shortly thereafter, I was co-opted to the Central Committee with the privilege of sitting in on meetings of the Politburo. B. D. Amis, the former head of the Negro Department, was sent to Ohio, and I was named to fill his position. In my new job, a large part of my time was devoted to the Scottsboro campaign, which was a major effort of the party in the Black liberation struggle.

It is difficult to fully assess the tremendous impact Scottsboro had on the party's political development in that period. Every area of work—every mass organization we were involved in—was strengthened by our participation in this defense campaign. Through our militant working-class policy, we were able to win workers of all nationalities to take up the special demands of Black people embodied in the Scottsboro defense. I'll never forget how the immigrant workers in the Needle Trades Union would sing "Scottsboro Boys Shall Not Die" in their various eastern European and Yiddish accents.

In the South, the movement awakened the great mass of the Black peasantry and resulted in the building of the militant Sharecroppers Union, which embraced thousands of land-starved Black croppers and poor farmers. Scottsboro helped pave the way for the growth of the Unemployed Councils and the Congress of Industrial Organizations (CIO). The ILD, which had been initiated by the party in 1925 to fight for the freedom of political prisoners like Tom Mooney and Warren K. Billings, became the main mass organization in Scottsboro.[1] The Mooney case and others like it were linked to the Scottsboro frame-up and became instrumental in winning white workers to the fight for the freedom of the Scottsboro Boys.

Scottsboro marked the first real bid of the party and the Black working class for leadership in the Black liberation struggle. Within the national movement, Black workers emerged as a force independent of the reformists and greatly strengthened by their role as part of the working class generally. By the end of 1931, we had effectively won hegemony in the defense efforts. Although the NAACP did not formally withdraw from the defense until January 1932, we were already in de facto control, the boys and their parents having signed up with the ILD.

The thrust of our policy, emphasizing the primacy of mass struggle for the freedom of the boys, had succeeded to a large extent in discrediting and isolating the reformist-liberal NAACP leadership. This fact, however, did not mean that the right reformist danger of compromise and capitulation in the Black freedom movement had been eliminated. On the contrary, its proponents continued to probe our positions, seeking weak spots that they could exploit to stage a comeback.

Within the party, these influences were reflected in the underestimation of the objective class role of the reformist leadership as an agency of the white ruling class within the Black movement. Underlying this was the tendency to ignore class differences in the Black community, the naive and anti-Marxist assumption that all Blacks, as members of an oppressed nation, were revolutionary or potentially so.

This attitude persisted despite the treachery of the NAACP leaders in the Scottsboro struggle. In practice, it was manifested in the tendency to rely on local Black leaders, particularly the clergy, in the building of local united fronts and the failure to involve the masses below. Often within these united fronts the party failed to place elementary conditions for struggle against the ruling class as the basis for unity and thus failed to maintain the independent role of the party, its freedom of action and propaganda.

This struggle against the right reformist danger was often made more difficult by left sectarian errors, manifested primarily in a resistance to building the broadest possible united front.

As head of the Negro Department, I felt it was my job to push the fight against reformism in the Black community and its reflections in the party. This I felt was essential, not only to the Scottsboro struggle but also to secure our long-term strategic objective, winning the hegemony of Black workers in the liberation struggle. I pursued this line in speeches, in lectures, in training classes for party cadres, and in my writings during this period.[2]

In those days the South was considered the main concentration point for the development of the Black liberation movement. As the head of the national Negro Department and the Central Committee representative to the South, I was expected to follow closely the development of the party's work in that region. It was therefore necessary to acquaint myself with its practical as well as theoretical problems. My plan was to spend at least three or four months a year in the South.

My first trip south was to Charlotte, North Carolina, in the spring of 1932. Charlotte, located near the foothills of the Piedmont, was the geographical center of the growing southern textile industry. The industry had grown up as the result of the runaway shops from New England—bent on tapping the cheap labor supply of poverty-stricken white farmers fleeing the uplands. Gastonia, the scene of the historic strike in the spring of 1929, which had been led by the party and TUUL, was only twenty miles from Charlotte.

Charlotte was also the headquarters of the party's North Carolina District. At the time of my visit it was quiet, but there were stirrings in the mills around the area, rumblings of a new wave of strikes that were to break out the following July. Unemployment was the main issue among both Black and white workers. Unemployment was growing as a result of the inhuman stretch-out (speedup) system. Blacks were still a minority in the mills, working only in cleanup jobs, sweeping and janitorial work. They were the lowest of the low.

The party had carried through some demonstrations for unemployment relief. Some of the stalwarts from the Gastonia strike who had been locked out of the mills had moved into Charlotte—providing the backbone of the party in Charlotte, at least among whites. The party had won sympathy among Blacks as a result of the Scottsboro issue and of its strong position against discrimination in the shops. An ILD branch had been set up, and there was a good Scottsboro movement in town.

The party was partially underground, and its members worked in the Unemployed Councils, the ILD, and the National Textile Workers Union (which had never really recovered after the Gastonia defeat). Downtown, there was an unemployed headquarters that consisted of an office and a fairly large hall where the ILD also held meetings. Party meetings were generally small and were held in the homes of comrades.

Most of the top party leadership was from the North. Richards, the district organizer, was of Finnish American extraction and hailed from Wisconsin, where he had formerly been district organizer. Amy Schecter was a Jewish cockney. Born in London, she was a college-educated intellectual, but she still retained a thick cockney accent. She was one of the original Gastonia Seven, who were charged with the murder of the chief of police. (Their case was finally won in the Supreme Court.) There was also Dave Doran of the YCL. He later became political commissar of the Lincoln Brigade and was killed on the Aragon front in Spain. The outstanding local comrade was a steadfast Black woman, Ann Withers.

My visit to Charlotte was brief. I sat in on a few meetings in the district, discussing preparations for marches on the issue of unemployment relief and the upcoming election campaign. I then returned to New York and reported on my visit.

That year, 1932, was a presidential election year. We Communists greeted it as an opportunity to popularize our program before the millions of people impoverished by the economic crisis and ruling-class offensive, as well as to stimulate and strengthen all the campaigns the party was engaged in.

By this time, the party had built considerable influence among the masses. We concentrated a good deal of attention on the struggle for unemployment insurance and immediate relief. Hunger marches on state capitals had taken place throughout the country, culminating with nationwide marches on Washington in December 1931 and 1932.

In the struggle of employed workers, the party found itself increasingly at loggerheads with William Green and the AFL. For instance, he supported Hoover's wage-cut policies, against which we had waged many successful battles. In direct defiance of the AFL's no-strike pledge, the party and the TUUL were leading strikes in the Kentucky mines and the needle trades.

Poor and middle farmers were then revolting against widespread evictions and foreclosures throughout the Midwest, and in December 1932 farmers from across the country held a National Relief Conference in Washington. As a result, the Farmer's National Committee of Action was set up—raising such demands as no forced sales or evictions of poor farmers, cash relief, reduction in rents and taxes, and an end to the oppression of Afro-American people.[3]

With mass demonstrations and meetings throughout the country to free the Scottsboro Boys, the party was becoming a respected leader among Blacks. We also helped organize the National Bonus March in July 1932. Some twenty-five thousand veterans marched to Washington, demanding adjusted service pay and standing against the danger of imperialist war and for the defense of the Soviet Union and the Chinese people.

We began preparing for the presidential campaign early in 1932, nominating a national slate of William Z. Foster for president and James W. Ford for vice president. Ford was called back from Germany, where he had been chairman of the International Trade Union Committee of Negro Workers. I had been briefly considered for vice president, but it was felt generally that my appearance was too youthful.

Though the party's vote was small—about 103,000—we used the campaign to broadly publicize our minimum and maximum programs.[4] We had a slate of congressional candidates, among whom were many Blacks. The party was on the ballot in forty states, and it conducted an aggressive campaign. Hundreds of mass meetings were held throughout the country, 7 million leaflets were distributed, and 1 million pamphlets were sold—all this in the face of vicious police harassment and repression. I don't really believe that the final vote was an accurate reflection of the party's influence at that time—particularly in the South, where the Black masses were almost entirely disenfranchised.

In the summer of 1932, nineteen-year-old Angelo Herndon, a YCL member, was arrested in Atlanta, Georgia. Herndon was charged with "incitement to insurrection" under an old 1861 fugitive-slave statute. Much of what I learned was from my brother Otto, who was in Atlanta at the time and worked actively in the campaign.

That June, the Fulton County Commissioners had announced that there was no more money for relief. After all, there was no need for relief, they said— there was no one in the city of Atlanta who was starving. Then they invited any stray soul who might be hungry to come to their offices and they would investigate the situation.

The Communist Party and the Unemployed Councils immediately took them up on their offer. They mobilized one thousand people—Black and white—to come to the county courthouse and demand relief. The meeting it-self was historic—the first time that such a large meeting of Black and white workers had taken place in the South.

Herndon described its significance in his autobiography: "It was a demon-stration of the Southern worker's power. Like a giant that had been lying asleep for a long time, he now began to stir."[5] Atlanta's ruling circles were appropriately alarmed, and the next day they found six thousand dollars for relief.

One week later, Angelo Herndon was arrested. His trial was an example of Georgia lynch justice, and the local rulers, through their newspapers, were to use it to sensationalize the "red Jew" scare for many years to come. I think the prosecutor's remarks sum up the situation pretty well.

Falling to his knees, the Reverend Hudson told the jury that he expected them to arrive at a verdict that would "automatically send this damnable anar-chistic Bolsheviki to his death by electrocution." The good reverend said that this would satisfy God and that the "daughters of the state officials can walk the streets safely. Stamp this thing out now with a conviction."[6]

Hudson didn't get everything he asked for, but Herndon was sentenced to eighteen to twenty years. Before he was sentenced, however, young Herndon told the court, "You may succeed in killing one, two, even a score of working-class organizers. But you cannot kill the working class."[7]

In the beginning stages of the case, the ILD had immediately taken charge of the defense, which was then in the hands of a young Black Atlanta attorney, Ben Davis Jr. The case was linked up with the Scottsboro struggle as a symbol of the racist persecution of Blacks.

A long legal battle ensued. Mass meetings and huge petition campaigns were launched as part of the defense effort. The case was fought through to the Supreme Court, which at first sustained the conviction but ultimately reversed it by a five-to-four decision. Herndon, out on bail, was finally freed in 1937.

As soon as we had received word of Herndon's arrest, we began planning a nationwide defense campaign. The Negro Department was responsible for developing and carrying out a campaign in support of the ILD. As part of this effort I made plans to go to Atlanta to see the situation at firsthand.

Shortly before I was to leave, however, Browder called me into his office and informed me that he had just received a CI request that the American party send three delegates to attend the Twelfth Plenum of the Executive Committee of the Communist International. Browder asked if I would like to go; the meeting was to be in Moscow in early September. He said that he was aware of my desire to bring my wife Ina to the United States, and he suggested that this might be a good opportunity. I, of course, enthusiastically agreed. Just a few days later, I was aboard ship—bound for the Soviet Union—with the other two delegates, Bob Minor and Henry Puro (a Finnish American comrade).

We arrived in Moscow in mid-August, and I had a joyous reunion with Ina. Not long after our arrival, the Twelfth Plenum of the ECCI convened as scheduled. Its purpose was to analyze the current international situation and check the work of the Comintern sections, the affiliated parties.

The tone was set in the resolution on the international situation. It noted that capitalist stabilization had ended, that we were well along in the third period, and that although a revolutionary upsurge was developing in a number of countries, a revolutionary situation had not yet arisen in any important capitalist country. The resolution stressed the danger of war and the "preparation for a counter-revolutionary war against the USSR." The enemy, it declared, was both fascism and social-fascism (social democracy), which stood for the maintenance and strengthening of capitalism. "Only by directing the main blow against social democracy, this social mainstay of the bourgeoisie," it said, "will it be possible to strike at and defeat the chief class enemy of the proletariat—the bourgeoisie."[8]

In the United States there had already been mass demonstrations of the unemployed, the veterans' march, and the strike struggles against wage cuts. The resolution called upon the U.S. party to continue to strengthen its efforts in mobilizing the masses, and toward this end to "concentrate chiefly on the struggle: 1. for social insurance, against wage cuts, for immediate assistance for the unemployed; 2. for assistance for the ruined farmers; 3. for equal rights of the Negroes and the right of self-determination for the Black Belt." It urged the defense of the Chinese people against foreign aggression and the defense of the Soviet Union. There was nothing new in all this.

I visited the Lenin School, where I reported on the Afro-American work in the party. The student body was completely new to me; there were a number of American Black students as well as several South Africans. One was Albert Nzula, the secretary of the South African Communist Party, a brilliant young Zulu Communist. Unfortunately Nzula died of pneumonia shortly after I left.

In Moscow I also met members of the Black and white film group who had come to the Soviet Union at the invitation of the Mezhrabpom (Soviet film industry). The twenty-two young men and women were there to film a story about race and class relations in the southern United States. Among them were the novelist and poet Langston Hughes; Louise Thompson (later Louise Thompson Patterson), secretary of the Committee for the Defense of Political Prisoners and a former social worker and teacher; Ted Poston, a New York journalist; Loren Miller, a young West Coast intellectual, later a lawyer and judge; and Henry Moon, a writer who later became publicity director of the NAACP. They seemed to be having a good time among the hospitable Russians, who went out of their way to show them courtesy.

After a stay of several months and a number of attempts to get started, the movie was called off. The reason, according to Mezhrabpom officials, was the inadequacy of the scenario. It was not worthy of the kind of picture they had hoped to make, nor were the actors quite what they had expected.

They were a group of intellectuals; there was not a genuine worker among them, and only one professional actor. Most were from the North and knew little or nothing about the South. Some members of the group, however, contended that the reasons for canceling the project were political—that the Soviets were backing away from the project in order to curry favor with the U.S. government.

They claimed that equal rights were being sacrificed and that the Soviets were betraying Blacks in exchange for diplomatic relations with the United States. At the time, the two countries were about to establish diplomatic relations, and a film depicting racial relations in the United States might be considered a violation of the proposed treaty of recognition, which enjoined both parties to refrain from hostile propaganda against the other.

This charge was picked up, embellished, and hurled throughout the world by the capitalist press. Added to it were accounts of "poor Blacks stranded in Moscow." The *New York Tribune* headlined a story "Negroes Adrift in 'Uncle Tom's' Russian Cabin—Harlem Expeditionary Unit Is Stranded in Moscow."[9]

A couple of years later, when George Padmore left his post as editor of the *Negro Worker* (organ of the International Trade Union Committee of Negro Workers in Hamburg), he made use of this incident to try to bolster his flimsy charge that the Communist International had deserted the African liberation struggles.

These charges were false. According to Langston Hughes, the group was on contract and continued to receive their salaries—higher than any of them had ever earned before. They were staying in a luxurious hotel, were wined and dined by the Russians, and were also invited by the theatrical union on a pleasure trip to the Black Sea to visit the resorts of the Crimea and the Caucasus.

Hughes also supported the Russians with respect to the inadequacy of the script. In fact, it was he who called their attention to it. He had read the script, written by a well-known Soviet scenarist whose knowledge of contemporary Black life was limited to the very few books on the subject that had been translated into Russian. He had evidently studied these and put together what he thought was a highly dramatic story of race relations in the United States.

The result, said Hughes, "was a script improbable to the point of ludicrousness. It was so interwoven with major and minor impossibilities and improbabilities that it would have seemed like a burlesque on the screen." He told studio officials that in his opinion, "no plausible film could possibly be made from it since, in general, the script was so mistakenly conceived that it was beyond revision."[10]

Mezhrabpom informed the group that they would be paid in full for the duration of their contracts and that transportation via London, Paris, or Berlin back to the United States would be available whenever they wished to depart. With regard to the future, three choices were offered: exit visas at any time, an extended tour of the Soviet Union before leaving, or permanent residence and jobs for any who desired to remain. All were invited to stay in the USSR as long as they wished.

Langston remained a year, visiting republics in central Asia and traveling in various parts of the Soviet Union. Two members of the group stayed permanently. Wayland Rudd, the actor, appeared in Moscow theaters and performed for the troops at the front during World War II. Lloyd Patterson, a scene designer who was a graduate of Hampton Institute in Virginia, married a Russian woman and stayed in the Soviet Union, where he died during the Nazi invasion of Moscow. His wife, Vera, also a scene designer, was a friend of Ina's.

Homer Smith, a former postal employee from Minneapolis, stayed in the Soviet Union until the beginning of World War II. He got a contract with the Russian postal service and introduced the first special delivery to Moscow.

While I was there, Mother Wright (mother of two of the Scottsboro Boys) was on a tour of Russia and spoke to a whole series of mass rallies, culminating in a huge demonstration and parade of tens of thousands of Soviet workers in Moscow. They went through the main streets of Moscow with placards and banners: "Free the Scottsboro Boys!" "Down with U.S. Imperialism!" "The Soviet Union—Friend of the Oppressed Black." This enthusiastic support of the Russians for the Scottsboro Boys further belied these slanders.

One day I dropped in at the Bolshoi Moscow Hotel to visit some members of the film group. Entering the lobby I saw my old KUTVA schoolmate Golden, and we ran into a Russian embrace. He had gone back to the States in 1928 and had now returned to the Soviet Union with a new wife, a Polish American woman. They had settled in Tashkent in central Asia, where he was professor of English literature at the university. His wife also taught there, and they had a baby daughter.

Golden told me what had happened to him in the past years. Back in the United States, he had found it difficult to fit into party work. "I was neither an organizer nor an agitator, and I felt I was too old to acquire these qualities," he said. (He was then about forty.) "As you know, I never had any party experience before coming to Russia."

He felt that he could, perhaps, eventually become a teacher of Marxian political economy. "You know I was good at that," he said. He was in fact an extremely modest and retiring fellow, not one to blow his own horn. I would say the comrades in the States did not know of his qualifications in this respect. He had worked awhile as the manager of the party restaurant in New York. Then he was sent as an organizer to Pittsburgh, but, as he himself admitted, did a poor job there.

He was a loyal Communist, however, and it occurred to him that there was one thing he could do for the Soviet Union, and that was to organize a group of Black technicians to go there to work. Approaching his old teacher at Tuskegee, the famed Dr. George Washington Carver, he solicited his aid in getting together a group of agricultural specialists to go to the Soviet Union. Dr. Carver seemed enthusiastic about the project and immediately sought volunteers from among his former students.

They eventually got together a group of nine agricultural specialists, agrono-mists, and agricultural chemists. There was also one young civil engineer, Charles Young, the son of Colonel Young—West Point graduate and highest-ranking Black officer in the U.S. Army at the beginning of World War I.

The whole group signed contracts through the Amtorg (Soviet trading orga-nization in the United States). Led by Golden, they left for the USSR. Otto told me he saw them off when they sailed from New York. He asked Golden when he was coming back. Repeating a verse of a once-popular song, Golden replied, "I'll be back when the elephants roost in the trees."

Golden died in Tashkent just before World War II. In addition to working as a professor, he was at that time a member of the city Soviet. He must have been a very popular man because we heard that the whole town turned out for his funeral.

Most of the young Black technicians remained permanently, married, and had families in the Soviet Union. One became head of the largest state poultry farm in the Soviet Union, and another, Sutton, an agricultural chemist from San Antonio, Texas, invented a process for producing rope from rice straw.

My desire to bring Ina back to the States was made known to the appropriate authorities. We had no trouble at all. She was immediately given an exit visa. Naturally, her mother was sorry to be separated from her only child, but she approved of Ina's leaving, saying she wanted her daughter to be happy.

We left Moscow for Riga, site of the nearest American embassy (the Soviet Union was not recognized by the United States at that time). Arriving in Riga, we proceeded at once to the American embassy to get the necessary papers that would allow Ina to enter the United States as my wife and become a permanent resident. At the time, I thought there was a possibility of getting immediate ap-proval so she could come through with me. I knew that this had happened in some cases, but I was quickly disabused of this naive hope.

At the embassy I was subjected to a quiz; the ambassador himself took part in the questioning. I could tell by his accent that he was a polite south-ern gentleman. Behind the mask, I could sense the hostility toward me. I told them I was a writer and had spent time in the Soviet Union a couple of years before. There I had met Ina, and we had gotten married. Now I had returned to bring her back with me. They asked me all sorts of questions about the Soviet Union—how I liked it, what it was like. I gave general answers. It was clear they knew all along who I was.

Finally I was told that they didn't handle visas from that office in this con-nection. I would have to go back to the United States and apply through the

Immigration Department to bring Ina in. They assured me I would have no problem. I should leave Ina in Riga. This, they said, was the normal procedure. The ambassador, keeping up the friendly facade, bade me goodbye in a polite way and wished me luck.

Fortunately, we had friends in Riga. The Armenian Vartanyan, a member of the YCI, had given us the name of his uncle, a wealthy doctor in the city, who had his own health sanitarium. Ina could stay there as a guest as long as she wanted.

The city of Riga was a notorious spy center. A listening post for the United States, it was the nearest place to gather information on the Soviet Union for U.S. intelligence. Many of the anti-Soviet "experts" were centered there, and the city served as a lie factory. For example, they reported 20 million people had starved to death in famines in 1932. I was there that year, and while I saw some tightening of the belt as a result of the bad harvest, there was no starvation. Then there was even cruder stuff about the "nationalization of women"—all invented by newspapermen in the bars in Riga.[11]

I was in Riga just three or four days and regretfully left Ina with the doctor and his family. He assured me everything would be all right. We went to the station, where I caught the train for Berlin; Ina and I embraced, and she watched as the train pulled out. I never saw her again.

From Berlin I went to Bremerhaven and got passage home on the liner *Bremen*. Immediately on arrival in the States I went to the immigration office on Ellis Island to apply for a visa for Ina. Here they were quite rude. One guy asked me, "Who is she—a Communist? We're not letting any Communists in, you know."

I said, "No. She's just a Soviet citizen." They gave me an application to fill out.

I then asked when I could hear from them, and they told me it would be a month or so. "Why does it take so long?" I asked.

They said they had to investigate.

I kept in close touch with Ina, assuring her that things would turn out all right. I also called the Immigration Department, constantly inquiring about the application.

After several months, I became convinced my application for Ina's visa was being deliberately obstructed by the Immigration Department itself. So I started my own campaign, assisted by my friend William "Pat" Patterson, then national secretary of the International Labor Defense. We felt the best way to get results was to threaten the immigration authorities with public exposure—it was a clear case of discrimination against a Black man!

We enlisted the support of several liberals, including Rabbi Benjamin Goldstein, the head of the Committee for the Defense of Political Prisoners, and

Malcolm Cowley of the American Civil Liberties Union. They addressed a telegram to the commissioner of immigration in Washington, demanding to know the reasons for the delay and denouncing this inhuman treatment. "Is it because she is white and Mr. Hall is Negro?" they asked.

We got an immediate reply from the commissioner himself. He denied the delay had anything to do with racial discrimination and said he would like to see Mr. Hall down in Washington so we could talk the matter over.

Pat and I went down to the office of the commissioner in Washington. Patterson, as my attorney, was on the offensive and launched right in. But the commissioner told him to hold back. There's no discrimination here, he told us, but of course, we're not going to let any Communists in. We objected, saying she was not a Communist, just a citizen of the Soviet Union.

Then the commissioner raised the question of my previous marriage. They as yet had no proof of the termination of that marriage. I replied that that was no problem; I would get the proof for them.

Shortly after I had arrived in Moscow in 1926, I had gotten a letter from my sister Eppa. She told me she had run into Hazel, my former wife. Hazel had told her that she had divorced me, was remarried, and had some children. So I assumed there would be no trouble getting confirmation of the divorce.

I immediately went to Chicago and saw my sister. She repeated what she had written to me, told me where Hazel was living, and then took me there to see her. I explained to Hazel that I needed to get confirmation of our divorce. But she said she hadn't divorced me.

"What do you mean?" I asked, amazed.

"You know, it's against my religion. My church doesn't approve of divorces," she said.

I was astounded. Here she was living with someone else and with children, but she couldn't approve of divorce!

I wrote Ina, telling her what had transpired and told her that I thought the best thing to do was for her to go back to Moscow. I would get a divorce as quickly as I could and then go back.

But I got bogged down in work. There was no money for a divorce, and no guarantee that even with the divorce, I would be able to get Ina into the country. I felt very sad about this, and we did exchange letters for a time, but I was unable to get back to the Soviet Union in the thirties, and we eventually lost contact. I later heard from friends who had visited Moscow that she had remarried.

10

SHARECROPPERS WITH GUNS:
ORGANIZING THE BLACK BELT

In the spring of 1933, Haywood Patterson of the Scottsboro Boys was declared guilty by a court in Decatur, Alabama. Following his conviction, a wave of indignation swept Black communities across the country. Mass protest rallies, demonstrations of all sorts, and parades culminated in the Free the Scottsboro Boys March on Washington on May 7–9, 1933.

The right danger took concrete form when the ILD leadership allowed themselves to be suckered into an agreement with the NAACP leadership. These leaders made overtures to the ILD, offering to help raise funds for the mounting legal defense expenses and particularly for those of the Patterson appeal.

This offer, however, was made with conditions that amounted to giving the NAACP veto power over all expenditures of defense funds, and thus over defense activities. It was a ploy that would allow NAACP leaders such as Joel Spingarn and Walter White to regain their position in the defense campaign and appear before the masses as leaders in this campaign.

Since the beginning of the campaign two years before, the Spingarn–White crowd had used every possible means to wrest the defense from the ILD. Their efforts were in vain, but they continued to attack—not the lynchers, but the defense. For example, shortly after the Patterson verdict, the NAACP board of directors stated that the only hope for the boys was to "remove . . . the additional burden of communism."[1]

Now these leaders, largely discredited and isolated, attempted to get back into the defense. The sharp rise in the movement under the leadership of the ILD, which followed the Patterson verdict, forced them to make a tactical retreat. Realizing they had misjudged the temper of the masses, they now attempted to regain a place within the defense in order to more effectively sabotage it. To this end, they made overtures to the ILD, offering to help raise funds.

In an ILD staff meeting that I attended as head of the party's Negro Department, the NAACP offer was discussed favorably by most of the staff. George Maurer, who played a leading role in organizing the Scottsboro defense, and myself were the only ones to object. William Patterson, national secretary, argued that there was no alternative if the organization were to gain the financial support we needed for the Haywood Patterson appeal and the future trials of the other boys.[2] As I recall, our objections were to no avail, and the agreement was carried through.[3]

The deal was obviously set up by Samuel Leibowitz, one of America's leading criminal lawyers, who had become quite well known for his defense of certain gangster types. He had volunteered his services free of charge to the ILD and was accepted as the chief defense lawyer in the trial of Haywood Patterson. He won national acclaim by his brilliant conduct of the defense and emerged as a hero of that trial. On his return to New York from Decatur, Alabama, more than three thousand people poured out of Harlem to greet him at Pennsylvania Station.

Leibowitz was a man of great personal ambition. (He later became a justice of the New York Supreme Court.) He was clearly uncomfortable in the company of revolutionaries and sought to avoid too close identification with the ILD. He brought the ILD and the NAACP together, ostensibly to achieve unity but in reality to weaken the hold of the ILD on the defense and pave the way for an eventual takeover by the NAACP leadership.

The ILD went on to compound this original mistake. They not only accepted the deal but hailed the NAACP leaders for their "changed attitude." In fact, the agreement reflected no change of heart by NAACP leaders. They continued to draw a line between defense in the courts and the mass movement. They tried to confine their support to the courts and moved to sabotage the mass defense movement, both from within and from without. They refused to support the Free the Scottsboro Boys March on Washington, but this proved to be a serious blunder for the already crisis-ridden and isolated NAACP.

Shortly before the march on Washington, our right opportunist mistakes were continued in the Scottsboro Action Committee, a broad united front that was under the leadership of the ILD. The NAACP had become largely discredited, and left reformists like William H. "Kid" Davis, publisher of the *Amsterdam News,* tried to step into the vacuum. Davis, along with Black politicians who served as fronts for New York's Tammany Hall, attempted to set up a new so-called nonpartisan defense committee for the purpose of the march. This was part of their effort to seize the leadership of the growing mass movement that was calling for a march on Washington. Davis attempted to divert it from a mass march into a committee of representative citizens who would present a petition to the president.

At the beginning of this move, the Scottsboro Action Committee tailed after the reformists. They failed at first to see through the left rhetoric of the group's criticisms of the NAACP. But within a short time, we corrected this mistake and regained leadership of the movement. We did the actual organization and formulation of the proposals for the march, which went over successfully.

I participated in the organization of the march on Washington along with Patterson, Ford, and others—helping prepare the program and working out technical details. The march involved people mainly from the cities of the eastern seaboard; there hadn't been time to organize a truly national demonstration. The demand of the march was "Freedom for the Scottsboro Boys," which was tied in with demands in the area of civil rights: an end to discrimination in voting, jury service, schools, housing, public accommodations, and trade unions and the death penalty for lynching. These demands were summed up in the Bill of Rights put forward by the LSNR. The three thousand marchers, led by Ruby Bates, Mrs. Jane Patterson (mother of Haywood Patterson), and William Patterson of the ILD, demanded to meet with President Roosevelt.[4] Roosevelt was in conference with Dr. Hajalmar Schacht, the special German envoy, and refused to meet the marchers.

We did visit various congressmen, who all said it was a matter for the courts; they could do nothing. Oscar DePriest, a Black congressman from the Thompson machine in Chicago, showed his true colors, declaring that we weren't going to get him into this mess! We left the petitions with Louis Howe, the president's secretary, and saw Vice President Garner and the speaker of the House. We then paraded through the streets of Washington and headed home.

After the march, the Politburo of the party reviewed the Scottsboro campaign since the Patterson verdict. The right mistakes before the march arose from a basic misconception of the united front. Behind this was the idea that a united front meant unity with everybody, under any conditions. Involved here was a definite underestimation of the class role of the Black reformist leaders as agents of the ruling class in the ranks of the Afro-American people. Their influence could only be destroyed in the course of building a united front with the masses from below. It was the same as the situation in the labor movement with regard to the labor bureaucracy.

We decided that a resolution should be developed in the light of our discussions; the Negro Department was given the task of drafting such a resolution. We summed up these mistakes in a resolution that was adopted by the Politburo. In its criticism of the ILD's deal with the NAACP, the resolution stated that the ILD should have offered the NAACP a "straight forward and clear proposal of mass struggle and mobilization of the masses against the capitalist frame-up courts and Jim-Crow legal system."

If the NAACP had accepted this program, it would have clearly discredited their past policy of relying on the courts. "If they had refused such an offer, this also would have cleared the issues before the eyes of the masses."

The resolution went on further to state:

In such a broad mass struggle as that of the Scottsboro conscious agents of the ruling bourgeoisie endeavor to come into the united front for the purpose of smashing the mass movement and thus serving the bourgeoisie. . . . It is necessary . . . to warn the masses constantly of the class role of these elements. . . . Under all conditions it is necessary to maintain the independent role of the Party and of the revolutionary forces in such a united front both in regard to our agitation and our actions.[5]

Southern Tour

Our line, projecting the question of U.S. Blacks as essentially that of an op-pressed nation, called for making the South the "center of gravity" for work among them. Though I had spent a brief period in North Carolina, it was not the deep, Black Belt South, the focus of the party's concentration. I was eager to visit the area, to see how our theory regarding the national question and the role of the "Black peasantry" were being worked out in practice.

The opportunity came in the early part of 1933. In consultation with the Alabama district organizer, Nat Ross; Elizabeth Lawson, acting editor of the *Southern Worker* (the party's southern newspaper); and Al Murphy, secretary of the Sharecroppers Union (all of whom were in New York at the time), it was decided that I should spend several weeks in the Alabama district.

Arriving in Birmingham, I had no difficulty in finding the hotel where the comrades had arranged for me to stop. It was on Fourth Avenue, downtown in a small Black business area, near the *Birmingham World,* the city's Black weekly.

When I registered, the owner and desk clerk said, "Oh, yes, Mr. Haywood. We've been expecting you. Your friends will be here shortly."

I was shown to my room, and a few minutes later two young Black com-rades, Hosea Hudson and Joe Howard, came to my room. Both were unem-ployed steelworkers. They had been assigned as my liaisons to the local party organization.

In Birmingham, the South's greatest industrial center, the ruling white su-premacist oligarchy expressed the interests of local capitalist Black Belt planters of the adjacent counties, local representatives of northern based industrial and financial corporations. Most of these latter merged socially with their southern counterparts. At the top of the corporate list was the gigantic U.S. Steel Corporation, sprawling over a section of the town itself.

The principle enunciated by Judge Taney in the Dred Scott decision—that the Black man has no rights that the white man is bound to respect—was still fully operative. Jim Crow laws in public places were strictly enforced. The purpose of it all was to preserve a cheap, subservient, divided, and unorganized labor force of degraded, disenfranchised Blacks and poverty-ridden whites. The latter were psychologically compensated by being accepted as members of a superior race.

In Birmingham, racism was all-pervasive and blatant. One could feel it in the atmosphere. Birmingham was a mean town, a place where the police periodically shot down Black people to "keep them in line," the latter being mostly young and unemployed.

When we walked down the street, Hosea and Joe told me, "If you expect to work down here, you gotta look like the rest of us. You gotta cut out that fast walking with your head up in the air—or these crackers'll spot you. Get that slouch in your walk. Look scared, as if you are about to run," he joked. These were big tough men talking now. Of course they were kidding—still, there was a grain of truth in these remarks.

Now a new element had entered the picture—the Communist Party. Formed in 1930 by organizers from the North, the party in Birmingham took the first steps toward building a union of steelworkers, laying the groundwork for building the CIO Steel Workers Union in 1935. It had initiated a movement of unemployed that organized a demonstration of seven thousand people on the steps of the Jefferson County Courthouse in November 1932.[6]

Though the numbers were not large, the party grew rapidly during the 1932 election campaign. Three hundred Blacks and fifty whites gathered to greet William Z. Foster at an election rally. Foster, however, failed to appear because of illness. The following week, four hundred Blacks and three hundred whites attended a meeting to hear Hathaway; this meeting was broken up by vigilantes throwing stink bombs from galleries. There were also a number of mass meetings called on the Scottsboro issue, including one of three thousand people at the Black Masonic Temple.

The party had chosen Birmingham as the center for its drive into the Deep South and as the logical jump-off place for the development of a movement among the small Black farm operators.

The most dramatic struggle was the movement of tenants, sharecroppers, and farm laborers centered in Tallapoosa County, southeast of Birmingham. The area bordered on the Black Belt plantation region and resembled the latter in respect to farm values, types of tenancy, and racial composition. The first local of the Sharecroppers Union was organized there in 1931. That was before the Federal Relief Crop Reduction Program had been instituted. The small owners, tenants, croppers, and farm laborers were hit the hardest by the crisis. Merchants and bankers had refused to "furnish" or provide them credit. Mortgages left them at the mercy of their creditors. Small operators lived under constant threat of foreclosure and eviction. The wages for farm laborers ran as low as fifty cents a day for men and twenty-five cents for women.[7]

The close proximity to the party organization in Birmingham facilitated the organization of these poor farmers in the area. A number of them had worked in mines north of Birmingham and in steel plants and factories in the city itself, returning to the land to eke out a living during the Depression. There was a continuous movement to and from the city, and those who didn't make the move themselves had close relatives who did. Thus, the development of the sharecroppers' struggle in Alabama, in contrast to other regions of the Black Belt where oppression was equally intense (for example, South Carolina or Mississippi), took a more organized and consciously revolutionary form. This accounts for what struck me as the relatively high political development of union members.

Local farmers sent a letter to the *Southern Worker* in Chattanooga, asking that organizers be sent to help them build a union. The party responded and sent several people, among them Mack Coad, a Black steelworker. Coad, arriving at the scene, met with the Gray brothers—Ralph and Tom—and other local leaders. It was decided that a meeting should be called for July 16, at Mary's Church near Camp Hill, to protest the Scottsboro convictions. Included in the agenda of the meeting would be plans for organizing a union around the minimum demands of the tenants. The most immediate aim was to force the landlords to increase the quantity of "furnishings" through the winter and to double the wages of the plantation laborers. A last-minute arrangement committee of the leaders met the night before, on July 15.

The county sheriff and local gentry were aware of the defiant moods among the sharecroppers. The sheriff had been tipped off by a local stool pigeon that an outside agitator was in the area and that radical meetings were being held. The same stool pigeon informed him about the meeting of leaders on July 15. He and his deputies, seeking the "outsider," raided the meeting. They found that they were all from Tallapoosa County, and they convinced the sheriff that the meeting was just a harmless get-together and that they knew nothing about an outside organizer.

The next night, July 16, the sheriff and his deputies approached the meeting, where they were confronted by Ralph Gray, who had been posted as a picket. Shots were exchanged in which both Gray and the sheriff were wounded. The sheriff and his deputies fled back to town, where a posse was formed amid cries of "Communist-instigated Negro rebellion," and a manhunt began.

In the ensuing battle, five Blacks were wounded in addition to Ralph Gray. A Black cropper helped carry him to his home, where Coad and several other armed Blacks had gathered. The posse approached Gray's home, and a battle ensued. The croppers, faced with overwhelming odds, decided to disperse. Gray, however, refused to be removed to safety and insisted upon "dying in his own home." The croppers insisted that Coad must flee and helped him escape to Atlanta. Gray's home was riddled with bullets by the posse, and when they broke in, he was found dead.

In addition to the wounded, thirty more Blacks were finally rounded up and arrested in the manhunt that followed.

The brutal repression following Camp Hill did not crush the movement; the union regrouped underground and continued to grow. By spring 1932, the union claimed five hundred members, mainly in Tallapoosa and Chambers Counties.

In December 1932, there were shoot-outs in Reeltown in Tallapoosa County involving Cliff James, a union leader in the area. The sheriff had tried to serve a writ of attachment on James's livestock as a result of his landlord's refusing him an extension on a year's rent.

The sharecroppers elected a committee to meet the sheriff, and when the latter arrived to seize the property, he found union members armed and barricaded in the house. In the ensuing battles, the sheriff and two deputies were wounded, one sharecropper was killed, and several were wounded, including James and Milo Bentley. The sharecroppers scattered through the woods. James and Bentley made it to Tuskegee Institute, where, according to several accounts, a Black doctor turned them over to the sheriff. They were then taken to Kilby Prison, where both men, with their wounds untreated, were forced to sleep on the cold floor; both subsequently died from exposure.[8]

This shoot-out was followed by mob action and violence exceeding that of the previous year after the Camp Hill affair. A posse of more than five hundred men went on a manhunt for Black farm operators and "Communist agitators."

Mobs raided homes of union members; several were reported to have been killed or beaten. Many union members fled to the woods for safety, and the number of Blacks killed in the four-day rioting was not known.

I was told that some white farmers had hidden Blacks in their homes during the rampages of the sheriff's mobs. At the time, I was told by someone that the racists had trouble getting enough men for their posses from Tallapoosa County and had to go outside the county to recruit vigilantes.[9]

The bodies of the two men were laid out in Birmingham, draped in broad red ribbons decorated by the hammer and sickle. The *Daily Worker* reported:

> Day and night, a guard of honor, composed of Negro and white workers, stood at attention by the coffins. The funeral home was filled with flowers and wreaths. . . . Thousands of workers filed past the coffins to, pay tribute to the martyred leaders of the sharecroppers.[10]

Some 3,000 people attended the funeral, 150 of whom were whites.

Again terror failed to suppress the union. Despite the arrest of some of its most active members, union members and sympathizers poured into Dadeville (the county seat) before dawn on the day of the trial of those arrested. The courtroom was filled, and the crowd overflowed into the square. On the second day of the trial, roadblocks were put up, and whites filled the courthouse to prevent Blacks from attending. Nevertheless, Blacks came along the bypasses and across streams, demanding to be seated. The judge was put on the spot and requested the whites to clear half the courtroom. The trial resulted in the sentencing and conviction of those accused.[11]

The union nevertheless continued to grow and by 1933 had three thousand members, including a few whites. Its membership and influence were extending to neighboring counties. The shoot-outs at Camp Hill and Reeltown brought into focus the explosive character of the struggle of the region's Black soil tillers. It revealed that the fight for even the smallest demands by the sharecroppers and tenants could lead to armed conflict. In fact, any demand that would give Blacks a voice in renting and determining wages was regarded as insurrectionary by the local gentry.

It was this explosive feature that distinguished the movement of Black soil tillers from that of the white farmers in the rest of the country or even the South itself. The demands of the Blacks were more revolutionary than those of the whites for they represented the demands of the agrarian and democratic revolutions, left unfinished by the betrayal of Reconstruction.

I was eager to visit Alabama and the sharecroppers and curious to know how the union had grown in the face of all that terror. What were the methods of organization they used? Al Murphy told me to go down to the area itself.

Murphy was a tall, jet-hued Black, an ex-steelworker and the most important organizer of the sharecroppers. Soft-spoken and modest to the point of self-effacement, he had given me a rundown on the Sharecroppers Union, playing down his own role and disclaiming credit for its achievements. Murphy was a self-educated Marxist, a genuine worker-intellectual.

He praised the local leaders and their high level of political development. He said that the people built the organization from their own experience and that the croppers had a tradition of underground organization. Any people who had experienced that kind of oppression, he said, would have done the same thing.

Discussing the matter with local comrades in Birmingham, it was agreed that I should go to Tallapoosa County, but I had to wait for them to arrange security. The opportunity came when Lem Harris and Hal Ware, leaders of the party's national farm work, passed through Birmingham on their way to an executive board meeting of the Sharecroppers Union. They were heading for Dadeville.

We left Birmingham at dusk, driving at night so as not to attract attention. The car was a Chevrolet coupe—the two-door model with a fold-down rumble seat in the back. I sat in the rumble seat. When we got to Dadeville it was dark. Hal turned to me and said, "You'd better pull down the top of the rumble seat over you." I hastily complied as we were in enemy territory and didn't want to attract attention.

We soon passed the lights of Dadeville. A short distance out, we came to a farmhouse and stopped. This was Tommy Gray's place. He was a small independent farm operator, and like most of his fellow operators in the area, he was deeply in debt. Greeted by Gray, who had expected us, we went into the house. He had met Hal and Lem at the Farmers' National Relief Conference the year before. He took our coats and put them in the bedroom, which looked like a small arsenal.

There were guns of all kinds—shotguns, rifles, and pistols. Sharecroppers were coming to the meeting armed and left their guns with their coats when they came in. Everyone came and left at night; the meeting lasted, as I remember, two days. There were fifteen or twenty people there, members of the executive board. I was impressed by the efficient manner in which Gray conducted the meeting; they were an impressive group overall.

I was introduced as a member of the party's Central Committee. As I recall, I spoke about the international situation and the Scottsboro and Herndon cases.

Hal and Lem said a few words about the farmers' movement in other parts of the country and the follow up of the national farmers' conference.

I was most impressed by the reports of the leaders of locals about their areas. They described conditions and how they were preparing for a strike, and gave reports on different landlords. I was also impressed that they could spread a leaflet over four counties inside of fifteen minutes. They had a tight underground organization.

I learned there of an attempt to assassinate Tommy Gray. It seemed that Tommy had been fishing at the creek, when he heard a shot and a bullet whizzed past his ear. He turned quickly and saw a man running whom he recognized as Charles Harris, a cropper and union member. The union had set up a committee to investigate the incident, and they brought a report back at the meeting I attended. One of the reporters told the group that they had visited the accused man and uncovered other information. He had evidently been hired by somebody from the town, a sheriff or landlord, to kill Tommy Gray. They had bribed the man with a promise not to call his loan in if he would do their work.

A discussion followed the report, as people wondered what to do with the turncoat. Some argued he should be permanently got rid of. But other, cooler heads, argued that this would only play right into the hands of the sheriff. He would use it as an excuse to come down on the whole group. The sober point of view prevailed. It was decided a committee would visit the man and tell him to get out of the area; if he didn't, then they would deal with him. I heard later that this tactic was successful, and the man and his family left after the delegation's visit.

I left Dadeville in high spirits, more than ever convinced of the correctness of our line; that the Black Belt peasantry under the leadership of the working class and the Communist Party was the motor of Black rebellion in the Deep South. I felt that the Sharecroppers Union was definitely a prototype for the future organization of the Black, landless, debt-ridden, and racially persecuted farmers of the area.

The union continued to grow after I left. By the fall of 1935, it claimed twelve thousand members, including some poor whites; twenty-five hundred of these were scattered in Louisiana, Mississippi, Georgia, and North Carolina. In 1936 in Alabama it had a membership of roughly ten thousand, spread over five counties in the Alabama Black Belt when it was liquidated—a victim of Browderism.[12] In October 1936, the Sharecroppers Union was dissolved and its membership merged into the Agricultural Workers Union and the Farmers Union of Alabama.[13] This latter was an organization of predominantly white small farm owners and tenants based in the northern part of the state, outside the plantation area. This union was strongly influenced by the racist and right-wing Coughlinite forces.[14]

In retrospect, I believe that those responsible for liquidating the Share-croppers Union were motivated by a sort of crude trade union economism, a desire to restrict the struggle of Black soil tillers to economic issues (as if this were possible) and a feeling that the existence of an independent and mainly Black union with the explosive potential of the Sharecroppers Union would frighten off our new democratic-front allies: the Roosevelt New Dealers, the southern moderates, and the CIO leadership. As Camp Hill, Reeltown, and Dadeville amply demonstrated, even the smallest move to change the status quo could lead to armed conflict. In fact, any demand to give Blacks a voice in determining sharecropping conditions or wages was essentially revolution-ary, as it threatened the existing setup. One could almost hear the opportunists sighing with relief upon the union's dissolution.

I recall in the late thirties listening to a garbled report by one of our agrarian specialists in which he tried to explain the reason for the move. The problem of Black soil tillers in the Deep South was just a part of the general agricultural problem, a matter of getting Blacks and whites together against the common enemy. The Sharecroppers Union, with its militant program mainly emphasiz-ing Black grievances, had become an obstacle to the unity of Black and white southern farmers. I took issue with this chauvinist position, pointing out that it contained a crass underestimation of the national character of the struggle of the Black peasantry in the South. I expressed surprise to hear, ten years after the adoption of our revolutionary line on the Afro-American question, what amounted to a reiteration of the old social democratic position that ignored the special position of Blacks in the name of unity. The problem of the Black peas-antry in the South was not exactly the same as that of the poor white farmers in the South or in the rest of the country. It was a struggle against semislave con-ditions reinforced by racist barbarism and, in the long run, for the completion of the land revolution left in default by the betrayal of Reconstruction.

The Sharecroppers Union had represented a renewal of that struggle, a struggle that required special forms and methods of organization and its own leadership. But by 1936, the union was dead, and a grievous blow had been struck against the movement in the South. In the face of the fiercest repres-sion, a sizable party organization with an active YCL and ILD and remarkably high political development had been built in the Black Belt. When the party backed down from the Sharecroppers Union, the whole party structure began to atrophy. By the end of 1943, all the major party concentrations in the South were formally dissolved and replaced by noncommunist education and press associations.

On my return trip to the national office in New York from Birmingham, I decided to stop over in Atlanta for a few days. This would be a chance for me to check on the party's activities in this important city and to see Ben Davis Jr. Ben was the young Black attorney who had courageously and dramatically defended Angelo Herndon in the famous "insurrection" case. It was this case that brought young Davis national attention. Along with Scottsboro, it had become a symbol of the fight for Black rights.

As I neared Atlanta, I tried to recall what I knew of Ben. Although we had never met, I had learned about his background from friends who were active with him in the Herndon defense. Ben's father was a self-made man from a poor Georgia family. He had worked his way into prominence and some wealth in Atlanta and was high in the councils of the Republican Party, once having served as a national committeeman. An old-style Republican in the tradition of Frederick Douglass, he was a determined fighter for civil rights, voting, education, and opportunity for Black business.

He had become owner and publisher of the *Atlanta Independent*, an influential Black newspaper. He was also the district grand secretary of the Negro Odd Fellows, the largest fraternal order in the state. From this position, he was able to build the imposing Odd Fellows business block on Auburn Avenue. Ben Senior had had ambitious plans for his only son. He had sent him to exclusive New England schools—Amherst and Harvard Law School. But the Depression had interrupted these plans.

The Depression had an especially devastating effect on the Black community. Not only were poor and working-class Blacks driven into deeper poverty, but the small and growing Black middle class, which was already on marginal foundations, was almost completely wiped out. Ben Davis Sr. became a victim of the Depression. He lost the newspaper, and the business block passed into the hands of an insurance company.

Coupled with economic decline was the inauguration of Hoover's "Southern Strategy" of replacing Black Republicans with a lily-white faction. Ben Senior was removed from his post as Republican national committeeman, with a corresponding loss of his powers of patronage.

Young Davis returned from his Ivy League education to find this devastated situation. A young Black attorney in the South was forced to work in a very narrow field. It was unheard of for a Black to argue a case against a white attorney. This left Ben Junior with drafting deeds, wills, contracts, divorces, and other such matters relating only to Blacks—a severely restricted arena for his Harvard Law School training. Ben hung up his shingle in the old Odd Fellows building and soon formed a partnership with another Black attorney, John Geer.

He was soon dissatisfied and angry; however, as his frustration grew, he found himself "challenged by the thought of what could be done if one put up a really tough fight for the constitutional rights of Negroes in a Georgia court."[15]

The Herndon case provided Ben with just such an opportunity. Effectively employing a working-class policy in the trials, Ben conducted a militant and aggressive defense. He appeared before the court as a tribune for Blacks and poor whites against Georgia's white supremacist oligarchy. The trial had been a high point of class militancy.

Arriving in Atlanta by car on a Sunday morning, I went directly to the Davis home. Ben and his father and sister (his mother had died the year before) lived in a large house on Boulevard off Auburn Avenue in a Black middle-class neighborhood. The family's past affluence was evident by the five-car garage in the rear of the house. I was warmly greeted by Ben, who had been expecting me. He was a huge, dark-skinned young man: six foot two inches tall with the bull shoulders of a football lineman, a position he had played at Amherst.

Ben showed me into their large living room. We had a long talk before his father and sister joined us. He filled me in on what was happening in Atlanta. By this time he had joined the party and a considerable movement had developed around the Herndon case. An ILD office and organization had been established. The party was still quite small, though there were a number of white members.

The next day Ben took me down to his office on the fifth floor of the Odd Fellows building. He spoke about the threats against him by the authorities and the Ku Klux Klan, which was virtually an arm of the state. Men took off their police uniforms to put on the robes of the Klan. He talked of the hounding and the threats as a result of his fight in the court.

He showed me a hole in the door between his office and an adjoining room. Just a few weeks after the trial, he was sitting at his desk and noticed a kind of tube sticking out of the hole in the door. Ben went up to examine it and discovered it was the barrel of an empty revolver that was set up against the door. He pulled a paper out of the barrel and read the message: "The Ku Klux Klan rides again. Georgia is no place for bad niggers and red communists. Next time we'll shoot."

He also told me about what had happened downtown, at the ILD office on Peachtree Street. A white comrade, the wife of ILD attorney Irving Schwab, was in charge of the office. Ben came into the office, which was in a white neighborhood downtown, fairly often. Once, as he was coming out of the door, a whole gang was waiting for him. He thought they were from the neighboring offices in the building. He was backed up against the wall, into a corner. No one touched him, but they shouted at him, calling him a nigger son of a bitch, threatening to get him or run him out of town.

With the jailing of Angelo Herndon, the authorities assumed they had disposed of one enemy. They now found themselves faced with another one—Ben Davis. In addition, the Atlanta movement had begun to grow. There were mass meetings around the Scottsboro and Herndon cases that had drawn many Blacks.

The ILD was militant and growing along with a small but active Communist Party. While I was in Atlanta, I visited a meeting or two of the ILD and the party. I recall a party meeting that was held in the home of the Leathers, an old white southern working-class family, long active in radical politics.

There seemed to be about three generations of the Leathers living in that house. This included Nannie Washburn, who was then a young mother. Otto had recruited her into the party, and she played a leading role in the Herndon and Scottsboro defenses. She was to remain active in the struggle long after the party's desertion of the South. Jailed in the civil rights and antiwar movements, Mrs. Washburn continued to be a staunch fighter in the cause of proletarian revolution.

I was worried about Ben Davis, about his safety. I didn't think the threats were idle—they could be carried out—especially after the trial, when there was a lull in the movement. Worries I had had in New York about the situation in the South were borne out by what I now heard in Atlanta. The more I thought about the matter, the more I felt Ben should be pulled out of there—for a time, anyway.

I had sized him up as an up-and-coming young Communist, with great leadership potential. He would be a good addition to our growing body of cadres—we didn't need another martyr, we needed living activists. He was such a dynamic aggressive person; if we got him to the center and national work, he would develop more fully as a Communist.

So upon my return to New York, I presented my opinions to the Politburo—we should draw him out of Atlanta. He agreed to come to New York, where he was first made editor of the *Liberator,* relieving Maude White; he later worked on the *Daily Worker.* He became a New York City councilman in the forties and a member of the Politburo of the party after Browder's demise. He grew into an important party leader with whom I was to have strong political differences in later years.

In March 1934, I was back in Birmingham, Alabama. On my previous visit, Nat Ross, the district organizer, had talked about building the revolutionary movement in Memphis, along with New Orleans, the great financial and commercial center of the lower Mississippi Valley. I had agreed on the necessity of such a step.

Memphis, however, would be a hard nut to crack. Twice the party had tried to build an organization there. Twice our organizers had been run out of the town by the Memphis police. First it was Tom Johnson, then, I believe, Mack Coad.

In those days Memphis had the reputation of being the murder capital of the nation. It boasted the country's highest homicide rate and had attained the distinction by police murders of Blacks.[16] In this respect, it was worse than in Birmingham, where the growth of the Communist movement had resulted in curbing police killings, to some extent.

In Memphis, the police were unrestrained; it was open season on Blacks, especially on weekends. Victims were usually among the lowest strata, unemployed, friendless, and homeless migrants from the countryside seeking employment in the city. They fell into the catchall category of vagrants, persons with no visible means of support.

Clearly a breakthrough in Memphis required careful planning and, most of all, capable organizers. Now, according to Nat, these requisites were present. He had received word from members of a Jewish branch of the International Workers Order (IWO) in Memphis that they were willing to subsidize an International Labor Defense organizer. The IWO was a left-wing insurance organization among whose members were a number of communist and party sympathizers. I knew the organization, but did not know it had a branch in Memphis.

Nat also informed me that there were two young comrades from New York available for the project—Forshay, an ILD organizer, and Boris Israel, a young Communist journalist who was writing a series of articles on the South for the *New Masses.* Israel offered to accompany Forshay.

"Now," Nat said, "if we could only find a good Negro comrade."

"When do we leave?" I asked.

He looked at me with feigned surprise and said, "You really think you should go, Harry? And that it would be alright with the Central Committee?"

"Of course," I replied. I was anxious to undertake this assignment, my first organizing job in the South. I could stay there a little while to help get things started and help make contacts with the Black population.

I was then introduced to the young comrades, and at midnight we were on our way to Memphis.

My two young friends, who shared the driving, were in the front seat. When I woke up it was dawn with the Mississippi countryside all around. It was Saturday morning, and we passed a number of trucks loaded with Black share-croppers and their families, apparently on their way to buy "stores" in Oxford. Some of the trucks were driven by white Simon Legree–looking characters, whom I assumed to be plantation riding bosses or planters.

We drew up to the gas station to fill our tank, just outside of Oxford. The attendant, a native cracker type, peered in at me with an expression of curiosity on his face. Then, as if he had figured it all out, he drawled, "What're yo-all doin' with that boy—takin' him home?"

"Yeah," said Boris, with a mock Mississippi drawl, "takin' him on home."

Then turning to me the guy said, "Yo glad to be home, boy?"

Falling into my "field-nigger" drawl, I replied "Yahza, cap'n, I shore am."

We pulled away and drove through the town of Oxford, passing the old state capitol and courthouse, dating from antebellum times. (Oxford's only claim to fame was that it was the home of William Faulkner and the University of Mississippi, "Ole Miss.")

A short distance out of town, we pulled up at the home of a comrade named Ufe, whose address had been given us by Ross. Ufe's wife and sister-in-law were the owners of a small plantation.

As a young man, he had emigrated from his native Denmark and settled in the South, where he married into a former slaveholding family. By this time, the plantation had been hard hit by the crisis and was mortgaged up to the hilt. There were, I believe, five sharecroppers on the place. I was to learn that they considered Ufe a fair-minded man. Their contracts included the right to sell their own crops and the right to plant gardens. The homes were equipped with electricity and running water. Recruited by Ufe himself, they were all members of the Sharecroppers Union.

Despite his wife, Ufe had never imbibed the white supremacist doctrine, and he insisted that he was not a planter but a farm manager. A member of the Socialist Party of Denmark, he had begun to read socialist papers in the United States, then the *Daily Worker,* and he was finally recruited into the party by the Birmingham comrades.

I pondered this unusual story, which I had heard from Ross and others, as we entered the driveway to his home. It was an old rundown antebellum structure with columns and all. Ufe, a small wiry man, had been expecting us and led us into the big living room, where a dozen or so sharecroppers and field hands were sitting before a large open fireplace. It was March cold and a huge log was burning. Ufe introduced us to the sharecroppers.

As we talked, I told them about my visit to Dadeville and other things in the outside world. They all listened attentively. We had supper and stayed overnight. His wife was strangely absent, although I'd seen her puttering around in the kitchen.

We left the next morning for Memphis. Arriving there in the afternoon, we drove directly to the house of a Jewish friend, where the IWO was meeting. Our hostess interrupted the meeting, introduced us, and suggested that the matter concerning our visit be discussed presently, under "good and welfare."

Israel, Forshay, and I sat in an adjoining room to wait. I picked up a newspaper lying on the table, I believe it was the *Commercial Appeal,* one of the city's big dailies. A front-page article—no more than three or four paragraphs long—caught my attention. It was a story about a young Black man named Levon Carlock who had been killed by police the night before, after allegedly attempting to rape a white woman.

According to the story, he had been shot while attempting to escape the scene of the crime. The article listed prominently the names of the officers involved and also the name and address of the alleged rape victim. The murder of Blacks by the police had apparently become such a routine matter that the latter didn't bother to present even a plausible story.

I passed the paper over to Israel and Forshay, exclaiming, "Here's our issue! Let's get to work."

After reading it, they simultaneously declared, "Jesus Christ! That's made to order."

By this time, the meeting in the adjoining room had come to our point on the agenda. I looked over the group. They were middle-class people, storekeepers and the like, several professionals, and, as I later learned, one wealthy jeweler. I was surprised that the majority of the group were young couples, some of them born in the South and speaking with southern drawls. They were very definitely revolutionary in sentiment.

Some were readers of the *Freiheit* (the Yiddish-language Communist daily) and the *Daily Worker.* Several of them, I was to learn, had participated in the two previous attempts to form a revolutionary organization in Memphis. They represented the left wing of the Jewish community in Memphis and reflected the hatred of an entire community for Boss Crump's reigning political machine in Memphis. Crump was not only a rabid racist, but a Jew-hater as well.

As regarded our mission, there was nothing much to be said. We had come there at their invitation. So they proceeded to the immediate question of the subsidy for Forshay, as the ILD organizer. They had agreed on a salary of sixteen dollars a week, with room and board. He was to stay with the jeweler, who had a large house.

Boris also was to stay with Forshay at the jeweler's, and I with a young couple—storekeepers who lived close to the Black neighborhood. That settled, I informed the group about the news article concerning the alleged rape.

Their response was, This happens every day—it was a common thing. They described the beating and killing of Blacks in the station house, of young Black boys disappearing after they were taken to the station by police, about Blacks being beaten unconscious right out on the street.

We were anxious to pick up on the issue while it was hot. We sent Boris Israel to check on the story while Forshay and I remained at the house, where we set up temporary headquarters. We were quite fortunate to have on our team a man like Boris, with his experience and training as an investigative reporter.

Several hours later he returned, having uncovered a shocking story of racism, murder, and police brutality. He had gone directly to the address of the "rape victim," whom he had found to be a prostitute living in the red-light district that adjoined the Black neighborhood. Interviewing her, he had found gaping irregularities in her obviously rehearsed story. At first she had talked openly, unrestrainedly about her "horrendous experience." Then suddenly she clammed up, blurting out, "The police cap'n said I was not to talk to anybody." Then she closed the door on Boris.

Boris then interviewed the widow of the murdered man. She lived in a rooming house not far from the scene. She was just a slip of a girl—sixteen she said, but looked even younger. The incident had left her in a state of shock. She was being consoled by an older woman, who turned out to be a maid who lived in the whorehouse.

She began to tell her story. She and her seventeen-year-old husband, Levon Carlock, were newly married and had just come up from Mississippi, where both their families were ruined sharecroppers. She had gotten a job as a maid in one of the white whorehouses. Levon, who was still unemployed, would come to pick her up every night at about 2:00 a.m. and escort her home.

On the night of the tragedy, he had been waiting out in the street for her as usual, when the police officers shot him down. Overcome by grief, Mrs. Carlock then burst into tears and could no longer continue.

At this point, the older woman led Boris into another room and continued the story. She had seen the whole incident from a second-story window above the alley.

She said four policemen had taken Levon around into the alley. She had heard noises and cursing, cries of "you Black son of a bitch." "You're the nigger that raped that white woman." They were beating the poor youth unmercifully with their clubs and fists, she said.

Levon kept protesting that he had come to take his wife home. Then one of the officers appeared escorting a white woman. She said, "I recognized her as one of the prostitutes that lives across the street."

Then the officers asked the woman if Levon was the one that had tried to rape her, and she said, "Yeah, he's the one." Then she went back to her house.

They started beating Levon again, knocking him to the ground and pulling out their revolvers. Levon begged for his life, but it did no good. "They shot him down in cold blood, right there in the alley," she said. As they turned and walked away, one of the cops said, "You know that nigger son of a bitch is still alive?" I guess they heard moaning. They stopped, and one of the officers went over and pointed his pistol at Levon's head and blew his brains out right there in the alley. Then a short time later, a Black undertaker came and took his body. The police must have had him lying in wait.

Mrs. Carlock had heard some of this but hadn't seen it. She had fainted, and after she had come to, was hysterical. We kept her in the house overnight; the landlady gave her some pills. In the morning, I went with her to the undertaker to identify Levon's body.

Later we got the maid to put her story in an affidavit.

Well, there it was. A perfect issue!

Hoping that through such a mass campaign we could build a party organization in Memphis, we immediately began our campaign to stir up Memphis. We knew that the issue would take hold of the Black population, and we hoped to take advantage of the anti-Crump sentiment among whites to win some of them to our side.

We set out to build a broad united front, under the auspices of the LSNR, which I represented, and the ILD. Then and there we worked out a leaflet, slogans, and plan of action. Our slogans were "Stop Police Murder of Negroes in Memphis!" "Levon Carlock Must Be the Last!"

We called for immediate expulsion of the officers involved, their arrest and prosecution on charges of first-degree murder, and indemnity to the widow. Our program of action called for the establishment of block and neighborhood committees and mass protest meetings.

The slogans caught fire. Within two or three weeks we had a considerable movement going. Outside of our Jewish friends, we knew no one in Memphis, but they introduced us to their few acquaintances among Blacks. Our most important contact was the editor of the *Memphis World,* Memphis's Black newspaper, and his staff. They were sympathetic and wanted something to be done about the murders. Then we met with a number of lower-echelon leaders— ministers, educators, lodge leaders, and a few businessmen. We soon had an ad hoc committee going, while we stayed in the background. A number of meetings were called at which Mrs. Carlock appeared, and some neighborhood or block committees were set up as a result.

At the beginning, we had contacted the national office of the ILD and informed Patterson of our plans. We called for a nationwide support campaign, linked up with the Scottsboro and Herndon campaigns. The national office gave us a green light to go ahead with our plans and get a local (white) lawyer to prosecute our case against the police.

A rain of telegrams from across the country poured into the Memphis mayor's office, and the *Memphis World* carried news of the campaign. Our Jewish friends succeeded in getting a local lawyer, a white anti-Crump man. "He didn't care so much about Negroes, but he sure hated Crump!" they said.

The campaign spread. Its effectiveness was confirmed by two incidents. Our friends on the *World* kept us informed about everything going on in the community. They told us that a delegation of Uncle Tom leaders had gone to see the mayor. They were alarmed by the threat our campaign posed to their leadership—they were unable to keep the Blacks in line. They pleaded for at least some token concession on the part of the police. For example, a statement from the mayor to the effect that an investigation would be held. Something they could use to counter the "red invasion" of the Black community.

The mayor not only refused to budge but told the delegation that the police were doing their duty—and they had better do theirs! The city and police, he asserted, would brook no rebellion from the niggers—and you'd better tell your folk that, too! As regards the "red invasion," the mayor said that he was aware that there were a dozen or so reds in the city and that they would be taken care of when the time came. They were apparently waiting for a lull in the movement to move in.

It was also through the *World* people that we met Robert E. Lee, a lieutenant of Bob Church, the Black Republican national committeeman from Memphis. Lee himself was a prominent man in the community. He sought us out to inform us (in private) that Bob Church liked what we were doing and wanted us to keep it up. He evidently felt that our campaign strengthened his position vis-à-vis Boss Crump.

Daisy Lampkin, national field secretary of the NAACP, came to Memphis in the midst of our campaign. She came there to help the local branch in its annual membership drive and was unaware of the growing movement initiated by the ILD. The whole thing was quite an unpleasant surprise for the woman. The party and the ILD had had run-ins with her regarding Scottsboro, and she became frantic when she found out about our work in Memphis. Her campaign was low key, conducted under the abstract slogan of "Equal Justice and Opportunity," which carefully avoided the burning issue of police murders right under our noses.

The NAACP was in an embarrassing spot. They called a mass meeting in one of the largest churches in connection with their membership-drive campaign. We invaded it, with Mrs. Carlock dressed in mourning black, and demanded a place on the platform for her. As I remember, she was given the platform and she spoke of the murder, asking for help from the NAACP to prevent anything of this sort from happening again. She proposed a united front of the NAACP, ILD, and LSNR against police brutality. The chairman passed it off by referring it to the local board. But after the meeting, Lee told us later, the proposal failed to pass the board by only one vote—he personally had voted for it.

This was to be the beginning of a downturn in our fortunes. Next was the disappearance of our star witness, the maid who worked at the whorehouse. The local attorney asked us to bring her up to his office, but when we went to get her, she had gone. She didn't work there anymore. We speculated that the police had frightened her into leaving town after we sent the affidavit she had given us to the national office and they had published it—either in the *Daily Worker* or the *Labor Defender*. We had had a weak reed in the first place, since she was vulnerable herself to a frame-up.

The legal side of the case was important, but now our attorney was helpless without a witness. Without the legal case, we couldn't keep up with the public campaign, and it began to lose momentum.

The situation was becoming threatening. The cops were getting ready to move in. We discussed this with our friends and they said we'd made a hell of a good fight, but it would be better to send someone else in, now that we were known. So the three of us went into the office of the *Memphis World* and the editor said we were lucky, we had just missed the four cops who were looking for us.

We decided it was time to leave town. We first decided to go by the telegraph station to pick up some money Patterson had wired us. Forshay and Israel went in to get the money. I stood outside waiting for them. Two cops came up and looked at the Alabama license plate on the car.

Then Forshay and Israel came out of the office—Boris took in the scene in a glance. He jumped into the car and shouted at me, "Come on, Sam! Let's get out of heah."

"Yassuh," I drawled, and climbed in the back. We kept driving until we got to Mississippi!

It wasn't a total defeat. Forshay stayed behind and continued to organize for the ILD. Our work put the cops on notice that they couldn't get away with the kind of crap they had been dishing out. The raw stuff had to stop; otherwise they would have trouble. The flood of telegrams had an impact. It also helped lay the base for future activity there.

At this time, the LSNR and the ILD were involved in a number of local struggles against police brutality and lynching, which raised similar slogans. Most notably, we helped to build a broad united front on Maryland's Eastern Shore. A reign of terror had struck the area after the legal lynching of Euel Lee and the lynching of George Armwood. Both men were Black, and both were innocent. At the initiation of the LSNR, we built the Baltimore Anti-Lynch Conference (November 18–19, 1933). Some 773 delegates, Black and white, attended, including Monroe Trotter, who along with Du Bois was a cofounder of the Niagara movement, Dr. Harry F. Ward of the Union Theological Seminary in New York, and Mary Van Cleek of the Russell Sage Foundation. Even some of the local NAACP types were forced to attend. I believe that the widely publicized movement around the conference was successful in bringing a temporary halt to the open terror on the Eastern Shore. Masses of people became aware that the deaths of Armwood and Lee were not isolated incidents. The antilynching movement won many new friends and supporters as a result of the conference.

11

CHICAGO: AGAINST WAR AND FASCISM

Back in New York, I began to take stock of myself as a party leader. I had risen rapidly in the party hierarchy during the four years since my return from the Soviet Union. I was now a member of the Politburo and head of the National Negro Department. Despite the importance of my post, I was dissatisfied with my own personal development. True, I was regarded as a promising young theoretician. But I felt a lack of experience in direct mass work.

Although the general orientation of the Negro Commission was toward promoting mass activities in the field of Afro-American work, I found my job mainly confined to inner-party activities. My actual work included checking on the work of the districts, particularly the Negro Commissions that existed on each district level, consulting with district leaders, training cadres, organizing education on the Afro-American question for national and district training schools, and preparing resolutions and articles on the question. I had little contact with the masses outside the party. Therefore, I had originally welcomed the decision to build the LSNR with myself as national secretary. I had expected it to be an opportunity to get into mass work. The failure of the LSNR, however, had eliminated that opportunity.

I was increasingly tied down to the office on the ninth floor of the party's national headquarters on Twelfth Street in Lower Manhattan and faced the specter of becoming an internal party functionary or bureaucrat.

In this situation my relations with James Ford became strained. Ford was the only other Black Politburo member and now headed the party's Harlem organization, a major concentration point in the party's work among Blacks. Ford and I had disagreements over such things as assignments of cadres, but I felt the main cause of friction was Ford's personal ambition. Ford was a man of considerable organizational ability, but Browder was able to play on his weaknesses and use him as a vehicle for winning the Black cadre to his developing liquidationist line on the Afro-American question. Thus, Ford, supported by Browder, built a power base—almost a clique—in Harlem.

I felt it was impossible to work in this atmosphere. Thus I requested to be transferred to Chicago, something I had thought about before these tensions had matured. My request was approved in late 1934, and I left New York for

Chicago. After my departure, Ford, with Abner Berry's assistance, took over as responsible head of the Negro Department.

As head of the Negro Department, I had kept in close touch with the Chicago comrades. The party in Chicago was beginning to grow. A large number of recruits were from the disintegrating Garvey movement, obviously attracted by the party's work among the unemployed, Scottsboro, and its program in favor of the right to self-determination.

Chicago was the country's second-largest Black city and had the greatest concentration of Black industrial workers. In the early thirties, the city was the scene of some of the fiercest battles of the unemployed.

In the summer of 1930, the city was the site of the founding convention of the National Unemployed Councils. Led by Communists, the councils fought for relief in cash and jobs, unemployment insurance, public works jobs at union wages, hot lunches for schoolchildren, a moratorium on evictions, and an end to discrimination against Blacks. Chicago's first Unemployed Council was formed on the Southside in the fall of 1930, with Black workers playing a leading role. Blacks constituted 11 percent of the city's population but were one-fourth of all the relief cases in the city. Chicago's Southside Blacks were among the worst sufferers of the Depression.

Chicago's unemployed, led by the Communist Party, were exemplary in carrying out energetic activities and demonstrations. Some fifty thousand marched through the Loop to Grant Park in the summer of 1931, halting traffic and forcing police to back off from a planned confrontation. Earlier that summer there had been a mammoth march on the state capital in Springfield demanding that relief cutbacks be restored.

But the real growth and consolidation of the movement followed the police murder of four Black workers (Abe Gray, John O'Neil, Thomas Paige, and Frank Armstrong) as they attempted to prevent the eviction of a seventy-year-old Black widow, Dianna Gross. This event—known as the Chicago massacre—occurred when police opened fire into a large crowd that was trying to put the woman's furniture back into her home.

A local party leader who was on the spot at the time described the tremendous demonstrations and actions that surrounded these brutal murders. The funeral of Gray and O'Neil was the greatest demonstration of Black and white solidarity that she had ever witnessed. Crowds of white people poured into State Street in solidarity with their Black brothers. They marched from Thirty-First Street, behind the coffins, south to the Englewood Station, where the bodies were put aboard a train to return to their homes in the South.

The crowd just took over State Street—there wasn't a cop in sight. As people walked, they carried open sheets with them; the crowds watching on the sidewalk threw money into the sheets to help defray the families' expenses. We estimated over thirty thousand people were there. For a considerable period of time following this march, the evictions were halted and the unemployment movement grew in leaps and bounds.[1]

There was a direct relationship in Chicago between this growth and our work on Scottsboro. The case had a tremendous impact on the Black community there. White comrades doing work among the unemployed told us that the case was really an entrée into the community. Once people knew that they were Communists, they were accepted because Communists were always associated with Scottsboro. The normal suspicion of whites in the Black community was greatly lessened.

The city administration's answer to this growing movement was unbridled police terror. A tool of the corrupt city government and allied with gangsters, Chicago's police force undoubtedly held the record for terror and lawlessness against workers. They were unsurpassed for sadism and brutality, regularly raiding the halls and offices of the Unemployed Councils, revolutionary organizations, and the party—smashing furniture, beating workers in the halls, on the streets, and in the precinct stations. Hundreds were arrested.

In 1930, the police murdered Lee Mason, a Black Communist candidate for Congress. Harold Williams, a party organizer in the Southside and an old schoolmate of mine from Moscow, was viciously beaten. Although hospitalized, he never fully recovered and died a few years later in New York.

It took courage and on occasion ingenuity to thwart the police terror aimed at forcibly stifling and demoralizing the workers' movement. One example of both was Herbert Newton, a Black member of the Central Committee and party organizer in the Southside. On one occasion he was speaking before a large crowd in Ellis Park. The police arrived, determined to stop Newton from speaking and to break up the meeting. But Newton, moving quickly, climbed up an old oak tree and kept right on talking. As the *Daily Worker* reported: "Some of the uniformed killers tried to climb up after him, but their graft-swollen bellies interfered."[2] The crowd laughed as they left and Newton climbed down.

When I arrived in Chicago late in 1934, the Depression was in its fourth year. The determined mass struggle had wrung some concessions from the Roosevelt government, and the spirit of the people was raised by these victories.

I stepped off the train on a wintry day in late fall. I was greeted by a surprise welcoming committee including Claude Lightfoot, Katy White, and John Gray.

They informed me of a banquet they had planned for that evening to welcome me to the district. During the day I visited with my family.

The hall that evening was filled. There were comrades from the district—many of whom I already knew and with whom I was to work in the coming months. There was Morris Childs, district organizer and former Lenin School classmate; Bea Shields, educational director; and Joe Weber, leader of the unemployed movement. From the Southside came Claude Lightfoot, a YCL leader; David Poindexter, from the LSNR; Brown Squire, from the packing houses; Delia Page, active in the unemployed work; Oliver Law, head of the Southside ILD; and other stalwarts. I knew I was among old friends. The speakers were enthusiastic, pledging support for the work on the Southside. They called on all the comrades to intensify their efforts and give me their full support. I was somewhat embarrassed by the overwhelming warmth and comradeship shown that evening, and left in high spirits.

Greetings from another source came the next morning. I was speaking at a demonstration in front of the "Fortress of Misery" relief station at 505 East Fiftieth Street. A police patrol wagon drove up, and several cops jumped out and rushed the speaker's stand. They dragged me off and hustled me, along with Tom Trent (Hyde Park YCL organizer) and Edelman (a young white University of Chicago student), off to the Forty-Eighth Street Precinct Station. They booked us on disorderly conduct or some such ridiculous charge. We then were taken to the Twelfth Street Detective Bureau for fingerprinting and "mugging." Here was my first encounter with Lieutenant Murphy of Chicago's Red Squad.

"Oh, *you're* the new nigger red from New York who they've been banqueting. Well, when we get through with you, you'll wish you were back east. By the way, how's old Williams doing?" (He was referring here to the severe beating that Harold Williams had received in 1931.)

They drove us back to the Forty-Eighth Street Station and threw us in a cell. Shortly after, two plainclothesmen appeared. "You Haywood?" they asked. "Captain Mooney wants to see you." They guided me toward the office and on the way one asked, "You ever met Captain Mooney? Well, you're going to meet him now and I'd hate to be in your shoes." (Mooney later led the Republic Steel Massacre of 1937.)

As they led me through the door, I saw Mooney—big, red-faced and brutal looking—sitting behind the desk. "So you're Haywood—you goddamn nigger son of a bitch, we'll banquet you all right! Now take him away!"

A few hours later I was taken back to see Mooney, and the same scene was repeated. In late afternoon we were taken out and lined up in front of the guards as the shift changed. There were several Black cops among them. "Now get a good look at these three," Mooney told them. "They're around here trying to stir up the poor colored people. Whenever you see them, I want you to run 'em in." After spending the day in jail, we were brought before the magistrate, fined, and released.

The greetings were over; it was now time to get down to work. Chicago District Eight included all of Illinois, parts of Wisconsin, Indiana, Iowa, and Missouri. I was installed as Southside regional organizer. My region included the Southside Black Belt wards, Hyde Park, and Englewood. At the same time, I was elected chairman of the Cook County Committee of the party.

When I first arrived, the mass struggles, particularly of the unemployed, had ebbed from the peak reached a year or so earlier. Strikes and unemployed marches throughout the country had wrenched limited concessions in the form of the first round of New Deal legislation—the National Industrial Recovery Act, Agricultural Adjustment Act, etc. The national economy had improved somewhat—profits had risen significantly, production was 15 percent higher than at the low point of 1932, and unemployment had dropped 3 million, although over 13 million remained jobless. These factors all helped to ease the situation of the masses somewhat. But this upturn didn't affect Southside Blacks much. Last hired, 50 percent were unemployed, as compared with only 24 percent of whites.

At the same time, these improvements signaled a new offensive by monopoly capital. With the depth of the crisis behind them, they were now confident they could put an end to the reforms they had temporarily accepted and move the country in a fascist direction. The Supreme Court declared key New Deal programs unconstitutional. Roosevelt chose to move a "little left of center" to strengthen his position among the workers, and presented the Congress with a second round of New Deal legislation—Works Progress Administration (WPA), the Wagner Act (National Labor Relations Act, which guaranteed labor's right to organize), the Social Security Act (which established small federal benefits for the aged and the unemployed).

The lull in mass activity, the growing conflicts in the ruling class, and the rapidly changing international situation marked the beginning of a new period. All the struggles of the future would be marked by the growing threat of fascism—at home and abroad—and our tactics would change accordingly.

We felt that what was needed was a clear program of action embracing the Black masses together with white toilers, aimed at building a broad united front movement. After much discussion in the region, a plan of action was adopted.

It called for concentration on the three most pressing issues of the time: relief, high rents, and the high cost of living. We called for a special focus on the rights of Blacks, for whom, because of Jim Crow, suffering was particularly sharp. We organized around the slogans of "Drive down rents!" "Abolish rent differences in Negro and white neighborhoods!" "Increase cash relief!" "Smash Jim Crow methods of relief distribution!"

Hands off Ethiopia

On July 25, 1935, the historic Seventh Congress of the Communist International opened in Moscow and met in session until August 21. The U.S. party sent a strong delegation, including an impressive group of Black comrades. Among them were Ben Careathers, Pittsburgh's "Rock of Gibraltar"; Claude Lightfoot (I was happy to see him go to further his political experience); and the share-cropper leader and organizer Al Murphy.

From Chicago, we followed the proceedings of the congress closely. How to prevent fascism, and how to overthrow it where it already had come to power, were the questions facing the Congress. In his main report, Georgi Dimitrov, hero of the Reichstag fire trial, defined fascism as "the open terrorist dictator-ship of the most reactionary, most chauvinistic and most imperialist elements of finance capital."[3]

The congress called upon the parties to build broad people's fronts against war and fascism. These antifascist fronts would include workers and farmers, intellectuals, and all democratic sections of the population. The parties were urged to take into consideration the changed conditions in the world situation and to apply the united front tactics in a new manner. While pointing out the need for such broad unity, at the same time Dimitrov warned against the Com-munist parties' losing their independence and freedom of action and abdicating their leading role within the antifascist front.

In February 1935, Italian troops were already massing in Eritrea, obviously preparing to invade. By summer, Italy openly proclaimed its goal of annexing Ethiopia. The fascist threat to Ethiopia aroused deep anger in the Black com-munities throughout the country. Anticipating the call of the Seventh Con-gress, we Southside Communists seized the initiative to build a broad united front struggle against the growing threat of war and fascism. An emergency Southside conference was held on July 10, 1935, to plan a campaign to defend and support Ethiopia. The response was overwhelming. Over eleven hundred delegates attended, representing all manner of Black community organizations:

churches, lodges, clubs, Black nationalist groups, and the Black YWCA, as well as a number of Italian antifascist groups.

Revolutionary-led organizations such as the ILD, the Unemployed Councils, and the League against War and Fascism, as well as the Communist and Socialist Parties, took part. It was a genuine citywide people's front with the Southside as its base.

From this enthusiastic conference, the Joint Committee for the Defense of Ethiopia was formed. Plans were immediately launched for a mass Hands off Ethiopia parade on August 31, 1935, and a petition drive for five hundred thousand signatures calling upon Congress to invoke the Kellogg Peace Pact and embargo arms shipments to Italy. A demonstration was also called in front of the Italian consulate on North Wells Street before the August 31 parade.

For Black Americans, Ethiopia had always been a symbol of freedom and independence in history and folklore. Masses of Black people strongly supported Ethiopia. Their readiness to defend Ethiopia from fascist invasion was linked to the struggle against the enemy at home. The defense of Ethiopia inevitably became a fight against the growth of fascism right in Chicago, against every petty persecution, Jim Crow degradation, misery, and discrimination.

The city administration made this strikingly clear by immediately refusing to grant a parade permit for the Hands off Ethiopia march. Mayor Kelly, who had just received an award from Mussolini himself, sought to justify this denial on the political grounds that the parade would be an affront to Italy—a "friendly power." (Ethiopia, while friendly, was not considered a power.) But the underlying reason for their fear was what might happen if the Black masses took to the streets—the specter of the massive 1931–32 unemployed upsurge that had shaken Chicago's Southside was still with them. The police and administration knew only too well that the deep-rooted emotion of the Blacks in Chicago for defense of Ethiopia could very quickly develop into a new wave of mass actions among the jobless starving families around the relief stations and against their domestic oppressors in the steel mills and stockyards.

It was evident that the Kelly administration brought pressure upon the joint committee and caused a number of ministers to bolt the coalition. Among them was the Reverend J. O. Austin, minister of the Pilgrim Baptist Church, one of the largest Black churches in the city and host to the July conference. The reformist leaders were afraid of the "red menace," afraid that they could no longer control the movement.

This temporary setback caused us to make a closer evaluation of our united front activity. We had relied too much on building the united front through negotiations at the top and had not emphasized mobilizing the party to work in the reformist-led mass organizations—churches, lodges, and unions. We had clearly underestimated the importance of work within these organizations. After a successful fight against these tendencies, we were able to rebuild the joint committee on a new basis, continuing our efforts to organize for the August 31 demonstration.

Our plan for escalating actions began on August 14, when more than two thousand Black and white workers attended three mass rallies on the Southside. I remember that on this occasion, young comrades in the YCL and the Young Liberators (a Communist-led predominantly Black youth organization) hanged an effigy of Mussolini, to the cheers of hundreds in the crowd.

A planning conference on August 19 at Lincoln Center drew together more than sixty-five delegates and many more unofficial observers and visitors from forty organizations. Reverend Kinsley of the Church of the Good Shepherd was elected chairman of the joint committee, and Arthur Falls, a prominent young Black surgeon, became its secretary. Delegations were chosen to visit leading churches and community organizations on the Southside to mobilize thousands for the upcoming parade. Everyone attending got copies of the call and Hands off Ethiopia buttons to take back to their organizations.

The following day, a delegation chosen at the planning meeting once again visited Mayor Kelly to demand a permit to march. Once again, we were refused. The coalition had by now received the endorsements of the local Socialist Party and the executive council of the Chicago AFL.

The actions continued with a protest at the Italian consulate. I was among a delegation who met with the consul to demand immediate withdrawal of Italian troops from Africa.

The young comrades on the outside, who were very adept at this type of dramatic action, carried on a demonstration during lunch hour. Two young girls, one white and one Black, were handcuffed to a light pole in front of the consulate. They wore white sweatshirts on which were printed the slogans "Down with Mussolini," "Hands off Ethiopia!" It took the police ten or twenty minutes to file through their chains, enough time for a huge lunch-hour crowd to gather and for them to make speeches and shout slogans. Sidewalk as well as street traffic was blocked. To add to the confusion of the police, others showered the crowd with leaflets from the nearby elevated station.

We had other flash actions in the downtown area. A hundred or so of us would blend in with the crowd in the busy Loop area and at a signal from the leader would draw out hidden placards and leaflets. I could see the looks of amazement and disbelief on the faces of the cops when this happened. Having received no instructions from their superiors, the police were shocked to see a full-sized sidewalk parade suddenly materialize seemingly from nowhere. After a few blocks, the demonstrators would discard their signs and disperse. All of these were buildups for our August 31 parade.

This groundwork was successful. The entire Southside community was in a state of anticipation, and in addition the Chicago party organization had mobilized support from all sections of the city. But there was still one hitch. Mayor Kelly and Chief of Police Allman continued to reject our application for a parade permit. The joint committee sent delegation after delegation of prominent people, Black and white, but the chief was adamant—there would be no permit.

Such was the situation at the final meeting of our joint committee on Friday, the eve of the demonstration, where we were to make the final preparations for the parade. Lincoln Center was packed with people. Spirits were not dampened; we were determined to go on with the parade. As the party's Southside spokesman, I was told that I made one of the most spirited speeches. It was unanimously decided that we would "assert our democratic rights" and march in defiance of the police ban.

Parade marshals were appointed and the line of march mapped out. The meeting adjourned amid defiant speeches. But we Communists were under no illusions. We knew that the police would not even allow us to assemble. Our intelligence had informed us that two thousand cops would concentrate in the assembly area, that all leaves had been canceled and extra duty assigned. They were preparing for a real showdown. The defense of Ethiopia had now become a fight for the streets of Chicago.

After the meeting adjourned, we Communists got together. As I remember, there was Morris Childs, David Poindexter, Oliver Law, Tom Trent, and myself. (Claude Lightfoot was in Moscow attending the Seventh Congress of the CI.) What we feared might happen was that the crowds would be dispersed without any kind of demonstration. We felt that this would be a demoralizing setback. Therefore we planned alternate demonstrations, dramatic actions of all sorts, including speaking from rooftops, burning of effigies of Mussolini, blocking traffic, and other actions. In order to carry this out, our people had to get into the assembly area that night (it was already midnight when the meeting adjourned) and stay. We knew that no known Communists would be allowed into the area the next day.

I chose to speak from the roof of a five-story hotel on the southwest corner of Forty-Seventh and South Parkway. I went straight from the meeting and rented a room on the fifth floor of the hotel, concealing a megaphone in my bag. I woke early, went to the roof, and surveyed the scene of the upcoming battle. It was a bright, warm day, and I could see that the police—hundreds of them—were already forming their lines. A string of patrol wagons were visible near the El station, waiting to be filled. I went back to my room and a comrade brought me coffee and a newspaper and reported on what was going on. Around one o'clock I went back up to the roof. The streets were filled with shoppers, men and women returning from work.

Then the demonstrators began arriving; streams of them, striding expectantly down the steps from the El station. And the action began. The police assumed most whites getting off the El in this part of town, the heart of Black Chicago, must be there for the demonstration. They began indiscriminately herding them into patrol wagons and hustling them off to the station. They limited the arrests among Blacks to a few well-known leaders. The whole police plan was orchestrated by Mike Mills of the Chicago Red Squad. Their strategy was to spare Blacks the brunt of the attack because a direct attack in this part of town could set off a full-scale riot. In this way, they hoped to split the demonstrators and thus make it easier to disperse them.

From my vantage point, I could see the scene unfolding. Pandemonium broke loose—the streets were crowded with demonstrators and shoppers alike. As arrests were made, people began shouting protests and slogans. I saw Oliver Law jump up and begin addressing the crowd from a roof very near the El station.

This caught the police off guard, and it took some time before they could get to him. But as soon as Law was pulled down and arrested, another speaker began on a roof across the street. This was repeated five or six times as the police moved frantically to silence the speakers. By this time, the crowd had grown considerably and the street and sidewalks were jammed. Every time we would outsmart the police, a great roar would go up from the crowd, and every time another arrest was made, they would jeer the cops. Milton Howard, the *Daily Worker*'s man-on-the-spot, described the scene:

> There were 2,000 uniformed police with revolvers and clubs lined up through a quarter mile radius from the corners where the demonstration was to have begun.
>
> But the 10,000 Negro and white enemies of war who gathered to raise their voices in solidarity with the independent Negro country facing the war menace of fascist troops were not easily intimidated. Driven

and herded from one corner to another, dispersed by proddings from clubs and revolver butts, scattered groups held stubbornly the immediate neighborhood from the early afternoon far into the night so that hundreds of police had to set a ring of isolation around the area several blocks on either side, blocking all traffic in their fear of a demonstration. Despite provocations, the assembled thousands permitted no breach of their peaceful discipline. The only violence was the slugging of helpless prisoners by the police and detectives in police cars and vans.

For many blocks on either side of Prairie and Forty-seventh Streets police cars guided by members of the "Red Squad" cruised everywhere, stopping and searching cars, seizing every white person in sight, chasing "suspicious" Negroes and whites down the alleys, swinging clubs and blackjacks in an organized sweep of brutality under the leadership of the "Red Squad" leader Lieutenant Mike Mills.

At various corners, Forty-seventh Street and Calumet, Forty-seventh Street and South Park, Forty-sixth Street and other places, speakers arose to speak to crowds only to be dispersed and seized.[4]

All this time the police were pushing the crowd in my direction. Now the crowd was below my building. Just as they arrested the speaker on a rooftop opposite me, I leaped up and began speaking. Because of the huge crowd and the increasing confusion and frustration of the police, I remember speaking for ten, maybe even fifteen minutes. I exhorted the crowd that they had the right to march and parade, scoring Chicago's Mayor Kelly and Chief Allman for importing Mussolini's tactics into the Southside. Indeed, Kelly had merited the decoration bestowed upon him by his friend Mussolini.

Then I felt a blow on the back of my head and spun around to face four plainclothes cops with riot clubs. They started to beat me but one said, "Careful, don't bloody him up. We have to get back through that crowd down there." They gave me a few kicks and dragged me down the back stairs outside the hotel. On the last flight, my spirit rose when I caught sight of an angry crowd of Blacks milling around the alley. "Look at that crowd!" exclaimed one of the cops as they nervously drew their guns.

A big Black woman in the crowd hollered out, "Don't you hit him, you sons of bitches!" The cops waved their revolvers menacingly.

The crowd in the alley pulled back grudgingly. The police pushed me out the Forty-Eighth Street side of the alley, commandeered a passing taxi, and ordered the cabbie to drive to the Wabash Avenue Station. I remember their sighs of relief as the cab got under way. They turned their attention to me, methodically beating my legs and knees, cursing me with every blow.

When we arrived at the precinct station. I was flung into the bull pen, which was already filled with demonstrators, all white, excepting three or four Blacks. I received a few parting kicks as the cops shouted, "Here's Haywood, your leader."

To one side, I could see bloodied people staggering and limping through the door. They were being herded from the patrol wagons, forced to run through a gauntlet of club-wielding, sadistic goons. I glimpsed a woman named Anna, our Chicago district office manager, with blood cascading down her forehead. A *Chicago Defender* reporter witnessed the incredible scene:

> If the people who saw the police break up the parade were surprised at the brutality that went on all afternoon on 47th Street they would have been astonished at the downright savageness with which the police amused themselves at the Wabash Avenue Station. The patrol wagons gathered in such numbers in front of the station to hold up traffic on 48th Street. Prisoners were unloaded in the middle of the thoroughfare. On each side of the wagon formed a long double line of 15–30 police. The unfortunate prisoners were pulled out of the vehicle and forced to run the gauntlet. Their heads, shins and bodies were clubbed by police-men who yelped in glee at the bloody sight.[5]

In the cell, my legs suddenly fell out from under me. It was a delayed reaction to the beating I had received in the taxi. I could no longer stand. My fellow cell mates began yelling and chanting, demanding that they take the more severely injured out to the hospital.

Finally we were taken to the city hospital. Expecting some relief from my injuries, I was greeted by another hellish scene. The emergency room was filled with people injured in the demonstration. The student doctors attending the injured were having a great time.

"Hey, look at this one! What a beaut! Hey, you have to give them cops credit, they sure know how to swing a billy. Look here, cut wide open but no skull fracture—perfect!"

I was given a quick going-over. I was unable to walk but the doctor mumbled, "He'll be all right; now get him out of here." I was taken back to the cell block. By this time the Red Squad was busy screening out the over five hundred arrested. Two cops were swaggering back and forth taunting us. "Goddamn Jews—stirring up all this trouble around here!" "There oughta be a Hitler over here."

"He's already here," someone yelled back.

A white man with his head in a bandage and blood stains on his shirt was explaining, "I'm just an insurance collector. I came over here on my regular rounds and look what happened."

Murphy, the Red Squad lieutenant, responded, "Oh, you don't look so bad, you'll be all right. We were protecting you—we just made a mistake. They must have thought you were one of those reds. You can go."

But there must have been a lot of "mistakes" that afternoon. When they finished, only thirty-five of us were charged with an offense. Late that night, bail was made and we were released. A Russian comrade, a huge man, picked me up and carried me like a baby to a waiting car and then to my apartment.

I was released on Saturday night. In its usual flamboyant and sensationalist style, the *Chicago Defender* reported that I was "beaten so badly that he may lose the use of his legs."[6] In fact, I did have to walk on crutches for a month as a result of the scientific beating from the Chicago police.

The party immediately took the offensive against this attack, linking it directly with the growing fascist menace abroad. Morris Childs, the district organizer, made a militant statement to the press in which he declared that the people of Chicago were against the "imperialist plunder of an independent country" and would stand up for their right to say so freely. He called for a "united people's front against fascist reaction in this city"[7] and urged the people of Chicago to flood the city with telegrams demanding the release of all demonstrators and an end to police suppression of political activity.

The party called for a huge protest meeting the following Wednesday at Boulevard Hall on Forty-Seventh Street. Despite the Red Squad's attempts at intimidation, it was packed with people. Speaking to the audience from a chair, as I was unable to stand, I told the audience that our demonstration had been a brilliant success in showing that the people of Chicago were ready to unite against war and fascism, both foreign and native, and in defense of their right to speak for peace.

There was indignation throughout the whole community about the police attack on our peaceful demonstration. A biracial committee of prominent citizens—including Dr. Arthur G. Falls, chairman of the Interracial Commission; attorney Edith Sampson, who later became a member of the U.S. delegation to the United Nations; A. L. Foster, secretary of the Chicago Urban League; and Robert Morse Lovett of the University of Chicago—was formed to investigate the police brutality. The committee urged that people send protest letters and phone calls to the mayor and to prominent members of the city administration.

The thirty-five of us who had been charged with inciting to riot demanded a jury trial. When we arrived in court, it was packed with our supporters. The prosecutor, on seeing the crowd, asked for the trial to be postponed. During the following weeks and months, the DA asked for postponements each time our case came up. It was clear that they were trying to drag things out, hoping that the momentum of our support would die down.

This tactic of theirs imposed a hardship on us, for we had thousands of dollars tied up in bail that would not be returned until after the trial. The money was desperately needed for defense work elsewhere. Finally, we accepted the deal they offered of pleading guilty in exchange for settling the matter quickly and reducing the charges to disorderly conduct, thus releasing the bail money. This went along with the understanding that the sentence would be a fine of one dollar and one day in jail, which we had already served.

The National Negro Congress

Our campaign in defense of Ethiopia helped lay the basis for the greatest Black united front movement of the period—the National Negro Congress (NNC). Founded in Chicago in mid-February 1936, the Congress brought together representatives of all classes in the national Black community, promoting unity in the struggle around the burning issues of Black rights.

Our activities on Ethiopia merged with preparations for the congress. We were glad that Chicago had been chosen as the host city because it provided impetus for consolidating and extending our contacts and associations. The National Sponsoring Committee for the congress, headed by John P. Davis, who was then secretary of the Joint Committee on National Recovery, set up headquarters in Chicago. We also established a local sponsoring committee with Charles Wesley Burton, a well-known leader in Chicago's Black community, as chairman.

An office was opened on Chicago's Southside. We set up a speakers' bureau and organized canvassing teams that distributed throughout the city the congress call and thousands of copies of the pamphlet *Let Us Build the National Negro Congress*. We approached local organizations for delegates to the congress. We were active in this preparatory work, and the result was reflected in an extremely large Chicago delegation.

The congress opened on Friday, February 15, at the Eighth Illinois Regiment Armory (my old World War I regiment). There was a large crowd milling around the entrance as Claude Lightfoot, Hank Johnson, and I arrived, flanked by several Black notables.

I recognized our old Red Squad enemies, Mills and Murphy, standing off to the side and watching the scene. Not only hatred, but frustration and surprise showed on their faces. And why not? It had been their job to isolate and discredit us Communists. Instead we had become respected members—even leaders—in the Black community. The overwhelming turnout and broad united front character of the congress were testimony to their failure. But we were to learn that they were not yet finished with us.

The armory was jammed with over five thousand delegates and visitors. Some 585 organizations from twenty-eight states and the District of Columbia were represented: sharecroppers' and tenant farmers' unions, 246 trade unions, eighty church and civic organizations, youth groups, political parties, cultural and fraternal groups, and women's organizations. About 85 percent of those attending were Black.

A. Philip Randolph, Black trade unionist and president of the Brotherhood of Sleeping Car Porters, gave the keynote address. He linked up the various issues in the Black community with the need for a united front organization. He pointed out the special significance of developing the antifascist movement and the need for special focus on organizing Blacks in industrial unions. He called for continuing and strengthening the "fight to break down the color line in the trade unions which now have it." He also urged independent political action in the form of a farmer–labor party.[8]

John P. Davis, secretary and a key organizer of the congress, stated its purpose and outlined the agenda for the meeting. Greetings of solidarity from many revolutionary movements throughout the world were read.

The one that excited me the most was that from Mao Tse-tung, then provisional chairman of the Chinese Soviet Republic. The message read in part, "I greet . . . the First National Congress of the fighting Negro people, 12,000,000 strong in America against every form of national and racial oppression." He went on to condemn the fascist invasion of Ethiopia and add that "this struggle must spur you on to strengthen your ranks in a united fighting front, guided by the program of the militant Negro leaders which today raises its voice for a determined struggle for freedom." Chairman Mao concluded by sending greetings from Chou En-lai and Chu Teh.[9]

The next day was devoted to panel discussions and workshops. The large armory floor was covered with groups meeting to discuss particular issues and hammer out resolutions. The largest workshop was on the trade unions, reflecting the significant working-class composition of the congress. The crucial importance of southern Blacks was emphasized by Robert Wood,

ILD organizer from Birmingham, and by Ozzie Hart, president of the Share-croppers Union.

Special sessions were held on fascism and war, civil liberties, and police terror. One of the highlights of the congress was the appearance of Lij Tesfaye Zaphiro, special envoy of Ethiopia's London legation, who addressed the gathering.

The militant spirit and determination of the delegates was continually brought out on the floor. At every mention of the Scottsboro Boys and Angelo Herndon there were prolonged cheers. Tim Holmes, Communist delegate from New York, led three cheers for the defense of Ethiopia, which shook the vast auditorium. When a resolution condemning the Hearst press and urging its boycott was unanimously adopted, the delegates staged a spontaneous demonstration in which every visible copy of the local Hearst sheet—the *Herald Examiner*—was torn to shreds and tossed in the air. Silence greeted the telegram from Mayor Kelly, who conveniently found that he had scheduled an out-of-town meeting and would be unable to attend. When his replacement, Judge Burke, telegrammed that he was suddenly called to the bedside of his dying sister, the audience responded with prolonged derisive laughter.

On Sunday, the closing session established the congress as a permanent organization and called for the formation of local councils throughout the country. The thrust of the program was basically as outlined in the keynote address by Randolph, centering on active support of industrial unionism and the need to combat the growing threat of war and fascism.

The congress passed resolutions calling for the formation of Negro labor committees to oppose discriminatory practices in trade unions and to undertake the organization of unorganized Black workers. The resolution read in part: "These Committees can be a powerful factor in the cause of Industrial Unionism and especially in mass production industry where there are many Blacks." Other resolutions supported sharecroppers' and tenant farmers' unions and called for social security benefits and improved unemployment relief.

On the front against war and fascism, the congress called for increased support of Ethiopia, passed a strong resolution opposing lynching and supporting the revised Costigan–Wagner antilynch bill and calling for continued support of the Scottsboro Boys and Angelo Herndon.

The speakers at the closing session included Norman Thomas of the Socialist Party; Roy Wilkins of the NAACP; Lester Granger, chairman of the Urban League; and Angelo Herndon, who received an enthusiastic ovation. Randolph was elected president of the new organization.

Throughout the congress, we Communists played an active role, participating on the numerous panels. James Ford stressed Black people's stake in the struggle for independent political action in the form of a farmer–labor party. Communists were on the local and national sponsoring committees. The seventy-member national council of the National Negro Congress elected at the conference included about ten Communists.

Our participation during the entire three-day session was, however, somewhat hampered by continual harassment from the Chicago Red Squad. They set up a loose dragnet around the armory and jailed a number of comrades on their way to or from congress sessions. They held them without booking until the congress closed on Sunday. These comrades were mostly second-line leaders. The police knew that any arrest of a well-known leader would have provoked large demonstrations and protests.

The Red Squad's disruptive activities were not confined to harassment outside, or to just the Communists. They clearly sought to disrupt the work of the congress itself. Congress leaders faced daily threats of being thrown out of the meeting hall. In this, the Red Squad had an amenable accomplice in Colonel Warfield, Black commander of the Eighth Illinois Regiment. He had obviously swallowed whole hog the Hearst propaganda accusations that the conference was organized and manipulated by the "reds" and was part of the "general plot" to overthrow the government by force and violence.

Colonel Warfield had even escorted friends of his around the armory, showing them hidden machine guns with standby crews to back up any ultimatum to clear the hall. The colonel, whom I remember as a lieutenant during my army days, was a "back-door relative" of Wallis Warfield. The old Virginia slaveholding family had recently gained some notoriety through their daughter's marriage to the Duke of Windsor. This connection had undoubtedly been helpful in the colonel's climb to eminence in Black bourgeois circles.

While this form of harassment failed, Warfield and his officers were successful in preventing Earl Browder from speaking at the closing session. Browder had been requested by the session's chairman to speak but was prohibited by order of the Eighth Regiment officers. This announcement was received with strong disapproval by the assembled delegates. The issue, however, was not forced because it was the last session and just before adjournment.

In all, the conference was a huge success. All our local activities were given a real boost, especially so in Chicago, with its large turnout at the conference. The party's prestige was also bolstered, and this was to be reflected in later campaigns, like the steel drive and the electoral campaign of 1936.

12

THE SPANISH CIVIL WAR: A CALL TO ARMS

Why did I go to Spain?

For me, as a Communist, Spain was the next logical step. Franco's rebellion in mid-1936 sparked a civil war that became a focal point of the worldwide struggle to halt fascism and prevent World War II. The generals' rebellion against the Spanish people's front government was backed by Hitler and Mussolini, who poured in troops, tanks, planes, and supplies in an attempt to topple the progressive Republican government.

The Spanish Civil War was a part of the worldwide drive for fascism. Spain had become the next item on their agenda, after north China and Ethiopia. The Soviet Union called for collective action to stop the aggression in Spain, but the Western capitalist democracies responded with a so-called nonintervention pact that allowed Hitler and Mussolini to flood men and munitions into Spain while the United States, France, and Great Britain refused to sell war supplies to either side.

Betrayed by these appeasement policies, the Spanish Loyalist forces faced seven-to-one odds in equipment and materials. Fascist atrocities shocked the world as the Nazis used Spain as a testing ground for new weapons.

On April 26, 1937, the small village of Guernica in the Basque province of Vizcaya was bombed by German planes from about four-thirty in the afternoon until eight at night. The population was strafed by machine guns as they fled, and 1,654 people were killed, 889 wounded.[1] Communist parties throughout the world rallied to the defense of Republican Spain and organized the International Brigades, made up of Communists and other antifascist fighters, to answer the fascist aggression.

Our party in the United States took up the call. It came during a time of deep domestic crisis and increasing radicalization of masses of Americans. We were already involved in the fight against domestic fascism and were developing a popular front under the leadership of Communists. There was widespread support for Republican Spain. Over three thousand American volunteers traveled there, making up the majority of the Lincoln and Washington Battalions of the Fifteenth Brigade. More than fifteen hundred died there.

As another step in the fascist plan of world conquest, Spain made the threat of fascism at home more immediate. Although there were relatively few Blacks—not more than a hundred—who volunteered for Spain, there was generally support and sympathy for the Republican cause in the Black community. Already alerted to the dangers of fascism through the defense of Ethiopia campaign, Blacks played an active role in the movement to support Republican Spain, with the National Negro Congress and the Southern Negro Youth Congress adopting strong resolutions against fascist aggression and for collective security.[2]

As a Black man, I was acutely aware of the threat of fascism. Blacks have always faced the most brutal, racist oppression in the United States, but fascism would mean a great heightening of the terror and oppression. I felt it was wrong to say that the conditions of Blacks "could not be worse under fascism." It was through this understanding that I felt the strongest solidarity with the Spanish people.

I was eager to go to Spain. We had carried on an active recruiting campaign for the brigade. Many of my coworkers in Chicago had volunteered—Oliver Law, Tom Trent, Oscar Hunter, and others. Also I felt it would afford me the opportunity to learn many lessons in revolutionary struggle that would be invaluable for our party and my people. Finally, I felt the presence of Black Communists in Spain would help emphasize the solidarity between the Afro-American and Spanish people in the struggle against fascism.

I was reminded of this later on in Madrid when Bob Minor introduced me to La Pasionaria (Dolores Ibárruri), the great woman Communist leader who embodied the whole sentiment of the Spanish people's struggle. She was happy to see me and related how impressed she had been when she had watched the parade of the International Brigades through Valencia on the way to the Aragon front. Leading them was a handsome Black youth carrying the American flag. "How remarkable that Black people, so oppressed themselves, see the relation of our struggles and are here to join us," she said. "What happened to that young man?"

"That was Milton Herndon, Angelo's brother," I replied. "He was killed a few days later on the Aragon front."

Despite heroic efforts, the civil war in Spain ended in a tragic defeat for the world's antifascist forces. The death of the Spanish Republic emboldened the fascists and led, six months later, to Munich, the invasion of Czechoslovakia, and, with that, the inevitable outbreak of the Second World War, in which millions died.

While the people's forces were defeated in Spain, their cause was not. The fascists could claim this initial battle, but the courageous example set by the Spanish people and the International Brigades, even in defeat, inspired millions across the world to stand up to the fascist tide. In the end, it was fascism that was crushed and the people's forces that triumphed. Those who fell in Spain were the vanguard of the victory.

Personally, I also suffered a defeat, a setback that would affect my life in the party for some years to come. My experience in Spain was short-lived, lasting only about six months. It, and its aftermath, which I relate in the following chapter, focus on some of the more negative features of the International Brigades. But they should not be allowed to detract from the overall epic struggle that Spain represented. I have not attempted to detail the political and military history of the brigades in Spain. This has been done in a number of books.[3]

Late in the winter of 1937 I raised the question of going to Spain with Browder, and he tried to dissuade me. I would be the highest-ranking member of the U.S. Communist Party in Spain and the sole member of the Politburo. He had been receiving reports about the problems in the brigade and probably questioned my ability to handle the job. I was persistent, however, and Browder brought it up before the Politburo, where it was reluctantly agreed upon. Within the next few weeks, the party took steps to strengthen its leadership in Spain and sent over several top organizers.

We sailed for Spain on the Île de France out of New York. Our large group of volunteers went through the usual charade of pretending not to know each other—just tourists meeting for the first time. The leadership group was composed of Bill Lawrence, Ed Bender of New York, and Dave Mates from Chicago—all old party functionaries whom I knew. The crossing was uneventful, and we docked at Le Havre, taking the boat train to Paris.

At the headquarters of the International Brigades on Rue de Lafayette we were taken in charge by the French party. We spent a few days in Paris, and I went to visit my friends Otto Huiswoud and his wife, Hermie Dymont. Huiswoud headed the International Trade Union Committee of Negro Workers, which had been in Hamburg until Hitler's rise to power. From Paris we went by train to Perpignan near the Spanish frontier, where a local committee took charge.

We were split up and lodged in a number of farmhouses outside the town. I was impressed by the strength of the antifascist forces, in which the local Communists were the moving force. We were treated with great courtesy and hospitality by our hosts. Lawrence, Bender, Mates, and myself were put up in the same house to wait for our turn to cross the Pyrenees.

While waiting I had a bad attack of asthma. It was the allergic type, which I attributed to some ragweed in the vicinity. I had had such attacks before, and I assumed this would go away once we got out of the area.

One night at about midnight we were roused and told to fall out with our baggage. We were to begin our march, and cars were waiting to drive us south toward the border. After about an hour's drive, we pulled up near a river and got out. This apparently was an assembly spot. A number of comrades were already there, and others were arriving by car.

We formed a column of probably a hundred men—including several guides and a doctor. We marched toward the river, where we were told to strip and wade across. As I remember, the rivet wasn't very wide or deep, but once we were in, we found the early spring water was ice-cold and chest-high. We got to the other bank, dried off, put on our clothes, reformed our ranks, and began to climb. We were told to keep close, not to straggle, because of the French border guards. There were guides in front and file closers in the rear to keep us together so there'd be no stragglers. They set a very fast gait.

We walked quietly, climbing steadily for a couple of hours. My asthma was bothering me, and I had difficulty breathing and found it hard to keep up with the column. It got worse, and I finally fell to the ground, completely out of breath. The column stopped. Two of the young men who were our file closers rushed forward. One stuck a pistol in my side as I lay there, saying, "Get up, you bastard; you volunteered, it's too late to change your mind!"

I knew what was on his mind. He was afraid that stragglers might disclose the secret trails to the French border guards, who were carrying out the orders of Premier Blum's noninterventionist French government to close off the borders.

My comrades immediately interceded, asserting that they knew me, that I was an important antifascist leader, that I must really be ill and wasn't faking. They called the doctor over and he checked me over with his stethoscope. He said, "Yes, this man can't go any further, to do so might cause irreparable damage to his heart."

What to do? The summit and the frontier were a couple of hours away. One of the guides, an elderly man, pointed to a hut on the mountainside, a short distance from the trail. He said it was vacant and suggested I should stay there, rest up, and come over in the morning.

One of my comrades said someone should stay with me; the old man volunteered. The column reformed and marched away, leaving me with the old man. I felt ashamed and somewhat humiliated at not being able to make it over the mountains. I had been in fairly good health ever since I had left the army, but, I thought to myself, I was getting old (I was thirty-nine and no mountain climber).

After resting in the road for a few minutes, I told the old man that I felt I could make it to the hut. He looked at me anxiously as if to say, Can you really go? He insisted on carrying my pack and helped me to my feet. Leaning on him, I made it to the hut. It was a one-room affair with a cot. I flopped down really fagged. He told me to get some sleep, that he was going down the mountain to get some food and would be back shortly. I gave him an incredulous look—You're going down there where we came from? "Oh, that's nothing. I've climbed mountains all my life."

After he left I fell fast asleep and woke when the sun was bright in my eyes. There was the old man sitting beside me, waiting patiently for me to wake up. He smiled—and produced some cheese and wine, which I ravenously attacked. He asked if I was ready to attempt the climb, that it was only a short distance, and we would go slowly, resting whenever I was tired. He carried my pack.

We reached the summit after a series of short hikes and pauses. There we met the guards of the Loyalist Spanish Republic. They greeted us; the old man knew them. They said our comrades had passed through several hours before. They insisted we have breakfast with them. The old man remained. The guards told me to follow the road to the Figueres, an ancient fortress now used as barracks for brigade volunteers.

A truck soon came by, and I hopped a ride into Figueres. I met up with my comrades again, as they had been detained there to wait for transportation. Worried about my health and the possibility of not being allowed to go to the front, I went to see a doctor. After a thorough examination, he assured me that my health was all right and that he saw no reason not to go to the front. The four of us in the leadership group were driven to Barcelona, where we spent the day.

During our stay in Barcelona we spent some time seeing the sights. Walking down the Ramblas de Catalunia, we suddenly stopped and did a double take. It was Bert Wolfe! He also stopped, startled at seeing us. He had been a leading member and chief lieutenant of the Lovestone group and had been expelled with Lovestone from the party in 1929.

What was he doing here in Spain, we wondered. We recognized each other, exchanged startled looks—and then turned and went our separate ways. We were sure he was up to no good, for he had turned virulently anticommunist. Looking back on it, our suspicions may well have been justified. For only a few weeks later, there was a counterrevolutionary putsch of the POUM, the

Trotskyite organization.[4] It was reasonable to assume that Wolfe would have made common cause in their struggle against the Communists.

We left Barcelona and eventually arrived in Albacete, a provincial capital, now the headquarters of the International Brigades. There were five International Brigades: the Eleventh, chiefly German, called the Thälmann Brigade; the Twelfth, chiefly Italian, known as the Garibaldi Brigade; the Thirteenth, mainly eastern European; the Fourteenth, chiefly French; and the Fifteenth, composed of Americans, Frenchmen, Belgians, and Balkans. The Fifteenth, due to the later predominance of Americans, was often incorrectly called the Abraham Lincoln Brigade.

At this time, all the brigades were under the political command of a triumvirate based in Albacete: André Marty, leader of the famous French Black Sea Mutiny and member of the Political Bureau of the French Communist Party, was commander; Luigi "El Gallo" Longo, second in command of the Italian party, was inspector general (he was later to become Togliatti's successor as party chief); and Giuseppi Di Vittorio was chief political commissar. The General Commissariat, under their leadership, was the multilingual command apparatus in which all nationalities were represented. Lawrence assumed the position of American political commissar of the Albacete base, Bender became his assistant in charge of cadre, and Dave Mates left Albacete for Tarazona de la Mancha to become political commissar of the Washington Battalion, which was then in training.

Even before we left the States, we had heard of the terrible losses suffered by the Americans of the Lincoln Battalion of the Fifteenth Brigade at Jarama. Upon our arrival in Albacete, George Brodsky, the acting American representative, filled us in on the details. The situation was much worse than we had expected. The action of February 27 on the Jarama front had resulted in a needless slaughter of American volunteers and their fellow battalion members, the Irish, Canadians, and Cubans. Ill-equipped, largely untrained, and without the promised artillery, air, or tank support, they were thrown against an impregnable fascist strongpoint, Pingarron Heights, in their first engagement.

This attack was carried through on the insistence of General Gal and Lieutenant Colonel Vladimir Copic, and over the protest of Captain Merriman, the American battalion commander. Charging up the hill, the Lincolns were caught in a murderous machine-gun cross fire. It was a virtual massacre.

The results were that our battalion, which had entered the lines with 450 men, had 200 killed or wounded, leaving only 250 effectives on the line. The casualties included most of the officers. Douglas Seacord, second in command; William

Henry, commander of the First Company; and Adjutant Eamon McGrotty were all killed in the attack. Captain Merriman was wounded, as was my old friend and schoolmate at the Lenin School the Englishman Springhall, known to all as "Spring," who was an assistant to the brigade commissar and along with Merriman had led the assault. My good friend from Hyde Park, our YCL organizer Tom Trent, was also killed that day.

The responsibility for this crime lay with Gal, the division commander, and Copic, the brigade commander. Their incompetence was exposed further when it was later learned that a little further down the line there were ill-defended enemy positions where a breakthrough could have been made.

Despite the handicaps and bungling by the brigade and division commands, the Lincolns fought with great heroism and determination. The International Brigades played an important role in halting the fascist offensive aimed at cutting the Madrid-to-Valencia road, the life artery of Republican Spain, and thwarted their efforts to encircle the capital.

After a few days in Albacete, I left for the front, accompanied by Lawrence and Bender. Our front lines were situated along the crest of a hill that rose in a gentle slope from the Morato road, about a kilometer away. About halfway up sat a small Spanish villa that was used as brigade headquarters. Entering the villa, we met Lieutenant Colonel Copic.

Much to my surprise, I recognized him as "Sanko," an old Lenin School student from the Slav language group. He had been one year ahead of me, and so I had known him only slightly. He seemed genuinely pleased that I was the brigade's new adjutant political commissar and embraced me warmly. I learned that he had been an officer in the Austro-Hungarian Army and had received some Red Army training. He spoke English fluently.

He introduced us to the members of the staff. There was Colonel Hans Klaus, chief of staff, a former Imperial German Army officer; George Aitken, brigade political commissar, my direct superior and a Scottish veteran of Passchendaele, the World War I holocaust of British and Canadian troops; Major Allan Johnson, on leave from the U.S. Army and the highest-ranking army officer in Spain (he had come to the brigade after the February 27 disaster); and Lieutenant George Wattis, former British officer and now in charge of brigade staff mess.

Copic took me aside to give me his account of February 27. According to him, the attack on Pingarron Heights was necessary and had to be carried out as General Gal had ordered. Of course it was difficult for the American volunteers to understand. After all, they were no soldiers, he said, but only raw recruits without training—pampered by easy living in the States and unprepared for the rigors of battle. He reminded me that it takes time to make a soldier. We all took a drubbing that day; the Americans were nothing special.

I listened, growing angry at his disparaging remarks. Of course all of this was true, but it still didn't explain the suicidal assault on Pingarron. These volunteers were not the do-or-die type. They were political soldiers, ideologically committed, and they knew who was responsible. Copic's account amounted to a disparagement of the American effort and a complete denial that the command was in error.

We went up to the trenches to meet the men. I was struck by their youth; many were YCLers, and I recognized only a few. Among those I knew was Oliver Law, a former Chicago comrade, head of the Southside ILD and one of the several American volunteers with military training. Law was a veteran of the Twenty-Fourth Infantry, a Black regiment, and was now commander of the Lincoln machine-gun company. He had been an important member of our Southside leadership. I remember him running the police gauntlet at the Forty-Eighth Street Precinct during the Ethiopia demonstration. He had been a victim of Red Squad sadism during the unemployed struggles in the early thirties, when he was beaten up and deliberately kicked in the groin. It seemed right and logical that Oliver should be in the front lines in Spain.

I was happy to see that he had survived the February 27 ordeal, but saddened when he told me that the young Irishman Tom Trent was among those who had perished in battle that day.

I also met Martin Hourihan, battalion commander, a former regular army cavalry man, teacher, seaman, and trade union leader. The fellows were happy to meet us and glad the U.S. party now had some leading members in Spain.

In hopes that we could be of some help, they poured forth their complaints. There were beefs concerning poor equipment, food, and clothing. They suspected some of these problems arose with the Spanish premier Largo Caballero. Rumor had it that the International Brigades were being discriminated against in terms of the limited amount of equipment available because Caballero, a right-wing socialist, hated the Communists. But the men's bitterest complaints were directed at the brutal incompetence and irresponsibility of Copic and Gal. The men had absolutely no faith in their leadership and were particularly angered by the fact that they had had no relief in four months. They wanted adequate American representation on the brigade staff.

I then spoke with Allan Johnson. He was very impressive and struck me as a first-rate officer, a graduate of the U.S. War College who had been a regular army captain assigned to the Massachusetts National Guard. Though he had arrived at the front after the Jarama battle, he felt that the men's complaints were justified. He was particularly outraged at what he considered to be the incompetence of the brigade and division leaders. He felt that they had failed to exercise common sense. His opinion was that something had to be done, at least the removal of Copic, because the colonel had lost the confidence of the men of the Lincoln Battalion.

Lawrence, Bender, and I talked it over and agreed that something had to be done. The two of them returned to Albacete and made an appointment with Marty's adjutant, Vidal. He was sympathetic and advised us to return in two weeks. We returned, and he explained that it was impossible to remove Copic. Vidal assured us that the men would be given relief—new weapons, clothing, and equipment. Also the brigades would be reorganized and divided into two regiments with Chapayev to lead the Slavic group. He then asked who we thought should lead the English-speaking battalions. I answered him immediately. Jock Cunningham was my choice, a well-respected rank-and-file leader. (Johnson probably would have been our first choice, but he had left Spain on a special mission to procure weapons for the Loyalist government and was not to return until September.) Vidal agreed and asked if I would be Cunningham's political commissar. I accepted. Vidal also explained at this point that we would be drawn back from the front for a long-deserved rest—though not right away—and that the plan would be implemented at that time.

These changes would be an important victory for our men, but I unfortunately paid far too little attention to the possible repercussions. I had made an enemy of Copic.

Our battalion was pulled back for a two-day rest at Alcalá de Henares. We were to take part in the May Day celebrations. At this time, Steve Nelson came up to the brigade. I only knew him slightly, but he had a reputation as a veteran Communist organizer and a leader in the eastern Pennsylvania anthracite coal–mining areas. When I met him, he relieved Fred Lutz as commissar of the Lincoln Battalion.

Shortly thereafter, on May 5, Bob Minor came over as a representative of the Politburo for a short inspection tour. We filled him in on the events with Copic. He spoke to the men on the May 3 attempted coup of the POUM, criticizing Caballero very sharply for his attitude toward the brigades, and left a new Dodge for my use.

In the middle of May, I accompanied Al Tanz, brigade supply officer, to Valencia on a matter of supplies and we learned more about the coup. At that time, the popular front government was in a crisis as a result of the POUM action.

Caballero had been hesitant to take military measures against the counterrevolutionary coup. His stand lost him the government, and he resigned on May 16.

A few days later, we heard La Pasionaria speak at one of the big halls in Valencia.[5] She stated the position of the Communists. I went to hear her with Langston Hughes and Nicolás Guillén, the black Cuban poet. I had heard great oratory before, but never anything like hers. She appeared to me tall and stately. She spoke in a calm manner with few oratorical flourishes, hardly raising her voice.

It was a damning bill of particulars, detailing the crimes of the Trotskyist POUM. She described how under their leadership the anarchist "uncontrollables" had set up a dictatorship of libertarian communes in Aragon where they were strong. Now, instead of agrarian reform for the benefit of the peasantry, they had imposed forced collectivization—this in the midst of a bourgeois democratic revolution. "You could win the war, but lose the revolution" was their slogan. She went on and detailed how they had refused to build the people's army and kept the arms in the rear, preparing for an uprising against the popular front government.

She charged fascist infiltration and collusion with Franco's agents. Finally, their activities culminated in the May 3 coup that left the Aragon front wide open to the fascists. Although I knew very little Spanish, I felt I could understand every word. Of course, I was acquainted with the subject, and that helped. La Pasionaria spoke eloquently, holding the audience in rapt attention for forty-five minutes. She built it up slowly and carefully, point by point, to the end of her speech. Lowering her voice, she asked, "What are you going to do with such people?"

Pandemonium then broke out in the hall. "Kill 'em! Shoot 'em!" I had never seen such a demonstration.

The meeting broke down spontaneously into a number of small meetings throughout the hall; people were bringing it down to their local situations, taking the lessons from her speech. She stood poised and calm, waiting for the commotion (which lasted fifteen minutes) to subside. And then a unanimous resolution of support for her and the Central Committee of the Spanish Communist Party was passed.

I returned to the front and pursued my duties as deputy brigade commissar. A political commissar's main job was to inspire morale and the highest spirit of discipline and loyalty among the men for the Republican cause. A crucial task was to establish a mutual confidence and close comradeship between officers and men. It was not a militaristic discipline, but rather one based on the conscious realization that the interest of the people and the army were one.

Our duties required keeping the men fully informed as to the progress of the war and our current military objectives. Our work extended to the smallest detail that contributed to the physical and mental well-being of the men—food, clothing, supplies, mail, rest, and leisure. Our jobs were an integral part of the brigade command structure. Political officers held parallel rank with the military command, and all orders to the troops needed the signature of both. The responsibilities and difficulties of the job were tremendous, and we could not always live up to them.

Our Fifteenth Brigade Commissariat was under the direction of Aitken. We published a daily memo sheet, *Our Fight,* in English and Spanish. There was also a larger periodical, the *Volunteer for Liberty,* which was published in French, German, Italian, Polish, and English. We used sound trucks for propaganda directed at the fascist troops calling on them to join the fight against their real enemies.

The heroic Frank Ryan, a flamboyant Irish journalist and former officer in the Irish Republican Army, was assigned to work with us. On one occasion, we drove into Madrid together to check up on the printing of the *Volunteer.* As we were driving from Grand Via, a main street in Madrid, I realized it was almost deserted. I wondered what was happening. Frank noticed also and exclaimed, "Damn! I didn't realize it was so late! It must be four o'clock!"

Suddenly a shell whistled over our heads and exploded down the street. It was the regular daily shelling that the fascists used to demoralize the valiant citizens of Madrid. The shelling came faithfully every day at four o'clock—you could set your watch by it. It came from Mt. Garabitas on Casa de Campo and was soon to be the objective of one of our offensives.

The men were finally withdrawn for relief to small villages near Madrid. The reorganization plan was put into effect, and the men were given new equipment and clothing. After a few weeks' rest, our brigade was given orders to move to the new front. Our first objective was Villanueva de la Cañada, a well-fortified town on the Brunete road. On the road to Villanueva, we passed many of the Listers and Campesinos, crack troops of the Loyalist army, lined up by the side of the road ready to move out. We realized this was to be a major battle.

We met with stiff resistance and became pinned down. The British Battalion in the Fifteenth Brigade circled to the west to cut the road leading south to Brunete. They crossed just to the right of us under machine-gun cover directed by Walter Garland, the young Black commander of a machine-gun company. Garland had been seriously wounded at Jarama and, after recovering, was sent to the brigade training camp at Tarazona de la Mancha, where he assisted in the training of the Washington Battalion. He served as acting commander until he left for the Brunete front, at which time he was relieved by Merriman.

I had made my way to the rear behind the lines to look over our positions. As I approached Garland's machine-gun company, he shouted a warning, "Get down, Harry, the snipers have a bead on that spot! Captain Trail's just been hit right there!" I ducked quickly, getting out of the line of fire, but a young Spanish soldier was not so lucky. Coming up behind me, he was hit and killed.

Walter was impressive, directing the very effective cover fire that allowed the British to cross the road. Standing behind his men, much like a quarterback barking signals, he would order his gunners into action, the fire pinning down the fascists long enough for the British to make it across.

Our Washington Battalion was under orders to move straight ahead for a frontal attack on the town. The town was well fortified, and we faced heavy machine-gun fire. Our only orders were to keep advancing. This we did, but very slowly. At one point, Martin Hourihan (adjutant to Cunningham) and I witnessed a suicidal charge by our cavalry in which they suffered terrible losses and were forced into a wild, disorganized retreat, nearly overrunning our position. Shaking his head in disbelief, Hourihan, an old cavalry man himself, asked, "Did you ever see anything like that? Horse cavalry attacking such a fortified position?"

Hourihan was severely wounded later that day in the final assault on Villanueva. Our attack proceeded very slowly, and it wasn't until early evening, after being pinned down the entire day in the sweltering heat with little water, that we forced the fascists to withdraw and were able to seize the town. But this delay was to have serious consequences, for it gave the fascists time to figure out our objective and to begin concentration of their troops and matériel on the Mosquito heights, the highest point in the area. Our offensive had lost its element of surprise.

In town I found Cunningham's headquarters; he had moved in with the British Battalion, which was on our right flank. Immediately he informed me that we were moving out. Moving south down the Brunete road, we soon encountered the horrible sight of the bodies of women and children lying in the road, as well as the bodies of members of the British Battalion. Among the latter I recognized George Brown, a member of the British Central Committee and formerly of the Lenin School. He had been a political commissar of one of the British companies.

What had happened? A group of fascists, fleeing the town, had seized some women and children as hostages, forcing them to march in front as a shield against the British fire. Passing the British they suddenly opened fire and threw grenades. Shoving the hostages aside, they rushed down the road. The British, caught off guard by this ruse, tried to defend themselves. But to avoid shooting the women and children, they were unable to effectively reply and took many casualties as a number of fascists escaped.

We continued to march in the direction of Brunete to our new attack position, avoiding the road as much as possible. Hitler's and Mussolini's planes were already bombing the roads. Toward evening we halted for the night. Cunningham was called to brigade headquarters to get the plan of action for the next day. At the time, I thought it was strange that I had not been called. Jock returned shortly and unfolded a military map, asking me if I could read it. Having no experience in military map reading, I said no. He abruptly folded the map and marched off without saying another word, apparently having confirmed some derogatory judgment of me.

I mention this incident because from that time on, there seemed to be a definite cooling in our relationship. At the time, I wondered if there was any connection between this action and an incident with Major George Nathan earlier that morning. I had been standing roadside waiting for the Washington Battalion to pass so I could fall in with them. Nathan, the chief operations officer for the brigades, marched past. Out of the side of his mouth he snarled, "You'll get yours."

This came so suddenly and so threateningly that I was taken aback. I yelled after him, "What did you say?" But he kept going without looking back. Now, putting these incidents together, I began for the first time to suspect that the hand of Colonel Copic was at work, that he had begun lining brigade staff up against me in order to even the score.

The next morning we were to be in position. I had only a general idea of the action. I knew our immediate objective was Mosquito Crest, the dominant ridge in the area, in the foothills of the Guadarrama Mountains, overlooking Madrid. If we took the hill, the fascists' positions at Mt. Garabitas, from which they shelled the city daily, would be outflanked and untenable. Franco would be forced to abandon his salient, and the siege of Madrid would be lifted.

We arose early and were in our attack positions by daylight. In our brigade sector, the British Battalion was on the right, where I was, the Franco-Belgian, Spanish, Washington-Lincoln, and Dimitrov Battalions were all on our left. At zero hour, our men charged up the hill with shouts, hurrahs, and vivas, dashing across the Guadarrama River, which at this time of year was practically dry. Under cover of machine guns, we took the first ridge. By this time, however, the surprise element in the offensive was lost.

The enemy had decamped, moving back to the heights beyond. We stood looking east; ahead of us, beyond a series of ridges and probably three thousand meters away, loomed Mosquito Crest, our objective. We established temporary regimental headquarters on the first ridge in a large dugout, vacated by the fascists. We established telephone connections with the brigade. Our orders were to continue the attack.

After a slight rest, all the battalions moved forward in an attack; British on the right, then Washington and Lincoln. Our regimental headquarters were closest to the British positions, and I watched the British battalion led by its commander Fred Copeman, leader of the naval mutiny of the *Enver Gordon*, move forward. Jock and I remained in our newly established headquarters, as all the battalions moved forward. The brigades came under withering fire from the crest and were forced to withdraw with heavy casualties. It was during this attack that Oliver Law was killed. The men brought back the wounded during a lull following the withdrawal.

During the next few days, a number of attacks and probes were made in the direction of the crest. Now seeing what we were up to, the fascists began a massive concentration of troops and weaponry, artillery, and planes. The air superiority that we enjoyed the first day or two was soon gone. The fascists brought in planes from everywhere. There were swarms of German Heinkels and Italian Cazas that bombed and strafed our ground positions, flying so low they showered us with hand grenades from the sky. All this amid the most murderous heat that I had ever experienced. The sun was a blazing inferno. The Guadarrama River, which the day before had been a trickle, was now completely dry.

By now the food and water problem was acute. The iron rations (reserve supplies) were running out, and we had lost our rolling kitchens; they had failed to keep up with our advance and were scattered along the road, almost to Madrid—sixteen miles away. A main duty of a commissar was to maintain morale; proper and sufficient food was an important item in this task. With the incessant bombing and strafing, the whole network of roads between Madrid and the front was disrupted and supplies were prevented from moving up. I suggested to Jock that I round up the chuck wagons and he agreed. I then left the headquarters dugout, walked down the hill across to the west bank of the river, and found the car Minor had left me at the brigade car pool in the woods. A young lad assigned to me as driver was there, and we drove back in search of the kitchens.

On the road I saw the devastation caused by the bombing. Villages that had been standing when we passed through on our offensive were now reduced to rubble, deserted by their surviving inhabitants. The sickeningly sweet stench of death filled the air. The bombing of the roads was so sustained that several times we stopped, abandoned our car, and took refuge in the woods.

We finally located some of the kitchens. They had pulled off the road to escape the planes. I remember running across an American mess officer from the Washington Battalion, Sam Kaye, who had drawn his whole outfit off the road into the nearby woods. He remained near the road, peering out from a culvert and trying to find directions to our brigade sector. There were several more of the rolling kitchens scattered along the way. I told him to wait until dark and some letup in the heavy enemy bombing and we would then guide them up to our positions. This is what we did, and we arrived late that night.

I spent the remainder of the night with the kitchen crew. In the morning I crossed the river with a Canadian comrade. We started up the hill to the regimental headquarters. Halfway up, we were halted by an ear-splitting and earth-shaking barrage of enemy artillery. We fled from the road and burrowed ourselves into the earth. We were showered with stones and dust but miraculously escaped without being harmed.

What had happened? The British, attacking east along Boadilla Road, ran into the withering fire of fascist artillery massed along the crest and were hurled back with heavy losses. The barrage lasted probably an hour. When the artillery finally stopped, we got up and continued up the hill to regimental headquarters. We found the entrance to the dugout blocked by a number of dead bodies. Among them I recognized Black, Canadian commander of our new antitank group. Charles Goodfellow, adjutant commander of the British battalion, lay dead in the road, cut down while trying to reach the safety of the dugout. We entered to find it crowded with men from the British battalion, those fortunate enough to have escaped the murderous shelling on the road. They had also dragged in a number of wounded comrades. In the dim light I saw Ted Allen, a Canadian newspaperman who was covering the Brunete offensive for the *Canadian Tribune,* a Communist paper.

Jock Cunningham was shouting excitedly over the brigade field phone. He hung up, turned, and continued shouting, this time at me. "Where the hell have you been?"

"Rounding up the kitchens; you knew that," I said

"Fuck the kitchens; you should have been here!"

I was incensed by his comment and even more by his tone. He was like a British sergeant dressing down a recruit. "You know goddamn well you agreed I should go get the kitchens!" I yelled back.

We confronted each other a few feet apart. Then Jock unleashed his crowning insult. "Aw, fuck off. You're no good anyway. You're scared now."

Furious, I started toward him. Ted Allen, sitting close by, jumped up and rushed between us. "Take it easy, Harry," he urged. "This can't be settled now in the midst of battle. You'd better go back to the brigade and settle this later."

I turned and walked out of the dugout, the confrontation over. I made my way down the road toward the river. The main shelling had stopped, but there was desultory fire. Walking down the hill, I thought over the events that had led up to this confrontation with Jock. Again I sensed the fine hand of Colonel Copic behind the whole matter. There had been the incident with Nathan. Our relationship had been cordial, but how was I to account for his actions on the road up to Villanueva? Then there was the fact that I hadn't been called into the operations meeting and the map incident with Jock that followed. Something wasn't right.

As I neared the river, engrossed in thought, I ran into Copic. He could see from my expression that I was troubled.

"What's the matter?" he asked eagerly.

I told him about the argument with Jock. "I told you those guys were no good, but you sided with them against me," he beamed. "What are you going to do now?" I told him I was on my way back to see Steve Nelson.

I found Steve at the Lincoln Battalion headquarters. He had had his own troubles; the Lincolns had also suffered heavy casualties. Oliver Law had been killed. Law's adjutant, Vincent Usera, an ex–marine officer, had left his post without permission and had been dismissed from the battalion staff by Steve and the other officers.[6] Nelson now assumed command of the battalion. I informed him about my quarrel with Jock. His opinion was that it couldn't be settled then in the midst of battle. He suggested that I return to Albacete, pick up Lawrence and Bender, and bring them up to the front within the next few days. Then we could find time with leading American comrades at the front to have a meeting on the situation and decide what to do. This made sense.

The meeting took place a few days later, when the battalion was given rest and drawn back on the other side of the river. Present were Steve Nelson; Mirko Mirkovicz, commander of the Washington Battalion; Dave Mates; two or three other comrades from the front; Bill Lawrence and George Bender from Albacete; and myself.

In the meeting, Steve repeated what he had said earlier. The issue couldn't be settled at that time, in the midst of battle. Jock Cunningham, he pointed out, was in effective command of the regiment. Thus he felt that I should be withdrawn from the front and things should be worked out later. This was unanimously agreed upon.

On my own part, I felt it was the only possible decision that could be made under the circumstances, but nevertheless, I didn't like it. I left the front bitter and frustrated. But now I had time to understand how this situation had come about. I had led the fight for improvement of conditions for the Americans and the removal of Copic. The main responsibility for the February 27 slaughter at Jarama was Gal's, the division commander. Copic, however, shared in it as brigade commander and became the main apologist for Gal—consequently he was the immediate target for the men's anger. The struggle for changes in the brigade brought about improved conditions, reorganization, and a marked boost in morale. It also meant a loss of prestige for Copic, even though he remained as commander.

Copic was aware of my role in all of this. At the front, where his power and influence were greatest, he was at last able to move against me.

Johnson had been the only American on the brigade staff. When he left the front on a special mission, Nathan took his place. Copic easily brought Nathan into his inner circle, which, I reasoned, enabled him to clear the way to isolate me in the brigade leadership. My confrontation with Jock was undoubtedly the end result of this effort to regain his lost prestige.

Shortly after the meeting at the front, Bob Minor arrived back in Spain, this time as official representative of the CPUSA. I was happy to see him. He listened sympathetically to my side of the story and told me that they had heard I was having difficulties. Browder had said that if I couldn't see my way through, I should come back home.

He agreed that my withdrawal was the only thing that could have been done at the time, and that at some future time it might be possible to work me into some position at the front. In the meantime, he suggested that I might consider taking over as political commissar in Madrid. I rejected this latter proposal, considering it a demotion. By this time, I was already beginning to feel that I was getting the short end of the deal. Rather than go to Madrid, I stayed in Albacete with Lawrence and Bender, accompanying them on their rounds of hospitals, checking up on Americans. Bob Minor took me to Valencia and introduced me to leaders from other countries and from Spain.

The battle of Brunete ended on July 28. Of the 360 men in the British battalion, only 37 were left on the line. The remainder were either killed or wounded. The Franco-Belgian battalion had 88 left. The Dimitrovs had 93 left from 450. Only 125 Spaniards remained effective out of 400. There had been two

American battalions with a total of 900 men. Now there were 280 effectives, who were merged into one battalion. They pulled back to rest in villages near Madrid, the same villages from which they had left for the offensive. Officers killed included Nathan. A number of volunteers were given "extended leaves" to return home if they wanted. Among those repatriated were Jock Cunningham and Aitken.

There was now, for the first time, an American ascendancy in the brigade. Although Copic remained commander, Steve Nelson replaced Aitken as political commissar; Merriman, now a major, became chief of staff, replacing the German Colonel Klaus. Gal was dismissed. Johnson returned to command the training camp at Tarazona. The brigade went on to Teruel and then to the Aragon front. It became clear to me that after all this reorganization, all of which passed me over, there was no place for me in the brigade. Minor raised again the question of repatriation, and I agreed.

The fighting in Spain continued for nearly eighteen months after I left. The internationals fought many more battles, and their heroism and fighting spirit became legendary.

But Loyalist Spain was not able to overcome the military superiority of the fascists, a condition forced on it by the nonintervention pact. On March 28, 1939, Madrid fell, ending the three years of bitter fighting. Republican Spain was clearly a victim of the Western imperialists' policy of appeasement. The fascist victory in Spain was another step toward World War II.

I left Spain bitter and frustrated. I was disappointed that I had not fully anticipated nor was I able to overcome the difficulties encountered there. It was for me a personal crisis, but nothing compared to what I was faced with on returning home.

I returned home from Spain in the fall of 1937. Soon after arriving, I heard for the first time the malicious rumors that had preceded me. I was being accused of leaving the front without permission, of running away.

Browder's first words to me were, "Harry, had you been a better organizer you wouldn't have gotten into that fix."

I had to admit that there was some truth in this. I'd done pretty well in Chicago, but there I had had the benefit of collective leadership. In Spain, a more experienced organizer would have moved cautiously, not impulsively as I had. He would have made a more careful analysis of the situation, would have arrived at an estimate of exactly what could be done, and would not have allowed himself to be pushed into premature action. As a staff officer, I lived in brigade headquarters, separately from the men in the trenches. A more experienced organizer would have made a greater effort to get out among the men and spend less time at headquarters.

I had made some mistakes in Spain. But I did not feel anything I had done warranted the type of rumor and slander that I was now confronted with. I had led the struggle to improve conditions in the brigade after Jarama. I had made tactical errors in carrying out this struggle, but I expected and felt I deserved the support of our leading comrades. Now I found myself the victim of a rumor campaign that could only have started in Spain.

I felt that at least the brigade leadership, which now included Steve Nelson and Lawrence, could have explained to the men why and how it was decided that I should leave the front. But they never did. Instead, it was left that "Harry Haywood left the front," providing fertile soil for rumor mongering.

I was in no position to fight the rumors, however. First, I hesitated to bring the whole business out into the open in the midst of the war. Also, to defend myself would necessitate bringing back to the forefront people and events that had drifted into history as the bitter fighting in Spain continued. Gal had been dismissed from the Republican Army for mistakes, including the criminal blunders at Jarama; Nathan was killed; Cunningham and Aitken were repatriated; Klaus had been transferred to the Thälmann Brigade; and only Copic remained of the old leadership.[7] The men who survived Jarama were veterans now. And most significantly, the gross command errors at Jarama's Pingarron Heights were not repeated, thus pushing these events into the background, where they lost the sharp significance they had had while I was in Spain.

I was demoralized and depressed. I had no other course but to accept the decision to leave the matter in abeyance until a later date. The rumors, however, persisted—undermining my role as a leading party member and questioning my integrity. At the time I saw this slander campaign as an unwarranted attack and, personally, as a tremendous setback. Only years later was I able to see how this attack on a leading Black cadre was part of the overall thrust in the leadership of the party to liquidate the national question and our leading role in the struggle. That is, the Browderite leadership made good use of the political infighting in Spain.

In December 1945, Charles Krumbein, an old Lenin School friend and then district organizer for New York, called me into a meeting. When I arrived, I found in addition to Krumbein Bob Minor (I had always had warm feelings toward Bob, which I thought were mutual, despite his close association with Browder); Steve Nelson, former brigade commissar in Spain; and James Ford, one of the few "casualties" from among the Browder leadership.

Charlie began the meeting by saying that they wanted to discuss my future work and resolve the Spanish problem once and for all. As I recall, he said that he did not believe the rumors that I had left the front without permission, and that Bob and Steve had been in Spain and could substantiate this.

It seemed to him that the rumors had been irresponsible accusations directed at "one of our leading Negro comrades." "One can just look—although it certainly isn't necessary—at Harry's World War II seaman's record and see that the rumors were not true," he said.

He concluded by saying that he felt it was time for all disparaging rumors, none of which were ever made into direct charges, to cease. And he added that "Harry should be encouraged to make the kinds of contributions to the party we all know he is capable of." Bob Minor said a few words along similar lines, and Steve Nelson agreed. Only Ford expressed reservations but did not make any specific charges.

Bob suggested that a restatement and elaboration of a revolutionary position on the Afro-American question was urgently needed. It had been nearly ten years since such a presentation had been made.[8] I agreed. I felt at the time that Krumbein and Minor were surely not acting on their own, but rather as a committee of the Politburo set up to investigate the matter. Therefore, I considered this meeting as an official clearance of all accusations stemming from Spain and felt free to concentrate all my efforts toward writing the book. For the next two years I spent the major portion of my time working on the manuscript and did a great deal of reading and research. In the fall of 1948 my book, *Negro Liberation,* was published.[9] It received great acclaim in the Communist press, both here and abroad, and was published in a number of languages: Russian, Polish, German, Czech, and Hungarian. It came to be regarded by the party as a basic text in its field.

13

WORLD WAR II AND THE MERCHANT MARINES

In October 1939, a few weeks after the fascist conquest of Poland, I found my-self in the Veterans' Hospital at Kingsbridge Road in the Bronx. I had suffered a serious heart attack. My condition was found to be service connected, the result of the endocarditis I had suffered while in the army during the First World War. This time the diagnosis was valvular heart disease. I was awarded full compensation, one hundred dollars per month, by the Veterans Admin-istration. After three months' recuperation, I was released from the hospital and advised to take a long rest. Thinking that I might be incapacitated for life, I decided to go to Los Angeles, arriving there in the winter of 1940. I rented a small bungalow on the property of a comrade in the San Fernando Valley and stayed there over a year. It was on Van Nuys Road near the Pacoima Reservoir.

My stay was very restful, and I became a member of the Southern California District of the party. There was a good party organization in the valley and a relatively large circle of sympathizers. The comrades were very solicitous to-ward me.

Our party branch actively organized in the valley for the American Peace Mobilization and we were able to send a strong delegation to Chicago as part of the Los Angeles contingent. Although still recuperating, I helped with this work by giving talks and leading discussions on the international situation and the progress of the war.

It was in California that I met an old comrade, Belle Lewis, who had also come from the East to recuperate from an illness. I was happy to see her again, having known her back east during the national miners' strike of 1931. She was a veteran Communist and organizer for the National Miners Strike Relief Orga-nization in "bloody" Harlan County. During the strike, she had been jailed along with five other women who were framed up and known as the Kentucky Six. Later she was a section organizer in Boston's Black ghetto.

Belle was a handsome, warmhearted woman in her early thirties. She had Slavic features, with a broad face and high cheekbones. We were both lonely and struck it off quite well together. She came to live with me in the valley and later we were formally married. Our union was to last fifteen years.

By the time Hitler hurled his war machine against the Soviet Union, my health had improved and I was feeling as good as ever. Belle and I decided to move into L.A. proper and become more active in party affairs. Browder had sent a letter to the district secretary, Carl Winter, to the effect that the Spanish incident was not to be held against me and that I was to be given an opportunity to make my contributions to the party. I went to the state rehabilitation office for a checkup to see if I was fit to work. To my surprise, I passed the examination with flying colors. The examining doctor told me my heart was in good condition, and he saw no reason why I couldn't do anything I had done before. Encouraged, I asked if I could go to sea.

"Certainly, but I wouldn't advise you to be anything like a stevedore," he said. Still, I was told I was unable to join the army.

Signing Up with the NMU

In June 1943, I enlisted as a seaman in the Merchant Marine at San Pedro, California, the port of Los Angeles. Just like millions around the world, I wanted to make some contribution to the fight against fascism. I knew the history of struggle of the National Maritime Union (NMU) and had long been an admirer of the militant seamen's union.

The NMU was the largest of all seamen's unions, reaching a membership of about a hundred thousand during the war. Its forerunner had been the Marine Workers Industrial Union, organized by the Seaman's International Union (SIU; an AFL-dominated union). The TUUL union dissolved and sent its membership into the SIU. They later helped to lead the rank-and-file revolt against the bureaucratic leadership of the SIU. This revolt led to the founding of the NMU as a CIO union in 1936. Its history was marked by bloody strikes in 1936 and 1937 in which several members were killed by thugs and police.

Through this fierce struggle and with the party's correct leadership, the NMU became one of the most militant, dedicated, and highly organized of all the CIO unions. The union was in the leadership of the antifascist movement both at home and abroad. It actively supported the antilynch bill and demanded full employment and a permanent Fair Employment Practices Committee (FEPC). When Italian fascists invaded Ethiopia, NMU seamen refused to sail ships to Italy. Later they refused to sail steel-laden ships and tankers for Japan. In the midst of very important union struggles, some eight hundred union members left their picket lines for Spain. Over two hundred died in the attempt to defeat the fascist offensive and prevent a new world war. NMU seamen were known as worldwide emissaries of labor: They would contact local unions wherever they docked, offering assistance and support and often participating in labor marches and demonstrations.[1]

As head of the party's Afro-American work, I had known many of the old-timers in the SIU and had worked with some of the men who helped to found the NMU. These included Al Lannon, Patty Whelan, Tom Ray, Johnny Rogan, Hursel Alexander, Roy Hudson, George Mink, Josh Lawrence, and Ferdinand Smith. The latter two were Blacks, and both were on the national board of the union. Smith became the national secretary and Josh, a boatswain, became port agent for the Great Lakes.

A few days after I enlisted, I signed on the Union Oil Company's tanker *La Placentia*. I had no training except as a waiter, so I chose the job of crew mess-man, serving the crew at meals and cleaning up. I was the only Black in the crew. We were bound for Pearl Harbor and Honolulu. Our tanker served as mother ship for a dozen or so PT boats on their way to the Pacific war zone, refueling them on the voyage across and relying on them to serve as our escort.

These boats (patrol torpedo craft) were small, fast, and heavily armed. They carried a minimal crew of three officers and eleven men. Armed with four torpedoes, two rocket launchers, twenty-millimeter antiaircraft guns, thirty-seven-millimeter cannons, and fifty-caliber machine guns, PT boats were pound-for-pound the most heavily armed ships in the war.

In the months following Pearl Harbor, the Japanese met with almost fantastic success in the Pacific and south Asia, despite the fact that their finest force, the Quantung Army, was tied down in northern and eastern China by the armies of Russia and China. By May 1942, most of the major islands in the South Pacific had fallen to Japan, either wholly or in part. Bangkok, Hong Kong, Java, Wake, Guam, and the Philippines were among the territories incorporated into Japan's "coprosperity" empire. Australia was threatened with invasion from the north; Darwin, a northern port city, had already been attacked by the Imperial Air Force. When Burma fell to the Japanese, land supply routes to embattled China were effectively cut, and Japan had a base from which to launch an invasion of India.

It wasn't until May 1942, at the Battle of the Coral Sea, that the Japanese met their first big setback. It was here that they were prevented from taking Port Moresby, Papua, New Guinea, and possibly invading Australia. In the next few months, they suffered major defeats at Midway and Guadalcanal. As we headed into the Pacific war zone, ten months after Guadalcanal, the Allies were preparing to launch their major offensive in the South Pacific.

After two weeks at sea, we landed at Pearl Harbor. In December 1941 it had been the scene of the massive Japanese raid on the Pacific fleet. Now, a year and a half later, the wreckage of Admiral Kimmel's once-proud fleet was strewn over the harbor. Thousands of victims still lay in the hulls.

I went ashore with some shipmates. We took a bus to Honolulu, a few miles away. I found wartime Honolulu pretty drab. The streets, busses, and amusement places were crowded with U.S. military and naval personnel.

We went into a bar on Bishop Street in downtown Honolulu and the white bartender-proprietor refused to serve me. He apologetically said that he had nothing against Blacks personally, but that there had been a bloody fight between Black and white soldiers there just a week before. For that reason he had decided not to serve Blacks at all. My white shipmates started to protest, but I said, "Aw, come on, don't bother." It wasn't worth the hassle. We just walked out and went to another bar.

The marines and the navy, serving as shore patrol in Pearl Harbor at the time, were generally arrogant and belligerent toward us civilian seamen. They called us draft dodgers, dollar chasers, reds, and slackers. We had to swallow hard and just take it. If we fought back, we'd be thrown in the brig, where we'd suffer even more abuse. We developed a real hatred for the navy and the marines.

Their hostility and the racism the military had brought over with it tended to sour my impressions of Hawaii. I had no regrets when, in a couple days, we were on our way back to San Pedro. We returned without escort, having left the PT boats at Pearl Harbor to supplement the Allies' Pacific fleet.

Two weeks later we left San Pedro again, retracing our last voyage back to Hawaii. By this time, the Allies were engaged in fierce battles to retake the Japanese-occupied territories on New Guinea and the Solomon Islands. In six months, as the result of these and later actions, Japan's eastern front would be wide open.

We brought with us another escort of PT boats. Again we dropped the PT boats at Pearl Harbor, but this time we headed southwest to Pago Pago in the American Samoas. It was not a busy port; we were the only ship in the harbor. The Polynesians there were among the friendliest people I had ever met. They had light brown skin and looked like any mulatto that one might see on the streets of Harlem or Chicago's Southside. Families would invite us to visit their homes.

Our next port was Noumea, New Caledonia, a French possession about eight hundred miles east of Australia that had formerly been a penal colony. The New Caledonians were Melanesians, big fine looking Blacks with wooly hair. My interest in anthropology had led me to read extensively about these "Asian Negroes," and I was glad to have the opportunity to meet them firsthand.

After about ten days there, discharging our fuel and refueling small naval craft coming in from the Solomons, we finally sailed out past the coral reefs and were on our way home.

At that time, merchant ships were more heavily armed than they had been earlier in the war. Our tanker mounted two three-inch cannons, fore and aft, and several twenty-millimeter rapid-firing Swiss antiaircraft guns. On our ship these guns were manned by a navy gun crew of eighteen men commanded by a lieutenant junior grade. We merchant seamen performed a vital support role for the armed guard detachment. I served as assistant loader on one of the antiaircraft guns.

In the early morning, about two days out of Noumea, a general alarm was sounded. An unidentified ship had been sighted on the horizon off the port bow. We all rushed to our battle stations and waited. In wartime, we had to maintain radio silence to avoid disclosing our position. We waited for the ship to come close enough to identify it. We knew we wouldn't have a chance against a Japanese warship; it would have blown us out of the water. We were all relieved when the alarm was finally called off; the vessel had been identified as the U.S. troopship *West Point*.

Back home after a couple of weeks in Los Angeles, we got the news that a big troopship was crewing up in San Pedro. It was the *Uruguay*, a former luxury liner on the New York–Buenos Aires run that had been leased to the military by Moore-McCormack Lines. She had now been converted into a troopship and had been carrying troops from the East Coast to Oran and other ports in North Africa. Now she had come through the Panama Canal and around to the West Coast.

Scuttlebutt had it that she was now to transport troops to the Pacific war zone. When they got the news that she was being transferred to the Pacific, half the original crew had gotten off in New York. She made the New York to San Pedro run with only half of her 450-man crew. She was carrying no troops at the time, so it posed no big problem.

San Pedro was mainly a freighter and tanker port, supplying crews of between forty and sixty. The NMU local was hard put for men to fill out the *Uruguay's* large crew and for the new crew ratings required for a large troop transport. The local had to send to San Francisco to help fill out the crew.

The NMU port agent in San Pedro at the time was Oliver Boutee, a progressive-minded Black from New Orleans. The chief union patrolman—the number one port union official under the port agent—was Neil Crow, a tough experienced seaman and a well-respected Communist. The union was determined to put together the best possible crew for the *Uruguay* and started by lining up a solid nucleus of good union seamen. One reason for the special effort was the rumors of racketeering aboard the *Uruguay*. It was a good opportunity to clean up the ship.

Racketeering on board ships—mainly gambling and selling illegal liquor to troops—was a crucial issue for the National Maritime Union. It was a matter of principle—the honor of the union was at stake. In spite of the NMU's 100-percent backing of the war effort, merchant seamen were often the target of the kind of slanderous remarks I have already mentioned. Shipboard racketeering played into these slanders.

Racketeering also prevented the union from handling legitimate beefs about ship conditions. It divided the crew against itself and made it difficult to wage effective struggles to improve intolerable conditions: crowded and inadequately ventilated quarters, unsanitary heads, poor food, and arbitrary disciplinary treatment from officers. Shipboard racketeers were strongly antiunion, undoubtedly often as the result of deals made with the officers to look the other way from the rackets. Having never worked on a big ship, I was, at the time, only dimly aware of these problems and what they meant for the union.

Rounding the Cape

When the day arrived to crew up the *Uruguay,* the hiring hall was crowded. I recognized some familiar faces. Red Herrick was there, a veteran Communist seaman and artist who had made the maiden voyage on the *Booker T. Washington.* The *Washington* was the first merchant ship to be commanded by a Black captain, Hugh Mulzac. Red was a fireman on the ship. I was surprised to see Hursel Alexander, a well-known Black Communist leader from Los Angeles who had never sailed before.

I stood in the crowded union hall, reading the long list of ratings that had to be filled. There were openings for cooks, bakers, waiters, pantrymen, utilitymen, and others in the Steward's Department. I knew my skills were limited, but I had no desire to take another messman job. Neil Crow approached me and said, "We really want you on that ship, Harry. Take the chief pantryman's job," he told me.

I hesitated, wondering why the job was posted when the third and fourth pantryman jobs were not. Why hadn't anyone from the old crew wanted to move up to chief pantryman? I didn't know if I was qualified; the job would put me in charge of about ten men, responsible for preparing salads and hors d'oeuvres, setting up and serving at steam tables, and making beverages, coffee, tea, and desserts for four hundred to five hundred officers. Several friends of mine standing nearby also urged me to take the job. A young man whom I had just met in the hall, Herbert Jeffries, said, "I'll support you, Harry. I'll throw in my card for first pantryman."

With the promise of their support, I agreed. When the dispatcher called out, "chief pantryman," I stepped forward and threw in my card. No one else applied; there was no contest. I felt uneasy all over again, but I had the job.

Upon boarding ship, my ability to perform the chief pantryman's job was immediately challenged by the chef. He was an Argentinian, an old chef from the *Uruguay*'s days as a luxury liner, and a rabid white chauvinist. When he saw me he scowled. "So you're the chief pantryman!" I said I was.

"Well, make me up four gallons of French dressing, four gallons of thousand island, four gallons of Russian dressing, a gallon of tartar sauce, and four gallons of mayonnaise."

It was clearly a challenge to my ability, especially making mayonnaise from scratch. I was taken aback because I'd never done it before. I sought out Jeffries, who had promised to back me up, but he didn't know how to make mayonnaise either. Fortunately the second pantryman, a Swede, stepped in and saved the day. I passed the chef's "test," to his great disappointment, and had no more problems of this type during the voyage.

We left San Pedro on November 9, 1943, bound for the South Pacific and eventually Bombay, India. Approximately five thousand troops were on board. In contrast to *La Placentia,* a large portion of *Uruguay*'s crew was Black, especially in the Steward's Department. On the first day out we organized a union ship committee that consisted of one delegate and an alternate delegate from each department—Deck, Engine, and Steward's. A meeting of the crew was called, and Red Herrick was elected ship chairman. The meeting was general, a statement of union principles was made, the need for a clean ship was emphasized, and every man was urged to do his job. There was no controversy and it was uneventful.

Two or three days out, however, racketeering became an issue. My third and fourth pantrymen were arrested by the ship's military police and charged with selling liquor to the soldiers. The military police had raided their bunk rooms and found the bulkheads packed with cases of liquor, a virtual warehouse of smuggled booze. How did they get all that contraband aboard, I wondered? Obviously these men had connections with shoreside gangsters. They were put in the brig for the remainder of the three-month voyage. Now it was clear to me why these men had not put in for the chief pantryman's job. They didn't need the extra pay and didn't want the extra responsibility.

But this was not all. The ship was swarming with a number of rackets. There was a cigarette racket, controlled by a storeman. He smuggled aboard entire cases of cigarettes and when we reached Bombay, sold them at fantastic profits. But the greatest of all the rackets was the nightly crap and poker games. They were run by two glory hole (crews' quarters) stewards, the lowest rating on the ship. The stewards were big-time professional gamblers and had the entire operation well organized. They were surrounded by toadies and sycophants who covered their jobs for them and even served them special food and the best scotch while they lay around all day in their bunks.

These men and their circle of cronies were corrupting a significant section of the crew and represented the main obstacle to any united action to improve conditions on the ship. In ship meetings they were always the greatest patriots and red-baited the union, warning against Communists that were out to "disrupt" the ship. We struggled against these phonies during the entire three-month voyage and after several tense incidents were finally able to isolate them.

Our first port of call was Hobart, Tasmania, an island southeast of Australia on the Tasman Sea. A few days before arriving, we picked up two army transports that continued sailing with us all the way to Bombay.

Our stay was short, only twenty-four hours, but a welcome break after the long, lonely Pacific crossing. Hobart, a very pleasant town, was a resort and vacation area for Australians.

Leaving Hobart, we stood for Freemantle, the port of Perth on the west coast of Australia, sailing the rough seas of the Great Australian Bight. In Perth, I had my first impressions of Australia. It seemed a white man's country to me then—I never saw any of the native inhabitants—but strangely I felt no antagonism. On the contrary, everyone was very friendly toward us Black seamen.

We were aware of the immigration bar against Asians and Blacks, which was rigidly enforced. When asked about this, the Aussies assured us it wasn't a racist law—"It's got nothing to do with you guys . . . and certainly we're friendly with the Chinese."

I thought to myself, "Well they should be, for the Chinese were a major factor in preventing a Japanese fascist invasion of Australia by pinning down Japan's main armies in north China."

They told us, "It's a law brought in by the labor government to prevent

Australian capitalists from importing coolie labor and undercutting the white Australian workers." The irony of this explanation didn't even occur to the Australians.

We found ourselves warmly greeted as we went sightseeing through the city of Perth. Several members of an Australian artillery regiment invited us to "bring all our friends" and come to a dance that night at their barracks just outside of Freemantle. We turned out in large numbers and were waltzing Matildas all night long. It was a great party and didn't break up until nearly daylight. When we sailed several days later, we bid them all goodbye.

We were glad to see the two Dutch cruisers that would escort us to Bombay. We felt these were particularly hostile waters since much of the territory on the coast of the Bay of Bengal was occupied by the Japanese, as were the Andaman Islands some eighteen hundred miles east of India. Even now, as we sailed through the Indian Ocean with our "cargo" of U.S. troops bound for Bombay, the Japanese were massing their forces in Burma preparatory to invading eastern India.

Six weeks out of San Pedro, we docked in Bombay. I wanted to find the Communist Party headquarters to see if it would be possible to meet with some of the Indian comrades I had known at KUTVA. This proved to be a simple task. I asked a longshoreman who gave me directions to the party headquarters. Several comrades, Hursel Alexander, Red Herrick, and I went downtown and found the party headquarters. It was an impressive four- or five-story building on a main street, with a red flag with hammer and sickle flying from its roof.

Walking in, we identified ourselves to the first person we saw—a young man who turned out to be a member of the Central Committee of the Indian party. I explained that we were American Communists and that I was interested in seeing some of the Indians I had known in Moscow. I didn't know their real names, but I gave the young man several descriptions. He asked what years I had been in Moscow. When I said 1926–30, his face showed real interest.

"Well," he said, "I think something can be arranged. Why don't you and your friends come back here at about six o'clock for dinner?"

Hursel, myself, and several others came back that evening and went upstairs. We took our shoes off in the hall, as was the custom, and entered in our stocking feet. There they were, my old friends from Moscow. Nada, a beautiful Indian woman, rushed to embrace me. There was Sakorov, my old roommate and close friend, one of the founders of the Indian CP. He told me he was now on the Central Committee and was party representative to the National Indian Congress for the Bombay District.

There was also Patel, who had toured the United States before the war as a representative of Indian students. His tour had been sponsored by the American Youth Congress. He was now Communist Party district organizer for Bombay. There were also several of the old Sikhs who grabbed me, "Harry! Harry!" My friends sat us down and we all ate and swapped tales about old times and about the political situation in our respective countries.

Nada was now president of the Bombay chapter of the Friends of the Soviet Union. Before, she had been a nationally known Communist youth leader. She invited us to come visit a group at the University of Bombay. The next day we met with a bunch of young students there and talked politics over cups of Indian tea.

Our troops disembarked at Bombay, and after about six days we pulled out of the harbor with a very light load: a handful of passengers, a few military hospital patients, and some diplomatic types. We headed for Cape Town, sailing down through the Indian Ocean ever watchful for the Japanese submarines that had been reported off Madagascar. As we neared Cape Town, a notice appeared on the ship's bulletin board, something to the effect that "the people of South Africa have certain customs and laws as to race. While they are not ours, we should all respect them; remember we are in their country and don't start any trouble."

A bunch of us, about half Black and half white, got off the ship together and went straight into a dockside bar. No sooner did we get in than the bartender started yelling, "Now wait a minute, fellows, the Blacks over here and the whites over there."

Some of our white shipmates started to protest, but we Blacks said, "What the hell, we want a drink, man. We know this is South Africa. Damn it, you know we can't fight this thing now—let's get a drink." We settled for salutes across the bar.

I went up to the Sixth District, Cape Town's Black ghetto, with some of my Black shipmates. I was never so depressed in my life. The oppression of the people was complete. I'd seen nothing like it, even in "darkest Mississippi." There Blacks at least had some kind of cultural institutions—churches, lodges, and so forth. Here they had nothing. They had been forced from the land and pushed into oppressive native "reserves." These reserves in turn served as labor reservoirs for the city, where Blacks were crowded into ghettos and their tribal structures and institutions completely destroyed. Their culture had been stolen from them. Whites were warned not to go into the area after dark, as a number of whites had been murdered there. This seemed like a kind of spontaneous rebellion to me.

As I walked down the street, I heard two Blacks speaking in a strange and beautiful language. I stopped and asked them what it was. They answered in perfect English that it was Xhosa, their tribal language. It sounded almost musical to me.

Back downtown, I went into a restaurant for natives, but the white owner refused to serve me. "But I'm Black," I protested. "Yeah, but you're not one of ours."

I made my way to the Communist Party headquarters and was surprised to find that, as in Bombay, it was located on a main street downtown. There was a young white woman at the office to whom I introduced myself. She seemed to recognize my name. She was the wife of an Indian member of the Central Committee. She said, "It's so unfortunate that you came through at this particular time. All the Central Committee people are in Jo'burg. There's a big plenum going on this weekend. I'm sure my husband and others would have liked to have met you!"

I asked about some of the South Africans I had known in Moscow. She said that Bunting had died and that Roux was no longer in the party, but still friendly.

"What's this I hear about the party in America?" she asked. I said that I didn't know what she meant. "Well, it came over the radio last night that your party is dissolving itself!"

This all came as a great surprise and shock to me. It was hard to believe. I knew there had been some backsliding and a general move to the right. But dissolve the party? I wondered if there could have been some misunderstanding.

Before we boarded ship, we all met at the USO by the docks. This was the first time since we had come ashore that Black and white shipmates had been able to get together. We made the most of it, drinking beer and swapping stories. Herb Jeffries, a very light-skinned Black man with blondish hair and blue eyes, was the target of a lot of kidding. Herb's brother, Howard, was a nationally known singer with the Duke Ellington band.

When we had split up on leaving the dockside bar, Herb had no choice but to go with the whites. Now we had some fun at his expense. "You goddamn white son of a bitch, you ratted on us. You left your own race."

"You ran out on us at the docks, man. I don't think we'll let you back in the race," said Hursel.

Herb was embarrassed and kind of felt bad. "What was I gonna do, man?" he asked. "They wouldn't serve me with you guys." Hursel winked at me and we kept putting poor Herb on for some time. What he said was true, though. In South Africa, he couldn't pass for Black.

The struggle against the racketeers had been going on since we left San Pedro, and by the time we left Cape Town we had them pretty well isolated. We had the goods on them, and they knew it. We had built up a core of about twenty-five guys who played a leading role in the fight for better conditions and against these crooks.

Things were tense though; one evening I was on deck, leaning on the rail, when Red came up from the engine room. "Harry," he said, "be careful about getting too near that rail at night. We're in the middle of a hell of a fight and those bastards would love to dump you over!"

The ship's committee met to draw up charges against the racketeers. Two or three of them were direct accusations. Clearly, we said, the racketeers were literally robbing the soldiers with their fixed games. They were obstructing the fight for better conditions on board by setting shipmates against each other. And finally, they were besmirching the name of the union.

As we headed up the South Atlantic, we called a general meeting to present the charges. A group of us got together beforehand to talk over the issues. Red Herrick, the ship chairman, was there, as was Hursel Alexander. Hursel was short, not more than five foot four inches, with broad shoulders and a big roaring voice. He'd been one of the party's finest orators. Red said, "After all these points are made I want you to sum it up, Hursel. Really stir the crew up. Then, when you're through, I'll call for a vote right away."

Red chaired the meeting and read the charges. Everybody had a say, and most everybody spoke against the racketeers. As I recall, they weren't there, but their toadies did their red-baiting for them. The discussion went on for a considerable time. Finally Red recognized Hursel and that clinched it. The crew confirmed the charges and referred the crooks to a shoreside committee of the union for trial.

Crossing the Caribbean, we were anticipating the time when we'd return to San Pedro and get rid of these parasites. This would be no problem since San Pedro was a small port and union grievances could be processed quickly. We thought we had everything sewn up. Then one night, while several of us were standing on deck, one old seaman noticed, "We're not sailing through any damn Panama Canal. We're too far north. Look at those lights; there's St. Thomas and that's Puerto Rico. We're going to New York, man!"

As the word spread, the crooks started getting cocky again. They knew the ropes in New York and stood a better chance of stalling things in such a large port. A few days later, the ship docked at the military base on Staten Island. Normally, crews were paid off at the end of a voyage with a union patrolman present who was able to handle grievances. But the military authorities would not allow our patrolman aboard ship. The crew was paid off outside the base, and everyone who had been active in our union caucus was fired for "inefficiency." By the time we could get through the red tape to raise the issues, the *Uruguay* was offshore, on its way to Oran, Algeria. The racketeers sailed with the ship while we were left in New York.

We put up at the Broadway Central Hotel and stayed there a couple of weeks. Nothing could be done about our grievances. Most of the guys went back to San Pedro—the shipping administration gave first-class fare back to your home port. I decided to stay in New York and take advantage of the union's program for members to upgrade their skills as cooks and bakers. I spent a month at Manual Arts High School on Thirteenth Street near Seventh Avenue, learning the rudiments of baking.

While I was in New York I went to see Bill Foster and check on what I'd heard in South Africa, about the party being dissolved. I went up to the ninth floor of the party headquarters on East Thirteenth Street.

There was Foster, alone in his office, his feet on the desk, his hat pulled down to his eyes. He appeared to be in deep thought. "Hello, Harry, I hear you're a seaman now," he said.

I told him I'd just returned from an around-the-world voyage, and we talked awhile about the sea. Foster had years before been a sailor himself. Finally I told him what I heard in South Africa about the party being dissolved.

"Yes," he said, "that is what Browder has in mind." When I asked what he planned to do about it, he said, "Let's take a walk; the walls have ears . . ."

As we walked down University Place toward Washington Square, Foster explained how he saw Browder's line. "It's a rightist line," I recall him saying. "One that just tails behind the bourgeoisie. He thinks they will voluntarily stick to the Teheran agreements. Browder is pushing the line that the American capitalists—for their own best interests—will continue the unity of the big three [the United States, USSR, and Great Britain—Ed.] after the war is over. He wants us to continue the no-strike pledge and is saying that there won't be any more economic crises or wars or class conflicts—only peace and prosperity."

Foster told me how Browder was then proposing to change the party into an "association," for this was in line with his view that the two-party system was adequate. What it all came down to was that he not only wanted to dissolve the party—he wanted to liquidate Marxism.

Again I asked Foster what he was planning to do. I remember that his greatest concern was to avoid a split in the party in the middle of a war.

"But," I asked, "isn't Browder going to dissolve the party in the middle of the war? There certainly is an opposition; why not lead it?"

He hedged, saying Browder was looking for the chance to expel him. By this time, we had returned to the party headquarters. We agreed to keep in touch. What I did not know then was that Foster had written a letter to the National Committee opposing Browder's line. This letter was read at the Political Committee a few days before our conversation on February 8, 1944, and was opposed by every other committee member except Sam Darcy of Pennsylvania. Further, it had been made clear at the time that Foster would be expelled if he attempted to take the struggle against Browder to the rank and file.

This was a difficult time for me. I knew from discussions with others, especially seamen, that there was fairly widespread opposition to Browder's position. But no one was sure what to do. The opposition existed, but it had no leadership. Browder was systematically violating democratic centralism by stifling any thorough discussion of his new policies. Thus the opposition in various parts of the country remained isolated from each other. I found myself feeling very much like many others. Browder's business was really bad, but it was being steamrollered through. At the time, it seemed the only thing that could be done was to bide our time, waiting for events to expose Browder's opportunism.

Life aboard the *Ericsson*

Late in March 1944, I signed on as assistant baker on the *John Ericsson* for the first of four voyages on that ship.

The *Ericsson* was a former Swedish luxury liner, now leased to the United States as a troopship. She usually carried about five thousand troops on her trips from New York to Liverpool. We would go in a big convoy with a number of other troopships and a number of escort vessels. The Allies by that time were building up for the opening of the second front and the invasion of Normandy, which was to take place in June of that year. It took us about a month to make the round-trip. We'd drop the troops in Liverpool and then sail up to Scotland.

There were four or five bakers and assistants in the *Ericsson*'s baking department. The chief baker was a Swede named Vidal. He had been chief baker on the *Ericsson* when it was a luxury liner. He was a fine pastry chef, and we baked bread for the whole ship, pastry for the officers.

Vidal outdid himself, making chocolate éclairs, bismarcks, and Danish pastry. I loved the work, and by the time I got off that ship, I could make all kinds of pastries. Vidal was a good teacher, but he was a little sore that all the young guys were learning so fast. He was from the old school and had been apprenticed to a baker at the age of twelve.

He used to tell us how the chief baker would stride in with his head up in the air and all the boys would greet him, "Good morning, Herr Chief Baker."

"I had to wash pans for a year before they'd even let me touch the dough," he would tell us, "and now you guys come on here and expect to be bakers in a few months."

I also met Jake "the bread baker" Rabinowitz on the *Ericsson*. He was a specialist in sourdough bread. He'd come up the gangplank with a little satchel and all the old bakers would say, "Here comes Jake with that same old mother dough he's had for twenty-five years."

After we dropped the troops off we had a chance to see Liverpool. It was an old port city that had suffered heavily from Hitler's blitz, and large sections of the city lay in ruins. The pubs were fascinating places. They were real social centers where people spent the evening drinking beer and playing darts. The British were polite and someone would always come up to my table and strike up a conversation. Perhaps because I was Black, they would often raise criticisms of Americans that they didn't mention to my white shipmates. They couldn't stand the way some Americans were always boasting and carrying on about American superiority. The British were proud too, but in a quiet way.

"What's wrong with the Yanks?" I'd ask when the subject came up.

"They're over paid, over sexed and over here," came the reply.

The German counteroffensive at the Battle of the Bulge was going on, and the British followed it carefully. "The Yanks are getting it now," they'd say. "Americans were so critical of our fighting, but they're finding out it's no easy road."

When we'd leave Liverpool, we'd go up to Glasgow, Scotland, and pick up German prisoners and wounded. It was easier to take them back to the United States than to ship food over for them. As our ship pulled out of Gourock, Glasgow's port, the German prisoners would be assembled on the deck.

We'd ask, "Are there any bakers here?" Inevitably some would step forward because they knew they'd get better food if they worked in the kitchen. So on the return voyages we ship's bakers could take it easy.

There were a lot of good fellows in our crew, but we were slow getting the ship organized. After my first voyage I got in touch with Al Lannon, the party's waterfront organizer and member of the Central Committee. I asked about the possibility of getting one or two good party men aboard to help us make the *Ericsson* a model union ship.

"Who's in port here?" I asked Al.

"I'll tell you just the guy you need. It's Harry Rubin."

"I'm not sure I know him."

"He's a man with tremendous drive and a hell of a dynamic organizer," Al said. "You put him on that ship and he'll be a real help. But I should warn you, he has a kind of puritanical streak. After a while he may do something or other and get himself isolated from the rest of the crew. You can use him for a couple of voyages, though." Rubin was a little fellow who walked with a limp as a result of being wounded in Spain. He signed on as wiper in the engine room, the lowest job there. Sure enough, he helped whip the whole thing together in short order. In no time at all we had the whole ship tightly organized. The committees and delegates in all the departments were functioning well. The crew was up to standard. We presented and won many grievances and improved the food and living conditions. There were classes for the crew on union history and on improving technical skills. As educational director, I taught a course on the nature of fascism.

A couple of voyages later, there was an incident that proved Lannon's cautions about Rubin to be correct. Rubin charged two Puerto Rican crew members with selling a couple pints of liquor to two of the soldiers on board. The union had a strict policy on this sort of racketeering, but the attitude of most of the crew was, We don't want to press this too hard. It's just a small case. Just tell them they can't do it anymore. There were no big racketeers aboard.

But Rubin took a hard line. He insisted that charges be brought against them and that they stand trial before the union port committee in New York. There was a division on the ship's committee, and many of us thought we should be a little flexible in this situation, but in the end we followed Rubin's lead.

The incident made for hard feeling among the crew and divided the ship that we had worked so hard to organize. The union meeting on board that we called to discuss the charges was very heated. The defendants claimed the charges were an example of discrimination against Puerto Ricans. There were about fifty Puerto Ricans in the crew and about the same number of Blacks.

The defendants were able to line most of them up on their side. In truth, Puerto Ricans and Blacks had some real grievances. They were mostly in the Steward's Department and many lived way down in the glory hole, the worst section of the ship. Also, the "evidence" against the defendants was flimsy and consisted of two affidavits signed by two soldiers long gone from the ship. The crew was split down the middle, and when the vote was called as to whether the defendants should be charged and stand trial in New York, about 60 percent voted no.

In later voyages, we were able to unite the crew under our leadership again. Rubin, however, didn't sign on again because he, more than any of us, had isolated himself from the rest of the crew.

I quit the *Ericsson* in early September 1944. I planned to return to Los Angeles, but I had followed the Soviet counteroffensive with intense interest. The victories at Stalingrad and Leningrad and in the Crimea had pushed the Germans back beyond the border. Thus, I was determined to make the Murmansk run before I returned to the West Coast.

I went down to the union hall on West Seventeenth Street. No one told where a ship was bound during the war, but when the dispatcher called out, "Here's that cold run. Get your heavy underwear on," everyone knew what he meant.

I wanted to sign on as second cook and baker, but that job was already taken. The only rating I could take was crew messman, so I threw in my card. The ship was the *Winfred L. Smith,* docked in New Jersey. I packed my bag, being sure to include my Russian grammar book and dictionary, and a Russian edition of Tolstoy's *War and Peace* so that I could bone up on my once-fluent Russian. I then hurried to New Jersey and signed on.

We sailed on September 26, 1944, for Halifax, Nova Scotia, where the convoy assembled. We had a heavy escort of destroyers, cruisers, and corvettes as we headed for Glasgow. After docking at Gourock on the Clyde, we headed north along the Scottish coast to Loch Ewe, where we reassembled for the last leg of the Murmansk run. A British commodore took over command of the convoy, calling a conference of captains to explain the procedures and route for making the dangerous run through the Norwegian Sea, around the North Cape to the Kola Inlet and Murmansk.

Leaving Loch Ewe, we were a formidable convoy of about thirty ships in all. Our escort vessels included frigates, destroyers, corvettes, and "baby" aircraft carriers (escort carriers). The cargo ships were also armed. Our liberty ship had, in addition to the normal crew of forty-four men, a navy gun crew of eighteen, which manned the two three-inch, fifty-caliber-type cannons, several twenty-millimeter Oerlikon antiaircraft guns, and lighter caliber machine guns.

The convoy, we understood, was also given distant cover by a British battleship and cruiser of the home fleet, which lay just out of sight. Further protection was afforded by the winter solstice, which provided virtually twenty-four hours of darkness.

The crew's quarters were midship, the portholes looking out on the aft deck cargo. There were several narrow-gauge train engines lashed to the deck.

Heading northeast, we entered the Norwegian Sea, one of the world's stormiest seas. It didn't take much imagination to visualize the engines breaking loose and crashing through our bunks. It certainly didn't make for a relaxed voyage, but then neither did the Germans.

German sub packs hounded us throughout the voyage. Our reminder of their presence was the constant dropping of depth charges, which shook everything and everyone on ship as the bulkheads quivered and the deck plates rattled. But we were lucky. It was later revealed that no less than eighteen U-boats had been lying in ambush for our convoy. When we arrived in Murmansk, we learned that only one escort frigate had been damaged by a torpedo.

Our convoy was routed unusually close to the Norwegian coast, probably not more than seventy-five miles offshore. The normal route took convoys far from German-occupied Norway. It was understood that we were attempting to lure the battleship *Von Tirpitz* out of the fjords. A year before, her sister ship, the *Scharnhorst,* had slipped out to attack a similar convoy and, after a long chase, was sunk by the British navy. But this time the *Von Tirpitz* did not accept the challenge and remained in the fjord.

Off North Cape we were attacked by a formation of sixteen German torpedo bombers. General alarm was sounded. I rushed to my position as assistant loader on the Oerlikon gun, life jacket slung around my neck and rubber suit under my arm. The engagement lasted only a few minutes. Heavy fire from our entire convoy quickly brought down three planes and drove the others off. They did manage to drop a few torpedoes, but they went astray, doing no damage.

We finally dropped anchor in the Kola Inlet in early November. Half our convoy, including our ship, unloaded our cargo in Murmansk. The remaining ships sailed across the White Sea and on to Archangel. Our first sight of Murmansk was the badly battered dock and railroad spurs. It was a prime target for the Luftwaffe, which had a base in Petsamo, Finland, barely sixty miles from Murmansk. By the time I got there, the Soviets had installed so many heavy antiaircraft guns and had brought down so many planes that the bombing was greatly reduced.

At last we were ashore in Murmansk. Formerly the Russians had given a $125 bonus to each seaman for making the run. This was a gesture of appreciation and provided money to spend in port. But at the behest of the U.S. government, they had stopped this practice. We drew money from the captain to spend ashore. At last ashore, the Russian language sounded beautiful to me. On the voyage over I had spent several hours a day boning up on my Russian. Once ashore, I became fluent again and found myself translating for my shipmates.

There was no doubt Murmansk was a frontline town. There were only two places to go for relaxation and diversion. There was the International Seamen's Club and the International Hotel. At the club there were often American movies and dances on a Saturday night.

The crews from the convoy crowded into the Seamen's Club and were soon drinking the good old Russian vodka. But we soon discovered that vodka, unlike whisky, was not a liquor to be drunk neat, as was the American custom. Under the influence of the vodka, the meekest fellows soon became roaring lions. Several fights broke out. The Russians looked on with amazement at this.

"What's the matter with you Americans?" they asked after finding that I could speak Russian. "Can't you take your liquor?"

"Ah well, they're just blowing off steam after the terrible tension of the voyage," I answered.

Thereafter, the Russians restricted the Americans to one drink of vodka in the club, which was equivalent to a double in our measure. On our part, a few of us union guys got together and constituted ourselves as an ad hoc committee to maintain order ashore. We served notice that henceforth any seaman who caused trouble and was giving the crew a bad name would have his shore leave taken away for the duration of our stay in port. We posted notices to that effect on the bulletin board of the club. The Russians were very pleased with our self-disciplinary action.

My Russian came right back, and I spent a lot of time in the clubs and met a whole number of Russians. They took me around to the factories and Russian clubs. Among my friends was the ship chandler, who took me out to his home and introduced me to his family. I was sitting in his office one day when two white American seamen came in. They asked the chandler if he could sell them some vodka. He told them that he wasn't permitted to sell to individuals, that they would have to get a permit from the captain of the ship. The chandler could understand a lot of English but he couldn't speak the language, so I volunteered to translate. My proffered help was met by a hostile stare by these two drunks. I heard their drawl and knew where they were from. One, the most belligerent, glared at me.

"Who's talkin' to you? Keep out of this," he growled.

"Well, I know Russian and thought I could help you."

"We don't need your help. We're from Texas."

"Well, good," I rejoined, "some of my best friends are from Texas."

I stood up and put my hand on the water bottle on the chandler's desk. They turned and walked out of the place.

The chandler was taking it all in, apprehensive that something was going to happen. "Comrade," he said, "I'm so glad you didn't allow yourself to be provoked."

He told me that a year ago, a Black seaman had been killed right there in Murmansk by white seamen. "Do Black people always have to fear for their lives in the United States?" he asked, puzzled. "Well, one can expect attack at anytime, but not all whites are hostile. And Blacks have their own communities."

He seemed puzzled by the whole thing. "I guess it's like the Jews under the old regime," he said.

"Precisely," I agreed.

I went over to the International Hotel and joined some of my white shipmates sitting around a table. I told them about what had happened at the chandler's. Just then the two fellows came in and sat down at the next table. One of my mates, a reconstructed Southerner—Texas Red, we called him—got up and started talking loudly about "goddamn rednecks." The two slunk out of the bar and that was the end of it. We figured they were members of the SIU, a Jim Crow seamen's union.

Another night I came into the International Hotel and, after checking my boots and coat, saw a group of young Russians, men and women, standing in the lobby. It was on the eve of the anniversary of the Russian Revolution. They saw me speaking Russian to the attendant, so one young Russian approached me. He was a small fellow, dressed in the Georgian manner with long coat, hat, and soft Caucasian boots.

"I think I know you," he said. "Weren't you in Moscow some years back?"

"Yes, I was," I answered, surprised.

"Don't you remember my sisters Vera and Era?" Vera and Era were two young women in our circle.

"Oh yes," I said, "how are they?"

"I was just a small boy when you would come around. Vera married Patterson, the American Black man who came over with the film troupe. He died in the evacuation from Moscow."

"Oh, I'm sorry," I said. "How is she doing now?"

"Fine," he said. "She has a nice apartment and her two sons are coming along well."

I was just about to ask about Ina, who had also been a part of that same circle, when he broke off, explaining that he had to go to a performance as he was a member of a dance troupe.

"Meet me back here tomorrow night," he said.

I came back to the hotel the next night, but he wasn't there. He probably had another performance. I didn't know his name or how to ask for him. Sadly, I never saw him again.

Not too long after we arrived in Murmansk, we received word that the *Von Tirpitz* had been sunk (November 12, 1944) in a successful attack by twenty-eight Lancaster bombers of the Royal Air Force. This was certainly welcome news, for it meant the end of the major German naval threat to convoys on the Murmansk run. We were relieved to know our return trip would not be threatened.

The human enemy was more or less taken care of, but the old enemy, the sea itself, was there to be reckoned with. The Norwegian Sea was a brutal sea, particularly rough at that time of year. Terrible gales buffeted the convoy and dispersed it over the whole area. Separated from the rest of the ships, we were forced to run alone. The decks, fore and aft, were awash continuously. We struggled into Loch Ewe one by one.

The return voyage was fairly uneventful. But even that late in the war, German submarines were still a very real threat. I remember we were almost home, just off Buzzards Bay in Massachusetts. There was a submarine scare, and depth charges shook the whole ship violently. One of our mates, a fireman, was down in his quarters counting up his hours. He came up frustrated as hell, "Every time I started counting, a depth charge would go off and I'd have to start all over."

It was seventeen below when we docked in Portland, Maine, on January 11, 1945. That night we took the train to New York City. The Russians had given every seaman at Murmansk a gallon of good vodka. On the way down to New York we broke them open and shared them with the passengers. The first thing we did when we got off the train was go to the Cafe Society downtown and see Billie Holiday, the Black singer.

After a week or ten days in New York, I took the train home to Los Angeles. I was happy to return to Belle and we had a warm reunion, exchanging stories, discussing the war and the political developments.

It wasn't long before I became anxious to get back to sea. In March I signed on a motorship we called the *Turk's Knot*. It was smaller than the liberty ship, but brand-new, just out of the yards. It carried the most modern equipment, along with a crew of thirteen plus the naval gun crew.

We sailed in early March for the Pacific war zone. It was understood that our destination would be the Philippines, with stops in Honolulu, Wake, the Truk Islands, and Guam. Our ship would then shuttle between New Guinea and Manila carrying installations and other war matériel the Americans had been forced to leave behind as they moved northward island by island.

Our first stop in the Philippines was the port city of Cebu, located on an island of the same name, right in the center of the Philippine Archipelago. Cebu was next to the island of Mactan. There, in 1521, Magellan was killed on the first circumnavigation of the earth.

Cebu, surrounded by lush tropics, was a beautiful town, as were its people. Paul, our Filipino chief cook, took me on the rounds of the town, introducing me to many friendly and hospitable people.

We left Cebu for Manila, the capital city on the big island of Luzon. The Bay of Manila was clogged with sunken vessels, a virtual graveyard of ships. They were undoubtedly an overspill from the crucial battle for the Gulf of Leyte, which took place on the eastern side of the islands in October 1944. It was here that Admiral Nimitz's fleet had put the finish on the Japanese navy and here that MacArthur's troops returned as he had vowed.

The wreckage was so great that we had to anchor a mile or two out in the harbor and go into town on water taxis.

In Manila, a friend and I ran into a group of revolutionary students and intellectuals who had ties with the Hukbalahap guerrillas, or "Huks." They had been active in the anti-Japanese resistance movement and in bitter struggles against the traitorous compradors and landlords who had aided them. They told us how, after the Huks and the underground had helped to recapture Manila, they had been disarmed by American troops. They were bitter and sharply critical of MacArthur's hostility toward the popular democratic movement. His clear intention was to return to the status quo of colonialism. They gave us lots of their literature, and during the following months of our shuttle we saw them whenever we were in Manila.

From Manila we would sail southward to New Guinea. Stopping at the small port towns of Hollandia, Wewak, and Oro Bay, all on the north coast of New Guinea, we would gather our cargo of war matériel and return to Manila. The round trip of some thirty-six hundred miles would take about fourteen to twenty days.

Homecoming at War's End

In April we received news that Roosevelt had died. The news saddened the crew; everyone seemed to realize that Roosevelt's death marked the end of an era.

We had scarcely left New Guinea on the trip home when news came over the ship's radio that an atom bomb had been dropped on Hiroshima. It was

August 6, 1945. Three days later we learned that a second and more powerful bomb had been dropped at Nagasaki. We knew then that it would not be long before the Japanese surrendered.

We spent a week or so relaxing and discussing what we should be doing now. We decided to go back to New York. I went first to find an apartment. Belle packed up our belongings in Los Angeles and closed the apartment.

EPILOGUE

The evil system of colonialism and imperialism grew up along with the enslavement of Negroes and the trade in Negroes, and it will surely come to its end with the thorough emancipation of the black people.

—Mao Tse-tung

By the late fifties, those of us who had defended the revolutionary position on Black liberation had been driven from the CP—either expelled or forced to resign. The party's leaders insisted that Blacks were well on the way to being assimilated into the old reliable American "melting pot."

But the melting pot suddenly exploded in their faces. In the sixties, the Black revolt surged up from the Deep South and quickly spread its fury across the entire country. Advancing wave upon wave—with sit-ins, freedom marches, wildcat strikes, and, finally, hundreds of spontaneous insurrections—the Black masses announced to their capitalist masters and the entire world that they would never rest until their chains of bondage were completely smashed.

This new awakening of the Afro-American people evoked the greatest domestic crisis since the thirties, and it became the focal point for the major contradictions in U.S. society, the most urgent, immediate, and pressing questions confronting the U.S. corporate rulers and the revolutionary forces. In its face, the ruling class employed counterrevolutionary dual tactics, both terrorist attacks on Black people, especially in the deep South, and reformist legal maneuvers in Washington.

First developing as a civil rights struggle against Jim Crow, the revolt increasingly took on a nationalist character, culminating in the Black power movement and projecting into the heart of modern U.S. society the demands of the unfinished democratic revolution of the Civil War and Reconstruction.

In a decade of mass movement, which saw demonstrations and uprisings in virtually every ghetto in the country, the Afro-American people put all existing programs for Black freedom to the test. Their struggle shattered the myth of peaceful imminent integration, revealing the bankruptcy of the "Free by '63" program of the old reformist leaders and their supporters in the revisionist CPUSA.

The Black upsurge had its fueling sources domestically in the combined influences of the failure of legal democratic integration and the catastrophic deterioration of the economic position of the Black masses, both absolute and relative to whites. In the fifties, the further monopolization and mechanization of agriculture had precipitated a deep agrarian crisis, throwing tens of thousands of rural Blacks off the land in the South. At the same time, the impending economic crisis, together with growing automation of industry, created an entire generation of ghetto youth in the urban areas, a "lost generation"—both North and South—with no work or prospects for work within the existing economic system. With the dispossessed Black population growing by leaps and bounds, the potential of the movement for Black power escalated.

The revolt was further fueled and inspired by the successes of the anti-imperialist movements of the third world, especially in the newly independent nations of Africa. This worldwide revolution of color broke the age-old feeling of isolation among the Black masses. As Malcolm X put it, "The oppressed people of this earth make up a majority, not a minority."[1]

Thus the struggle was transformed from an internal, isolated one against an apparently "invincible" ruling class into a component part of a worldwide revolutionary struggle against a common imperialist enemy. U.S. defeats in Korea, China, Cuba, and then Vietnam further exploded the myth of U.S. "invincibility." Many Black power militants drew upon the experiences of the third-world liberation struggles in developing a strategy for the movement here, as well as in many instances openly expressing solidarity with liberation struggles in Vietnam, Palestine, and Africa.

This anti-imperialist outlook reflected the rising mood of the times. Thus the revolt's development confirmed our thesis that the Black movement would inevitably take a national-revolutionary, anti-imperialist direction, culminating in the demand for political power in the areas of Black concentration. Far from being simply a fight for reforms, as the revisionists claimed, the Black liberation movement became a spark, a catalyst pushing forward the whole working-class and people's struggle in the United States.

This latter point underscored the treacherous depths of the revisionist betrayal. The CPUSA did not even attempt to mobilize labor support for the Black struggle, and the labor aristocracy maintained hegemony over the workers' movement. Thus abandoned to the leadership of the chauvinist bureaucrats, sharp divisions were sown between Black and white workers. This was in clear contrast to the unity built by Communists in the thirties, when the party and the working class had played a leading role in fighting for the special demands of Blacks, making the Scottsboro Boys a household word from the tenements of New York to the ghettos of Watts.

Though the revolutionary outlook and organization of Communists never became the leading factor in the revolt, the movement nonetheless made considerable gains in the course of its development. As I see it, the revolt developed in three periods. The first began with the Montgomery Bus Boycott of 1955–56 and ended with the 1963 March on Washington. This latter protest event brought in its wake a widespread disillusionment with the reformist, legalistic, and nonviolent strategy of such organizations as the Southern Christian Leadership Conference (SCLC), the Urban League, and the NAACP.

The growing isolation of these "responsible" leaders and the breakup of the Kennedy-backed civil rights coalition (the "Big Five"—SNCC, SCLC, CORE, Urban League, and NAACP and NAACP Legal Defense and Education Fund) ushered in the second phase of militant open revolt. This period was marked by widespread rebellions in the cities and the demand for Black power. But lacking a Leninist vanguard linked to the masses, the movement at this point was unconsolidated. Its nationalist leadership splintered into a variety of petty-bourgeois tendencies—separatist, pan-Africanist, cultural nationalist, and even some terrorist tendencies. Thus the bourgeoisie was able to usher in a third phase by buying off the right wing of the Black power movement and establishing its own brokers within it. The 1969 Black Power Conference in Newark, which was generously funded by the Ford Foundation, was the signal that this phase of the movement had begun in earnest.

From the Courtroom to the Streets (1955–63)

The stage for the Black revolt was set in 1954, the year of the Supreme Court decision outlawing school segregation. This decision, historic in its effects upon the future of the Black movement, was a tactical concession forced by the rising movement at home and especially by criticism of Jim Crow from third-world and socialist countries. NAACP leaders, however, hailed the decision as a vindication of their legalistic policies.

For its part, the federal government gave hard-core southern reactionaries the opportunity to organize and unleash the most planned and purposeful campaign of anti-Black terror since the defeat of Reconstruction.

In response, the Black movement in the South burst out from under the wraps of the old elite leadership of the NAACP and took on a mass character—defying segregation laws and directly attacking the Jim Crow system. The spark was ignited in the Montgomery, Alabama, Bus Boycott of 1955–56 under the leadership of Martin Luther King. The flames spread. In 1960, the Student Non-violent Coordinating Committee (SNCC) began sit-in demonstrations which swept the South.

Freedom riders under the leadership of the Congress of Racial Equality (CORE) took over the spotlight in 1961 and won national support for their campaign to integrate transportation facilities. In the spring of 1963, the struggle reached a highpoint in the battle of Birmingham and from there leaped over regional boundaries and spread throughout the country, uniting various classes and strata of Black people under the slogan "Freedom Now!"

The movement exerted tremendous attractive power on all sections of the population, especially the youth, drawing sections of the white community into support and participation. The summer of 1964 saw hundreds of college students travel to Mississippi to participate in a voter-registration project.

It was also in the South that the armed self-defense movement was initiated in North Carolina by Robert Williams, whose NAACP local was suspended for these activities. Based upon Black workers and war veterans, other armed groups like the Deacons for Defense and Justice in Louisiana and Mississippi won important victories against the Ku Klux Klan in the midsixties. It was during the Meredith March through Mississippi, which was protected by the Deacons, that the slogan "Black power" first gained national prominence in 1966.

As Chairman Mao wrote, the movement became "a new clarion call to all the exploited and oppressed people of the United States to fight against the barbarous rule of the monopoly capitalist class."[2] Movements developed among students and women and Chicano, Native American, and Puerto Rican people, as well as among activists against the Vietnam War.

Alarm bordering on panic struck the ruling circles. *Time* magazine expressed the fear that the civil rights movement "will crash beyond the framework of passive resistance into new dangerous dimensions."[3] U.S. efforts to build a neo-colonial empire in the third world were further impaired as the grotesque contrast between its high-flown moral posture and the brutal reality of an organized system of racist barbarism nurtured within its own borders was further exposed. Racist police employing such methods as electric prodding irons, police dogs, high-pressure hoses, and the brutal beating of women provoked angry outrage throughout the world. Its impact was especially felt in Africa, where concern about racism in the United States was expressed by the Addis Ababa Conference of African Ministers.[4]

The alarm of white ruling circles was also reflected among the top leadership of the NAACP and other reformist organizations. In order to maintain their role as "honest" brokers between the Black masses and the white rulers, they had been forced to grant some autonomy to the southern dissident wing led by King and SCLC. Representing ministers and the Black bourgeoisie of the South, King favored a policy of nonviolent, mass action. But he in turn was faced with a growing challenge from the more radical elements of the movement, especially the youth of SNCC, sections of CORE, and the NAACP youth—the shock troops of the revolt. It was among these frontline fighters that the inherent conflict between King's nonviolent philosophy and direct mass action first came to a head. Under conditions prevailing in the Deep South, direct mass action and civil disobedience campaigns could develop and grow only if accompanied by organized armed self-defense. In renouncing self-defense, the movement inevitably reached an impasse there.

In situations like the heroic but unsuccessful battle of Albany, Georgia (1961–62), the moral and political bankruptcy of making nonviolence a principle was revealed. In Jackson, Mississippi, even after the assassination of NAACP leader Medgar Evers, little or no progress was made. Similarly, in Greensboro, North Carolina, two thousand demonstrators were jailed over the integration of two restaurants. And in Birmingham, the South's most important bastion of white supremacy, it was fourteen years until a token indictment was brought against a few of the child-murdering bombers. The upsurge of 1963 resulted in gains in other parts of the country, but practically none in the Deep South.

Even the victories that were won in desegregation and legal reforms produced no improvement in the conditions of poor and working-class Blacks. These experiences cast doubt on the whole program of "peaceful democratic integration." Riding the tiger of the Black revolt, King and fellow advocates of nonviolence were rescued by President Kennedy. Trying to walk a tightrope between the hard-core Dixiecrat defiance and surging Black militancy, the administration sought to divert the mass movement back into legalistic channels by proposing a civil rights bill. The bill's declared purpose was to get the Black movement off the street and back into the courtroom where the hundred years of litigation promised by the southern governors could proceed. Instead of being the militant protest originally planned, the 1963 March on Washington was converted into a peaceful demonstration in support of the president's civil rights bill. But even this much-vaunted march could not succeed in diverting the rising tide of rebellion. It did, however, openly expose to the masses the collusion between the Kennedy administration and men like Whitney Young of the Urban League, Roy Wilkins of the NAACP, and A. Philip Randolph. At the same time, the march leaders censored John Lewis's speech for SNCC because it attacked Kennedy's civil rights bill.[5]

Malcolm X showed how the government used bribery to bring these reformist leaders to its aid in controlling the masses in the March on Washington.

> When they [the administration—Ed.] found out that this black steamroller was going to come down on the capital, they called in Wilkins, they called in Randolph, they called in these national Negro leaders that you respect and told them, "Call it off." Kennedy said, "Look, you all are letting this thing go too far." And Old Tom said, "Boss, I can't stop it, because I didn't start it." I'm telling you what they said. They said, "I'm not even in it, much less at the head of it." They said, "These Negroes are doing things on their own. They're running ahead of us." And that old shrewd fox, he said, " If you all aren't in it, I'll put you in it. I'll put you at the head of it. I'll endorse it. I'll welcome it. I'll help it. I'll join it."[6]

Black Power

Following this event, mass rejection of peaceful democratic integration became apparent in the growing wave of ghetto rebellions. There were 24 in 1964, 38 in 1966, 128 in 1967, and 131 in the first half of 1968, the year of King's assassination.

These urban uprisings put into sharp focus the alienation of the Black masses from the old-line leaders like Roy Wilkins, A. Philip Randolph, and Bayard Rustin. As the Kerner Report lamented, "Those who come forward to discourage rioting may have no influence with the rioters." The report also contained another ploy of the bourgeoisie, designed to get itself off the hook. It charged, "What white Americans have never understood—but what the Negro can never forget—is that white society is deeply implicated in the ghetto. White institutions created it, white institutions maintain it, and white society condones it."[7] By blaming everyone, including the masses of white working people, the ruling class in effect blamed no one and covered up their own crimes.

Black power became the rallying cry of the uprisings because it summed up the main lessons learned by the masses during the civil rights phase of the movement; legal rights meant nothing without the political power to enforce them. Black power expressed the growing consciousness of the Afro-American masses that they are an oppressed nation whose road to freedom and equality lies in taking political power into their own hands. Thus Blacks should become the controlling force in the areas of their major concentration—in the urban ghettos of the North as well as the Black Belt area of the South.

The emergence of Black power as a mass slogan signaled a fundamental turning point in the modern Afro-American liberation struggle, carrying it to the threshold of a new phase. It marked a basic shift in content and direction of the movement, from civil rights to national liberation, with a corresponding realignment of social forces. It indicated that the Black revolt had crashed beyond the limited goals set by the old-guard reformist assimilationist leadership of the NAACP and associates, beyond the strictures of Reverend King's nonviolent holding operation, into channels leading to direct confrontation with the main enemy—the "white power" oligarchy of the imperialists. Inevitably, this struggle moved toward juncture with the anti-imperialist revolutions in the third world and with the working-class movement for socialism.

The vehicle of the revolt was an indigenous grassroots nationalism, upsurging from the poor and working-class masses of the urban ghettos and the poor and dispossessed farmers and sharecroppers of the Black Belt. The movement reflected their strivings to break out of the bind of racist economic and cultural subjugation, to establish for themselves the dignity of a free and equal people. Here was the mass base of SNCC, the Black Panther Party (which raised the question of armed self-defense for the urban ghettos and popularized the writings of Mao Tse-tung), Malcolm X (recently split from the Black Muslims), and other revolutionary nationalists.

Afro-Americans were caught up in an assertive drive for a viable, collective identity adapted to the peculiar conditions of their development in the United States and their African background. Further, it was a drive to recover a cultural heritage shaped by over three hundred years of chattel slavery and a century of thwarted freedom. This quest for identity as a people in its own right led ever-greater segments of the Afro-American community to a fundamental reassessment of their actual status as an oppressed nation—virtual captives in the metropolitan heartland of one of the world's most powerful and predatory imperialist powers.

A growing body of young Black radical intellectuals assumed an active role in fostering Black power nationalism. Their efforts, reflecting the spirit of the masses, produced a new cultural renaissance surpassing that of the twenties. The vanguard was an angry, alienated Black youth—a proud and sensitive young generation that refused to stagnate and die in a system that sought to destroy it.

The above developments led to a mass defection from the old-guard leadership that became morally and politically isolated from the masses. The trend of

Black power nationalism rose to dominate the Black community in the second phase of the struggle. The nationalism of the sixties differed from the Garvey movement and its latter-day spiritual descendants, the Black Muslims, neo-Garveyites, and others. In the main, the Black power movement called not for escapist withdrawal but for a fight here where Blacks live. Among some narrow nationalist sects, however, the old backward utopianism persisted.

The leadership of the Black power movement, while having a profound and positive effect on the struggles of the Black masses, displayed its own major weakness—that of being primarily based in the Black intelligentsia and petty bourgeoisie. The movement was hamstrung in attempting to fight U.S. imperialism without the benefit of a program of class struggle. It also deeply underestimated the potential strength of unity with the overall workers' movement in achieving the goals of the national struggle. These weaknesses contributed to the ability of the U.S. corporate establishment to temporarily cool out and buy off the Black upsurge by employing both reformist and narrow nationalist schemes.

At first Black power activists submerged class conflicts in the movement. But soon a right wing emerged, with its base in a sector of the ghetto bourgeoisie: businessmen, ministers, professionals, poverty-project leaders, Black studies professors, newly hired lower management and token upper management. This right wing found its spokesmen in elite intellectuals like Roy Innis, Floyd McKissick, and Harold Cruse. They aspired to the role of economic and political administrators of a Black "internal colony," still owned and controlled by white monopoly capitalism.

Co-opting a Right Wing

This perspective of pursuing the Black bourgeoisie's class interests within an imperialist framework was not fundamentally different from the integrationism of the old-guard Black leaders. The more nimble members of this group hopped on the bandwagon, while others, like Whitney Young, kept a foot in both camps.

This emerging Black right wing was met halfway by a white establishment in search of new allies. Facing defeats abroad and burning cities at home, the establishment was haunted by the specter of a national rebellion in its urban nerve centers. As McGeorge Bundy pointed out, if Blacks burn the cities, "the white man's companies will have to take the losses."[8]

This new kind of broker spoke the language of the Black power movement and might better lead it into safe channels, away from the confrontations that threatened domestic tranquility and international credibility. So the buffer zone between the establishment and the Black masses was extended to include the new right-wing nationalists and their social base. A wide range of corporate leaders united behind this strategy, bringing into play their tremendous powers of co-optation and manipulation. This does not mean that the bourgeoisie gave up on the old-line leadership; rather, it means that they concentrated their efforts on the right-wing nationalists in this particular period.

Bundy's Ford Foundation led the way, putting some of CORE's leadership on the payroll. The establishment and its new allies moved to redefine Black power in more acceptable terms. Harvard's Kennedy Institute of Politics defined self-determination to mean community development corporations and tax incentives for investors in the ghetto; Roy Innis endorsed this formula.

Fifty corporations jointly sponsored two Black power Conferences under Nathan Wright's leadership. To Wright, Black power meant Black capitalism, or, as he expressed it, "The most strategic opportunity which our American capitalistic system has to preserve or strengthen itself lies in the possibility of providing the Negro community with both a substantial and immediate stake in its operation at every level."[9]

In fact, "Black capitalism" was the centerpiece of the power elite's strategy. This included a stepped-up policy of piecemeal concessions to contain and reverse the revolutionary trend by buying up and corrupting potential and actual community leaders. Richard Nixon articulated this strategy in 1968: "What most of the militants are asking is not separation but to be included in—not as supplicants, but as owners, as entrepreneurs—to have a share of the wealth and a piece of the action."[10] Sections of the ghetto entrepreneurs and professionals were ready to misuse the collective strength of the Black community to get "a piece of the action."

The crisis and ebbing of the Black power nationalist movement was precipitated by the rise of this thoroughly reformist trend, which was backed directly by the imperialists. This new Black elite moved systematically to take over the movement, sap its revolutionary potential, and restrict it to goals that U.S. capitalism was willing to concede. In this, they were aided by a growing apparatus of repression—police, FBI, CIA, National Guard, and U.S. Army Intelligence—which murdered, jailed, and suppressed many uncooperative leaders. This came on the heels of Nixon's law-and-order, white-backlash campaign of 1968. The full story of intrigue, murder, character assassination, splittism, and provocative activities is only now beginning to come to light. The exposure of the FBI's notorious Counter Intelligence Program (COINTELPRO) operations was but the tip of the iceberg.

Where were the forces to give leadership to the movement in the face of this both open and covert assault by the imperialists?

Certainly they were not to be found in the CPUSA, which made every effort to attack and downgrade the movement. James Jackson summed up the basic attitude of the CPUSA toward nationalism. "The main function of nationalism," he wrote, "*whatever its form* [our emphasis], is to split and divide and fragment the international working class and the advanced contingents of the national liberation movements."[11] Genuine Communists, of course, must distinguish between the nationalism of the oppressor nations and that of the oppressed, as well as between nationalism's progressive and backward aspects.

The limitations of the nationalist outlook (as I have already shown) became clear. Its leadership was unable to make a class analysis of the Black community, thus overestimating the unity between the Black masses and the Black bourgeoisie, while underestimating the need for unity with the general workers' movement.

To be sure, the upsurge spurred the political development of the Black proletariat, building on the foundations laid by the Black caucus movement of the post–World War II period. Beginning in the early sixties, a new wave of Black caucuses sprang up in basic industries across the country, reaching perhaps their highest political development in the Detroit League of Revolutionary Black Workers.

I believe that if we had had a revolutionary party in the sixties, much of the spontaneity and reactionary nationalism of the period could have been combated. Undoubtedly, the ruling class would still have tried to split the Black power movement, but the left wing would not have been nearly wiped out as an organized force in the Black community. If the CPUSA hadn't liquidated Communist work in the South and in the factories, the sixties would have seen a consolidated proletarian force emerge in the Black Belt and the ghettos. The Communist forces could have come out of the revolt with developed cadres rooted in the factories and communities, with credibility among the masses.

The Road Ahead

Despite such shortcomings, the sixties revolt did force concessions from the ruling class—breaking down a great deal of legal and occupational Jim Crow, enlarging the Black middle class, and extending the franchise to Blacks in the South.

But have these gains exhausted the revolutionary potential of the Black movement? Have the mechanization of southern agriculture, massive outmigrations from the Black Belt, and civil rights laws wiped out the consequences of the old plantation system? Most important, have these changes wiped out the existence of an oppressed Black nation in the Deep South, as so many have claimed? Is the right of self-determination for the Black Belt nation still a demand that Communists should raise?

Let's take a look at current conditions. Despite the imperialist offensive against the Black masses, which resulted in tremendous outmigrations from the Black Belt homeland, there remains a stable community of Black people in the rural South and a growing Black population in the urban areas. The actual number of Blacks has steadily increased. In 1940 there were over 9 million Black people in the South, and by 1970 the number had increased to nearly 12 million. Over 70 percent of all Black people in the United States were born in the South and still have roots there. Within the Black Belt territory itself, despite fierce economic and political coercion, there has remained since 1930 a stable community of over 5 million. The "escape valve" into the northern cities is being closed by the crisis, and outmigration from the South has slowed considerably, with reverse migration now becoming the dominant trend.

It is no accident that the civil rights movement first arose in the South, where Blacks face the most terroristic oppression and are often denied even the most basic democratic rights. In fact, the mechanization of agriculture, which drove so many Blacks off the land in the South, provided one of the main fueling sources of the rebellion. SNCC did some of its best work in its southern rural projects, where it took up the struggles of sharecroppers and the displaced peasantry.

Today the spiraling inflation and recession of the worst crisis in forty years still hits Blacks hardest, the victims of continued last-hired, first-fired policies and an unemployment rate twice that of whites. Recent statistics show the highest rate of unemployment among Black youth since World War II, while at the same time there have been cutbacks in Black studies and other affirmative-action programs. The result is yet another "lost" generation of Black youth condemned to the margins of the workforce. Once again, the sensitive ghetto youth and students are becoming a flash point for all the contradictions of the system.

In the midst of the biggest strike wave in twenty years, the ruling class is desperately trying to exacerbate existing race differences. This accounts for the new rise of antibusing and segregationist movements in northern cities, the rise in membership of the Ku Klux Klan, and the increasing attacks on social welfare and affirmative action programs.

The crisis is also undermining the existence of the expanded Black middle class, which was created by the ruling class's strategy of concessions during the "boom" years of the sixties. Business failures and service cutbacks are weakening this group economically, while fascist attacks and growing class divisions inside the Black community are eroding the political credibility of Black elected officials. In cities like Atlanta, Detroit, and Newark, where Black mayors have been elected, the living and working conditions among Blacks have continued to deteriorate. Far from indicating the attainment of real political power for Afro-Americans, these politicians have been elected merely to serve as administrators for the white power structure.

This domestic situation is combined with an international situation more explosive than in the sixties, symbolized particularly by the fierce liberation struggles in southern Africa and the increasing threat of war between the two superpowers. It is only a matter of time before the smoldering embers of Black revolt burst into flame again. Whenever the next Black upsurge comes—whether as part of a general revolutionary upsurge or as signal of the movement to come—we must be prepared to bring out mass support for equality and self-determination as a special feature of the struggle for socialism.

Most assuredly, the next wave of mass struggle will begin from a higher level of consciousness, based on what the last upsurge taught the masses about the nature of the enemy and the path to liberation. In fact, the revolt sparked an irreversible growth of Black national consciousness and brought forward a new generation of revolutionaries. A section of this movement has turned to the best experiences of the socialist countries in fighting for equality of nations and nationalities.

In this regard, a great deal has been learned from the People's Republic of China, its Communist Party, and its great leader Mao Tse-tung. The emphasis on testing ideas in practice, care and flexibility in applying united front tactics, relying upon and serving the people, realism in dealing with power relationships, respect for the integrity of national minorities and for the rights of the third-world nations against great-nation chauvinism, the concrete analysis and application of Marxist-Leninist principles to one's own country, and the pursuing of the two-line political struggle inside the party are all part of China's great legacy. For me, this has been a cause for great optimism for the future, especially for the new generation of Communists.

This generation, left without guideposts after the betrayal of the CP, was forced to start almost from scratch. It has carried out a long march through the mass struggles of the sixties to recapture our revolutionary heritage. It is heartening that they, along with some of us veteran fighters, are building a genuine communist party—the first in this country in decades. To this new revolutionary movement falls the task of giving leadership in the coming upsurge.

The ever-deepening crisis and the increased threat of war between the two superpowers are affecting the living conditions of the broad masses of American people. At the same time, the ability of the imperialists and the labor aristocracy to grant concessions, and thus buy off dissents, has been somewhat hampered by the crisis. Under such conditions and with the leadership of a new party, there is a strong possibility of building a movement based on the alliance between Blacks and other nationalities and the working class. As Chairman Mao wrote in 1968:

> The struggle of the black people in the United States is bound to merge with the American workers' movement, and this will eventually end the criminal rule of the U.S. monopoly capitalist class.[12]

I hope that this book, which sums up some of my experiences and that of many other comrades, will make some contribution to this lofty goal.

ACKNOWLEDGMENTS

Many friends and comrades, directly or indirectly, helped me with the writing of this book. Unfortunately, they are too numerous to all be named here.

A number of young people assisted with the editorial, research, and typing tasks and moved the project along through political discussions. Special thanks to Ernie Allen, who gave yeoman help with the early chapters. Others whose assistance was indispensable include Jody and Susan Chandler, Paula Cohen, Stu Dowty and Janet Goldwasser, Paul Elitzik, Pat Fry, Gary Goff, Sherman Miller, John Schwartz, Lyn Wells, and Carl Davidson. Others who helped me are Renee Blakkan and Nathalie Garcia.

Over the past years, I have had discussions with several veteran comrades and friends who helped immeasurably in jogging my memory and filling in the gaps where my own experience was lacking. I extend my warmest appreciation to Jesse Gray, Josh Lawrence, Arthur and Maude (White) Katz, John Killens, Ruth Hamlin, Frances Loman, Al Murphy, Joan Sandler, Delia Page, and Jack and Ruth Shulman.

A political autobiography is necessarily shaped by experiences over the years and by comrades who influenced me in the long battle for self-determination and against revisionism. My earliest political debts are to the first core of Black cadres in the CPUSA: Cyril Briggs, Edward Doty, Richard B. Moore, and my brother Otto Hall, all former members of the African Blood Brotherhood.

To Harrison George, outstanding son of the working class, charter member of the CPUSA, former editor of the *Daily Worker* and the *Peoples' World,* who gave his all to the Communist movement and died alone, victimized for his "premature" antirevisionism.

A special tribute to my comrades in the battles against revisionism within the CPUSA and after: Al Lannon, veteran director of the Waterfront Section and member of the Central Committee of the CPUSA; Charles Loman, executive secretary of the Brooklyn Party Organization; Isidore Beagun, executive secretary of the Bronx Party Organization; Allen and Pearl Lawes, Al and Ruth Hamlin, Olga and Victor Agosto. And to my wife, Gwendolyn Midlo Hall, my closest collaborator from 1953 through 1964 in the writing of manuscripts as well as in the political battles, who has since established her own reputation as a historian and essayist.

A tribute to Ed Strong, former Communist youth leader and director of the Southern Negro Youth Congress, whose premature death in the midfifties cut short his uncompromising stand within the Central Committee for the right of self-determination for the Black nation.

To the editors of *Soulbook Magazine*, who published my writings in 1965–66 and invited me to Oakland, California, in the spring of 1966 during the formative stages of the Black Panther movement.

To Vincent Harding, who provided me with funds to return to the United States from Mexico in 1970 and gave me technical and material assistance to begin this autobiography.

Thanks to John Henrik Clarke and Francisco and Elizabeth Cattlett de Mora for their enthusiasm and moral support.

To Robert Warner, director of the Michigan Historical Collections, for his help and his sensitivity to the need to collect and preserve historically relevant materials from the Black movement in the United States.

NOTES

Introduction

1. Steven Hahn, *A Nation under Our Feet: Black Political Struggles in the Rural South, from Slavery to the Great Migration* (Cambridge, Mass.: Belknap Press of Harvard University Press, 2003).

2. V. P. Franklin, *Living Our Stories, Telling Our Truths: Autobiography and the Making of the African-American Intellectual Tradition* (New York: Oxford University Press, 1996).

3. Robert A. Hill, "Racial and Radical: Cyril V. Briggs, the *Crusader* Magazine, and the African Blood Brotherhood, 1918–1922," introductory essay to *The Crusader* (New York: Garland Publishing, 1987); http://www.marxists.org/history/usa/groups/abb/1922/0400-abb-program.pdf.

4. Michel-Rolph Trouillot, *Silencing the Past: Power and the Production of History* (Boston: Beacon Press, 1995).

5. Brenda Gayle Plummer, *Rising Wind: Black Americans and U.S. Foreign Affairs, 1935–1960* (Chapel Hill: University of North Carolina Press, 1996).

6. Jacquelyn Dowd Hall, "The Long Civil Rights Movement and the Political Uses of the Past," *Journal of American History*, March 2005, 1233–63, http://www.historycooperative.org/cgi-bin/justtop.cgi?act=justtop&url=http://www.historycooperative.org/journals/jah/91.4/hall.html.

7. A. B. Davidson, *South Africa and the Communist International: A Documentary History*, 2 vols. (London: Frank Cass, 2003), 1: xxiii (entry for Harry Haywood). The Resolution on "The South African Question," adopted by the Executive Committee of the Communist International at the Sixth World Congress of the Comintern in 1928, can be found at http://www.marxists.org/history/international/comintern/sections/sacp/1928/comintern.htm.

8. Nelson Mandela, *Long Walk to Freedom* (New York: Little Brown, 1994), 366.

9. See "The 1928 and 1930 Comintern Resolutions on the Black National Question in the United States," http://www.marx2mao.com/Other/CR75.html. For the discussion during the Sixth World Congress and its implication for the work of the CPUSA in the South, see Glenda Elizabeth Gilmore, *Defying Dixie: The Radical Roots of Civil Rights, 1818–1950* (New York: W. W. Norton, 2008), 63–105.

10. Thomas J. Sugrue, *Sweet Land of Liberty: The Forgotten Struggle for Civil Rights in the North* (New York: Random House, 2008).

11. Claude Mckay, "Report on the Negro Question: Speech to the 4th Congress of the Comintern, Nov. 1922," http://www.cddc.vt.edu/marxists/history/usa/groups/abb/1922/1100-mckay-cominternspeech.pdf.

12. Gilmore, *Defying Dixie*, 154.

13. Ibid.

14. James S. Allen, *Organizing in the Depression South: A Communist's Memoir* (Minneapolis, Minn.: MEP Publications, 2001).

15. Edith Rosepha Ambrose, " 'Thar's Reds in Them Thar Bayous!' Labor Politics in Jim Crow New Orleans, 1923–1949." Unpublished manuscript.

16. Gilmore, *Defying Dixie*; Mark Naison, *The Communist Party in Harlem, 1928–1936* (Urbana: University of Illinois Press, 1983); Mark Solomon, *The Cry Was Unity: Communists and African Americans, 1917–1936* (Jackson: University Press of Mississippi, 1999); Randi Storch, *Red Chicago: American Communism at Its Grass Roots, 1928–35* (Urbana and Chicago: University of Illinois Press, 2007).

17. John Erickson, *The Road to Stalingrad: Stalin's War with Germany* (New Haven, Conn.: Yale University Press, 1999); John Erickson, *The Road to Berlin: Stalin's War with Germany* (New Haven, Conn.: Yale University Press, 1999).

18. Harry Haywood, *Black Bolshevik* (Chicago: Liberator Press, 1978), 532–33.

19. William J. Chase, *Enemies within the Gates? The Comintern and the Stalinist Repression, 1934–1939* (New Haven, Conn.: Yale University Press, 2001).

20. Report to the NKVD by Colonel Sverchevsky, August 22, 1938, document 77, in *Spain Betrayed: The Soviet Union in the Spanish Civil War,* ed. Ronald Radosh, Mary R. Habeck, and Grigory Sevostianov (New Haven and London: Yale University Press, 2001), 488–96.

21. Cecil D. Eby, *Comrades and Commissars: The Lincoln Battalion in the Spanish Civil War* (University Park: Pennsylvania State University Press, 2007), 173–74.

22. Ernest Hemingway, *For Whom the Bell Tolls* (New York: Scribner, 1995), 233.

23. Eby, *Comrades and Commissars,* 149, 179.

24. Alvah Cecil Bessie, *Men in Battle: A Story of Americans in Spain* (New York: Charles Scribner's Sons, 1939). See also Alvah Cecil Bessie and Dan Bessie, *Spanish Civil War Notebooks* (Lexington: University Press of Kentucky, 2002).

25. Civil Rights Congress (U.S.), *We Charge Genocide: The Historic Petition to the United Nations for Relief from a Crime of the United States Government against the Negro People* (New York: Civil Rights Congress, 1952).

26. Patricia Sullivan, *Lift Every Voice: The NAACP and the Making of the Civil Rights Movement* (New York and London: New Press, 2009), 361–62, 366–67.

27. Solomon, *The Cry Was Unity*; Ambrose, " 'Thar's Reds in Them Thar Bayous!' "; Ellen Schreck, *Many Are the Crimes: McCarthyism in America* (Boston: Little Brown, 1998).

28. Mindy Thompson, *The National Negro Labor Council: A History* (New York: AIMS, 1978); Dayo F. Gore, *Radicalism at the Crossroads: African-American Women Activists in the Cold War* (New York: New York University Press, 2011).

29. Numan V. Bartley, *The Rise of Massive Resistance: Race and Politics in the South During the 1950's* (Baton Rouge: Louisiana State University Press, 1969).

30. Michael C. Dawson, *Black Visions: The Roots of Contemporary African-American Political Thought* (Chicago: University of Chicago Press, 2001), 172–237.

31. Noel Ignatin and Theodore Allen, *White Blindspot: Can White Workers Be Radicalized?* (Detroit, Mich.: Radical Education Project, 1969); Theodore Allen, *The Invention of the White Race*, 2 vols. (London: Verso, 1994). I typed and kept most of the records of the POC; they are available at the Harry Haywood Collection, Bentley Historical Library, University of Michigan, Ann Arbor.

32. Jack O'Dell, *Climbing Jacob's Ladder*, edited by Nikhil Singh (Berkeley: University of California Press, 2010).

33. Works in progress by Akinyele Umoja and Timothy B. Tyson.

34. Lance Hill, *The Deacons for Defense: Armed Resistance and the Civil Rights Movement* (Chapel Hill: University of North Carolina Press, 2004).

35. Sugrue, *Sweet Land of Liberty.*

36. Harry Haywood, with Gwendolyn Midlo, "The Crisis and Growth of Negro Reformism and the Growth of Nationalism," *Soulbook* 3 (Fall 1965): 203–7; Harry Haywood, with Gwendolyn Midlo, "The Two Epochs of Nation-Development: Is Black Nationalism a Form of Classical Nationalism?" *Soulbook* 4 (Winter 1965–66): 257–66; Harry Haywood, with Gwendolyn Midlo, "Is the Black Bourgeoisie the Leader of the Black Liberation Movement?," *Soulbook* 5 (Summer 1966): 70–75; Harry Haywood, with Gwendolyn Midlo, "The Nation of Islam: An Estimate," *Soulbook* 6 (Winter–Spring 1967): 137–44; all as they appear at http://people.umass.edu/eallen/haywood/haywood_selected.html.

37. Haywood, with Midlo, "The Crisis and Growth of Negro Reformism and the Growth of Nationalism," 207.

38. Dan Georgakas and Marvin Surkin, *Detroit, I Do Mind Dying: A Study in Urban Revolution*, rev. ed. (Cambridge, Mass.: South End Press, 1998).

39. Robin D. G. Kelley and Betsy Esch, "Black Like Mao: Red China and Black Revolution," in *Afro-Asia: Revolutionary Political and Cultural Connections between African Americans and Asian Americans*, ed. Fred Ho and Bill V. Mullen (Durham, N.C.: Duke University Press, 2008), 97–155; also available online in four parts, http://kasamaproject.org/2010/03/01/red-china-and-black-revolution/, http://kasamaproject.org/2010/03/01/black-like-mao-red-china-black-revolution-part-2/, http://kasamaproject.org/2010/03/06/black-like-mao-red-china-black-revolution-part-3/, and http://kasamaproject.org/2010/03/14/black-like-mao-red-china-black-revolution-part-4/.

40. Gwendolyn Midlo Hall, "Socialism and Political Democracy: Recent Developments in the Peoples' Republic of China," in *International Human Rights: Contemporary Issues*, ed. Vera Green and Jack P. Nelson (Stanfordville, N.Y.: Human Rights Publishing Group, 1980), 183–98; Henry Kissinger, *On China* (New York: Penguin Press, 2011).

41. Harry Haywood, *For a Revolutionary Position on the Negro Question*, http://marxistleninist.wordpress.com/2009/11/18/harry-haywood-for-a-revolutionary-position-on-the-negro-question-2/#comments.

42. Komozi Woodard, *A Nation within a Nation: Amiri Baraka (LeRoi Jones) and Black Power Politics* (Chapel Hill: University of North Carolina Press, 1999).

43. Harry Haywood, "China and Its Supporters Were Wrong about USSR," *Guardian*, April 11, 1984, http://www.marxists.org/archive/haywood/1984/04/11.htm.

1. A Child of Slaves

1. W. E. B. Du Bois, *Dusk of Dawn* (New York: Harcourt, Brace, 1940), 96.

2. On April 12, 1864, six thousand Confederate soldiers commanded by an ex–slave trader, Major General Nathan Forrest, overran the six hundred defenders of Fort Pillow, Tennessee, including 262 Blacks. After the fort was surrendered, Forrest's troops massacred every Black soldier who failed to escape. Some were shot; others were burned or buried alive. This was in line with the official Confederate policy that Black soldiers would be treated as stolen property, not prisoners of war. Reference to the incident can be found in the following works: Lerone Bennett Jr., *Before the Mayflower: A History of the Negro in America* (Baltimore, Md.: Penguin Books, 1966), 175–76; John Hope Franklin, *From Slavery to Freedom*, 3rd ed. (New York: Alfred A. Knopf, 1967), 292; Carl Sandburg, *Storm over the Land* (New York: Harcourt, Brace, 1942), 245–48; Bruce Catton, *A Stillness at Appomattox* (New York: Doubleday, 1953), 233.

2. A Black Regiment in World War I

The epigraph is from "An Essay Toward a History of the Black Man in the Great War," in *The Seventh Son: The Thought and Writings of W. E. B. Du Bois*, ed. Julius Lester (New York: Random House, 1971), 2: 130–31.

1. Branches of Manasseh also existed in Milwaukee and Chicago, but they had dissolved by the late twenties. See St. Clair Drake and Horace R. Cayton, *Black Metropolis* (New York: Harper and Row, 1962), 2: 145–46.

2. Herbert Aptheker, "Negroes in Wartime," *New Masses*, April 22, 1941, 14.

3. John Hope Franklin, *From Slavery to Freedom*, 4th ed. (New York: Alfred A. Knopf, 1974), 474–75.

4. Martha Gruening, "Houston, an N.A.A.C.P. Investigation," *Crisis*, November 1917, 14–15.

5. This was the story as we heard it from Company G. Slightly different versions appear in the following: Jack D. Foner, *Blacks and the Military in American History* (New York: Praeger, 1974), 113–16; Robert V. Haynes, "The Houston Mutiny and Riot of 1917," *Southwestern Historical Quarterly*, April 1973, 418–39; and Charles Flint Kellogg, *NAACP* (Baltimore, Md.: The Johns Hopkins University Press, 1967), 1: 261–62.

3. On to France

1. This document was first published in the *Crisis*, May 1919, 16–17, with this note: "The following documents have come into the hands of the Editor. He has absolute proof of their authenticity. The first document was sent out last August at the request of the American Army by the French Committee which is the official means of communications between the American forces and the French. It represents American and not French opinion and we have been informed that when the French Military heard of the distribution of this document among the Prefects and Sous-Prefects of France, they ordered such copies to be collected and burned."

2. This was how Roberts impressed many of us in the ranks at the time. Black officers, however, later told W. E. B. Du Bois that Roberts let them run the regiment while taking credit for their exploits and conniving behind their backs to replace them with whites. See Lester, *The Seventh Son*, 140–41.

3. Charles H. Williams, *Sidelights on Negro Soldiers* (Boston: B. J. Bremmer, 1923), 74–75.

4. Robert R. Moton, *Finding a Way Out* (Garden City, N.Y.: Doubleday, Page, 1920), 254.

5. Quoted in Monroe N. Work, ed., *Negro Year Book* (Tuskegee Institute, Ala.: Negro Year Book Publishing, 1922), 192.

6. For a detailed description of Black stevedore units, see Lester, *The Seventh Son*, 117–19; and Williams, *Sidelights on Negro Soldiers*, 138–55.

4. Searching for Answers

1. Arthur I. Waskow, *From Race Riot to Sit-In* (New York: Doubleday, 1966), 12, 111–12.

2. Claude McKay, *Selected Poems* (New York: Harcourt, Brace and World, 1953), 36.

3. Allan H. Spear, *Black Chicago: The Making of a Negro Ghetto* (Chicago: University of Chicago Press, 1967), 36–41, 151–55. Also see William M. Tuttle Jr., "Labor Conflict and Racial Violence: The Black Worker in Chicago, 1894–1919," *Labor History*, Summer 1969, 408–32.

4. Spear, *Black Chicago*, 141.

5. In the wake of mass actions in Philadelphia and Boston, the film was temporarily banned in many cities, including Chicago, where the NAACP and the *Chicago Defender* were active in the campaign.

6. These states included New York, Indiana, Michigan, Illinois, and some in New England. The Klan was first reorganized in 1915 by William J. Simmons, who advertised the reborn KKK in an Atlanta paper, alongside an ad for the opening of *The Birth of a Nation*. According to David Chalmers, the KKK grew from several thousand members in 1919 to nearly a hundred thousand by summer 1921 and up to 3 million by the mid-twenties. See David M. Chalmers, *Hooded Americanism* (Garden City, N.Y.: Doubleday, 1965), 29–31, 291.

7. See W. E. B. Du Bois, *Black Reconstruction in America* (New York: Harcourt, Brace, 1935), 711–28.

8. Martin Madden, the white congressman from the first district, was the grand patron of Black post office employees. From his position on the House Postal Committee, he built a reputation for getting his Black constituents a good share of post office jobs. See Harold F. Gosnell, *Negro Politicians* (Chicago: University of Chicago Press, 1935), 307–8, 316–17.

9. Ibid., 302–18; and Henry McGee, "The Negro in the Chicago Post Office" (master's thesis, University of Chicago, 1961), 31–36.

10. Quoted in Du Bois, *Black Reconstruction in America*, 718–19.

11. *Philosophy and Opinions of Marcus Garvey,* edited by Amy Jacques Garvey (New York: Atheneum, 1969), 1: 4, 8.

12. There are many examples of pre-Garvey nationalism in the United States, but Martin Delany is one of the most modern sounding. In the conclusion to his book *The Condition, Elevation, Emigration, and Destiny of the Colored People of the United States, Politically Considered* (New York: Arno Press, 1968), he writes, "We are a nation within a nation; as the Poles in Russia, the Hungarians in Austria; the Welsh, Irish and Scotch in the British Dominions. . . . The claims of no people, according to established policy and usage, are respected by any nation, until they are presented in a national capacity" (209–10).

13. Edmund David Cronon, *Black Moses* (Madison: University of Wisconsin Press, 1955), 197.

14. Quoted in Spear, *Black Chicago,* 135.

15. Garvey, *Philosophy and Opinions,* 2: 69–70.

16. W. E. B. Du Bois, "Back to Africa," *Century Magazine,* February 1923, 547. History repeated itself forty years later when the Black Muslims' public contacts with ultra-racists caused them to lose many of their more revolutionary followers. This was exposed in the March 1966 issue of the radical monthly magazine *Now*: "If Americans—and Negroes in particular—were astonished when a member of the American Nazi Party was accorded a place of honor at a Black Muslim conclave not long ago, Malcolm indicated that Muslim ties with the oil-rich supporters of the Ku Klux Klan were deep and vast. James Venable, a Klan lawyer, had defended the New Orleans mosque following a raid by police and charges of insurrectionist activity. Malcolm said he himself had accompanied Elijah Muhammad to an incredible meeting in 1961 at Magnolia Hall in Atlanta, Georgia, at which Elijah's dream of a Black nation within the United States was solemnized in a treaty with officers of the Klan. Maps were drawn 'ceding' the Black Muslims parts of South Carolina and Georgia, an act to be effectuated when the right wing forces came to power." *Now,* March 1966, 10.

5. An Organization of Revolutionaries

1. Frederick G. Detweiler, *The Negro Press in the U.S.* (Chicago: University of Chicago Press, 1922), 77.

2. *Amsterdam News,* September 5 and 19, 1917, quoted in Theodore Draper, *American Communism and Soviet Russia* (New York: Viking Press, 1960), 323.

3. "Liberty For All!" *Amsterdam News,* 1918, quoted without full date in Draper, *American Communism and Soviet Russia,* 323.

4. *Crusader,* November 1921, quoted in Draper, *American Communism and Soviet Russia,* 505–6.

5. In 1946, while researching material for *Negro Liberation,* I had occasion to look over the file of the *Crusader* in the Schomburg Collection of the New York Public Library. It seemed at the time to be almost complete. I learned later from Briggs, who sought to consult these files in 1967, that they had disappeared. Theodore Draper, in preparation for his hatchet job on communism, *American Communism and Soviet Russia,* was

able to track down fourteen copies in the Howard University library. For the present, pending my own research, I am relying partially on Draper's quotes, but not, of course, upon his interpretation.

6. *Crusader*, April 1921, 9, quoted in Draper, *American Communism and Soviet Russia*, 324.

7. Bughouse Square was a corner of Washington Park used for open-air speaking in the twenties and thirties. The Dill Pickle forum gathered on the Northside on Saturdays under the leadership of the anarchist Jack Jones. A wide variety of radicals attended the meetings and spoke there, including Emma Goldman.

8. See Spear, *Black Chicago*, 198–99.

9. Quoted in Ray Ginger, *The Bending Cross* (New Brunswick, N.J.: Rutgers University Press, 1949), 260.

10. *International Socialist Review*, November 1903, 258–59.

11. Ibid., January 1904, 396.

12. Sterling D. Spero and Abram L. Harris, *The Black Worker* (New York: Atheneum, 1968), 425.

13. James W. Ford, *The Negro and the Democratic Front* (New York: International Publishers, 1938), 82.

6. A Student in Moscow

1. The January 17, 1926, edition of the Sunday *New York Times* carried an article titled "Communists Boring into Negro Labor." It included such sensational subheads as "Taking Advantage of the New Moves among Colored Workers Here to Stir Unrest"; "Not Much Progress Yet"; "Ten Young Negroes Are Sent to Moscow under Soviet 'Scholarships' to Study Bolshevism"; "Nuclei Sought in Unions"; "Labor Federation and Older Leaders of the Race Seek Antidotes in Real Labor Unions."

2. John Reed, *Ten Days That Shook the World* (New York: Boni and Liverwright, 1919).

3. Stalin saw the university as having two lines of activity: "one line having the aim of creating cadres capable of serving the needs of the Soviet republics of the East, and the other line having the aim of creating cadres capable of serving the revolutionary requirements of the toiling masses in the colonial and dependent countries of the East." J. V. Stalin, "The Political Tasks of the University of the Peoples of the East," in *Works* (Moscow: Foreign Languages Publishing House, 1953), 6: 382.

4. See J. V. Stalin, *Foundations of Leninism* (Peking: Foreign Languages Press, 1975), 72–83.

5. Ibid., 77.

7. Self-Determination

1. Lenin, "Preliminary Draft Theses on the National and Colonial Questions," in *Collected Works* (Moscow: Progress Publishers, 1964), 31: 144–51.

2. "A historically constituted, stable community of people, formed on the basis of a common language, territory, economic life, and psychological make-up manifested in a common culture." Stalin, *Marxism and the National Question*, in *Works*, 2: 307.

3. Speech of James Ford, *Inprecorr*, August 3, 1928, 772.

4. H. J. Simons and R. E. Simons, *Class and Colour in South Africa* (Baltimore, Md.: Penguin Books, 1969), 390.

5. "The South African Question (Resolution of the E.C.C.I.)," *Communist International*, December 15, 1928, 54.

6. Ibid., 52.

7. Ibid., 54, 56.

8. Simons and Simons, *Class and Colour in South Africa*, 395.

9. Edward Roux, *Time Longer Than Rope: A History of the Black Man's Struggle for Freedom in South Africa*, 2nd ed. (Madison: University of Wisconsin Press, 1964), 13.

10. Simons and Simons, *Class and Colour in South Africa*, 398.

11. Ibid., 398.

12. See Simons and Simons, *Class and Colour in South Africa*, 406.

13. Speech of Sidney P. Bunting, *Inprecorr*, August 3, 1928, 780; and *Inprecorr*, September 19, 1928, 1156.

14. Ibid.

15. Speech of Sidney P. Bunting, *Inprecorr*, November 8, 1928, 1452.

16. I know of no written record of either Rebecca Bunting's or Manuilsky's remarks since they were made at the commission meetings, and these were not recorded in *Inprecorr*.

17. This position was stated in the section on South Africa in the "Theses on the Revolutionary Movement in the Colonies."

18. "CI Resolution on Negro Question in USA," *Daily Worker*, February 12, 1929; "Theses on the Revolutionary Movement in the Colonies and Semi-Colonies," *Inprecorr*, December 12, 1928, 1674.

19. "Theses on the Revolutionary Movement in the Colonies and Semi-Colonies," 1674.

20. Cyril Briggs, "The Negro Question in the Southern Textile Strikes," *Communist*, June 1929, 324–28; Briggs, "Further Notes on Negro Question in Southern Textile Strikes," *Communist*, July 1929, 391–94; "Our Negro Work," *Communist*, September 1929, 494–501.

21. Briggs, "Our Negro Work," 494.

22. *Daily Worker*, October 4, 1929.

23. Briggs, "Our Negro Work," 498.

8. Return to the Home Front

1. See Dan T. Carter, *Scottsboro: A Tragedy of the American South* (London and New York: Oxford University Press, 1969), for a detailed account of the trial.

2. As quoted in Harry Haywood and Milton Howard, *Lynching* (New York: Daily Worker, 1932), 13.

3. "Is the N.A.A.C.P. Lying Down on Its Job?" *Crisis*, October 1931, 354.

4. William Z. Foster, *History of the Communist Party of the United States* (New York: International Publishers, 1952), 285.

5. Ibid., 257.

6. United Press International dispatch, quoted in the *Daily Worker*, June 9, 1931.

7. Formerly a member of the Central Committee of the German Communist Party, Ewart led an opposition to the Thälmann leadership. As a result, he was pulled out of Germany and assigned to international work. Later, while representing the Comintern in Brazil, he was captured and tortured to death by the regime of the dictator Vargas.

9. Reunion in Moscow

1. Mooney and Billings were arrested in July 1916 for their activities in opposition to World War I. Their frame-up and conviction attracted support from workers all over the world. Due to this mass movement and, in particular, the efforts of the ILD, Mooney was finally released in January 1939 and Billings in October of that year. Mooney's health was ruined by his twenty-two years in prison, and he died in 1942.

2. See "The NAACP Prepares New Betrayals of the Negro Masses," *Daily Worker*, May 28, 1932, and *Daily Worker*, May 30, 1932; "The Scottsboro Decision," *Communist*, May 1932, 1065–75; Haywood and Howard, *Lynching*.

3. Foster, *History of the Communist Party of the United States*, 289.

4. Ibid., 291.

5. Angelo Herndon, *Let Me Live* (New York: Arno Press, 1969), 192.

6. Ibid., 238.

7. Ibid., 240.

8. "The International Situation and the Tasks of the Sections of the Communist International: Theses on the Report of Comrade Kuusinen," *Inprecorr*, October 6, 1932, 939–43.

9. Langston Hughes, *I Wonder as I Wander* (New York: Hill and Wang, 1964), 69–70, 73–80, 89–90, 94–99. See also the *Crisis*, January 1933, 16. See Louise Thompson's response in the February 1933 issue, page 37. Delegation members Poston and Moon issued a statement in Berlin claiming that the "forces of American race prejudice have triumphed" in canceling the film. This statement was published in the *New York Times* and the *Amsterdam News* of October 10, 1933. Similar statements were also issued by two other members of the twenty-two-member delegation. Hughes and fourteen others issued a statement repudiating these slanders. See the *Daily Worker*, October 5, 1933, and October 15, 1933.

10. Hughes, *I Wonder as I Wander*, 76–77.

11. Walter Duranty of the *New York Times* is the only American newsman I know of who wrote favorable and accurate reports about the Soviet Union in this period.

10. Sharecroppers with Guns

1. *New York Times,* April 12, 1933, as quoted in Carter, *Scottsboro,* 247.

2. In 1932 my close friend, William L. "Pat" Patterson, had been elected national secretary of the ILD at its Cleveland convention. Earl Browder and I attended as delegates from the party's Central Committee. We pushed for Patterson's election, but Pat, a brilliant dynamic man, needed no pushing! He was quite popular, having played a leading role in publicizing the Scottsboro case.

Louis Engdahl, former national secretary of the ILD, was on tour in Europe and the Soviet Union with Scottsboro mother Ada Wright at the time of the convention. He was elected chairman of the ILD at that time, but he died while on tour in Europe.

3. See Carter, *Scottsboro,* 248.

4. Ruby Bates was one of the two women supposedly raped by the nine youths. She recanted her testimony at the Decatur, Alabama, trial of Haywood Patterson and became an active member of the defense movement.

5. "The Scottsboro Struggle and the Next Steps: Resolution of the Political Bureau," *Communist,* June 1933, 575–76, 578–79.

6. Hosea Hudson, *Black Worker in the Deep South* (New York: International Publishers, 1972), 57.

7. The following account of the sharecroppers' struggles is based on what I learned at the time from personal observations and reports of comrades. Much of it is confirmed by Stuart Jamieson, *Labor Unionism in American Agriculture,* Bureau of Labor Statistics Bulletin no. 836 (Washington, D.C.: U.S. G.P.O., 1945), 290–98; and Dale Rosen, "The Alabama Sharecroppers Union" (Radcliffe Honors Thesis, 1969), 19–20, 30–41, 48, 56, 130–35.

8. *Daily Worker,* December 28, 1932.

9. Ibid., December 21–22, 1932, and April 17, 1933.

10. Ibid., January 7 and 9, 1932.

11. Ibid., April 27, 1933.

12. Jamieson, *Labor Unionism in Southern Agriculture,* 298.

13. The Farmers Union of Alabama agitated for populist-style cooperatives and federal regulation of markets and prices. Traditional reformist demands, rather than the right of the tiller to the land he tilled, characterized its work. Although the Sharecroppers Union was always overwhelmingly Black, it was an integrated union and stood in principle for unity. Particularly after the reputation of the Sharecroppers Union was established, many white croppers and tenants joined up. In contrast, a Farmers Union organizer explained that "the Farmers Union is proud of its large colored membership. But just as America had more white farmers than colored, so has the union. In Opelousas, Louisiana, we had an instance of colored farmers crowding out the white at an open meeting. They later realized that their enthusiasm had worked against them. Both white and colored generally prefer to have their own locals and meet separately." Rosen, "The Alabama Sharecroppers Union," 116.

14. Rosen, "The Alabama Sharecroppers Union," 112–16. Reverend Charles Coughlin, a fascist demagogue, violently criticized everything progressive, and he aimed at

establishing a fascist United States. He had an estimated 10 million listeners to his weekly radio broadcast and launched the National Union for Social Justice in 1934, along with the notorious Christian Front with its organized groups of hoodlums and storm troopers.

15. Benjamin J. Davis, *Communist Councilman from Harlem* (New York: International Publishers, 1969), 44; see also 27, 34, 40, 43, 46–48, 51.

16. Kenneth E. Barnhart, "A Study of Homicide in the United States," *Birmingham-Southern College Bulletin,* May 1932, 9. Figures for 1930.

11. Chicago

1. *Daily Worker,* August 5–8, 10, 11, and 13, 1931.
2. Ibid., September 29, 1932.
3. Georgi Dimitrov, *The United Front* (New York: International Publishers, 1938), 10.
4. *Daily Worker,* September 2, 1935.
5. *Chicago Defender,* September 7, 1935.
6. Ibid.
7. *Daily Worker,* September 2, 1935.
8. As quoted in James W. Ford, "The National Negro Congress," *Communist,* April 1936, 323–24. I plan to speak of Randolph a number of times during the course of this book, and therefore, I feel it necessary at this point to briefly give my estimation of the man. Randolph is a social democrat. At the height of his career, he was probably the most influential Black union executive in the United States. His role in the AFL-CIO, however, has always been the loyal opposition. At every annual convention, he would make the same criticisms of discrimination in the unions, but always in a manner acceptable to the bureaucrats.

Randolph was a board member of the NAACP and had broad influence, not just among Black workers but in the Black community as well. As one of the very few Black labor bureaucrats in the United States, he was widely claimed to represent Black labor. In reality, he shared the basic ideology of the labor aristocracy: support for U.S. imperialism, belief in the common interests of labor and management, negotiation by bureaucrats as a substitute for militant rank-and-file action, and consistent anticommunism. Randolph helped to legitimize the labor aristocracy's claim to speak for Black working people. Despite his anticommunism, our leadership of the mass struggles of Blacks often forced him to unite with us. Such was the case with the NNC.

9. *Daily Worker,* February 17, 1936.

12. The Spanish Civil War

1. Hugh Thomas, *The Spanish Civil War* (New York: Harper and Row, 1961), 419–21.
2. Certain nationalists asked why the International Brigades had not intervened in Ethiopia. This question struck home, touching the genuine sentiments of the masses in support of the Ethiopian people's cause and was used to confuse matters in the Black community. Indeed, there was worldwide support among the international Communist

and antifascist forces for the Ethiopian people, but Haile Selassie had neither called for nor desired the assistance of the International Brigades.

3. I have relied on these works to refresh my memory and found them to be some of the best: Arthur Landis, *The Abraham Lincoln Brigade* (New York: Citadel Press, 1967); Robert Colodny, *The Struggle for Madrid* (New York: Paine-Whitman, 1958); and Hugh Thomas, *The Spanish Civil War*.

4. The POUM—the Workers Party of Marxist Unification—was a Trotskyist group; their line denied the bourgeois–democratic nature of the struggle in Spain and called for immediate direct revolution for socialism. The POUM's followers charged that the united people's front government was betraying that revolution and put forward the slogan "You may win the war and lose the revolution." They staged an uprising in Barcelona on May 3, 1937, and virtually opened up the Aragon front to the fascists.

5. With the defeat of Republican Spain in 1939, Dolores Ibárruri (La Pasionaria) fled to Moscow. She remained there until May 1977. I was sorry to see that Ibárruri supported the revisionist takeover in the Soviet Union and, by the late fifties, became a leading spokesperson for revisionism worldwide. Since her return to Spain, she has become a supporter of the Euro-Communist brand of revisionism.

6. According to Landis, Usera was later found to be working for U.S. Army Intelligence. Landis, *The Abraham Lincoln Brigade*, 207, 325.

7. Copic was dismissed from command on July 4, 1938 (Landis, *The Abraham Lincoln Brigade*, 505). He then went to the Soviet Union, where he was purged in the course of Soviet preparations for war with Germany. See Vincent Brome, *The International Brigades* (New York: William Morrow, 1966), 276–77.

8. James Allen, *The Negro Question in the United States* (New York: International Publishers, 1936).

9. Harry Haywood, *Negro Liberation*. The revisionist clique quickly let the book go out of print, and it remained largely unavailable until it was reprinted in 1976 by the Liberator Press.

13. World War II and the Merchant Marines

1. For the history of the NMU, see William L. Standard, *Merchant Seamen: A Short History of Their Struggles* (New York: International Publishers, 1947), 54–128, 170, 190–94. See also Joseph P. Goldberg, *The Maritime Story: A Study in Labor-Management Relations* (Cambridge, Mass.: Harvard University Press, 1958), 130–97.

Epilogue

The epigraph is from *Statement Calling on the People of the World to Unite to Oppose Racial Discrimination by U.S. Imperialism and Support the American Negroes in Their Struggle against Racial Discrimination* (Peking: Foreign Languages Press, 1964), 6.

1. *Malcolm X Speaks*, edited by George Breitman (New York: Grove Press, 1965), 218.

2. *Statement by Comrade Mao Tse-tung, Chairman of the Central Committee of the Communist Party of China, in Support of the Afro-American Struggle against Violent Repression* (Peking: Foreign Languages Press, 1968), 2.

3. *Time,* June 6, 1963.

4. Held in Addis Ababa, Ethiopia, in May 1963, this was the founding conference of the Organization of African Unity (OAU).

5. James Foreman, *The Making of Black Revolutionaries* (New York: Macmillan, 1972), 331–37.

6. *Malcolm X Speaks,* 14–15.

7. *Report of the National Advisory Commission on Civil Disorders* (New York: E. P. Dutton, 1968), vii.

8. Robert L. Allen, *Black Awakening in Capitalist America* (Garden City, N.Y.: Doubleday, 1970), 72.

9. Ibid., 161.

10. Ibid., 229.

11. James Jackson, "On Certain Aspects of Bourgeois Nationalism," *Political Affairs,* September 1977, 39.

12. Mao Tse-tung, Statement in Support of the Afro-American Struggle against Violent Repression, 4.

INDEX

ABB. *See* African Blood Brotherhood
Abbott, Robert S., 91
Abd el-Krim, 99
Abraham Lincoln Brigade, 233–34, 236
Abyssinian affair (1920), 91–92
academic world: Black scholars, 82; pseudoscience of racism in, 81–82
ACTC (American Consolidated Trades Council), 109, 111
Adams, Henry, 8
Addams, Jane, 113
Addis Ababa Conference of African Ministers (1963), 274, 299n4
adolescence: problem of race in, 34
affirmative action, 281
AFL. *See* American Federation of Labor
Africa: Cape Town, experience in, 257–58; promoting trade union organization in, 156–57; South African question, 144–48, 149, 150
African Blood Brotherhood (ABB), x, xi, xiii, 70, 103–11, 162; Communist core of, 109; decline and absorption by Communist Party, 107, 108–9; first association with Black Communists in, 110–11; fraternization ritual, 104; history of, 104–7; main efforts of, 111; membership, 104–5; purpose of, 104; rejection of Garvey's racial separatism, 106
African Motor Corps, 90
African National Congress (ANC), xii, 144, 145
agrarian crisis in 1950s, 272
Agricultural Adjustment Act, 215
Agricultural Workers Union, xvi, 198
agriculture: mechanization of, 281
Aitken, George, 234, 238, 245, 246

Alabama: Montgomery Bus Boycott (1955–56) in, xi, 273, 274. *See also* Birmingham, Alabama; Scottsboro Boys case
Albany, Georgia: battle of, 275
Alexander, Hursel, 250, 253, 256, 258, 259
Allen, Ernie, xxiii
Allen, James S., 288n14, 298n8
Allen, Norval, 109
Allen, Robert L., 299n8
Allen, Theodore W., xxi, 242, 289n31
Allman, Chief (Chicago police), 219, 221
All-Southern Scottsboro Defense Conference, 168–70
Ambrose, Edith Rosepha, 288n15
American Communism and Soviet Russia (Draper), 292n5
American Consolidated Trades Council (ACTC), 109, 111
American Federation of Labor (AFL), 94, 97, 98; Chicago, 218; discriminatory policies of white, 109; no-strike pledge, 180
American Negro Labor Congress (ANLC), 118–20, 121; Anti-Lynching Conference called by (1930), 160, 162–64; launching of, 118–19
American Peace Mobilization, 248
American Railway Union, 75
American Samoas: experience in, 251
Amis, Ben, 160, 164, 168–69, 177
Amsterdam News (Black New York newspaper), 104, 105, 190
Amtorg (Soviet trading organization in United States), 186
ANC (African National Congress), xii, 144, 145

301

battles for self-determination within, xxi, 138–59; Central Committee, 117, 153, 154, 177, 178–79; dissolution of, xix, 258, 260–61; founding of, xii; Haywood's fall from leadership in, xvi–xix; joining, xi, 101–2, 116–17; members sent to Moscow, xi–xiv, 121–59; national revolutionary sentiment in, 109; Negro Department, 153, 177, 178, 182, 189, 191–92, 212; during 1930s, xv; organizing in the South, 154–55, 192–210; Otto in, 70, 100–101, 103, 107; overall thrust in leadership to liquidate national question, 246; post–World War II, xix–xxi, 271, 272–73, 280; presidential election of 1932 and, 180–81; red scare and, xx; revisionist betrayal of, 271, 272–73, 280; Scottsboro Boys case and, 167–70, 177–78, 179, 180, 191; Sixth Party Convention, 153; training of organizers by, xxi–xxii; underestimation of revolutionary potential of Black struggle for equality, 141, 145, 156; white paternalism in, 103–4
Compiègne front: hanging of Black soldier for rape on, 55, 58
Condition, Elevation, Emigration, and Destiny of the Colored People of the United States, Politically Considered, The (Delany), 292n12
Congress of African Peoples (CAP), xxiii
Congress of Industrial Organizations (CIO), xv, 177; National Maritime Union, xix, xxi–xxii, 249–50, 253; Steel Workers Union, 193
Congress of Racial Equality (CORE), xi, 273, 274, 275, 279
Congress of the Friends of the Soviet Union, 146
Conventional Lies of Our Civilization (Nordau), 83
Copeman, Fred, 241
Copic, Vladimir, xviii, 233, 234–35, 236, 245, 246, 298n7; undermining of Haywood by, 240, 243, 244

Coral Sea, Battle of the (1942), 250
CORE (Congress of Racial Equality), xi, 273, 274, 275, 279
Costigan–Wagner antilynch bill, 226
Coughlin, Charles, 296n14
Council of Nationalities, 130
Counter Intelligence Program (COINTELPRO), FBI, 279
Covington (battle cruiser), 48
Cowley, Malcolm, 188
CPUSA. *See* Communist Party of the United States
Crimea: visit to (1927 and 1928), 131
Crisis (NAACP), 39, 290n1
Cronon, Edmund David, 292n13
Crow, Neil, 252, 253
Crump, Boss, 206, 207, 209
Crusader (ABB), 104–7, 109, 117, 118, 292n5
Crusader News Service, 105
Cruse, Harold, 278
Cudahy, Ed, 31
cultural resistance: underground Black power movements for, x
Cunningham, Jock, 236, 239–46

Dadeville, Alabama: meeting in, 197–98
Daily Worker (CPUSA), 75, 117, 152, 154, 163, 203; on funeral of Bentley and James, 196; Hands off Ethiopia parade description in, 220–21; Scottsboro Boys case and, 167, 168
Dalton, Mary, 162, 163, 164
Daniels, Rufe, 39
Dante's Inferno (silent film), 28
Darcy, Sam, 261
Darrow, Clarence, 100
Darwin, Charles, 81, 83, 84
Darwinism, social, 81–82, 84
Davidson, A. B., 287n7
Davis, Ben, Jr., 182, 200–203, 297n15; background of, 200–201; Herndon defense by, 200, 201; law practice, 201; move to New York, 202–3
Davis, Ben, Sr., 200

Chicago Defender (newspaper), 114, 162;
Abyssinian affair and, 92; attack on
Garvey's movement, 91; police brutality
at Hands off Ethiopia parade described
in, 222
Chicago Federation of Labor, 94
Chicago massacre, 212–13
Chicago Red Squad, 214, 220–23; National
Negro Congress and, 227
Childs, Morris, 214, 219, 223
China: break with Soviet Union, xxiii;
Chinese students in Soviet Union, 128;
Great Cultural Revolution, xxiii; Mao
Tse-tung, xxiii, 225, 271, 274, 277, 282,
283, 299n12; People's Republic of China,
282
Chou En-lai, 225
Christian Front, 297n14
Christophe, Jean, 20
Church, Bob, 209
churches mobilizing for Hands off Ethiopia
parade (1935), 218
Chu Teh, 225
CIO. See Congress of Industrial
Organizations
Civil Rights Congress (U.S.), ix, xix–xx,
288n25
civil rights movement, 271, 273–76; alarm
of white ruling circles over, 274–75;
civil rights bill, 275–76; Kennedy-
backed coalition, 273; lessons learned
by the masses during, 276; LSNR Bill
of Rights, 191; in the North, xxii–xxiii;
roots of, xi. See also Black liberation
movement
Civil War, x, 10–11, 290n2
Clansman, The (Dixon), 80
Clarke, Edward Young, 95
class, social: class warfare in mines, 170–73;
conflicts in Black power movement,
278; co-optation of Black bourgeoisie, 278–80; Herndon case and class
militancy, 201; interclass character of
nationalist movements, 94–95; rift be-

tween masses and upper class NAACP
policies, 90–91; tendency within party
to ignore class differences in Black community, 178, 191
Coad, Mack, 194, 195, 203
Coal and Iron Police, 172–73; murder of
Filipovich, 174
coal miners' strikes: class warfare in mines
and, 170–73; of 1927, 170; of 1931, 170,
175–76; of 1932, 176, 180
Coe, Joe, 8
college students: voter-registration project
and, 274
Colodny, Robert, 298n3
Commercial Appeal (Memphis newspaper),
205
Communist (newspaper), 152
Communist International (Comintern),
103, 182; end of, xvi; Executive Committee of (ECCI), 120, 144, 145, 151; Executive Committee of (ECCI), Twelfth
Plenum of, 182–83; Fourth Congress
(1922), 120; in Moscow, 124; Negro
Commission of, 148–51, 152, 160, 211;
resolutions prioritizing Black freedom
movement in South, xiii–xiv, 151–58;
revolutionaries trained by, xii; Seventh
Congress (1935), 216; Sixth World Con-
gress (1928), 97, 138, 141–42, 148–58,
287n7, 287n9; United Front against Fas-
cism policy (1935), xv–xvi
Communist Manifesto, The (Marx and
Engels), 100
Communist Party Marxist Leninist
(CPML), xxiii–xxiv
Communist Party of China, xii
Communist Party of Japan, xii
Communist Party of South Africa. See
South African Communist Party
Communist Party of the Soviet Union, 129
Communist Party of the United States
(CPUSA), ix; African Blood Brother-
hood and, 107, 108, 109; in Atlanta,
Georgia, 202; Black Communists'

Harry Haywood (1898–1985) was a worker-intellectual. After studying at the Lenin School in Moscow, and strongly backed by the Third Communist International (the Comintern), he returned to the United States in 1930 to lead the Negro work of the Communist Party of the United States, initiating the fight to save the Scottsboro Boys and supporting the Sharecroppers Union, the Unemployed Councils, and interracial industrial trade union movements. He helped develop and apply the theory that Blacks are an internal colony in the United States, a suppressed nation with the right of self-determination. Among his best-known publications are *Negro Liberation* (1948) and the pamphlet *For a Revolutionary Position on the Negro Question* (1957).

Gwendolyn Midlo Hall is professor of history at Michigan State University and the widow of Harry Haywood. Her many publications include *Africans in Colonial Louisiana: The Development of Afro-Creole Culture in the Eighteenth Century* and *Slavery and African Ethnicities in the Americas: Restoring the Links.* She has received many honors and awards. Her pioneering and ongoing work in digital history began with the construction of the Louisiana Slave Database in 1984 and continues with the construction of the Atlantic Slave Data Network, funded by the National Endowment for the Humanities.